COMMUNICATION THAT WORKS

Second Edition

Edited by:
Katherine Allen

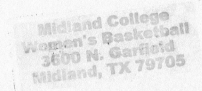

Kendall Hunt
publishing company

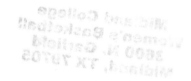

Cover images © 2016, Shuttestock.com

Kendall Hunt
publishing company

www.kendallhunt.com
Send all inquiries to:
4050 Westmark Drive
Dubuque, IA 52004-1840

Contents

COMMUNICATION BASICS

DEFINING COMMUNICATION

What is communication? That's a deceptively easy question. All sorts of job advertisements use the word "communication," and it seems that every employer wants someone with "good communication skills." In relationships, we beg for friends and partners who are "good communicators." Yet when you ask someone to define what a good communicator is, you get a lot of puzzled looks and confusing answers. Although communication surrounds us, we have a hard time specifying exactly what we mean by the term. Communication covers a lot of territory, but the following definition should reveal the basic characteristics. Human **communication** is a process of interacting through symbol systems to create and share meanings. It's a short definition, but one that requires elaboration.

Process

As a **process**, communication is ongoing and dynamic. The *ongoing* nature of communication appears when we try to separate when communication starts and stops. For example, you might not speak to someone for years, but the silence definitely sends a message. When you interact with a friend today, can you say that your previous conversations and observations had no impact at all what you said or did? Every time we communicate, our communication is shaped by past instances and can affect future communication experiences. If you ever noticed how various conversations overlap and evolve in social gatherings, you can see how difficult it is to count discrete individual occurrences of communication.

The *dynamic* quality of communication deals with how it can change. What began as a joke might be taken as an insult. Words that signified friendly courtesy later intensify into declarations of love. Your tone of voice adjusts when a young child enters the room. Whether through time or as the crafting of communication to different audiences, communication can alter intentionally or accidentally.

One result of communication being a process is that all of its components are interdependent. If one part of communication malfunctions, then the entire process breaks down. To communicate effectively, every element in communication has to run smoothly.

Interaction

Since communication involves **interaction**, it places some obligations on all participants. Everyone involved in communication bears some responsibility for its proper operation. In a relationship, for example, whenever two people experience conflict, both of them should try to find ways they can resolve it. There is no such thing as "That's *your* problem" if people are engaged in genuine communication. When people interact through communication, they operate under certain basic principles. One of the most fundamental underlying principles is to treat others as potential participants, not merely objects to be manipulated. The idea that others have basic value and can contribute something important is fundamental to communication as an interactive process.[1]

Symbolic

Communication operates by means of symbol systems. A **symbol** is a representation of something else. The relationship between symbols and what they symbolize is arbitrary, established by custom and usage. There is no necessary reason why the gooey, oozing corn glob next to my eggs must be called "grits." Different languages have different words to stand for the same things, and no word is "better" than another—they're simply different. Symbols also are ambiguous: They can be interpreted in more than one way. This ambiguity makes sense if symbols are arbitrary, since different languages and cultures might vary in how they understand the same symbol.

Our definition mentions symbol *systems*, indicating that how we refer to things might be arbitrary, but there is order. Symbols are systematic because their signification is governed by custom, not by personal whim. The systematic nature of languages is revealed in their grammar. To qualify as a system, symbols must obey some basic rules of consistent usage. There is no such thing as a private language that would be impossible for anyone else to access.[2] Communication requires that symbols be—at least in principle—sharable with others, even if we choose not to reveal them at a particular time. Examples of symbol systems include spoken and written languages, American Sign Language, and "body language" such as gestures and use of space.

Meaning

Communication moves toward creating and sharing meanings. Note the plural: meaning*s*. Since symbols are ambiguous, the same symbol can be interpreted differently by different people. Aside from ambiguity, all communication operates on two levels of meaning: informational and relational. The **informational meaning** of communication consists of the literal content. An information-centered concept of communication, however, fails to capture much of what we want and expect communication to accomplish. A world filled with this kind of communication might be efficient, but would it be bearable? Would you want to live in a world consisting only of facts and equations (the world of television characters Sheldon Cooper from *The Big Bang Theory* or Sergeant Joe Friday from *Dragnet*)? Gathering "just the facts" might yield lots of data but would make you humorless robot.

Linguist Deborah Tannen[3] observes that if we think all communication focuses on relaying information to each other, we miss much of what communication actually accomplishes. Another significant aspect of communication is **relational meaning**, or how communicators define their connections with each other. Relational meaning may concern degree of intimacy, power and status, and other interpersonal factors that the informational content of the message alone does not reveal. Informational meanings and relational meanings are equally important, and ignoring either level can cause serious communication breakdowns. In particular circumstances, one level often will assume more importance, but informational and relational meanings are always present.

Sometimes the informational meaning carries far less weight than the relational meaning that the overt message infers. For example, close friends might exchange remarks that appear to outsiders as insults:

Paco: "Hey, you lazy fool, are you still asleep?"

Chi-Lo: "No, stupid. If you had half a brain, you'd realize I was meditating."

Sounds terrible, doesn't it? Only on the informational level. Paco and Chi-Lo in this example use a ritual exchange of insults to signal their friendship. The relational meaning each of them shares here is: "We're such good friends that we can pretend to be angry without offending each other." Communication not only conveys information but also shapes and sustains human relationships.

CONTEXT OF COMMUNICATION

By now you probably realize that communication is much broader than you had thought. This book helps you develop skills in several areas of communication, most of which emerged as distinctive areas only gradually over the 2,500 years that communication has been studied.

Intrapersonal Communication

An often-ignored realm is known as **intrapersonal** communication. This type of communication is the internal dialogue you have with yourself, the self-talk that also affects how you present yourself and relate to others. Howard Gardner[4,5] includes *intra*personal and *inter*personal skills as two of the eight basic types of human intelligence. To function smoothly in life, we need to understand our own perceptions, perspectives, and feelings. Although not directly shared with others, intrapersonal communication can have enormous consequences. Perhaps the most important intrapersonal communication students have when they enter this course is the image about themselves as communicators. If you remind yourself daily, "I'm a lousy speaker" or constantly tell yourself, "I'll mess up and look like a fool," then your negative intrapersonal communication actually can cause you to perform poorly. That's right, you do as you're told. The good news is that you can and do control the messages you send to yourself, so you can program your intrapersonal communication to enhance your skills. Try it now. What positive intrapersonal messages can you send instead of the negative ones stated earlier?

Interpersonal Communication

One type of communication that we often take for granted and rarely examine is the **interpersonal** realm. Interpersonal communication includes all the conversational and relational interactions among friends, family members, co-workers, and anyone else we might associate with. The challenge of interpersonal communication is that we do it so automatically that it becomes easy to forget that we can adjust our ways of interacting with others. We forget, of course, until a relationship goes bad or someone takes offense at something we said. Interpersonal communication researchers deal with issues such as how to improve conversational skills or why relationships begin, continue, and fade. Ultimately, a better understanding of interpersonal needs and patterns can lead to the development of healthier relationships.

Group Communication

Group communication, often called small group communication in research, covers the interactions that occur between three or more people who gather together for a predetermined purpose. Groups can convene for many reasons, such as solving problems, providing emotional support to members, sharing members' interests or backgrounds, or to accomplish tasks too large for one person. Much of the communication research in this area deals with groups that are small enough for all the members to have some direct interaction with each other. A growing body of literature is devoted to the impact that electronic media have on groups, especially Web-based interest groups. On average, some researchers estimate that a manager spends at least 17 hours per week in group meetings and more than six additional hours preparing for them.[6] Considering the enormous amount of time business executives report spending in group meetings, competence in group communication should be a high priority.

Interviewing

We usually associate **interviewing** with the job search process, but interviews actually encompass a wide range of activities. Although usually conducted in one-on-one pairs known as **dyads**, interviews can occur in groups. Regardless of the format, all interviews use a turn-taking format with questions designed to gain information from the person being interviewed. Psychological and career counseling, disciplinary meetings, performance appraisals, adoptions, diagnoses of health problems, loan applications, and many other activities use an interview as at least part of the process.

Public Speaking

You are probably most familiar with communication as **public speaking**. In the public speech, a single speaker addresses an audience that can number from a handful to, with the help of broadcast media, millions at once. The roles of speaker and audience in this type of communication usually are clearly separated, with the speaker responsible for most or almost all of the oral delivery while the audience might interrupt briefly during the presentation with applause or other reactions. In a public speech, the speaker has a definite purpose and the content is more structured than an ordinary conversation.

These types of communication might be mixed in some circumstances. *The Daily Show* with Jon Stewart operates as a public speech when Stewart or one of the show's correspondents presents a story. Then the show shifts to an interview format when host Jon Stewart brings the guest onstage for a question-and-answer session. The different formats of communication do demand rather different sets of skills. A polished orator might deliver superb public speeches but perform very poorly in group settings. You might know people who are dynamic group members but interview poorly. This imbalance of skills shows why it is important to become competent in all the types of communication we cover in the textbook. A broad base of communication skills will equip you to function better whether the situation calls for groups, pairs, or individual performance in a variety of settings.

MODELS OF COMMUNICATION

Sometimes models can help clarify abstract, complicated, or new concepts. Since we experience communication as a process, a model could help us observe how the process works. For example, how easy would it be to understand the structure of DNA without the double helix model proposed by Watson[7] and Crick? Models also isolate the various components of systems so we can keep the system operating smoothly. Models certainly cannot tell us everything about communication. Since communication is a process, a model in a textbook can only sample the ongoing flow of communication, much like a still photo or freeze frame captures one image of something in motion. Communication models, however, enable us to understand ways we can identify and improve the ingredients of the communication process.

Linear Models

Linear models treat communication simply as messages sent from a speaker to a listener. In linear models, as shown in Figure 1.1, communication flows in one direction: from speaker to listener. You might have experienced a classroom where the teacher practiced a linear philosophy of communication. The teacher's job was to impart knowledge, so the teacher spoke while you listened silently. In an online environment, the linear model simply presents text, graphics, or video (such as the instructor lecturing) that require and ask for no response from the user. The advantage of these models is their simplicity. The limitations, however, are serious. The speaker has total control, determining everything about the communication. The listeners are totally passive, mere objects that receive whatever the speaker decides. Linear models do not account for adaptation to different listeners, so the speaker would talk at people, since there is no explanation of how communication changes over time.

Some simplistic views of mass media effects still show signs of linear models. These outlooks presume that television and film viewers, for example, are

FIGURE 1.1 A Linear Model of Communication.

empty receptacles that simply absorb, accept, and imitate uncritically whatever they watch on the screen. Cultural critic Stuart Hall objects to this naïve position, arguing that audiences are not "cultural dupes".[8] According to the linear view, my adolescent preferences in movies (action films), computer games (violent combat and fantasy quests), and music (heavy metal) probably should have resulted in me becoming a serial killer. Listeners evidently do more than the linear model depicts.

Interactive Models

Interactive models treat communication as a turn-taking activity. Speaking and listening are distinct; you either speak or listen, but you cannot do both at the same time. Just as two people play catch, as seen in Figure 1.2, there is process of turn-taking required in this model. Interactive models add to linear models the listener's reaction and response, known as **feedback**. We will hear much more about feedback later in this chapter, but for now consider how an interactive view improves our understanding of communication. You might have experienced a classroom based on the interactive view: The teacher still imparts information, then reserves time for student questions and comments. Listeners now at least can become somewhat involved in the process. Instead of listeners merely absorbing whatever the speaker offers, they can act as speakers when their turn comes. In an online environment, an interactive approach would give users opportunities to respond to communication through means such as e-mailing comments. Returning to our television example, interactive models can explain changes in programming based on viewer preferences. When the original competitive "reality show," *Survivor*, proved immensely popular, other reality shows quickly appeared and will remain on the air as long as the viewers keep watching them. The success of one show prompted response (or feedback) from other networks.

Interactive models also advance our understanding of communication in relationships. In linear models, everyone in a relationship simply tries to do what he or she thinks is right and hopes for the best. Interactive models enable listeners to play more of an active part because the speaker-listener roles will alternate during communication.

FIGURE 1.2 An Interactive Model of Communication.

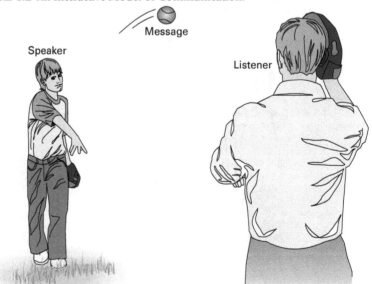

Despite its advantages over linear models, interactive models still fail to account for much of communication. Many questions remain unanswered by interactive models.

- What psychological and environmental factors might affect communication?
- How does understanding emerge from communication?
- How can we account for ongoing communication (such as families, friends, and co-workers) instead of single, discrete instances?
- What about communication environments where there is no definite turn-taking (such as one person telling a story while another person laughs)?

These persistent questions require a more sophisticated treatment of communication.

Transactional Models

In **transactional models**, communication becomes a shared venture between speakers and listeners. The term "transaction" captures the idea of participants working together to move toward understanding (which does not necessarily mean agreement). "Transaction" also implies that the results of communication are negotiated between speakers and listeners in their mutual adaptations. Actually no one is a pure speaker or listener in transactional models, because these roles are fluid while each communicator constantly both sends and receives messages. This allows both parties to co-create meaning as seen in Figure 1.3. Unlike the linear and interactive models, communication can flow in different directions. In a transactional classroom environment, discussion occurs often, students actively question and comment, and the teacher adjusts to student input. An online employment of the transactional view would invite user control of content through hyperlinks and participatory activities such as discussion forums and chats that engage communicators.

No longer does the speaker monopolize control over communication. Speakers and listeners rely on each other to know how well communication is going. Instead of being discrete as they were in linear models, speakers and listeners in interactive models are interrelated as partners in the shared quest to manufacture meaning and reach understanding. Although transactional

FIGURE 1.3 A Transactional Model of Communication.

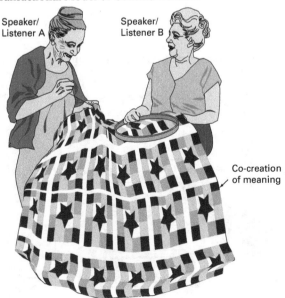

models offer an attractive overall way to approach communication, we still need to examine the individual parts of the communication process to get a better idea of how communication actually works.

COMPONENTS OF COMMUNICATION

Suppose your friend Narendra's car breaks down. She takes it to a mechanic. What will the mechanic do? The breakdowns of machines resemble communication breakdowns. We take our vehicles, our appliances, our electronic devices, our communication for granted—until something goes wrong. As communicators, we can learn something from the repair people. When a machine breaks down, the technician examines its individual parts, because one defective part can damage the entire mechanism. We can approach communication similarly: If we experience or witness a communication breakdown, we need to examine the elements that go into communication to diagnose the problem and fix it. Fortunately, because all of us communicate, we can understand the interconnected parts not only to recover from communication breakdowns, but hopefully to prevent them from occurring.

This idea of diagnosing potential problems means that studying communication has some very practical benefits. Following the language theorist I. A. Richards,[9] we could define the basic task of learning about communication as the "study of misunderstanding and its remedies" (p. 3). We will examine each component of communication, the problems that could arise with that component, and concrete ways you can fix or avoid misunderstanding. These components and their relationship are represented in Figure 1.4.

Interference

Effective communication always seeks to eliminate, prevent, or reduce the impact of **interference**—anything that hinders or reduces effective communication. Interference is the great enemy of every communicator. In the earliest discussions of communication components, modeled after research on electronic circuitry, interference was called noise because it literally was noise: static that reduced the efficiency of electronic transmissions.[10] Our understanding of interference has broadened substantially.

FIGURE 1.4 The Basic Components of Communication.

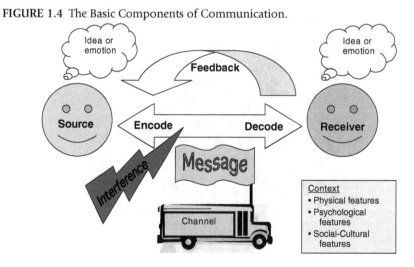

Rarely do we find only one type of interference operating alone. Interference operates on two basic levels. **Internal interference** consists of any conditions or perceptions that are within the communicators themselves. **External interference** includes anything about the environment that might disrupt the flow of communication. What kinds of things can cause interference? The possibilities are almost endless, but three roots of interference qualify as the most common. **Physical interference** covers any physiological challenges (internal) or concrete conditions in the environment (external) that can impede communication. **Psychological interference** encompasses perceptions or preconceptions that could threaten successful communication. Perceptions held by the communicator qualify as internal, while those held by others about the communicator would be external. **Social-cultural interference** involves a combination of internal and external factors that arise from the different backgrounds of communicators or mismatches between the communication and the audience's expectations. Figure 1.7 details the various causes of interference with examples of how they operate.

Interference can arise at any point in the communication process. Since interference can emerge anywhere, we should recognize that there are two ways to deal with it: prevention and reduction.

Option 1: Prevention

Prevent interference from arising. If possible, predict where interference might invade the communication process and take concrete measures to reduce the likelihood of it happening.

Examples: Prevention

1. Presentation (external physical interference)
   Interference. PowerPoint or other presentations might not display properly in the room.
   Prevention. Prepare samples of your slides and practice displaying them using the equipment you will have for your presentation.
2. Group interaction (external psychological interference)
   Interference. My group members don't know me so they might shun me.
   Prevention. Actively communicate with group members before your first group meeting. Arrange some informal interactions with at least one group member outside formal meetings.

The more thoroughly you can anticipate interference, the better you can use careful preparation and practice to control whether it happens. You will not necessarily foresee all potential interference by yourself, so get input from others regarding what might get in the way of effective communication. Then you can build in methods to reduce the chances that these problems will arise.

Option 2: Reduction

Reduce the impact of the interference. Sometimes we do not anticipate interference, but then recognize that communication has fizzled. One of the best things you can do in this situation is to focus on building some common ground with your listeners. If you and your listeners can envision yourselves as experiencing the problem together, the impact will not be as serious.

Examples: Reduction

1. Interview (social-cultural interference)
   Interference. You badly mispronounce the interviewer's name, which derives from an unfamiliar language.
   Reduction. Briefly apologize and note how this shows you have a lot to learn from each other.

2. Conversation (social-cultural interference)
   Interference. You stand too close to someone whose cultural custom is to keep more distance between people.
   Reduction. Alter your behavior and mention that you understand how frustrating it is for people to invade each other's space.
3. Presentation (external physical interference)
   Interference. The room is small and cramped.
   Reduction. Acknowledge the limitation as affecting everyone equally.

Although we never can eliminate all interference, we can prepare for it and manage it whenever possible.

Message and Medium/Channel

The **message** is the substance, or what is transmitted during communication. Message is not equivalent to meaning. To understand the difference, think of messages as the raw materials that contribute to constructing meanings. The words on this page form a message, but their meaning depends on how you understand and react to them. Messages can be intentional or unintentional. **Intentional messages** include whatever a communicator wants to convey. These messages are deliberate and may require advance preparation. If you are a candidate at an employment interview, your intended messages include confidence (ability to make and stick to decisions), competence (ability to do the job well), and collegiality (ability to get along with co-workers and supervisors). **Unintentional messages** consist of all the information a communicator conveys without realizing it. While unconscious, the unintended messages can carry great significance. A rich realm of research documents the unintended behaviors called *leakage cues* that liars accidentally exhibit why hiding the truth. Returning to the job interview example, you probably will need to continue your job search if your unintended messages show apprehension (shaky voice, minimal eye contact), incompetence (mispronouncing the company's name), and abrasiveness (insulting a previous employer).

A growing source of interference at the message level is sheer oversupply. As communication technologies expand, humans can produce messages at astronomical rates. The total amount of information stored electronically, optically, and in print throughout the world *doubled* just from 1999 to 2002.[11] The volume of messages outpaces the ability to process them, a condition known as **information overload**. This condition would not be problematic if the ability to process information kept pace with information production. Humans physically cannot increase their listening and reading speed to keep up with the storm of incoming spoken, written, electronic, and visual messages.

A related type of message-related interference is **message competition**, which compounds the problem of information overload. Message competition refers to the difficulty of sorting incoming messages because they become harder to distinguish from each other: high priority vs. low priority, personal vs. professional, uplifting vs. depressing, substance vs. spam, etc. With so many messages competing for our attention, which should we deal with, which should we defer, which should we ignore? As the volume of incoming messages increases, it becomes ever more difficult to make distinctions to decide which messages to process. Now that we have hundreds of television channels to choose among, what do we do? We spend a lot of time channel surfing, unable to decide amid this baffling buffet of broadcasting. Many of us even struggle to decide which should have higher priority: talking on the cell phone or driving?

The variety as well as quantity of messages has very real effects. A study reveals that workers who tried to complete problem-solving tasks suffered a

10-point drop in IQ when constantly bombarded by e-mails and telephone calls.[12] The effect of this information overload was twice the intellectual damage inflicted by being high on marijuana! London psychiatrist Glenn Wilson comments: "If left unchecked, 'infomania' will damage a worker's performance by reducing their [sic] mental sharpness. . . . This is a very real and widespread phenomenon".[12] Other research finds that people who multitask heavily are more easily distracted and demonstrate lower levels of attention to the tasks they are trying to do. The researchers note a "reduced ability to filter out interference from the irrelevant task set".[13]

To deal with information overload and message competition may require more **gatekeeping**. Any method that filters information to make it more usable to communicators qualifies as gatekeeping. The essential task of gatekeeping is to select messages based on quality. The editors of newspapers, televised news, and online news services select only some stories to cover. The *New York Times* slogan "All the news that's fit to print" is a terrifying prospect, since it is equivalent to saying your dinner consists of all the food that's in the kitchen. To limit and sort information, communicators can employ various gatekeepers. Concerned parents use v-chips, Internet content filters, and other parental control devices to shield children from inappropriate material. Spam filters and pop-up blockers restrict incoming e-mails and online advertisements so computer users can concentrate on messages relevant to their tasks. The challenge when gatekeeping is to try to filter out as many undesired messages as possible without losing important information.

Tech Talk

What are some of the pros and cons of spam filters, pop-up blockers, and parental control devices for gatekeeping? In your experience, how well do these devices work?

The **channel** of communication, often called the **medium**, concerns how communication is sent and received. The choice of channel may be as important as the message itself. Canadian media theorist Marshall McLuhan believed "the medium is the message",[14] meaning that *how* we communicate, the means of communicating, can play a central role in interpretation and reaction. The form of messages affects the way they are perceived. More than any other component of communication, the medium is affected by technology. The first students of communication in ancient Greece knew face-to-face interaction and a bit of writing. Now we have to add mass-produced printing, radio, telephone, texting, television, faxes, computer-mediated communication, and other media.

People's communication skills can vary drastically depending on the medium. Many students who are quiet and reluctant to speak in a traditional classroom open up and participate more in online settings. For example, due to cultural differences some Japanese and Chinese students tend to remain quiet in U.S. college classrooms, yet these same students become full participants in electronic learning environments.[15]

The main way interference seeps into the channel is through mismatching the message with the means for conveying it. Every medium brings advantages and drawbacks. The key to successful communication lies in choosing the best medium. If your best friend is seriously depressed about work, would you call, send a card, drop an e-mail, or visit? The telecommunication company AT&T used to promote its long distance phone service by saying, "It's the next best thing to being there." But even the most sophisticated media will not bring your loved one to your side, unless you build a *Star Trek*-type transporter.

Quite a few people are starting relationships in an online medium rather than in person. Online dating services boasted an estimated 12 million subscribers in 2008.[16] Interference enters very easily online, as people can accidentally or intentionally misrepresent or misinterpret identities, motives, or appearances.[17]

Aside from deception, the speed and ease of online communication invites hasty and sometimes offensive communication. How often have you received a harshly worded e-mail from someone who would never treat you so rudely in person? These incidents happen a lot with e-mails because they are so easy to send. If you are tempted to write a very angry e-mail message, go ahead and write it—but then save it as a draft for a while. Given a bit of time, you may calm down or want to reconsider by editing or deleting your message. Also remember that even the most confidential e-mails are not private. Anyone can—accidentally or intentionally—forward an e-mail message to people you never wanted to address. Treat all electronic communication, especially e-mail, as potentially public because it can be circulated without your knowledge or consent.

Source and Receiver

The **source** is where communication originates. Often we identify the source as the speaker, which is true as long as we refer to verbal communication. A source can be anyone or anything that generates information someone can interpret. Individual people, collective bodies (corporations, groups and organizations, governments, institutions, etc.), or even objects (such as the clothes someone wears) can qualify as a source. Here are a few examples of sources:

Individual sources. Barack Obama, George Lopez, Beyoncé Knowles, your roommate

Collective sources. The Republican Party, the Internal Revenue Service, Toyota, Aerosmith, the financial aid department at your school

Objects. The U.S. Holocaust Memorial Museum, the Eiffel Tower, the Sistine Chapel, the Statue of Liberty, the Mayan Ruins, an office cubicle

The source of communication also might be anonymous, such as the Valentine's day card or gift from a "secret admirer" or the unnamed donor of $10 million to a university's scholarship fund.

The wide variety of potential sources also opens the way for interference. We have to be able to identify the source to judge whether communication is credible. An anonymous tip can't be trusted on face value. Sometimes the identity of a source remains fuzzy or deceptive. Consider some of those amazing business opportunities you might have seen on television or online. Just go to the Web address listed and you'll get rich. Isn't it strange that these advertisements avoid describing the nature of the business or the identity of the company that sponsors the promotions? Stay on the lookout for deceptive or unknown sources, since communication from them should raise suspicion.

Morality Matters

Modern presidents of the United States have so many speeches to give that they cannot write much of their own material. They depend on a staff of speechwriters to craft their words. Audiences almost never know the identity of the speechwriters, and the words are uttered by the president. Who, then, is the source of communication we get from the president? What moral concerns arise from reliance on unidentified speechwriters? What, if anything, should we do about this situation?

Another type of interference lies in how we react to sources. Too often we have immediate, uncritical reactions to a source simply because of the source's prestige, rank, or status. Sources sometimes offer credentials that are only empty titles. A careful communicator needs more than an impressive sounding title to earn or trust and belief. Too often we find so-called "experts" offering all sorts of information. Always ask: "What makes this source believable?"

The **receiver** is the audience, whoever gets the message and can interpret it. Be careful: The identity of receivers is more complex than you might think. Receivers are not simply the people who are physically present. According to how we just defined receivers, children too young to understand verbal language would not count as part of the audience for a public speech. On the other hand, any preserved and archived messages can reach audiences the source never intended or even imagined. William Shakespeare's plays and sonnets were not composed for American college students in the twenty-first century, yet you count as part of Shakespeare's audience. Television and movie actors, musicians, and speakers can entertain audiences who enjoy their work long after the performers have died. Computer simulation technology led to conceiving of **virtual audiences**, people who are not physically present but who still receive messages. Online chats sometimes serve as virtual group meetings because participants perform all the functions of a group remotely, apart from other members of the group. Receivers also can be unintended, such as someone who accidentally overhears a conversation or receives an e-mail intended for someone else.

Interference with receivers poses special challenges, because receivers determine whether communication succeeds or fails. If the goal of communication is to create meaning and these meanings arise from interpretation, then receivers hold the key to effective communication. As a source, you should carefully gather accurate information about how your receivers' culture and context shapes what they consider appropriate. Since receivers determine the success of communication, adapt to receiver needs and standards for proper interactions.

Encoding and Decoding

Have you ever known what you wanted to say, but you just couldn't seem to express it properly? If so, then you already are acquainted with the challenge of **encoding**. The encoding process converts our private ideas and feelings into a public symbol system (words, objects, or behaviors) that others can access. For years, the florist industry has recognized the challenge of encoding by their slogan "Say it with flowers," presumably because affection, apology, sympathy, and other sentiments can be felt much more easily than they can be communicated to others. Many of my students have admitted that flowers often encode an apology, a way of saying "I'm sorry" when the verbal apology just doesn't seem to do the job. Elton John recorded a song titled "Sorry Seems to Be the Hardest Word," and he may be correct. Deep emotions often resist easy encoding.

Encoding is vital because it is the only way that private thoughts and feelings can go public. Without encoding, whatever you want to express remains just an idea or a feeling trapped inside your brain, inaccessible to others. The rock band Boston had a hit song, "More Than a Feeling," that described the sensation an old song caused. If you want to understand how much effort encoding can take, try explaining to someone else the feeling you get when you hear your favorite song or after reading an amazing book.

Interference arises in encoding simply from the difficulty of transforming ideas and feelings into symbols. Internally, a communicator might have problems encoding because of insufficient access to public symbols. For instance, someone might have a limited vocabulary, which restricts the ways ideas can be communicated. To address this limitation, practice expressing yourself more thoroughly using all the resources at your disposal: words, tone of voice, and body language (topics discussed in Chapters 4 and 5). For example, try conveying the widest possible variety of different emotions through your facial expressions and voice—the type of skill mastered not only by the best actors but by effective storytellers and teachers.

A second sort of interference with encoding lies in the assumption that everyone else encodes exactly the same way as we do. To avoid disappointment in relationships, try to discover how others encode values that are important to them. Perhaps an employee encodes hard work as staying late at the office, but the supervisor encodes hard work as doing things efficiently and leaving early. These co-workers may begin to appreciate each other more if they understand how each other encodes the concept of "hard work" or "dedication to the job."

Decoding is the process of interpretation that occurs on the receiver's side of communication. Through decoding, we give meaning to messages. Think of decoding as the reverse of encoding. While sources attempt to capture ideas and encode them in ways that others can access, receivers are trying to reconstruct those messages into meaningful information. But there's a catch, and that is where interference arises.

Ideally, there would be perfect understanding if every receiver decoded exactly the same way the source encoded. The receiver would be able to reconstruct the source's original thoughts and emotions. Can such perfect understanding ever occur? Since everyone interprets reality according to his or her own experiences and no two people have exactly the same experience, we should not expect or seek perfect matches between intended meaning (what the source wants to encode) and interpreted meaning (what the receiver has decoded). The risk of interference increases as the differences between the source and receiver grow.

Nowhere is the encoding/decoding gap more obvious than in the familiar and weighty words "I love you." Suppose for Leslie "I love you" encodes: "I want you as my life partner and we will be faithful exclusively to each other forever, an inseparable pair." Dakota, the recipient of this message, also hears the same statement: "I love you." Dakota, however, decodes those three words as: "I'll treat you as special but each of us is free to date others and there is no long-term commitment while we see each other whenever it is convenient." Chances are high that this relationship is headed for trouble. Who is right? Both Leslie and Dakota are correct *within their own perspectives for encoding and decoding*. Since they have different experiences, they interpret a declaration of love differently. Dakota and Leslie could have avoided serious interference problems by sharing with each other what they recognize as love. This negotiation of meaning is vitally important in human relationships.

Feedback

All responses to communication comprise **feedback**. These reactions can be immediate, such laughing at a joke when you hear it, or delayed, such as the comments you get on an essay you turned in last week. In any communication, the source and receiver constantly exchange feedback. In fact, feedback is absolutely crucial because it is the only way a communicator can determine how well the communication is going. A speech, for example, is only as successful as the audience and analysts judge it to be. Feedback has special importance for students: How else would you know how you are doing in your courses?

Without feedback providing concrete suggestions, evaluations would seem random because they lacked explanation. Educators and corporate executives prioritize feedback, since it provides ways for students and employees to improve performance.

Feedback should be prompt. Sometimes slow feedback causes interference in threaded discussions online.[18] In a group project, some group members might post important ideas or proposals that require quick input. If other members fail to post promptly, not logging in for days or weeks, the entire group might suffer by having to delay its vote, slowing the decision-making process. Expectations for feedback have become much higher with the expansion of electronic communication. While most of us can wait at least a week to receive a reply to a written letter, how long would you expect to wait for a reply to a text message?

Feedback also should be expressed clearly. In transactional communication, communicators always are seeking reactions from each other and taking those reactions into account. Blank looks and total silence give a communicator no clue about how someone is interpreting messages or whether he understands at all. Think of a time you have been on the telephone and had to ask whether the other person was there because she offered no response. Frustrating, isn't it? Beyond frustration, unclear feedback makes communicators guess at whether the message is getting through as they intended.

Feedback needs to be specific. The more specific the feedback, the more useful it can be. How would you like to receive a performance review during your first job after college with feedback such as "B: pretty good work" or "F: you're fired"? You would be upset because you would have no idea what you should continue or change in the future. Feedback should allow you to interact with other communicators. In casual conversations, how can others recognize your feelings if you reply only with grunts of agreement?

Finally, get feedback from others. To improve performance, we need to get the perspective of other people. They might provide valuable observations and suggestions that we miss if we rely only on ourselves. Former New York City mayor Ed Koch used to solicit feedback by walking the streets and asking ordinary citizens, "How am I doing?" Sometimes students in communication courses mistakenly believe they need only to rehearse their presentations in front of a mirror or in their mind. Researchers have found that self-generated feedback is less effective than feedback from others in leading to positive change.[19]

Checkpoint

To be effective, feedback needs to be:

- Prompt
- Clearly expressed
- Specific
- From others

Communication Context

Perhaps the broadest component, **context** refers to all the factors surrounding communication that could influence it. Think of communication context as the overall setting of interaction, including the audience, time of day, cultural background, and spatial environment. Because it is so broad, the communication context breaks down into several categories. To help you recognize and remember the types of communication context, the categories mirror the kinds of interference described earlier in this chapter. Figure 1.5 lists the three main communication contexts and examples within each category.

FIGURE 1.5 Communication Contexts.

Physical	Psychological	Social-Cultural
Definition: objects, environmental conditions, space, time	Definition: attitudes and beliefs about communicator, audience, or topic	Definition: expectations based on customs and heritage
Examples: size of room, time frame allowed for presentation, temperature, availability of podium	Examples: knowledge of topic or communicator, prior experience with topic	Examples: political affiliation, age, educational level, ethnic background of listeners, national traditions

Take into account the context to reduce the chances of interference. Before engaging in communication consider the following contextual factors:

- What are the basic expectations for this type of communication in these circumstances?
- What do these specific listeners expect to get from our interaction?
- What similarities and differences between myself and my listeners should I consider?

If you at least recognize the features of the context that might affect your communication, you can anticipate interference that might arise.

CONFUSIONS AND CORRECTIONS

Now that we have reviewed the components of communication, it's time to set the record straight. This section discusses some features of communication that often cause confusion. We will examine where common misconceptions might arise and how to avoid them.

Meanings Are in People, Not in Words or Symbols

This chapter earlier referred to transactional communication as a shared quest to "manufacture meaning." That phrase might sound strange. After all, don't words already have meaning? Not exactly, at least not if you study communication.

Meanings are created, not found. Since meanings come from experience and no two people's experiences are identical, meanings must be negotiated between communicators.[20] Creation of meaning, therefore, involves forging connections between people whose worlds of experience may differ radically. "In so far as we experience the world differently, in a sense we live in different worlds" (pp. 21–22).[21] The components of communication described earlier in this chapter do not include meaning, since that is an outcome of how receivers interpret messages. When you send a message, you cannot legislate its meaning, guaranteeing that everyone will share your interpretation. If meanings were in words or other symbols, then a quick trip to the dictionary would solve all misunderstandings. Instead, we must carefully search for why the encoded message and the decoded message may not correspond.

Because symbols always stand for something else, they do not have meanings in themselves.[22] How people interpret symbols such as the Confederate flag from the U.S. Civil War depends on their perspective. People whose ancestors fought for the Confederacy may recognize the flag as a symbol of proud Southern heritage and an independent spirit. People whose ancestors were enslaved under that banner may perceive it as a symbol of racial bigotry and inhumanity. The flag itself is literally a piece of cloth. Throughout the debates that surround the Confederate flag, the same question reappears: "What does the flag really mean?" From a communication angle, that's not the most accurate question. The flag—and any symbol—means what people interpret it to mean. What the flag symbolizes will depend on people communicating with each other, discussing how they construct meanings.

Unfortunately, people don't always communicate effectively with each other and often develop inaccurate beliefs as a result. **Prejudgment** occurs when receivers reach conclusions about communicators or communication based on assumptions instead of evidence. The word "prejudice" reflects this jumping to conclusions. Whenever we interact, we tend to make predictions to ease communication. For example, we might know that one person enjoys humor so we make lighthearted conversation, but another person prefers getting straight to the point so we are direct and concise.

Prejudgments are more problematic than predictions because they lack sufficient grounds for reaching conclusions. A student of mine once delivered a persuasive speech with the thesis "Black people deserve all the abuse they get" (yes, that's the exact quote—I still remember twenty years later). The class was appalled. Meeting privately with the student, I asked why she would make such an offensive and unsupportable claim. Her contention was based solely on two or three African American students who picked on her in high school. That was her total body of experience to support the position that an entire race deserved mistreatment. Moral of the story: Gather sufficient data before you judge.

Recall the components of communication and how they interconnect. Communication is about the transmission of messages, not the transfer of meaning from one person's mind into another. If meanings were in words or other symbols, we could simply grab a meaning, shove it into someone else's mind, and achieve complete understanding. "The" meaning of a symbol lies in how we and other communicators use it and react to it. Instead of asking for "the" meaning of a word, ask for the user's meaning.[20]

Communication Concerns Quality, Not Quantity

Although communication plays a central role in almost every facet of our lives, it is easy to think that communication, in itself, will solve all problems. A mystique surrounds communication, as if communication holds the solution to all problems and the more communication we have, the better. This attitude is not only unrealistic, it also reflects some serious misconceptions.

More communication is not always better. Don't confuse quantity with quality. According to the National Communication Association,[23] "We are living in a communications revolution comparable to the invention of printing. . . . In an age of increasing talk, it's wiser talk we need most." In some relationship situations, the wisest move is to reduce the quantity of communication and focus on utilizing communication strategically. For example, if two people become very angry, the exchange of harsh words might reach a point when every additional remark escalates the anger and makes the situation worse. In this case, the communicators may need to take a "time out" and refrain from communicating with each other until anger subsides and sensibility emerges. Effective communication also sometimes requires ending a relationship. A skillful communicator knows when to stop talking, and the best communicators may listen a lot more than they speak.

Sometimes more communication might actually hurt more than it helps. Earlier in this chapter, we discussed the challenge of information overload. Piling on more communication without a clear purpose simply adds to the oversupply of messages. In addition, more communication can be harmful if a communicator has learned poor habits and continues them. For example, should we always encourage more communication from people who degrade others? Instead, we should strive for more appropriate and thoughtful messages, not just more miscommunication.

Communication Is "Inevitable, Irreversible, and Unrepeatable"

Many introductory communication texts contain this statement, almost a slogan within the field. The inevitability of communication often has been captured with the comment, "You cannot *not* communicate".[24] Even when alone, we find ourselves engaging in intrapersonal communication: "Why can't I ever find my keys?" "Come on, who am I kidding? Of course I can have that speech ready by next Tuesday." Whenever you are around other people, you cannot help conveying messages that others can receive: clothing, tone of voice, gestures, grooming, and posture qualify as potential messages. Since many messages are unintentional, we don't have to plan communication for it to happen anyway. If you ever spend time "people watching," then you become a receiver of messages, trying to construct explanations of people's behavior.

"You're ugly! No—disregard that." But you can't; the insult has been made. Messages, once sent, cannot be retracted. You might have heard judges say to juries in a courtroom: "Jurors, ignore that last remark. Strike it from the record." The problem is that we cannot "take back" communication, although we have all wanted to at times. We might forgive it or forget it, but every message received makes some sort of impact. One useful but bizarre feature on Microsoft Outlook e-mail is the option to "recall" a message you sent earlier. The idea behind it is that you can realize, "Oops—I shouldn't have sent that" and retract the message. If the message already went through to the recipient, then that person receives a message saying that you wish to "recall" the previous message. Yet there it sits in the recipient's inbox. Once sent, messages are available to be received, interpreted, misinterpreted, or ignored. So choose your messages wisely.

The ancient Greek philosopher Heraclitus claimed, "You can never step into the same river twice." His statement aptly describes communication. You can never communicate exactly the same way twice, because—as we discussed earlier—all communication is tied to its context. In a long-term relationship, the bonds of love endure, but the nature of that love matures and adjusts through time. What started as perhaps shared sporting interests and physical attraction might evolve into more of a focus on spiritual connections. Richard Nixon's speech when he resigned from the presidency had a different impact on audiences in 1974 than it does on people who view the speech today. Not only do audiences change, but the same people's attitudes and perspectives alter over time. Science fiction films that dazzled audiences a few decades ago often look ridiculous now because special effects technology has raised our expectations. You probably recall someone telling a story about an event he thought was hilarious, but you don't find it amusing at all. The narrator says, "Oh, you just had to be there." Exactly: The same communication changes when retold or re-enacted. Each communication event is a unique experience.

Good Communicators Are Made, Not Born

Often students entering an introductory communication course worry about the performance components. I hear remarks such as: "I'm not a naturally good speaker," or "I don't have the gift of communicating well." Everyone brings some natural talents and limitations to a communication course. Regardless of how well you think you communicate now, everyone can learn and improve. Communication is definitely a learned skill. The more you practice effective communication skills, the more confidence you will have in your own abilities.

All people are born with the capacity to communicate, which leads to the mistaken belief that communication doesn't have to be taught in a formal course. If communication is natural, why bother with a course? Communication certainly is natural, but effective and appropriate communication is quite rare. If anyone could simply pick up communication skills on the street or absorb them through the course of life, formal study would serve no purpose. But how many people do you know who are wonderful listeners, inspiring group leaders, awe-inspiring speakers, or gripping conversationalists? Chances are that your list is quite short. Communication involves concentrated effort and dedication; otherwise, models of excellent communication would surround us.

WHAT ARE CRITICAL THINKING STYLES?*

Browne and Keeley suggest that there are two alternative thinking styles that people use.[5] The first, the *sponge* approach, allows you to absorb as much information as you can, just as an absorbent sponge soaks up water. It is a pretty easy way to take in information, because you can remain passive, especially if the material is not too complex. Being a sponge is not necessarily bad: The more information you soak up, the greater your ability to understand how complex issues can be. Knowledge can always be saved and retrieved later; think of this as summary without analysis (like what you might do when you underline in a textbook!). But the problem with sponge thinking is that you end up with gobs of information and no real means for deciding which to keep and which to eliminate. If you cannot select which information to maintain and which to reject, then you might only know what you ran across last. You may end up taking ideas for granted, not considering what to accept or reject, and you may ignore the limits of your perceptual ability. You will find it difficult to create a message based on so much unsorted data.

Most of us prefer to consider ourselves as people who think critically or analytically. That is, we like to keep certain pieces of information and eliminate others, based on some type of criteria. If you want to choose wisely, however, you need to interact with the incoming data. The *panning-for-gold* style of thinking, according to Browne and Keeley, requires active participation as you try to determine the worth of what you hear and read.[6] It requires a questioning attitude that is the heart of critical thinking. It is a challenge to the intellect to utilize this method, because it means that you have to plan how to think, which can be tedious. But in the end, your thinking will probably be stronger and more reliable, and you should be better able to develop a strategic, vaudience-oriented message, which is essential for successful communication.

To understand the difference between the two thinking styles, put yourself in the shoes of each type of thinker. If you are a sponge thinker, you are focused on getting as much knowledge as you can. You develop skills in memory, note taking, and summarizing. It is not really that important to understand the information or to decide if the information is important or worthy of remembering; you just want to soak it all in. Now consider panning-for-gold thinking. Although you want to gain new information and understanding, you consider the information in light of personal standards for uncovering the truth. You try to comprehend in order to create a stronger base of belief for yourself.

Consider an example of the two styles: You hear from your friend that your school is thinking about changing athletic conferences. If this happens, your friend has heard, the school will need to change its mascot because there already is one of those in the new conference. Your friend tells you that everyone is upset

---

*From *Communication: Principles of Tradition and Change* by Wallace et al. Copyright © 2008 by Kendall Hunt Publishing Company. Reprinted by permission.

about this change, because it will probably mean that your sports team will not be the best of the conference. He admits, though, that his advisor thinks that this change will probably result in more academic scholarships, greater study-abroad opportunities, and more national recognition for your school. However, your friend reminds you, "Nothing good has ever happened when a school enters a conference. That school loses its identity and becomes something no one recognizes." Your friend then asks you for your opinion on changing conferences.

A sponge thinker would take all this information in, trying to create a judgment, as the friend has requested. If you are using this approach, you probably will rely on your own feelings about your mascot, your sports team, your current conference, members of the new conference, and academic offerings. You will know whether your friend has been trustworthy in the past in what he tells you. But do you know if the information you have just gotten really can form the basis of a judgment on your part? A panning-for-gold thinker would ask questions about the information:

- What does "thinking about changing" really mean? Does this mean that preliminary negotiations have begun? Does it mean that an idea is being floated?
- Who is "everyone" that is upset? What is the source of that statement?
- What are the facts of the potential merge? Are they even known yet?
- Is your friend's advisor in a particular position to be able to offer expert testimony about the outcome of such a merger?
- What are the pros and cons of a merger? What have the mergers of other schools into conferences resulted in for those schools? Can you compare your school to those situations?

Questioning the information you receive allows you to choose what to believe and then to make more critical judgments. When you ask questions, you might discover that the information is incomplete or faulty, that the sources are not credible, or that the assertions being made are unsubstantiated. In every sense, the panning-for-gold thinker will approach thinking as an interactive activity. It is much more difficult than sponge thinking, partly because you have had more experience in sponge thinking, and partly because panning-for-gold means that you have to expend energy. But be honest: most of us *are* lazy, and panning means that you have to work hard at thinking.

HOW DO I BECOME A CRITICAL THINKER?

Let us now assume that you want to be the panning-for-gold type of thinker; you want to question what you hear and to determine what you will believe. This analysis and evaluation is essential for critical thinking. You sense that this type of thinking will not only help you to understand your world more clearly, but it might also result in your creating a more effective message. But in order to know *what* to ask about, you need to know about the kinds of knowledge that are important for critical thinking and the lenses that help to focus us.

The Hallmarks of Critical Thinking

Critical thinking provides us with three kinds of knowledge: organized knowledge, skill knowledge, and understanding.

- *Organized knowledge.* The first, **organized knowledge,** is often called your intellect. It consists of your informed beliefs, what you think is real. For instance, do you know what day it is? Do you have mathematical knowledge of what addition and subtraction rules are? Do you know what is meant by the *Final Four?*

- *Skill knowledge.* **Skill knowledge** consists of your grasp of how to do something. Can you apply those mathematical rules to balancing your financial accounts? Are you able to discuss the method by which teams are chosen for the Final Four?
- *Understanding.* **Understanding,** the third type of knowledge, combines skill with intellect to create insight. In understanding, you grasp the complexity of ideas and evaluate how they impact other concepts. Can you articulate why the Everyday Math program used in public schools employs practical applications of mathematics, rather than asking children to memorize by rote the times tables? Can you discuss the pros and cons of various teams' selections for the March Madness tournament?

The three kinds of knowledge are useful in different situations, and you may be called to use them for different reasons. If you are following instructions, then you need to have skill knowledge. But if you plan to explain how to do something to someone else, transferring that skill knowledge to someone else, you need to be able to go beyond skill into understanding. Organized knowledge is essential for living day to day; you have to have beliefs that serve as the fundamental basis of who you are. If you don't know what a term means, then you can't go past that most basic intellect that constitutes organized knowledge.

Essential Skills for Effective Critical Thinking

To think critically, you apply different skills to gather and focus information. The skills that are essential are perceptual skills, knowledge-gathering skills, and researching skills:

- *Perceptual skills.* **Perceptual skills** engage physical and psychological dimensions, resulting in an interaction between the senses and the external environment. If you wear contact lenses and lose one, your physical ability to see things at a distance might be impaired, possibly causing you to miss something important. If you think that taking a communication class is the sure way to an easy A, you might be disturbed by the reality that the theories and strategies of communicating with others is complex. Your perceptions in both cases will lead your thinking astray.
- *Knowledge-gathering skills.* Here, we are not talking about the physical or mental ability to decode words; it is something much more. **Knowledge-gathering skills** include your ability to read and to listen. Listening involves more than hearing, as you will learn later in this chapter. In the same way, reading is not "just" decoding symbols; it is comprehending meaning, grasping tone and spirit, and evaluating the worth of the material.

What skills do you need to apply to think critically?
© Dainis Derics/Shutterstock.com

- *Researching skills.* **Researching skills** consist of your ability to seek and to gather information. What sources can you access? You have a repertoire of sources such as databases, Internet-based resources, personal interviews, books, journals, and magazines, surveys, and focus groups.

Let us try some simple exercises to discover these skills before we explore them in greater depth.

Copy these nine dots on a sheet of paper. Then connect them using four straight lines. You may cross over lines, but you may not pick your pen or pencil up off the paper, nor may you retrace a line.

Your ability or inability to do this task is a result of your perceptual skill. Do you expect to be able to connect a box-shaped series of dots when you have four lines to use? Most of us expect to be able to make a box. But the directions disallow that, because you cannot connect all the dots with four lines (that one in the middle becomes problematic with a box shape). You feel constrained by the presumed (and perceived) shape, and you cannot think outside of the box!

Now let us imagine that your instructor has just announced in front of the whole class that she wants to see you at the end of the hour. No other information is given. Your mind begins to race. You wonder about the instructor's tone: Did she sound angry? Was she looking at me? You consider what you have possibly done that would require having to see the instructor. You may even have flashbacks to the last time you were called into the instructor's presence! You are engaging in knowledge-gathering. You record the information and try to establish its worth and meaning in a context beyond "simple" decoding.

Try this problem from Marilyn vos Savant's column in *Parade* magazine to test your knowledge-gathering skills:[7] What can you find in these words: dogma, resin, minor, facet, somber, labor, tirade, dormer. *Hint:* Try whistling while you work out your answer. (*Answer:* The first two letters of each word spells out the tones of the musical scale: do, re, mi, fa, so,la, ti, do.)

Finally, what if you were asked to complete this analogy: George Washington is to one as William Howard Taft is to ———. Now, you might know that Taft was a president of the United States, and you might know that an analogy requires you to do some type of this-is-like-that thinking, so you can employ your knowledge and perceptual lenses. But unless you memorized the presidents sometime back in elementary school and can retrieve the correct rank number, it is likely you would need to go to an outside source to discover the answer. Where exactly would you go? You might do an Internet search, ask your great uncle or political science professor, or even remember to look the answer up in a book. Your researching skills require you to know what kind of information to seek and where likely sources of information might be.

In the remainder of this chapter, let us probe these skills more closely in order to appreciate their importance for critical thinking.

WHAT ROLE DOES PERCEPTION PLAY IN CRITICAL THINKING?

To engage in critical thinking, we have to begin with the most fundamental of our skill abilities: our perceptions. The concept of **perception** can be defined in many ways, but simply put, it is our set of beliefs concerning what is out there. For more detail, let us consider two views. John Chaffee, a professor of humanities specializing in critical thinking, says that perceiving involves actively selecting, organizing, and interpreting what is experienced by your senses.[8] Thus, perception involves what you can see, hear, feel, smell, and taste; you use these sensations to experience and to make sense of the world. Communication Professor Julia T. Wood says that perception is an active process of selecting, organizing, and interpreting people, objects, events, situations, and activities.[9] It is how we attach significance to the world around us.

Process of Perception

If we combine the previous definitions, perception involves our senses, employs a process of interaction, and results in an understanding of some experience in order to make sense of the world. Returning to Wood's definition, perception involves three interactive processes: selection, organization, and interpretation:

Selection

First is **selection.** Because your senses are bombarded by sights, sounds, and smells (at the minimum), you have developed a method of focusing that narrows your attention to selected stimuli. Stop reading right now and focus on the sounds around you. Did you notice them as you were holding this book? Can you close your eyes and picture what page you were on? Are there any pleasant or unpleasant smells around you? Reflect on the stimuli you were actively conscious of and those you eliminated from awareness. This selection of stimuli is necessary and typical of perceptions; you cannot make all stimuli relevant, so you focus on the ones that you have defined as important to whatever task you are currently engaged in.

Perhaps you remember a time when a pot boiled over. Even though dinner was important, your attention had been drawn away by a phone call. One perception (the phone's ring) shifted your perception away from the boiling pot. This perceptual process is important for a communicator, because you can use it to your advantage. We know that some stimuli will draw attention because they are particularly relevant, immediate, or intense. If you talk about something that your listener relates to, it is likely that issue will draw greater interest. If you attempt to catch initial attention by a soft voice, it is unlikely that will work, simply because it is not very intense. If your audience cannot see what you are showing them, their visual limits will likely result in their tuning out.

Organization

The second perceptual process is **organization.** We all try to structure perceptions in order to make sense of them. You will learn later that there are many strategies for structuring public speeches, group meetings, and interviews to accomplish desired goals. For now, we will simply say that each of us applies certain cognitive patterns, or perceptions. Those patterns are developed through experience. If you have never smelled certain spices, then you cannot sort them into the correct meaning of what kind of food is cooking; if you have developed stereotypical patterns that suggest all members of a certain ethnic group have a certain intellectual level, then you might assume that a new colleague from that group has that intellect.

Interpretation

Interpretation happens when you assign meaning to your perceptions. Once your brain has selected and organized the stimuli, it has to create meaning. For instance, if you are given a set of numbers, how do you know what they mean?

231 7620

904 38 7231

5468 9960 0075 1234

The first set appears to be a phone number, without the area code. The second set might be structured like a social security number. The third set appears to be similar to a credit card number. How do you know this? Part of your interpretation comes from the way the numbers are structured (organized), but part has to come from your experience. If you have never seen a social security number, you cannot interpret the second set in that way; it might not have any meaning. Similarly, if someone you know suddenly stops talking to you, you recognize the change in a pattern, but you interpret what has "caused" this silence to occur based on your own experiences, beliefs, values, and attitudes. Did Joan stop talking to you because you hurt her feelings? Is she sick and hoarse? Each of those interpretations is different, but they are based on the same initial perception of silence. Depending on your interpretation, your next communication encounter with Joan will be markedly different.

Other strategic perceptual techniques will be developed later in this text, but you need to remember that an audience's perceptions will greatly influence your ability to communicate successfully with them. The process of perception, involving selection, organization, and interpretation, describes the active steps we engage in to develop meaning.

Perception Principles

Three basic principles of perception might offer a deeper understanding of the complexity of the perception process. Subjectivity, stability, and meaningfulness describe the various filters that each of us employs when we attempt to create meaning from stimuli.

Perception Principles

Subjectivity—Perceptions that are unique to your personal experience, views, or mental state. Sources include:
   Physiology: physical sensory ability
   Culture and experiences: beliefs, values, norms and ways of interpreting experiences
   Psychological: affected by the perceptual choices you make
      Selective exposure: you choose consistent information
      Selective attention: you choose to pay attention to known stimuli
      Selective interpretation: you interpret ambiguous stimuli to be consistent with what you know
      Selective retention: you remember more accurately those things that are consistent with what you know
Stability—The predictability that we need in life; managed in two ways:
   Assimilation: you interpret the stimuli you receive to fit what you already know or expect
   Accommodation: you change what you know to fit the incoming perceptual data
Meaningfulness—Refers to the ways that we project comprehension or understanding onto perceptions; achieved in several ways:
   Contrast: you say something is like (or unlike) something you know
   Familiar versus the novel: you understand what you've experienced, but something new is much more difficult to understand
   Closure: you fill in details of an incomplete picture
   Repetition: if it happened before, you expect it to happen again

Subjectivity

Subjectivity refers to perceptions that are unique to your personal experience, views, or mental state. The most obvious source of subjectivity is your **physiology**; you differ from another in your physical sensory ability. Next time you are at the grocery store, look at what people are wearing on their feet. Some will be in sandals, others in boots, some in shoes, and some may try to shop barefoot! Each person's footwear choice indicates a degree of sensitivity to temperature and texture. Similarly, what might be hot chili to you might be mild to another. Music that is "too loud" for some may be "too quiet" for others. Ten million American men—7 percent of the male population—either cannot distinguish red from green, or see red and green differently from most people. This is the most common form of color blindness, but it affects only 0.4 percent of women.[10] That knowledge might impact your strategic choice of color on a graph. In the same way, about 10 percent of the population is left-handed; this means that some of us experience an anti-lefty bias that assaults us; scissors are useless, power tools (such as circular saws) are dangerous, and pens smear and make writing illegible. In giving instructions, it might be important to consider handedness. Consider how awkward it might be for a leftie to learn to use a tool meant for the right-handed worker. Many physiological states can influence perception. When you are tired or ill, you may be less able to react to a friend's humor and may take offense at a comment that normally would not make you blink.

A second subjectivity source involves psychological aspects created by our culture and experiences. **Culture** refers to the community of meaning to which we belong (beliefs, values, norms, and ways of interpreting experience that are shared by those around us). As Americans, we tend to subjectively view the world through basic assumptions of various rights: to freedom of speech, to pursue religious beliefs, to be all that we can be. Other cultures do not have those assumptions, yet we do not become aware of that until we are questioned. For instance, in the United States, many adoptive families openly celebrate how their families were created, and they consider the birth parents as part of their extended family. In other countries, adoption is still a shameful state, and if one is forced to make a decision to place the child for adoption, it is shrouded in secrecy and mystery.

To envision this aspect of subjectivity, consider your reactions to the following examples. Past Olympic media coverage highlighted the adoption stories of 2006 American bronze medalist (men's mogul) Toby Dawson, adopted at age three from South Korea, and 1984 gold medalist Scott Hamilton, adopted at six weeks from the United States. Run-D.M.C. group member, Darryl "D.M.C." McDaniels, revealed on a 2006 VH1 documentary that he was adopted as an infant but only learned that at age thirty-five.[11] Wendy's founder Dave Thomas started a foundation to celebrate adoption, because he had been adopted from foster care. Your beliefs and experience with adoption, whether you have a member of your family who is adopted or if you are adopted, will impact the way that you view these stories, and, in turn, whether you donate to adoption causes, watch programs about adoption, or even consider adoption yourself.

In the same way, modern Western culture integrates technology and speed into nearly everything about living: we expect things to happen quickly (instant messages, instant photos, instant oatmeal). How does our speed expectation impact our perceptions of other cultures where patience and leisure are the norm, such as Mexico and Nepal?

It's not easy to be left-handed in a world that's more accommodating to right-handed people.

© Glen Jones/Shutterstock.com

Psychological subjectivity is affected by the perceptual choices that you make, either intentionally or not.[12] *Selective exposure* suggests that you choose to seek consistent information or to expose yourself to certain contexts where you will feel comfortable with the stimuli. For example, you may attend only one style of play (let's say musicals) rather than going to Greek tragedies, comedies, farces, or melodramas, because psychologically, a musical is pleasant to your eyes and ears. You know what to expect and feel at ease with the context, story line, characters, and addition of music to the overall experience.

Selective attention suggests that people choose to expose themselves or pay attention to certain stimuli already present, to key in on certain phenomenon, because these are more similar to their experiences or beliefs. Perhaps you listen only to one kind of music because that is what you know; the thought of going to a country concert when you are an opera fan may just be too much to ask! If you engage in *selective interpretation*, you interpret ambiguous stimuli so that it becomes consistent with what you know. Imagine that you are given some new food to taste, and it looks pretty much like chicken. You may interpret what you taste as a unique flavor of barbeque chicken, only later to find out that it was alligator! *Selective retention* suggests that you will remember more accurately messages that are consistent with interests, views and beliefs than those that are in contrast with your values and beliefs. Because of the vast amounts of information you are bombarded with, you decide what to keep in the memory, narrowing the informational flow once again. When parents ask children to do household chores, those children seem to have an uncanny ability to remember only the chores that are the easiest or the ones they want to do. Perhaps you are more likely to remember the parts of your professor's lecture that you agree with and to forget the parts that do not correspond to your beliefs.

Stability

A second perception principle, **stability,** refers to the predictability that we need in life. The concept of organization suggests that we pattern what we perceive in order to get stimuli to "fit" into our preconceived ways of thinking. Stability can be managed in two basic ways. *Assimilation* is when you interpret the stimuli you receive to fit what you already know or expect. In simple terms, you "bend" the incoming information so that it fits what you know. If you know that your family always orders sausage pizza, that first bite you take of that pizza will taste like sausage, because you are certain that's what they order. Until you are informed that the topping is really tofu, you expect that the pizza guy has brought you sausage. *Accommodation* occurs when you change what you know to fit the incoming perceptual data. For instance, if you believe that your friend is honest but you see her looking on someone else's test, you might change your perception of what constitutes cheating.

Meaningfulness

Finally, **meaningfulness,** the third perception principle, refers to the ways that we project comprehension or understanding onto perceptions. This is achieved in several ways. You might employ *contrast*, where you say that something is like (or unlike) something that you know. Is the latest reality show anything like *Survivor*, which you cannot stand? You might compare a political candidate to an earlier politician you admired, giving him your vote. Someone you are interviewing with might think that you are too similar to the person she just fired, so she cannot take a chance on you.

A second technique is through the *familiar versus the novel:* You can understand something that you have experienced, but something new is much more difficult to understand. Until you have had your house burn down around you, it is hard to really understand the range of emotions of those who have lived through this. You might never have heard of being a CASA volunteer, so you cannot imagine volunteering for this valuable child advocacy service when you hear a speech about it.

With *closure*, you fill in the details of an incomplete picture. You are given an assignment, but once you try to complete the task, you realize that you do not know exactly what is expected. When you cannot reach your instructor,

Have you ever been surprised to learn what's really in that new food you just tasted?
© Simone van den Berg/Shutterstock.com

If you expect that you're eating sausage pizza, the first bite will taste like sausage.
© Mariusz Szachowski/Shutterstock.com

you make some decisions about what you think she means for you to do. Even *repetition* is a means for creating meaningfulness; if something has happened before, then you expect it to happen again. If you have been snubbed by a colleague several times, you will not be able to attribute friendship meaning when that person suddenly treats you as his best buddy in a meeting; you might assume his behavior is a political move.

Errors in Perception

Perceptions are fundamental to critical thinking, and they are confounded by multiple opportunities to be imperfect. There are many reasons for these perceptual errors, and understanding their source may make for a more perceptive communication event. One reason is that we are influenced by the immediately obvious. You observe two children fighting on a playground, and you immediately assume that the one who is hitting the other must have started the fight. When you intercede, you concentrate your message on the "guilty" one. We also cling to those first impressions, because again, our interpretations are rarely questioned. If a church is the place you first meet someone, you might think that she is a devout member of that church, even though it might be her first time there. Third, we assume that others think like we do, so we do not question our perceptions. Maybe you like junk mail, cyberjokes, and the like, so you pass them on. Others may despise getting bombarded with this same material. Maybe your mother appreciates "constructive criticism," but you do not. As previously noted, we have different sensory abilities, so our facility to see or hear something is likely different from someone else's; where a road sign may be perfectly clear to you, the passenger, your friend the driver may miss it because he cannot see that far.

How do your own experiences affect your perception of other cultures?
© 2008, JupiterImages Corporation.

We also have different experiences through our culture, education, character, and activities, so our perceptions are impacted. If you are a football fan, you may watch the game from a technician's point of view, noticing how the linebackers play defense and the variety of coaching plays. A non–football-loving friend who attends the game with you may focus on the cheer squad and the band. In another example, a builder sees the new house construction differently than the first-time homeowner. Finally, different perceptual expectations may be part of the context: Where you are may determine what you expect to see or to hear. A car accident is perceived quite differently by the drivers, witnesses, and attending officer. What each party communicates about that experience will likely be significantly different. If you are at a concert, you probably expect to hear music and not a political pitch, so your perception of the politician who uses the concert as a fundraiser will probably be negative.

What can you gain from this brief foray into perception? The knowledge you gain from your perceptions is vivid, personal, and often accepted uncritically. Your perceptions are experiential, selective, perhaps inaccurate, and likely evaluative. Every dimension of what you know is directly impacted by your perceptions. You cannot engage in critical thinking without considering your perceptions. The same is true of your listener: you cannot communicate with another until you have considered his or her perceptions.

ENDNOTES

1. Arnett, R. C., & Arneson, P. (1999). *Dialogic civility in a cynical age: Community, hope, and interpersonal relationships.* SUNY Series in Communication Studies (D. D. Cahn, Ed.). Albany: State University of New York Press.

2. Wittgenstein, L. (1958). *Philosophical investigations* (3rd ed.; G. E. M. Anscombe, 3. Tannen, D. (1986). *That's not what I meant!* New York: William Morrow.

3. Tannen, D. (1986). *That's not what I meant!* New York: William Morrow.

4. Gardner, H. (1983). *Frames of mind: The theory of multiple intelligences.* New York: Basic.

5. Gardner, H. (1999) *Intelligence reframed: Multiple intelligences for the 21st century.* New York: Basic.

6. Lockwood, G. (2005). So your day is a waste of time? Retrieved May 30, 2005, from http://www.bizsuccess.com/articles/time.htm

7. Watson, J. D. (1997). *The double helix: A personal account of the discovery of the structure of DNA.* London: Weidenfeld and Nicolson.

8. Hall, S. (1981). Notes on deconstructing the popular. In R. Samuel (Ed.), *People's history and socialist theory* (pp. 227–239). London: Routledge and Kegan Paul.

9. Richards, I. A. (1936). *The philosophy of rhetoric.* New York: Oxford University Press.

10. Shannon, C., & Weaver, W. (1949). *The mathematical theory of communication.* Urbana: University of Illinois Press.

11. Festa, P. (2003, Oct. 29). Knowledge experiences exponential growth. CNET News.com. Retrieved July 14, 2009, from http://news.zdnet.co.uk/hardware/storage/0,39020366,39117457,00.htm

12. Info-overload harms concentration more than marijuana. (2005, April 30). *New Scientist.* Retrieved July 14, 2009, from http://www.newscientist.com

13. Ophir, E., Nass, C., & Wagner, A. D. (2009). Cognitive control in media multitaskers. *Proceedings of the National Academy of Sciences of the United States of America, 106*(37), 15583–15587.

14. McLuhan, M. (1964). *Understanding media: The extensions of man.* New York: McGraw-Hill.

15. Warschauer, M. (1999). *Electronic literacies: Language, culture, and power in online education.* Mahwah, NJ: Lawrence Erlbaum.

16. Haley, J. (2008, February 14). Be a savvy consumer when looking for love online. CNN.com. Retrieved February 27, 2010, from http://www.cnn.com/2008/LIVING/personal/02/14/roym.online.dating/index.html

17. Ellison, N., Heino, R., & Gibbs, J. (2006). Managing impressions online: Self-presentation processes in the online dating environment. *Journal of Computer-Mediated Communication, 11*(2). Retrieved February 26, 2010, from http://jcmc.indiana.edu/vol11/issue2/ellison.html

18. Benbunan-Fich, R., & Hiltz, S. R. (1999, March). Educational applications of CMCS: Solving case studies through asynchronous learning networks. *Journal of Computer-Mediated Communication, 4*(3). Retrieved July 14, 2009, from http://jcmc.indiana.edu/vol4/issue3/benbunan-fich.html

19. Booth-Butterfield, M. (1989). The interpretation of classroom performance feedback: An attributional approach. *Communication Education, 38,* 119–131.

20. Lee, I. J. (1952). *How to talk with people.* New York: Harper.

21. Laing, R. D. (1969). *Self and others.* New York: Pantheon.

22. Katz, D. (1947, March). Psychological barriers to communication. *Annals of the American Academy of Political and Social Science, 250,* 17–25.

23. National Communication Association. (1999). *Credo for ethical communication.* Retrieved July 14, 2009, from http://www.natcom.org/index.asp?bid=514

24. Watzlawick, P., Bavelas, J. B., & Jackson, D. D. (1967). *Pragmatics of human communication.* New York: W. W. Norton.

Chapter 1
Outlook paper

Write a paper with 1″ margins, word processed, double spaced with a font no larger than 12. In this paper be sure to:

- Describe what you anticipate learning from this course.
- Describe briefly your values and attitudes toward communication. For example, how does your family communicate? How do they communicate celebration? How do they communicate when dealing with conflict?
- Describe briefly your and your family's attitudes toward education.
- State challenges you anticipate to doing well in this course. Tell me how we can work together to overcome any challenges you anticipate in doing well in this course.
- Staple if more than one page.

Write four separate paragraphs each covering one topic. Spelling, grammar and punctuation errors will affect your grade. Be sure to proofread it carefully!

PERCEPTION AND LISTENING*

Listening is often considered THE most important communication skill, especially in interpersonal situations. Without it, messages frequently go unheard or are misunderstood. Without skillful listening (often referred to as "active listening"), positive situations can deteriorate into negative situations, and negative situations can disintegrate into chaos, hostility, even warfare.

Consider the following scenario. Does it sound familiar? You're hungry and don't have much time. You need to grab some food quickly, so you decide to go to the Bubba Burger drive-through window. You place your order. "I'd like a Bubba Burger with cheese, no mayonnaise, and extra pickles. And I'd like a large order of fries and a chocolate milkshake." You pick up your order and zoom away. You arrive at your destination, open the bag, and: Surprise! Remember what you asked for? You actually got a Bubba Burger with no cheese or pickles, a thick blob of mayonnaise oozing out the side of the bun, a small order of fries, and a strawberry shake. Infuriating, isn't it?

Or try this situation. In the midst of a heated disagreement, your partner blurts out: "That's the problem with our relationship—you never listen to me!" Frustrated, you reply, "Oh, yeah? Well, *you* never listen to *me*!" Then you both go to separate rooms and slam the door. Animosity builds. You think, "Why can't I find anyone who's a good listener?"

All of us witness or experience situations like these daily. They annoy us, they cause pain, they cost money. Yet they continue. Why? The answer lies in our failure to value and consciously try to improve our listening skills. This chapter provides a guided tour through the listening process. First, we explore what listening is, discovering that our careless definitions of listening may be one reason why we listen so poorly. Next, we examine why we usually do not learn to listen well and the costs incurred by poor listening. Then our tour takes us to the stages of the listening process, where we learn about how to improve each stage of listening. We then deal with barriers to effective listening and how to overcome them. Our final destination offers ways to apply our listening skills in specific contexts such as classes, relationships, and oral presentations.

One of the best ways to prevent, diagnose, or cure poor listening habits is to take inventory of how we listen. For your own information, write the answers to the following questions about your listening behavior.

1. In your interpersonal or social communication, to whom do you listen best? To whom do you listen most often? Why do you listen to this person?
2. In your interpersonal or social communication, who is your best listener? Why do you think this person is your best listener?

* This chapter was written by Roy Schwartzman, Ruthann Fox-Hines, and Bob Bohlken.

3. What topics do you find most interesting? What do you enjoy listening to others discuss?
4. How do you respond when you are listening effectively? How do you indicate you are listening carefully? (take notes, ask questions, make eye contact with the lecturer, facial expressions, body attitude, etc.)
5. What communication situations make you the most anxious or nervous about listening and why?
6. What is your most common distraction when you are trying to listen? (the topic, the language, the speaker's appearance, your own fatigue and/or preoccupation, incoming text messages, etc.)

You might want to compare your answers with others in your class for a better awareness of listening skills. Also try comparing your answers to those of your friends. How might you learn better listening habits from each other? With these questions in mind, let's explore listening in more detail.

WHAT IS LISTENING?

Too often we tend to take listening for granted. After all, I listen to everything anyone says—don't you? Of course not! We often have mistaken notions about listening, then the costs of poor listening become apparent only after our listening has failed. So, what does listening involve?

To understand what listening is, we first should recognize what it is not. **Hearing** is the physical process of receiving sound. If someone has difficulty hearing, the challenge may lie in physical barriers such as a distracting communication environment or damage to the person's auditory abilities (for example, nerve damage). Hearing also can be unintentional. While waiting outside a professor's door, we may accidentally catch part of a private conversation. In a classroom, you might notice a classmate's stomach growling. At other times, we might strain to hear, making a conscious effort to catch every word. Many medical devices are available to assist with various types of hearing reduction or loss. For example, hearing aids can amplify sound volume and reduce distortions. Yet there are no prospects for any sort of technology that can serve as a listening aid. Why not?

Listening does include hearing, but it goes far beyond the physical process of receiving sounds. Figure 2.1 summarizes these differences between hearing and listening. The International Listening Association[1] defines **listening** as "the process of receiving, constructing meaning from, and responding to spoken and/or nonverbal messages." For our purposes we restrict our study to listening to spoken language (verbal) and the nonverbal elements that accompany the spoken verbal message. Let's examine the main ingredients of our definition.

In the definition, *process* indicates that listening is a complex series of activities and events that are ever changing, ongoing, and irreversible—just as communication itself is a process (Chapter 1). In your past you have failed to listen to messages that you later wished that you had listened to, and you have listened to messages that you wished you had ignored. The process begins with an event in time with many available sensations such as sights, sounds,

FIGURE 2.1 Hearing Versus Listening.

Hearing	Listening
Can be accidental or purposeful	Intentional
Automatic	Requires effort and training
Physiological process	Interpretive process
Receive sounds	Decode messages

aromas, etc. The listener chooses to hear a spoken verbal message and the accompanying nonverbal elements such as voice inflection, rate, and tone. The listener then interprets the words and phrases and makes the association with his or her mental concepts (such as recognizing a voice as belonging to a friend). The listener then makes inferences, generalizes, abstracts, and/or concludes from the mental associations and responds verbally and/or nonverbally and activates degrees of memory. So we find that listening requires effort and decoding or interpreting sounds once they are heard.

Receiving refers to the initial step in the listening process in which the verbal message is taken in or perceived through the sense of hearing and the nonverbal messages perceived through sight and hearing and sometimes touch. You as the listener choose or select whether you attend the spoken verbal message among a multitude of stimuli within a particular situation or environment. It is like sitting on the bank of a country pond or lake while hundreds of insects are buzzing around your head competing for your attention. When you are conversing with a friend and the sounds of passing traffic begin to disrupt your interaction, you become painfully aware that you can only attend to and process effectively one message at a time. In other words, it is very difficult to listen to someone speaking, while reading or hearing a different verbal message and expect to comprehend both. CNN Headline News, MSNBC, and Fox News (and many other news networks) give you the opportunity to prove it for yourself. Try reading the scripted news at the bottom of the screen at the same instant you are listening to the commentator. You may tune in and out but cannot perceive both at the same time. Similarly, we find it very difficult to process verbal and visual messages that conflict. Try to say aloud the *color* of the words printed below (not the words, but the color of the type) in the order they appear:

ORANGE RED GREEN PURPLE BLUE BROWN WHITE

Why was that apparently straightforward task so difficult? You were receiving inconsistent messages. Your visual perception told you the color of the type, but your verbal perception cued you to say the word. The lesson: When we send mixed or competing signals, reception suffers.

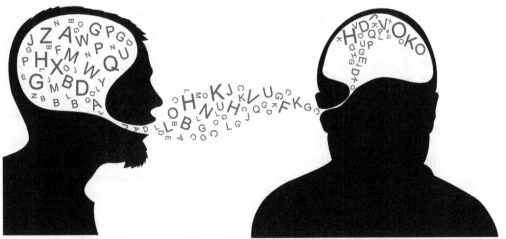

Listening is a more complex process than simply pouring information from one person's mouth into another person's brain.

© Petr Vaclavek/Shutterstock.com

Constructing meaning is the association of words and phrases with references or concepts previously experienced and established in one's mind. Meanings have to be negotiated between communicators. Listeners decide what words mean and how much importance they have. The meanings for the words "freedom" and "democracy" are very abstract and rely on each listener to create verbal meaning. The same point holds for collections of words. Anthologies of "great speeches" emerge from audiences reacting to those presentations over time, not by the speakers deciding how they should be interpreted. More broadly, listeners ultimately have the power to decide whether someone's communication is understood, laughed at, respected, preserved, or ignored.

Responding to spoken verbal and accompanying nonverbal messages is a physiological reaction to what speakers say and the way they say it. The listener's verbal response may be in the form of questions, paraphrased messages, or repeating what the speaker said. The nonverbal, visual responses may be change in eye behavior, nod of the head, shrug of the shoulders, turning away, smiling, altering body posture, or hand gestures.

WHY CARE ABOUT LISTENING?

Listening is one of the four fundamental language skills along with reading, writing, and speaking. Listening is the first language skill we use, yet ironically the skill that we least study and develop. It is the skill that employers respect most in an employee, and the skill that lovers admire most in loved ones. It has been said, "No one ever listened themselves out of a job" and "A person would rather marry a poor financial provider than a poor listener." Throughout formal schooling, the average student spends at least half of the time listening.[2] The typical manager spends about 60 percent of each day listening.[3] As much as 80 percent of an ordinary person's time awake is spent doing some sort of listening.[4]

Amazingly, although we use listening more than any other communication skill, we tend to spend the least time learning how to do it. How many years did you spend learning to write? If you are taking a course in writing, you are still learning! You probably recall entire classes throughout elementary school devoted to teaching you how to read. Speaking usually gets far less attention, but formal practice in speaking is widespread at colleges and universities. Many high schools offer speech courses or formal speech activities such as competitive debate.

What about listening? Chances are that until this course relatively few of your classmates received specific instruction in listening. Curricular studies confirm this experience. On the average, "students get 12 years of formal training in writing, 6–8 years in reading, 1–2 years in speaking, and from 0–½ year in listening".[5] An estimated 5 percent of the population has any formal training in listening,[6] and businesses are scrambling to address this lack of listening background because it could reduce employee performance.[7,8]

Why haven't we learned how to listen? Traditionally, the study of communication has focused on the speaker or the message source. The speaker does indeed have the highest profile. In public speaking, the audience trains its attention on the presenter. In groups, the person who is speaking commands attention. For centuries, texts on public speaking never mentioned listening. Instead the authors preferred the more visible communication skill of presenting speeches. We also may be self-centered as communicators. In the competitive worlds of academics and business, people prefer to promote their own viewpoints instead of allowing time for others to express theirs.[9]

Somebody definitely *should* teach us listening. Measurements of listening performance show abysmal results. Since we tend to take listening for granted, we assume that listening is easy and natural. We often develop false confidence that we listen well, claiming that we are good listeners.[10] Yet the average listener, including students and employees, understands and remembers only about 50 percent of a conversation, and within two days it drops to only 25 percent. Imagine studying for a test and remembering only one-quarter of the material 48 hours later! Overall listening accuracy hovers around 25 percent.[2,4,11]

We need to learn how to listen because the stakes are high. Poor listening incurs tremendous costs. First, consider the financial costs. Listening specialist Don Stacks estimated that poor listening causes businesses to lose $1 billion per day.[12] That figure seems almost conservative if you think about how often errors such as our Bubba Burger fiasco occur. "Listening is a critical skill for success. The impact of ineffective listening can be significant. If poor listening habits caused every worker in the United States to make just one $5 mistake a year, the total cost would be more than half a billion dollars!".[13] Within professional organizations, the ability to listen accurately proves to be a key factor in how far and how fast an employee will advance.[2] Listening to customers has been rated the top factor in successful selling and the number one reason for poor sales performance.[8] Supervisors also rate listening to employees as the most vital tool in evaluating and directing them.[14] If you want to be considered an effective communicator on the job, you had better learn to listen. Co-workers associate good job performance with good listening.[15]

Next, think about the emotional toll of poor listening. Marital and familial ties weaken under pressure of poor listening. "Ineffective listening is also acknowledged to be one of the primary contributors to divorce and to the inability of a parent and child to openly communicate".[11] We know how frustrating and insulting it can be to interact with someone who seems not to listen. People commonly list "good listener" as one of the most desirable characteristics in a friend or mate.

Finally, listening has academic consequences. Improving your listening skills has immediate and long-term benefits. Considering that the average student retains only one out of every four words uttered in the classroom, the better listener will have a more accurate record of class discussions. Your notes should become more precise and more helpful as a study guide. In the long term, as you become a better listener you will get more involved in your classes. You will be more likely to ask questions and engage in discussion, so you will deepen your understanding of the subject. Faculty agree. Surveys indicate that faculty consider effective listening highly important for the academic success of students—especially those who speak English as a second language.[16]

That's Debatable

Effective listening is so important and poor listening so costly that proposals sometimes arise calling for mandatory listening skill tests as a condition for graduation or employment. Weigh the various opinions on two issues: (1) What should be the content of listening tests? (2) Should schools or employers require passage of a listening test as a requirement for graduation or employment?

THE LISTENING PROCESS

Although we may have developed the bad habit of listening haphazardly, listening is a structured process. Listening consists of five stages: receiving, understanding, evaluating, recalling, and responding. This section explains each stage of listening, identifies challenges associated with each stage, and offers ways to improve that component of listening. Before delving into those stages, let's consider what we listen to in the first place and how we process it.

Listening Filters

With the number of messages coming toward us in the communication environment, it is impossible to process everything. The challenge is to get and process the important, relevant messages while ignoring or de-emphasizing the distractions and distortions. **Listening filters** help sort the confused mass of incoming messages into sensible, manageable information. When our listening filters work well, we receive and deal with only the information we need. An effective filter keeps useful material while screening out everything else. Problems arise, however, when our filters interfere with the listening process.

Initially, **selective attention** determines which incoming messages we process at all. Selective attention leads us to seek out and concentrate on communication that we find acceptable. We hear what we want to hear. A rally of Republicans will tend to attract a Republican audience, for example. Selective attention does help listeners sort through the mass of messages competing for attention. The problem is that selective attention also can restrict our exposure to new and possibly beneficial information because we never leave our comfort zone. You might see a college dining hall filled with tables of students who seem racially or culturally segregated, with everyone sitting at a table alongside people of similar identity. Selective attention contributes to this self-segregation. Since listeners tend to prioritize familiar, agreeable messages, they may avoid a novelty such as a different culture. We need to expand our selective attention when we seek to widen our knowledge and understanding.

Selective interpretation can lead us to alter message content to conform with our beliefs. We can protect ourselves against possibly distorting messages through selective interpretation. We can take a cue from scientists, who recognize that our conclusions should be shaped by our experiences instead of force-fitting our experiences to conform to pre-existing beliefs. Scientists recognize that we often must modify our beliefs to accommodate new experiences. Another precaution would be to check our interpretations by comparing them to those of other listeners. How do you know your class notes are accurate and do not reflect only your own perspective on the course material? Don't wait until the next test to find out. Compare your notes with the notes of several other students to improve accuracy and escape from the biases of your own worldview.

Step One: Receiving

At the **receiving** stage, listening is equivalent to hearing. Reception involves the ways that we obtain sounds. This step must come first in the listening process. With all of the sounds we encounter, we must strategically select what we will receive. If sounds are inaudible, garbled, or otherwise distorted, we should not proceed with listening until we can clarify what was heard. If we receive only part of a message, trying to listen is like trying to read a book with random pages missing.

Challenges to Receiving

Information Overload. Reception becomes a bigger problem year after year because of **information overload**: The number of incoming messages exceeds our ability to process them. I distinctly recall the days prior to cable television when "good" reception meant three or four channels. Now a cable or satellite package with fewer than 150 channels seems meager. The Internet allows us to access most major newspapers in every country throughout the world. Bloggers (people who post online diaries/commentaries) track events throughout the world as they happen. Electronic gadgets beg for our attention as we can check text messages, play video games, take photos, and browse the Internet all through our cell phone that might ring at any moment. The problem is that while the sources of information expand exponentially, we still process the information at about the same speed as our grandparents and great-grandparents did. We might get 500 channels on TV, but a 30-minute program still takes 30 minutes to watch. We can bookmark 50 newspapers on our Web browser, but we still have to read them one page at a time. A 10-minute speech still takes 10 minutes to listen to. With all this data coming to us so fast, it's no wonder we miss a lot.

Aside from the sheer number of messages heading toward us, we may not prioritize messages well. Often we find ourselves preoccupied by irrelevant stimuli that lure us away from the speaker's message. If you have many incoming messages, try to focus only on the most important ones (the ones most relevant to your task or to your relationship) and defer or ignore the other messages.

Examples: Poor Prioritization

1. Your mother is having a serious conversation with you about finances. You answer a call on your cell phone. Mom's conclusion: "My child doesn't value me." Better choice: You can return the call, so delay responding to it until after the conversation.
2. (True story) A professor returns a call from a student. After a minute of conversation, the student places the professor on hold to talk with a friend. What would you do in this situation if you were the student? If you were the professor?

Consider what you want to accomplish in the communication situation. If you receive messages from other sources (a friend enters the room, etc.), decide whether the new message can improve the communication you are in already. Ideally, you might connect competing stimuli. For example, suppose you notice a rare, expensive sports car pull up next to the window while a speaker is giving a presentation on air pollution. Instead of ignoring the speech and admiring the sports car, connect the new stimulus (the fancy sports car) to the speaker's message. You might consider, "I wonder how much pollution that car emits," or "The speaker just mentioned the Clean Air Act reducing factory smokestack emissions. Would the Clean Air Act apply to cars like that as well?" Instead of distracting you, the new experience (the car's arrival) has urged you to expand your understanding and application of the speaker's topic.

Speed of Speaking and Listening. Another challenge to reception is the **speaking-listening gap**: We can listen much more rapidly than most people speak. Generally, a rate of about 150 to a bit more than 200 words per minute sounds "normal" in a conversation or lecture. Yet we can listen at a rate of 400 to 800 words per minute with minimal loss of comprehension.[2,11] Since we process speech at two to four times the rate most speakers are talking, we have a lot of time for our minds to wander. How do you occupy this "spare time"? Chances are that you, like most of us, start thinking of all sort of irrelevant things. Try to occupy your listening time with activities that can enhance your listening experience: take notes, think about questions, or try repeating to yourself the speaker's most recent point.

Self-Centered Listening. Focusing only on yourself—what you want from the message rather than what the speaker has to offer—distorts messages by not considering the speaker's motives. Self-centered listeners tend to listen only long enough to reach a hasty judgment, usually one that confirms a pre-existing opinion. Show respect for the speaker by taking his or her views seriously and giving him or her a hearing even if you disagree.[17] To maximize your listening ability, focus on the speaker's rationale for sharing the information. Instead of listening only for what pleases you or confirms your own beliefs, allow the other person a chance to have his or her say. Wait to speak until there is a natural lapse in conversation or an appropriate time for questions.

Making Time to Listen. Finally, you might discover that you simply cannot devote adequate time and effort to the listening situation. If you find this happening, you should try to defer the communication until a time when you can devote more energy to it. For example, I am amazed at the students who will attend class while they are dreadfully ill, semi-conscious, and clearly cannot attend to what is happening in the classroom. They would benefit more by informing the instructor of the situation and then reviewing the class notes or discussing the class when they can process the information fully. In group situations, you should recognize when you cannot take the time or have the mental focus to listen properly. Listening does take time and effort, so choose to listen only when you can invest in the endeavor.

How to Improve Receiving

Reduce Distractions. A vital way to improve reception amid this message glut is to reduce distractions. Anything that competes with the communicator's message qualifies as a distraction. Students claim that some of the most distracting elements in classrooms are the noises and behaviors of the students sitting near them. Other distractions include room temperature, the student's own preoccupations and tiredness, and the lack of the student's interest. When studying in an online environment, the distractions multiply. Do you work on your online course units while keeping several unrelated windows open on your screen—maybe your e-mail, a social networking site, and research for a project in another course, or all of the above? How many times has your online coursework been interrupted by an instant message or a Facebook chat request?

All of these distractions can be alleviated by the student listener *and* by the design/delivery of the message received. The most common excuse for not attending or receiving the instructor's message is that either the professor or the material is "boring." This excuse puts all of the responsibility on the speaker or message source when in reality at least half of the responsibility is with the listener.

Distractions fall into two categories: external distractions and internal distractions. *External distractions* consist of everything in your environment that could draw your attention away from the communicator's message. For example, my students have identified the following sorts of things that could become external distractions for them: harsh lighting in the room, noisy air conditioners, crowded seating, cell phones ringing, unusual clothing worn by the presenter or audience members. *Internal distractions* are physical or psychological aspects of the listener that reduce focus on the communication. For example, my students have admitted to the following items as some of their internal distractions: hunger, fatigue, uncomfortable clothing, focusing on a test in another class, planning for an event later in the evening, and even a hangover.

Reducing distractions requires identifying them as early as possible (preferably before they arise) and taking proactive measures to prevent them or reduce their impact. It is never enough simply to know what your distractions are; you must gain control over them. When you complete your inventory of distractions, you may be surprised to find that you can eliminate most of them by taking specific—sometimes simple—actions.

You can control the communication situation not only to help you as a listener, but to aid the presenter. Avoiding interruptions is also a way of granting the speaker a sense of importance. In an office you could close the door, hold calls, not read materials on your desk, and not write except to make notes related to what you and the person are talking about. If you are in a classroom, clear your desk of anything unrelated to the class. Turn off your cell phone if you brought it. Just turning off the ringer isn't enough, since you still might be tempted to check text messages.

Maintain Eye Contact. Another excellent way to improve your ability to receive communication is to establish **direct eye contact** with the presenter. When your parents shouted, "Look at me when I'm talking to you!" they did so for a reason. In most American cultures direct eye contact with another communicator signals involvement and interest. As a listener, you benefit from direct eye contact because you can pay attention to all the nonverbal messages a communicator sends. Some researchers estimate that more than half of message content comes from gestures, facial expressions, and other body language that we must watch to comprehend.[18] Studies by Mehrabian[19] show that people decide whether they like a speaker's message based mostly on the speaker's facial qualities (accounting for 55 percent of liking) and vocal qualities (38 percent), with only 7 percent of liking or disliking derived from the words themselves. So *listen with your eyes* by maintaining eye contact with the person speaking to you. Not only will you gain a better understanding of the message by being receptive to visual stimuli, but you will signify that you care about what the speaker has to say. Direct eye contact also has payoffs in the classroom. If the speaker is your instructor, you will find you get more direct attention and interest—and probably better conversations—when you look at him or her during class. That sort of direct interaction enhances relationships and can't hurt grades!

Step Two: Understanding

The second stage of listening is **understanding**. In listening that term has special significance. To listen effectively, we must comprehend communication *in the presenter's own terms*. We must temporarily set aside what we as listeners want or believe and try to remain as open as possible—at least during this stage—to the speaker's viewpoint.[20] Understanding comes only after reception. If the message we receive is incomplete or distorted, we cannot get an accurate idea of what was communicated.

Challenges to Understanding

It seems so simple. All we need to do as listeners is figure out what the other person is saying. But we know better. Understanding can be quite elusive.

Mutually Assumed Understanding. A common error at the second stage of listening is **mutually assumed understanding:** We believe our messages are clear and rarely doubt the perfection of our listening skills; therefore, we always assume we have the correct information. Each of us thinks everybody else interprets things exactly the way we do. But how can we be sure? The problem is that 10 different people have at least 10 different ways of understanding the world, and all 10 think their way is the right way for everybody else. To prevent this problem, Wendell Johnson[21] recommended that we should assume <u>mis</u>understanding until we get positive proof that others share our interpretations. Tell other people when we don't understand something they say. Don't rely on puzzled looks or frowns—people interpret the signals differently. Say the magic words: "I don't understand" or "Could you clarify that?" The next time someone gives you important instructions, for example, check for misunderstanding. Paraphrase the message. Say something like, "If I get your point, you were asking me to do *x*."

Confusing Understanding with Agreement. Understanding has nothing to do with agreement. I might understand how to make a taco, but that does not imply that tacos are my favorite food. So far we have not reached the stage of listening that involves judging communication in any way. Ultimately, the test of understanding would be whether we could state the communication's cognitive and emotional content and the presenter would respond, "Yes, that's exactly what I was trying to get across." As listeners, we should not respond to communication until we get some indication that we have understood the message first. If nothing else, confirming understanding can clarify where you and the other communicator disagree.

How to Improve Understanding

Suspend Judgment. Probably the biggest threat to effective understanding is the rush to judge. We must resist that urge for now and recognize that understanding precedes judgment. It is especially tempting to react quickly to people different from ourselves, jumping to conclusions about someone's motives, intelligence, or ability. I sometimes encounter people who assume that anyone with a southern accent must lack intelligence. People who communicate in sign language may find that they are judged as mentally deficient because they do not communicate verbally. These inaccurate perceptions result from placing judgment as the first step in communicating with others. Unfortunately, hasty judgments suffer from inaccuracy and they may prevent us from gaining knowledge and enjoyment from communication that was dismissed as unimportant.

Paraphrase. An excellent way to check understanding is to **paraphrase** a presenter's message, restating content in your own words. A paraphrase goes beyond parroting back a speaker's words. A parent might say to a child, "Take out the trash now. Do you understand me?" The child replies, "Yeah. Sure. Take out the trash now," and does nothing. That is a parrot, not a paraphrase. A paraphrase shows that you recognize not only the words someone says, but the emotional and cognitive substance of the message. Skill at paraphrasing also will help you in your research. If you can capture the gist of what someone says or writes, you can refer to that information without the legal and academic risk of copying someone else's words.

Ask Questions—Even if Only to Yourself. Some of my colleagues and I conducted an informal study involving lectures in classes. We required the student listeners to write a question about the material being presented every five minutes. We compared their scores on a pop quiz immediately after the lecture with those in another class having the same instructor on the same material. The students required to write questions about the lecture material did significantly better on the 10-item unannounced quiz after a 40-minute lecture. Not a very scientific study, but enough proof for you to try it for yourself. In the class where you believe you are not an effective listener, along with your regular note taking behavior, write at least one question every five minutes about the specific information being presented at the time. You don't even have to have your questions answered, but it would help if you asked for answers from the lecturer or someone else who had experienced the same class session. Personally, as a speaker or lecturer, I am very pleased to have questions by listeners because I know one has to listen to ask questions.

Receiving Versus Perceiving. When you attempt to understand, carefully distinguish the messages you receive from your opinions of the messages. Contrary to reception, which involves physically getting messages, **perception** refers to how we view ourselves and the world. Earlier in this chapter, we recognized that we tend to fall prey to selective interpretation, understanding what we experience in ways that distort message content. These distortions systematically tend to protect ourselves and put us in the best possible light. Selective interpretation can strongly influence understanding.

We engage in **self-serving bias** by accepting responsibility for whatever is good and blaming others for problems. Avid American sports fans who watch the same football game, for example, will claim to "see" the opposing team play miserably, deserve far more penalties, and commit more unfair plays, even when both teams play almost identically.[22] Of course, the fans thought any penalties against their favorite team supposedly resulted from poor officiating.

We often listen to *confirm pre-existing beliefs*. Why? Because we attend to what we need, are interested in, or what we expect. It is more comfortable to reinforce what we already think and feel, so we may skew information to avoid challenging assumptions. To avoid this trap, do not try to rationalize or guess the motives behind a message. Instead, remain faithful to the original message content.

Step Three: Evaluation

Only after we have received all relevant information can we reach the evaluation stage. In **evaluation**, we judge the merits of messages. Evaluation includes several layers of judgments.

- Should listening continue? We must decide whether the message is important enough to remember and whether it deserves a response. When we check our voice mail, we first decide whether to erase the message or make a note of it. Then we also consider whether to return the call. The same judgments apply to e-mail. Should we keep the message or delete? Should we hit the reply key or archive the message?
- How important is the communication? Is the matter urgent? Should we interrupt other communication to shift attention to this interaction?
- What are the strengths and weaknesses of the message? At this point we engage in **critical listening** by considering the pros and cons of what the speaker has said. How reliable is the information? What are the advantages and disadvantages of the position the speaker takes? What has the speaker left out?

Challenges to Evaluation

Polarized Judgments. The greatest challenge to careful evaluation is the temptation to make sweeping overall judgments that oversimplify the value of the message. A common trap is falling into the tendency to evaluate only in all-or-nothing terms such as good/bad, right/wrong, or yes/no. While you may want to reach an overall judgment of this type, there usually are other alternatives. Remain open to the possibility that a message may be partially accurate and not just 100 percent true or 100 percent false. For example, how often have you watched a movie and adored every scene? Usually, you will find some parts of the movie appeal to you and others turn you off. The movie critics who give a film a simple "thumbs up" or "thumbs down" have oversimplified evaluation.

Evaluating People Instead of Performance. If you ever watched the television show *American Idol*, you know how the judges sometimes crush the dreams of the contestants, ridiculing them mercilessly when they sing badly. This behavior exemplifies poor evaluation. Just because someone sings poorly in an audition does not mean he has no talent whatsoever.

Many of your classes, including this one, may require you to evaluate presentations by other students. To help the presenter, you should always focus your comments on specific behaviors that can be improved. Whenever you find something that the presenter does not do well, identify what should change. If you concentrate on evaluating what someone *does* instead of who someone *is*, the presenter will recognize the criticism as constructive and not become defensive.[23]

Be careful how you phrase evaluations, since that can make the difference between insulting a presenter and improving the presenter's performance. Consider the following evaluations. Which would you rather hear from a listener? Which would help you become a better communicator?

Examples: Evaluations

1. "You did a terrible interview. What was wrong with you?"
2. "Your questions in the interview were vague and difficult to follow."
3. "Your questions in the interview could be more specific. Try listing categories of information you want, then write individual questions that could generate that information."

The third evaluation identifies a specific area needing improvement and offers a suggestion. The first two evaluations sound more like accusations and provide no foundation for improving communication.

How to Improve Evaluation

Evaluate Along Many Dimensions. An excellent way to become a better evaluator is to consider the various types of values that might affect your judgment. Using the basic judgment of quality, begin with the most general overall value of good/bad. To reach a more precise evaluation, break down the good/bad quality into several categories and expand your range of judgment. This expansion might seem to take a lot of effort, but values rarely operate in isolation. For example, an attractively served main dish at dinner might influence how tasty we judge the food to be.

To help you expand the range of your evaluations, here are several categories of values that you might consider applying to the ideas a speaker presents.

- Aesthetic
- Moral
- Practical (time, cost, resources, etc.)
- Health
- Emotional (frightening, humorous, sad, etc.)

A quick visit to the contents of a good thesaurus (such as *Roget's International Thesaurus*) will give you long lists of qualities that can guide your evaluations.

Use "I" Statements. To respect other people's feelings, evaluations should not sound like accusations. Take ownership of your evaluations. State what

FIGURE 2.2 "You" Statements and "I" Statements.

Compare the examples of "you" statements with the examples of "I" statements. Which would you rather hear and why?

"You" Statements	"I" Statements
1. "You're wrong."	1. "I disagree with you."
2. "You speak unclearly."	2. "I could not understand what you said."
3. "You make me so angry when you say ____."	3. "I feel angry when I hear you say ____."

you experience, observe, or feel instead of claiming you already know what the other person means, feels, or believes. Notice the different impact each of statements has in Figure 2.2. The "I" statements claim responsibility for feelings instead of seeming to blame the other person. If you begin your evaluations with "I" statements, you can express your feelings without getting into attack and defense.[24]

Step Four: Recalling

After you decide that information is valuable enough to keep, **recalling** encompasses remembering and using the information. Recall can be long-term or short-term. We may need to retain information only long enough to write an answer on an exam and then forget it. Other information, such as how to ride a bicycle or a favorite recipe for lamb kidneys, might stick with us for a lifetime. Effective recall extends past regurgitating individual facts. Recall allows us to relate new information to what we already know, so we recognize when to use what we learn. Since almost all academic tests place high value on recall, improving our recall skills can lead to handsome payoffs in academic performance. Remembering important occasions such as birthdays and anniversaries can improve relationships. Even more important: Listen to input from your relational partners. If your father expressed dissatisfaction about getting a necktie for his birthday, listen to that reaction and remember to select a different gift next year.

Challenges to Recalling

The main barrier to effective recall lies in the information glut discussed earlier in this chapter. Too many messages, too little time. But if we can't reduce the sheer amount of incoming information, maybe we can improve the way we sort messages and file them away in our memory. If you surf the Web for a few minutes, you will find all sorts of memory improvement courses and techniques. Every truly effective memory enhancement program shares the same trick: patterning information in systematic ways. These techniques of patterning information in ways that make it easier to remember are known as **mnemonics**. The reason we seem plagued by poor memory is that we fail to notice relationships among the isolated items that we encounter. Suppose you meet 50 people at a party. Unless you have some ways to organize these names and faces, they will remain an anonymous blur afterwards.

How to Improve Recalling

Connect the Unknown with the Known. Unfamiliar information often presents problems because we don't know how it fits with our current knowledge. How can we file something in our memory if we don't know where it belongs? The best way to cope with new information is to relate it to something you already know. For example, you meet an important client for the first time and you want to remember her name. She introduces herself as Julia, so you could make a connection with the actress Julia Roberts. If you prefer visual associations, try connecting new information with colors or objects. Perhaps you would write each of the five stages of listening in a different color so you recall, for example, that recall is green. Finding or creating associations between new and known information makes the task of recall far less threatening. Sometimes vivid visual associations help us remember names and terms. You might not remember General Norman Schwarzkopf by name, but your recall might get a boost if you recognize that his name means "black head" in German (it's true). Now you have a clear visual image that could help you recall the name.

Show as Well as Say. Effective listening involves more than mere repetition. An effective listener is able to act appropriately. An effective listener never simply claims to understand. The effective listener demonstrates understanding. One of my students was a supervisor at a turkey processing plant. Part of his job included training new employees how to use the meat slicers. These machines were huge assemblies of razor-sharp, rotating blades. He showed a group of newcomers how to use the equipment. As usual, he concluded by asking for questions. Naturally, there were none. After all, what new employee would want to look foolish or seem not to understand? A few weeks later, one of the trainees was slicing turkey, and along with slicing the turkey, she sliced off a good portion of her finger. This was the first serious accident one of this supervisor's trainees had. He was distraught and desperately asked, "What should I have done to prevent this accident?"

The answer lies in listening. I would redesign the training so that every trainee had to demonstrate proper cutting technique (with the blades turned off so that mistakes could serve as education, not amputation). Instead of relying on the claim to recall the training, the trainees would have to *prove* they could put the information into practice. This example shows how recall goes beyond just knowing information and includes knowing how to put information into practice.

As a speaker, you can verify accurate recall. If you ask "Do you understand?" or "Is that clear?" who will say no? Nobody wants to admit publicly to being a poor listener. This reluctance explains why when teachers ask such questions in the classroom, they usually encounter silence. The teacher then proceeds to the next topic, unaware that students may remain confused.

Checkpoint: How to Verify Listener Recall

- DON'T ask, "Are you listening to me?" or the equivalent. Almost nobody will admit to not listening.
- DON'T just repeat what you said and think that guarantees better listening.
- DO ask the listener, "On the basis of your listening, what will you do now?" to check for the desired response.
- DO anticipate misunderstanding. Be prepared to offer several ways for listeners to understand. Include visuals and hands-on experiences as well as lecturing.

Use Grouping and Patterns. Why trying to remember large volumes of information, break up the material into smaller chunks. How small? The number of items people tend to remember in a cluster of information is between five and nine, often referred to as the "magic seven".[25] Check the groupings of numbers that you remember easily, and they follow this pattern. American ZIP codes consist of five digits followed by a group of four.

American telephone numbers are sequences of three digits followed by four. So if you need to recall a lot of information, divide it into groups of about seven items apiece.

Your recall also will improve if you develop patterns that connect different bits of information. We tend to remember better when we organize material in some systematic manner. For example, how might you remember the stages in the listening process? The five stages of listening are: receiving, understanding, evaluating, recalling, and responding. Since these stages occur in a particular order, you need to preserve the sequence. So you could begin by remembering the first letter of each step—RUERR. If you look at the terms, you find that all end in –ing, so you might order the steps by creating a short version of the steps that you can recite as a reminder: -ving, u-ding, -ting, -ling, r-ding. You can continue to find patterns in any group of information. These patterns give structure to information that otherwise might be an indistinguishable mass. Methods of structuring information for recall include

- *Rhyming*. Search for rhyming words or construct a short poem or song to help you recite the rhyming items.
- *Drawing*. Write key terms, names, or numbers in a pattern that illustrates the concept. For example, write the word "circle" by arranging the letters in a circle.
- *Acronyms*. Selected letters in key words might spell something that will stimulate recall.

These suggestions might seem silly now, but they can dramatically increase the amount and duration of recall. Listeners tend to discover which tricks work best for them. Try some of these recall methods the next time you need to study for a test and you will see their value.

Step Five: Responding

The final step in listening, **responding**, is equivalent to feedback: offering explicit verbal or nonverbal reactions to communication. The reactions we give are crucial in maintaining positive relationships with others: family, colleagues, friends, customers, and teachers. To avoid causing the people you care about to feel ignored, unimportant, or rejected, do not react to their communications with silence, an immediate change of subject, or interrupting with your own personal stories. Take the time to acknowledge what was said and even allow for expansion on it.

Example:

Elvis: "I got an 'A' on my roadkill recipe project."

Priscilla: "Oh, I bet you feel good about that. What do you think was the best part of the project?"

Challenges to Responding

False Feedback. To give the impression that they are listening carefully, some listeners will aim to please the speaker by giving visible signs of positive reaction regardless of their genuine feelings about the communication. In their eagerness to appear attentive, listeners may offer misleading responses such as direct eye contact and nodding even when they disagree with or fail to understand the presenter. For example, someone might address you in an unfamiliar language, yet you smile and say, "Oh, really?" although you have no idea what the person is saying. False feedback confuses speakers by sending the wrong message. Since speakers respond to the reactions of their listeners, nonverbal signals of understanding signal the speaker to move on and assume the listeners are following. In the classroom, show your confusion or puzzlement if you don't follow what the instructor is saying. Skilled teachers quickly recognize when a student does not grasp an idea. If you find your instructor tends not to explain concepts well, it might be because the student reactions are saying "We understand" when their facial expressions and questions should indicate "Slow down and help us."

Morality Matters

Consider and discuss the following scenarios.

1. Responding in the Classroom

The description of false feedback often resonates with students, who respond, "Oh, yes, I've done that!" Imagine you are teaching a class where all the students want to impress you by offering false feedback constantly. How would this affect your teaching? How would it affect student learning? What would you say or what policies would you implement that would generate more honest feedback?

2. Romantic Responses

Have you (or has someone you know) been misled into believing that someone cared about you when they actually didn't? What false feedback gave you (or the other person) the impression of affection? What effect did this misleading feedback have on the relationship? How will you encourage more genuine responses in the future?

Conflicting Responses. Communicators sometimes face a challenge reacting because the communicator offers mixed signals. If a presenter's words conflict with the nonverbal behavior, listeners may not know whether to believe their ears or their eyes. For example, I have interviewed many candidates for jobs who say they are confident and outgoing, yet they mumble their answers and avoid direct eye contact with me during the interview. Most listeners tend to respond more to what a person does than to what they say. In the interview example, the interviewer probably would get a negative impression because the applicant's actions speak louder than words. To determine how you should react, look for cases where the presenter's words and behaviors reinforce each other. In those cases, you can be more confident that the presenter is sending a clear message. When the verbals and nonverbals conflict, indicate your puzzlement by asking questions or showing facial expressions of confusion. In the interview, I might respond to the interviewees by asking how confident they feel right now speaking with me. If they admit some nervousness, I recognize the reasons for their behavior. But if these interviewees continue to claim confidence while displaying signs of fear, I begin to doubt their sincerity.

How to Improve Responding

Offer Explicit Reactions. Reactions keep a conversation going and keep a presenter tuned in to the audience, ready to adapt to their feedback. Don't expect others magically to guess what you are thinking and feeling, even in intimate relationships. Often we mistakenly think that our close friends should know our reactions even when we offer no visible indication of our emotions. Those people you identify as your best listeners probably show they are listening by visible signs such as their eye contact. Eye contact here means short durations of perhaps 5 seconds at a time and not a stare. Experiment for yourself by looking someone directly in the eyes. How long did it take before you became uncomfortable? If the listener stares into space or never changes expression, you can bet that the person is not listening.

Facial expressions and body attitude offer important nonverbal visual responses. Do you let other communicators know how you feel about the subject or their behavior by your expressions? Or do you expect others magically to guess how you feel? With our eyes, facial expression and body attitude, we communicate our feelings and whether we agree, disagree, or are indifferent.

Choose Questions That Build Dialogue. We already discussed the value of questions to improve understanding. Here we examine how you can use questions to generate the mutual openness of **dialogue**, a conversation where each communicator can participate fully and openly express him- or herself. Even if you think of yourself as a skilled conversationalist, you can do your part by identifying your own and the other person's feelings and asking clarifying or open-ended questions.

Good questions show your attentiveness and encourage reactions in return. "What?" questions can perform this function. "How?" "When?" and "Where?" questions also can be useful invitations to dialogue. "What did you like about the movie?" stimulates a more informative response than simply "Did you like the movie?" The "what" question encourages a fuller reaction. The yes/no question invites only a single syllable or a grunt in response. Questions that can be answered only with yes or no are poor choices for dialogue because they do little to keep a conversation going.

Poor questions, especially in relationships, tend to be "why?" questions that place others on the defensive. Although "why?" questions can be useful, beware of "why?" questions that sound like accusations.

Examples of poor "why?" questions:

1. "Why would you say such a thing?"
2. "Why didn't you look at me when you said that?"

These questions immediately place the other communicator in the position of justifying a claim or behavior. If you rephrase your questions, they sound less accusatory.

Examples of better questions:

1. "What did you mean when you said _____?"
2. "What were you thinking about when you looked away from me?"

The revised questions ask the other communicator to discuss ideas and feelings without having to justify them.

LISTENING ROADBLOCKS AND REMEDIES

We now turn to factors that affect whether the entire listening process succeeds. The five stages of listening can work properly only when we cultivate good listening habits. These good listening habits include the techniques of active listening and recognizing the obligations communicators assume in listening.

Active Listening

Effective listeners do not simply sit passively and absorb information like a sponge absorbs water. Effective listening goes beyond merely regurgitating information after it was absorbed as if we were squeezing water from a wet sponge. Healthy listening is **active listening**: being fully engaged in the speaker-listener relationship, using all the steps of the listening process, and taking deliberate actions to improve communication.

Active listening requires the ability to listen with **empathy**—the willingness to set aside our own agendas and understand reality as the other person does. When we empathize, we place ourselves in the other person's shoes and try to recognize her perspective. When we empathize, we are able to explain the content of a communicator's message *and* acknowledge the feelings that are being expressed.[24]

Empathy differs from sympathy. Empathy enables us to imagine how someone else feels. **Sympathy** involves feeling sorry *for* someone; empathy allows us to feel *with* them. When I accidentally shut the window on my cat's tail, I sympathized with her because she obviously was in pain. But I could not empathize with her because I don't have a tail and cannot possibly imagine what it would feel like to have one.

Active listening truly involves the listener as well as the speaker. It is not merely going through the motions of listening, simply nodding your head as you think about other things or what you are going to say next. The skill of active listening requires three subsidiary skills:

1. *Attending behaviors.* Nonverbal signals that signify you are attentive. These behaviors communicate "I am interested in what you have to say," "I want to hear what you have to say," or at least, "I am willing to hear what you have to say," or "I'm not afraid of what you have to say, I can handle it." Attending behaviors include:
   - Eye contact with the other person.
   - Facing the other person.
   - Body open to the other person (arms and legs uncrossed).
   - Body inclined body toward the other person.
2. *Verifying content.* Listening for the substance of the message and letting the other person know you have heard the main ideas and facts. Check the accuracy of your understanding as soon as possible, before distractions arise or the message fades. This content check allows for misunderstanding to be cleared up quickly; it also gives the speaker a sense of truly being valued.
3. *Listening for feelings.* being communicated and letting the other person know you heard and accept those feelings by tentatively naming them. This identification of feelings is a wonderful way to show the other person you accept them as a whole person, someone with feelings as well as ideas.

Example:

"It sounds as if you are pretty upset with your boss because when she criticized you for being late, she had not criticized others and you think you were treated unfairly."

Checkpoint: Components of Active Listening

- Empathize: Understand ideas and feelings from the other person's perspective.
- Perform attending behaviors: Visibly show you are focusing on the communicator.
- Verify content: Check accuracy of comprehension before evaluating.
- Listen for feelings: Acknowledge the other person's emotional state.

Listening as a Shared Responsibility

We often think of the physical and psychological aspects of listening, but listening also has an ethical side. We conveniently accuse others of poor listening and place the burden of improving listening entirely on them. My favorite examples are the contradictory complaints I hear from students and teachers. Walk into a teacher's lounge and you will hear: "Our students don't pay attention. They refuse to listen. They won't follow instructions. It's their fault if they get bad grades." Go to the student union or school cafeteria and you will hear students saying: "Our teachers don't help us out. They refuse to tell us what they want. They won't give clear instructions. It's their fault if we get bad grades." Who is correct? Everybody is half right and half wrong. Since communication is transactional (Chapter 1), speakers and listeners share a relationship by affecting how each experiences the interaction. Speakers and listeners share the responsibility for effective communication. This shared responsibility places obligations on all communicators, whether the context is groups, interviews, conversations, or public speeches.

Speakers need to respond to reactions from the audience. If a speaker encounters signs of impatience such as checking watches, looking at clocks in a room, drumming fingers on desks, and tapping feet, the audience is sending a message that requires a response. In this case, the speaker needs to move on to the next point or conclude. Few things alienate an audience more than being ignored, so speakers should "read" the audience and prepare to adjust accordingly.

Listeners incur the obligation to be assertive and take action to improve the communication situation. Speak up or alter your communication environment if you are unable to listen effectively because of poor timing, distractions, or other factors. Several years ago, I was distressed to receive a comment on a course evaluation from a student in a large class who complained of never being able to see the whiteboard in our classroom and blamed me for not making the notes more visible. I wish this student had spoken to me so we could have made some arrangements to improve listening. I could have reserved a seat for the student near the front of the room or enlarged the visuals, for example. I remained ignorant of the problem and the student missed important information.

Speakers and listeners share another obligation: knowing when to keep silent. Let the other communicators have their say—that is the only way you can be sure you receive the entire message. Interrupting a speaker is not only rude, but it may deprive you of information that you need to understand and evaluate the message. Interruptions also signify that you value your own ideas and feelings more than those of others, so you may create an impression that you are self-centered and domineering.

That's Debatable

Throughout this book, you'll notice the term "debatable" appears as a way to recognize and respect differing viewpoints. Generally debates are designed to render decisions, so that's why you see this term instead of "discussions" (which have no definite closure). Try testing or challenging a few of the points in the next section of this chapter. When have you found listening for advice or listening in relationships to be the most successful? What would you add to the discussions below as recommendations for listening in these contexts?

LISTENING IN CONTEXT

Sometimes the communication context places special demands on listeners. The final stop on our tour of listening takes us to two situations beyond the classroom: listening to give advice and listening in close personal relationships.

Listening to Give Advice

One of the most important everyday situations that requires us to become active listeners is when someone turns to us for advice. Our ability to give good advice depends on our ability to listen carefully enough to diagnose what the other person needs from us. Offering advice is part of your "job description" as a parent, supervisor, or friend.

Contrary to what we might think, advice-giving is the *last* step in the process. We need a clear grasp of the individual's problem, issue, or needs before accurate advice can be given and accepted. First, the advice/help seeker needs to feel comfortable, respected as a person totally, and that his or her problem—whatever it is—counts as important and is understood. Without this security of being appreciated, all your great wisdom and knowledge will fall on deaf ears.

Nonverbal communication assumes paramount importance: It communicates respect and raises the comfort level of the interaction. Invite the individual into your office or another private space that you can dedicate entirely to your conversation. Do as much as you can to ensure privacy, and demonstrate respect by avoiding interruptions. Be open and nonjudgmental to the advice-seeker (open body language, no barriers such as big desks between you and her) to show respect and promote trust. Engage in all the attending behavior skills of active listening.

Verbal input is also important. Paraphrase what the speaker tells you, both the content and the feelings expressed. Active listening helps you get a clear handle on the problem of this particular individual so your advice can be more accurate and specific. Active listening also helps the advice-seeker feel or believe that you do understand his or her problem. Before giving advice inquire as to what ideas, actions, plans, or options the individual has considered. Often advice is not really what the person wants. The advice-seeker may actually want validation of what she or he has already figured out, or the individual may simply need someone to listen so the speaker can ventilate.

We need to become adept at listening to advise and to validate. Researchers such as Deborah Tannen[26] contend that men tend to gravitate toward giving advice, feeling fulfillment from guiding others toward solutions. By contrast, women often want listeners to validate their right to have opinions and feelings, not necessarily to provide suggestions for solutions. Not all men or women listen in the same way, and the research points to different approaches rather than genetic absolutes. Given these different perspectives, Tannen cautions that we need to develop sensitivity toward the other communicator. Does the advice-seeker want the listener to play "Fix-It," or does the communicator prefer confirmation of thoughts and emotions?

Listening in Relationships

Listening in relationships requires some special considerations. We need to listen in ways that assure a safe place to share emotions so we draw closer to each other. Relational contexts place priority on revealing emotional content instead of on winning a point or establishing superiority. Relational listening employs several techniques.

1. *Tune-in time.* Take time to listen within, to be aware of and responsible for your own feelings. Do not use this time to set up your "arguments." Use the time to really listen to yourself and to consider how best to express the feelings you are becoming aware of. The word "best" is used in terms of getting your feelings across—not in the sense of how well crafted or how good they will sound.

2. *Expression of feelings.* Both partners should agree to be as open as possible, both in expressing their own feelings and in allowing the other freedom to express. If only one partner deeply shares, that partner often develops negative feelings of having to carry the relationship alone. Try to share the awareness you developed during the tune-in time. Avoid intellectualizing. Avoid generalization. Avoid labels and accusations. Stay in the first person

as much as possible ("I," "me," "my"), as discussed in the evaluation stage of listening. Own your feelings and your perceptions—as perceptions, not as The Ultimate Truth.

3. *Empathic listening* Try very hard to hear what your partner is saying, to actually feel what your partner is feeling. Try to see and feel things as your partner is seeing and feeling them. Avoid planning your "retort."

4. *Summarizing.* Before sharing one's own feelings, the listener should work on trying to indicate through summary that what the other person was trying to communicate was heard and understood. Do not use this summary as a weapon. ("See how well I know you"; "You can't fool me.") The tone of voice and manner are very important. Use this process in the most helpful way possible: demonstrate that you are truly *with* the other person.

5. *Processing.* Stop occasionally to process the interaction. Note the communication patterns. Is the communication working? Do you feel you are being heard? Do you feel you are getting enough opportunity to express your feelings and views? Do you feel your partner is being receptive? Do you feel your partner is being open? Do you feel you are being open, receptive, and specific?

Throughout your conversation, avoid accusations that place your partner on the defensive. Sometimes it is best to start with what you feel is positive so far about the exchange, especially if either you or your partner starts getting verbally aggressive or defensive. If the process is not working well, perhaps some more tune-in time is needed so you can individually clarify the emotions you want to communicate.

Tech Talk

Sometimes we need to "listen" online or on the telephone when face-to-face interaction is impractical. What concrete indicators of effective listening could you offer in these mediated conditions? Identify some situations where this sort of "listening" has frustrated you. What could you or the other person have done to enact active listening?

Our tour of listening should have provided you with several souvenirs in the form of listening habits that you can implement in your academic, personal, and professional life. Hopefully you not only read this chapter, but experimented with practicing the techniques of effective listening. A lot is at stake in listening, since remaining content with merely hearing exacts a hefty price economically, intellectually, and personally. Every stage of the listening process—receiving, understanding, evaluating, recalling, and responding—allows us to examine our own listening behaviors and find how we can become more active listeners. Communication succeeds only to the extent that people listen well.

HIGHLIGHTS

1. Listening is probably the most crucial communication skill, since it determines whether communication succeeds or fails.

2. As a deliberate, interpretive process that seeks meaning, listening is distinct from the physical act of hearing sounds.

3. Listening is rarely taught, and the costs (emotional and financial) of poor listening are high.

4. Listening filters determine how much and we listen to and what we make of it.
   a. Selective attention directs which messages get processed at all.
   b. Selective interpretation determines how message content gets processed.
5. Receiving, the first step in listening, involves acquiring sounds.
   a. Challenges to receiving include information overload, speed differences between speaking and listening, and personal factors that compete with devoting attention to listening.
   b. Receiving can improve by reducing distractions and maintaining eye contact.
6. Understanding, the second step in listening, involves comprehension of a message in the presenter's own terms.
   a. Challenges to understanding include assuming automatic clarity of our own communication and confusing understanding with agreement.
   b. Understanding can improve by suspending judgment, paraphrasing in our own words, asking questions, and avoiding traps of selective interpretation such as self-serving bias.
7. Evaluation, the third step in listening, involves judging the value of messages.
   a. Challenges to evaluation include polarized judgments that unnecessarily limit options and evaluating the person instead of the communication.
   b. Evaluation can improve by evaluating along several dimensions to avoid all-or-nothing thinking and using "I" statement to avoid blaming others for miscommunication.
8. Recalling, the fourth step in listening, involves remembering and using information.
   a. Challenges to recall include having too many competing messages to process.
   b. Recall can improve by connecting new information with what is known, verifying recall with demonstrations of comprehension, and grouping information to form memorable patterns.
9. Responding, the final step in listening, involves reactions to communication given as feedback.
   a. Challenges to responding include false feedback that imitates careful listening and conflicting feedback that offers mixed messages about reactions.
   b. Responding can improve by listeners offering explicit reactions and by encouraging thorough dialogue through questions that invite discussion.
10. Effective listeners practice active listening.
    a. Active listeners can empathize with others to be sensitive to their messages.
    b. Active listeners demonstrate attending behaviors that show attentiveness.
    c. Active listeners verify the content of messages for accuracy.
    d. Active listeners listen for feelings as well as for factual information.
11. Speakers and audiences share responsibility for effective listening.
12. When giving advice, offer advice only after listening to the entire problem and exploring available options.
13. Listening in relationships calls for tuning in to expressing feeling, prioritizing empathy, summarizing what the other person is communicating, and taking time to process communication rather than leveling accusations.

ENDNOTES

1. International Listening Association. (1996). Retrieved August 3, 2009, from http://www.listen.org

2. Atwater, E. (1992). *I hear you* (Rev. ed.). Pacific Grove, CA: Walker.

3. HighGain.com (2004). *The business of listening*. Retrieved August 3, 2009, from http://www.highgain.com/html/the_business_of_listening.html

4. Pearce, C., Johnson, I., & Barker, R. (1995). Enhancing the student listening skills and environment. *Business Communication Quarterly, 58*, 28–33.

5. Hyslop, N. B., & Tone, B. (1988). *Listening: Are we teaching it, and if so, how?* ERIC Digest Number 3. ED295132. Retrieved August 3, 2009, from http://www.ericdigests.org/pre-928/listening.htm

6. Lindahl, K. (2003). *Practicing the sacred art of listening*. Woodstock, VT: Skylight Paths.

7. Cooper, L. (1997). Listening competency in the workplace: A model for training. *Business Communication Quarterly, 60*, 75–84.

8. Shepherd, C. D., Castleberry, S. B., & Ridnour, R. E. (1997). Linking effective listening with salesperson performance: An exploratory investigation. *Journal of Business and Industrial Marketing, 12*, 315–322.

9. Hayakawa, S. I. (1955, Autumn). How to attend a conference. *Et Cetera, 13*, 5–9.

10. Halone, K. K., Cuncoran, T. M., Coakley, C. G., & Wolvin, A. D. (1998). Toward the establishment of general dimensions underlying the listening process. *International Journal of Listening, 12*, 12–28.

11. Alessandra, T. (1995). The power of listening. *Speakers platform*. Retrieved January 12, 2010, from http://www.speaking.com/articles_html/TonyAlessandra, Ph.D.,CSP,CPAE_107.html

12. Arthur W. Page Society. (2004, September 13). *Page Society annual conference closes with a world-view of listening*. Retrieved December 24, 2004, from http://www.awpagesociety.com/newroom/apsconf091504.asp

13. McKeone, L. (2004). *The executive extra. Listen up!* Retrieved August 3, 2009, from http://www.executiveextra.com/listen_up.htm

14. Hunsaker, P. L., & Alessandra, A. J. (1986). *The art of managing people*. New York: Simon & Schuster.

15. Johnson, I. W., Pearce, C. G., Tuten, T. L., & Sinclair, L. (2003). Self-imposed silence and perceived listening effectiveness. *Business Communication Quarterly, 66*, 23–45.

16. Johns, A.M. (1981). Necessary English: A faculty survey. *TESOL Quarterly, 15*, 51–57.

17. Smith, A. (2004). *The communication gap*. Institute for Youth Development. Retrieved January 12, 2010, from http://www.youthdevelopment.org/articles/fp059901.htm

18. Burley-Allen, M. (1982). *Listening: The forgotten skill*. New York: John Wiley.

19. Mehrabian, A. (1981). *Silent messages: Implicit communication of emotions and attitudes* (2nd ed.). Belmont, CA: Wadsworth.

20. Nichols, M. P. (1995). *The lost art of listening*. New York: Guilford Press.

21. Johnson, W. (1956). *Your most enchanted listener.* New York: Harper.

22. Snibbe, A. C., Kitayama, S., Markus, H. R. O. S. E., & Suzuki, T. (2003). They saw a game: A Japanese and American (football) field study. *Journal of Cross-Cultural Psychology,* **34,** 581–595.

23. Blanchard, K., & Johnson, S. (1982). *The one minute manager.* New York: William Morrow.

24. Burns, D. D. (1999). *The feeling good handbook* (Rev. ed.). New York: Plume.

25. Miller, G. A. (1956). The magical number seven, plus or minus two: Some limits on our capacity for processing information. *Psychological Review, 63,* 81–97.

26. Tannen, D. (1990). *You just don't understand: Women and men in conversation.* New York: William Morrow.

Chapter 2
Listening Journal

Students are asked to choose **only** three listening skills from the verbal and nonverbal lists* given in class and **apply one at a time** when listening in 3 **separate** communication situations with 3 different people resulting in a total of 9 communication exchanges. Use each behavior/skill once on each person. Use this assignment as an opportunity to practice new listening behaviors on your friends, family, co-workers, or other acquaintances. Then write about the speaking-listening exchange and the results of using the skill.

Be sure to:

- Label each paragraph with the skill used in that conversation
- State whether the skills helped or hindered the exchange
- Describe your perceived reaction of the speaker to the use of the listening behavior/skill
- Describe your own reaction to use of the listening behavior/skill: were you comfortable, uncomfortable, at ease, scared, concerned, etc.
- Will you use this particular skill/behavior in the future
- Then write a 4–5 sentence summary of what you learned through this assignment

The Listening Journal must be **typed** and **stapled**.

SAMPLE LISTENING JOURNAL ENTRY LABEL

Skill used: Leaning forward

Person talking: Mom

---

*I use Pearson, Nelson, Titsworth and Harter's verbal and nonverbal communication effectively lists in *Human Communication*, 3rd ed, McGraw-Hill, 2008, 121–123.

3

VERBAL COMMUNICATION

"Sticks and stones may break my bones, but words can never harm me." Almost everyone remembers that saying from childhood. But do you believe it now? How many times have you noticed your own words hurt others? How often have you felt the pain of sharp words hurled toward you? Yes, words can harm, but they also can heal. Words chosen and used wisely can bring peace, build relationships, and fill rooms with laughter. Inconsiderate, harsh, or inaccurate word usage has caused untold human misery, from broken marriages to broken bodies. The philosopher Ludwig Wittgenstein commented, "The limits of my language . . . mean the limits of my world" (1961, §5.62). The New Testament affirms the centrality of language: "In the beginning was the Word, and the Word was with God, and the Word was God" (John 1:1). More than we realize, our ability to express ourselves verbally intertwines with the ways we think, how we act, and even shapes what we consider as real.

Oral communication occurs in three main realms: verbal (the words we say or hear), vocal (qualities of the voice—how we say things rather than the words themselves), and visual (physical characteristics such as body movement). This chapter approaches the verbal side of communication. The next chapter discusses the vocal and visual domains. Whether we like it or not, people will judge the quality of our ideas by how well we express those ideas. Just ask the public relations firm responsible for purging the word "prunes" from our local grocery stores.

> Prunes suggested "old," "stodgy" and "shriveled" and it needed a name that was more hip, upbeat and healthy sounding. Our consumer research revealed that "dried plums" did not elicit negative images like "prunes" did and, in fact, better represented the true nature of the food product we wanted to sell.[1]

The agricultural industry agreed, so the identical dried fruit reappeared in stores as "dried plums." Words matter. Our verbal ventures begin with an overview of how language operates in the construction of meaning and stylistically. Then we cover the four verbal virtues that we label PIES: precision, inclusiveness, expressiveness, and sensitivity. Finally, we move to specific language devices that can enliven your verbal delivery.

HOW LANGUAGE OPERATES IN COMMUNICATION

Language doesn't get much respect or attention—until something goes wrong. You've probably heard people remark, "Actions speak louder than words," as if what someone says doesn't matter. Yet, we often talk our way into—and out of—relationships, jobs, and opportunities. Communication is a complete package that requires attention to verbal and nonverbal dimensions. If you want to inflict the ultimate punishment on a family member, what do you do? Give the person "the silent treatment" and refuse to speak. So verbal communication must make a difference if people use deprivation of it as a weapon. Careful use of language may seem frivolous, dismissed with a wave of the hand and the comment, "It's only semantics—just a matter of words." Well, the difference between "yes" and "no" is just a matter of words. If you doubt the seriousness of careful language usage, just speak with anyone who has ever signed a legal contract. Terms of treaties that end wars rely on the clearest possible language. Lives depend on it.

Words Are Symbols

Try this experiment. Introduce a newcomer to a group of people simply by mentioning the person's name and that he or she was just released from prison. Say nothing else, then watch what happens. You may find that, despite their apparent interest in the newcomer, people in the group begin to behave differently even though they know nothing about the person other than the association with the label "prison." Some folks may hold their purses tighter, others check their wallets frequently. Some might move farther away from the supposed "criminal." Others might avoid this person entirely. Is the "criminal" actually guilty? What is the nature of the supposed crime? No one knows, yet the power of the words alone can influence how people treat the one you labeled an ex-prisoner. These reactions are based on a fundamental and common error, the mistaken belief that **the word is the thing**. When we treat words as things, we fail to question the circumstances that might confirm or disprove the label. Instead, we react to the power of the words themselves without examining the realities and possibilities that underlie the words. The confusion doesn't have to be negative. Just introduce someone as a "film director" or "professional athlete" and observe how the individual becomes instantly popular and admired—regardless of how accurate these labels are.

The remedy for this problem of treating words as things lies in a better understanding of how language operates. Words are **symbols** that represent real objects or events, but the relationship between symbols and what they stand for is **arbitrary**. Words are arbitrary because there is no necessary reason why something must be called one thing or another. Words do not have to look like or sound like what they stand for. What we call **meaning** is a product of our experience—what we have learned about the associations between words and the things they represent. Meanings always are communal matters. There's no such thing as a meaning that one person decides individually, since meanings have to be understandable by others. "Meanings of words are shared between people—they are a kind of social contract we all agree to—otherwise communication would not be possible".[2] So if someone tries to excuse confused communication with "Well, I know what I meant," the person misses the social basis of language use.

Meanings are interpretations of messages that arise from experience. Arbitrariness does not imply that we can make up meanings randomly, since they arise from collective custom.[2] The arbitrariness of meaning explains why different languages have different words for the same objects. Comedian Steve Martin used to remark that French was a difficult language to learn because it seemed that the French had a different word for everything. Of course that's true, which is why the terms of various languages sound strange to people unaccustomed to them. The words "house," "la maison," "la casa," and "das Haus" certainly don't look like houses, and there is no specific reason why houses are feminine in French and Spanish but neuter in German.

FIGURE 3.1 Symbols and Referents.

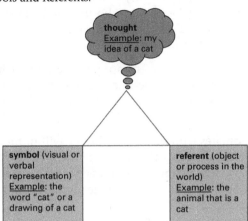

C. K. Ogden and I. A. Richards originated a helpful way to describe the process of constructing meaning.[3(pp140-143)] Figure 3.1 offers an adaptation of their approach. Whatever words stand for is known as the **referent**. In Figure 3.1, the referent would be the actual cat that we discuss by using the word "cat." The relationship between symbol and referent is arbitrary. There is no reason why we call a feline animal "cat" instead of calling it "hootenanny." We simply have become accustomed to assigning the three letters c-a-t to domesticated felines.

What is the relationship between language and reality—the word "cat" and the fuzzy, striped beast lounging across my keyboard? Most people think that words simply label things, but language does not just reflect reality. Language actually can affect what we see as reality. This is the **Sapir-Whorf hypothesis** (named after the theorists Edward Sapir and Benjamin Lee Whorf): Language shapes reality; it does not just mirror reality. This primacy of language explains why one of the first duties of new parents is to name the child. Much thought goes into selecting a name, since the chosen name shapes perceptions and expectations regarding the child.

Language Unites and Separates Communities

Our choice of words can build bridges or barriers between communities. Have you ever had a computer specialist fix your computer, and then you asked what the problem was and how it was fixed? If so, you probably got an answer that was so technical your brain wanted to explode. The specialized language adopted by a particular group of people is known as **jargon**. Sometimes jargon is technical, as in the preceding example. At other times, jargon helps to identify an ethnic group, age group, or other community of people. In fact, many groups are recognizable by their unique terminology more than by any visible identification.

Regardless of the type, jargon always plays two distinct roles. On one hand, jargon serves as a way to connect with other members of the "in-group" that uses the specialized terms. Proper use of the jargon can indicate you are a member of the group that communicates with those particular terms and phrases. So if you overhear two computer experts conversing in English but in technical terms you cannot comprehend, they are doing more than sharing information: They are reinforcing their social bond through the jargon they share. The second role jargon plays goes along with its unifying function. Jargon also divides people. While the computer technicians were drawn together by their shared jargon, the layperson was left out of the conversation. Jargon unifies the insiders (the people who use the jargon) while alienating the outsiders (people who are not fluent in the technical terms). To experience both effects, consider the following example:

> As East defending to three no-trump, you see partner lead a heart, and your jack holds the trick, declarer playing the four. Partner must have king-fifth of hearts since declarer denied a major in response to Stayman.[4(p.D7)]

Huh? But your classmates who avidly play bridge will immediately recognize someone is discussing their favorite game of cards. The jargon interests the bridge players but also tells people unfamiliar with bridge that they are in alien territory. The same language that unites bridge players forms a barrier between them and non-players.

When jargon becomes a way to obscure truth or prevent understanding, it qualifies as a type of **doublespeak**, or language designed to confuse and mislead.[5,6] Unlike ordinary jargon, doublespeak does not clarify understanding even for specialized communities. The doublespeak version of jargon overwhelms its audience with complicated messages that short-circuit interpretation. For instance, when you hear a building inspector say your new apartment has a "discontinuity," you might want to find another place to live. Your apartment actually has a cracked support beam that could lead to structural collapse.[7(p320)] Incomprehensible language not only puzzles audiences, but its very complexity prevents thoughtful discussion. Speakers easily evade responsibility by concealing their wrongdoing or errors in impenetrable language.

Connotation and Denotation

Whenever we speak, the words we use evoke two separate but often related meanings, known as denotation and connotation. The **denotation** of a word is the literal meaning assigned to it, what we might consider the dictionary definition. Referring back to Figure 3.1, the denotation would be the referent, the thing or event in the world that people associate with a word. So far, so good. If meanings operated only on a denotative level, then all misunderstandings could be resolved by checking the dictionary. Some very simple words, however, have a huge array of denotations. Browsing an unabridged dictionary, I discover 39 distinct definitions for "have," 91 for "go," 33 for "bear," 82 for "make," and 25 for "man." With each word forced to do so much work, no wonder we find it difficult to comply when someone pleads, "Why don't you just say what you mean?" How do we know which meaning our listeners will select?

Verbal communication, however, involves more than just checking dictionaries. We must attend to a word's **connotation,** or its emotional impact. Words carry emotional baggage and generate feelings in addition to dictionary definition. Different word choices carry different connotations. For example, each of the following terms has the same literal denotation (a female), but what connotation does each term carry if you are addressing an adult woman?

- lady
- girl
- chick
- babe
- ma'am (madam)
- piece
- broad

Since meaning operates on both levels, we should recognize that misunderstanding could arise with denotation or connotation. Developing a clear understanding of word connotation is a continuous challenge as connotations depend on the circumstances and on the interpreter. It is wise to determine connotations based on your audience, not on your own assumptions about how people will react. Usually, you have a range of terms that carry varying degrees of positive or negative connotations. When in doubt, ask others how they want to be addressed and respect those preferences.

Oral Style

We don't talk the same way we write. Often when we hear someone read a speech directly from a manuscript, it sounds oddly stiff and artificial. On the other hand, if you read an exact transcript of a conversation, the written text seems a bit disjointed, perhaps too folksy and informal. Speaking and writing call for different styles of language. Playwrights agonize over writing scripts that sound natural when spoken onstage; the conversion from writing to speech is not automatic. Figure 3.2 summarizes some differences between oral and written style.

Oral style and written style are matters of degree, not absolute opposites.[8] Most speech contains some features of writing, while most written work displays some oral components. Employing more oral style in an oral presentation, however, will sound more "natural" to the audience. Compare the following versions of the same basic content.

Example (written style): This writer is of the conviction that the opposing party's position has little merit.

Example (oral style): I truly think my opponents are wrong—just plain wrong.

The oral style version sounds more appropriate for a face-to-face conversation. The written style version sounds more appropriate for a scholarly article.

One vital difference between speaking and writing is that readers can adjust their pace at will, but listeners remain at the speaker's mercy. Listeners depend on the speaker to indicate which points are important and which emotional responses are appropriate. As a speaker, you must verbally highlight the portions of a presentation you want to emphasize. Writers do this by use of space: larger fonts, more pages, or other textual effects such as italics and boldface. As a speaker, you can use tone and time. The tone of your voice should match the emotion you want to convey. Saying "I'm delighted to be here" in a flat, barely audible mumble signals that your feelings do not match your words. As

FIGURE 3.2 Oral Versus Written Style.

(Stylistic features derived from Thomas[9] and McLaurin.[10])

Feature	Oral Style	Written Style
Sentence complexity	Shorter, simpler vocabulary, possibly includes sentence fragments	Longer, more complicated vocabulary, often includes compound sentences with several clauses
References to audience and speaker	Direct references to immediate audience, speaker refers to self	Few or no references to immediate audience, minimal self-references
Style of reasoning	Employs more stories, personal examples	Employs more fully developed logical proofs, chains of arguments
Style of delivery	Repetitive, may include slang, more frequent interjections ("oh," "hey," etc.), more frequent pauses and variance in pacing	Linear, organized by logical sequences, obeys more conventional grammatical patterns, consistent speed of delivery
Emphasis	Primarily on social relationship with audience and connection to context, affects audience emotionally, stresses speaker-audience interaction	Primarily on proof or knowledge, affects audience through transmitting information

for time, listeners tend to connect time spent on a topic with its importance. The longer you talk about something, the more important the audience will consider it to be. Devote the most time to the portions of your presentation you consider the most important.

VERBAL VIRTUES: DEVELOPING HEALTHY LANGUAGE HABITS

Effective language usage conveys an image of a polished, competent professional. Sloppy language signifies sloppy thought, and audiences quickly judge poor language usage as a sign that the speaker lacks education, has little competence, and might not deserve trust. Fortunately, developing healthy language habits can clarify our communication. In this section, we review four verbal virtues that effective communicators should develop. The first letters of these virtues spell PIES: *precise, inclusive, expressive,* and *sensitive*. We now turn to how PIES can enhance your language skills.

PIES Virtue 1: Precise Language Use

Precision in language refers to how specifically we speak. The more precise we are, the more exactly our symbols and referents align. As we become more precise, there should be less confusion and uncertainty about meanings. Clarity counts. If others cannot decipher what we are talking about, little else in communication matters.

Abstraction

Imagine you are trying to get a description of a criminal from several witnesses. When you ask them to describe the person they saw, they offer the following description:

> above average height, medium complexion, rather thin, reasonably attractive, dark eyes.

Not much help, is it? This type of description, quite familiar and frustrating in law enforcement, demonstrates imprecise language. Millions of people fit the description because it contains little detail. Now consider a more precise version of the same description:

> six feet tall, olive complexion, 175 pounds, looked like Tiger Woods, brown eyes.

Now we have a better chance of finding the criminal. We have a set of qualities that applies to far fewer people. Precision doesn't always require more time and more words—just more carefully chosen terms. The more precisely we use language, the easier our listeners can distinguish between possible referents. The more referents a word or phrase can have, the more **abstract** it is. As language becomes more precise, it becomes more **concrete** by narrowing the range of interpretations it can have.

To improve precision, try using the ladder of abstraction, illustrated in Figure 3.3. The higher terms get on the ladder, the more abstract and distant from reality they become. The lower terms get on the ladder, the more concrete and precise they become. The number of possible referents increases the higher one goes on the ladder, increasing the chance of misunderstanding. *Animal* includes billions of creatures—insects and reptiles as well as dogs. *Pugsley*, especially in the context of my roommate's pet, pinpoints the reference to one creature.

Precision improves when you stay low on the ladder of abstraction. As you get lower on the ladder, language becomes more concrete. With fewer

FIGURE 3.3 The Ladder of Abstraction.

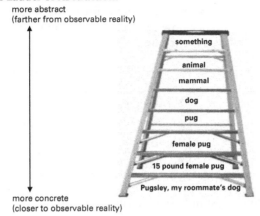

possible referents, the less likely your listeners will misinterpret your words. Highly abstract language works like a multiple-choice question with hundreds of options for answers. Different interpretations will abound. Concrete language presents listeners with fewer options, like a multiple-choice question with only a couple of possible solutions. Think of the abstract sources we sometimes use for information. We "heard from someone" that a course has a lot of reading or that it requires certain types of assignments. We could determine the accuracy of these rumors by using a more concrete source, such as the course syllabus.

Euphemisms

Sometimes, when discussing sensitive topics, we need to select words and phrases that minimize the chance of offending others. For example, instead of saying that someone "died," we might say that the person "passed away" or "met his maker," and refer to "the deceased" or our "late friend" instead of "the corpse." These substitutes for unpleasant terms are called **euphemisms**, and they provide diplomatic ways of discussing bad news or delicate issues.

Euphemisms serve some important positive functions. By masking unpleasant subjects in more pleasant terms, we feel more comfortable discussing these topics.[11] Circumstances or social customs might prohibit discussion of certain topics. Such prohibited areas are knows as **taboo**, so euphemisms provide handy ways to avoid these forbidden zones.[12] For example, in everyday, polite American conversation, open discussion of human sexuality or bodily excretions would qualify as taboo topics. Parents might explain "the facts of life" or "the birds and the bees" to children, since many parents would feel uncomfortable openly dis-cussing "sexual intercourse." Elaborate euphemisms refer to bodily functions such as urination, which we finesse by "using the restroom," "making water," "relieving ourselves," or "obeying Nature's call." Besides reducing inhibitions, euphemisms provide polite ways to spare people's feelings. If a student performs poorly on an assignment, a considerate professor would prefer saying "This work needs revision" instead of "This is miserable garbage." The euphemism offers potential for improvement, while the cruel criticism treats the situation as hopeless. Euphemisms can save face for speaker and audience by preventing embarrassment.[13]

Euphemisms also carry substantial risks, so use them cautiously. Used too often, euphemisms can mask the seriousness of topics and might prevent others from understanding or facing reality.[14] When euphemisms deceive or mislead, they become a type of doublespeak.[5,6] As we noted earlier in this chapter, doublespeak uses language to confuse or distort reality. It includes not only overly complex language, as we saw when discussing jargon, but also malicious euphemisms. Consider how the following military euphemisms distort the horrors of war and obscure the loss of lives.

Euphemism	Translation
Friendly fire	Shooting your own troops
Collateral damage	Accidentally killing or wounding civilians
Sortie	Bombing mission
Strategic withdrawal	Retreat

Sometimes doublespeak simply sugar-coats the truth. A company that chooses to "downsize" sounds much gentler than the same company deciding to "fire" workers. Euphemisms also can become downright evasive or deceptive.[13] An evaluation form for staff at a university where I worked listed the performance levels as outstanding, very good, good, and "below good," a sign that we no longer call poor work what it is. Deceptive euphemisms abound in education. Many American elementary and junior high schools practice "social promotion," which advances a student to the next grade level despite inadequate performance. Such doublespeak avoids confronting "failure."

Contrary to euphemisms designed to spare people's feelings, doublespeak causes confusion by deceiving listeners about what the euphemism signifies.[12] Doublespeak has serious consequences. It "alters our perception of reality. It deprives us of the tools we need to develop, advance, and preserve our society, our culture, our civilization. It delivers us into the hands of those who do not have our interests at heart".[15(p233)] When "taxes" become "revenue enhancement" and "death" becomes a "negative patient outcome," how can we understand what language refers to anymore? Mary Bosik[16] offers some practical suggestions:

- Recognize evasive language, whether it takes the form of euphemisms, jargon, or unnecessary complexity.
- Determine whether or why the source might want to mislead you. What might the source be trying to hide? How does the source benefit from the evasive language?
- Offer some type of response. Clarify the terminology by asking questions, summarizing, requesting examples (which tend to be specific), or challenging the accuracy of the terms.

Two-Valued Orientation

Two-valued orientation, sometimes known as black-white thinking, divides the world into polar opposites. As a result, language paints every situation and issue as a contest between two extremes that cannot combine or be reconciled.

Examples (Two-Valued Orientation)

- Abortion: Positions are pro-life or pro-choice.
- In labor disputes, you must side with management or labor.
- In every competition, there are only winners and losers.
- "Either you are with us, or you are with the terrorists".[17(p.1349)]

We can slip easily into two-valued orientation because the structure of language and thought invites it. Most important decisions, however, have more complexity than a simple for/against, yes/no, true/false. Furthermore, two-valued orientation fuels the assumption that the two sides must be bitterly opposed. A vivid and shameful result of two-valued orientation in parts of the United States was racial segregation, with "black" and "white" legally treated so differently that all public facilities, including restaurants, busses, and restrooms, physically separated the races. With signs proclaiming "White Only" and "Colored Only," public life was split along the two-valued color line. Yes, two-valued orientation has serious consequences.

Two-valued orientation can be cured. **Multi-valued orientation** offers more precise (and thus more accurate) classifications. In the example of racial segregation, the two main categories begin to break down once people realize that "black" and "white" do not describe human skin color accurately or completely. What about olive-skinned people? How dark must brown be to qualify as black? How pale is white? These sorts of questions might help people think beyond the familiar two values that have structured their world. A good place to begin a multi-valued orientation would be to search for some middle ground between the two supposedly opposite values.

PIES Virtue 2: Inclusive Language Use

If you want the audience to connect with you, be on your side, or even if you simply want them to give you a fair hearing, you must speak *with* them and not *at* them. Depending on how we use language, we can ally with an audience or alienate them.

Connect with the Audience

How would you react if you heard someone make the following comments in a public presentation?

Example 1 (student addressing other students in the same course): "Students need to realize their limits so they can avoid stress. Many students actually cause more stress by overloading their schedules."

Example 2 (Caucasian addressing an African American audience): "I'm pleased to talk to you people about Campus Ministries. We need more of your kind of people in our organization."

Example 3 (professor addressing students): "How would one begin to solve this problem? What could one do to simplify it?"

All three examples suffer from a shared problem. **Inclusive language** makes all audience members feel as if the speaker considers their background, beliefs, and needs. These examples use language in ways that create barriers between speaker and audience. The solution is simple: Use inclusive pronouns ("we," "us") to connect speaker and audience. Example 1 talks at the audience, referring to them as "students"—almost as if they weren't there. To understand how odd this language pattern sounds, conduct a conversation while referring to yourself by name instead of with "I" or "me." Inclusive pronouns would improve Example 1, especially since speaker and audience share the same group identity (as students).

Improved Example 1 (student addressing other students in the same course): "We need to realize our limits so we can avoid stress. A lot of us—I know I do, and I'll bet some of you do, too—actually cause more stress by overloading our schedules."

Example 2 creates an "us" versus "them" mentality through language that might create racial tension. Inclusive language would address the entire audience as prospective members of the group.

Improved Example 2 (Caucasian addressing an African American audience): "Let's discuss Campus Ministries. We welcome you to campus and hopefully to our ministry. Hopefully by the end of the semester, we'll all be meeting together in the new Campus Ministries social hall instead of in this classroom."

Example 3 renders class discussion impersonal, distancing students from the professor. A slight change in language could help students feel more like partners in learning.

Improved Example 3 (professor addressing students): "How would we begin to solve this problem? Let's see—how could we simplify it?"

In all these examples, inclusive language builds bridges between speaker and audience.

Use Unbiased Language

Inclusive language goes beyond changing pronoun references. It also involves selecting terms that respect the dignity, value, and individuality of people who might differ from us. As we discussed in Chapter 2, stereotyping is common and often leads individuals to use biased and insensitive language.

Sexist Language. Sexism, defined as the treatment of women as less important or inferior compared to men, infuses language in many ways. Generic male language—referring to people in general as male—shows sexist bias. Traditionally, the word or suffix "man" was used to designate all people. The "man in the street" or "the average man" supposedly referred to the average person, yet the terminology sounded as if the average person always were male. The generic pronoun "he" historically has referred to all groups of people, as in "Everyone will get his share." Many professions have included "man" as a generic term for all workers: "policeman," "fireman," "postman," "serviceman." Construction signs along roadways used to read "men working." Repeated use of generic "man" to describe professions ignores the possible presence of women and implies they do not belong.[18] When women or men are asked to describe workers in professions with the "-man" suffix, they are more likely to imagine the workers as male. Gender-neutral job titles correct this tendency.[19] "Humanity," "humankind," or "people" includes men and women. "Police officer," "firefighter," "postal worker," or "letter carrier," "soldier," and "road workers" or "construction zone" offer easy modifications that include women.

Other sexist tendencies include referring to women in disparaging or dismissive terms. How often have you heard adult females called "girls" (not "women") while males of the same age are called "men" (not "boys")? For a quick orientation to sexist language, scan a good thesaurus for derogatory terms that refer primarily or exclusively to women. This list would include terms such as "bimbo," "ditz," "dumb blonde," and a long list of less flattering vocabulary. Compare the number of such terms reserved for men, and you begin to realize how language easily can work against women.

Some people might say that language really has no sexist bias and deny the need for non-sexist language. More than 30 years of research has shown that audiences tend to interpret masculine-oriented language as referring only to men[20]—a finding that makes perfect sense once we recognize that language shapes reality. Many professional organizations such as the American Psychological Association, the Modern Language Association, the American Medical Association, the American Marketing Association, and the American Association of University Professors explicitly instruct authors and members to avoid gender bias, including the use of generic "he" and "man."

Sexist language suggests a mindset that is unwelcoming or dismissive toward women. Gender bias in language may actually contribute to discrimination by affirming the presumed superiority of men over women.[18] The switch to non-sexist language might sound awkward at first, but research on audiences reveals no negative reactions to speakers who use non-sexist replacements for sexist language.[21] Substituting "they" for "he" or "she" and "them" for "him" or "her" has become widely accepted when no reference to gender is necessary. Switching to the plural avoids the more clumsy "he/she" and "her or his" phrasings.

Heterosexist Language. Inclusiveness also has relevance to **heterosexist language**, which ignores or criticizes gay men or lesbians. Heterosexist language reflects an attitude that heterosexism (opposite-sex affection) is superior to other sexual orientations. Heterosexism can infuse language in many ways, such as:

- Assumptions that everyone is heterosexual (Examples: "Will all the women please introduce their husbands to the audience?" or "Sir, what is your wife's name?").
- Comments that stereotype homosexuals as having certain physical or vocal mannerisms.
- Remarks that make value judgments about sexual orientation (Examples: "Too bad you're gay," or "Why is such an attractive woman a lesbian?").
- Statements that pathologize sexual orientation (such as, "Maybe my friend will recover from homosexuality").

The American Psychological Association's Committee on Lesbian and Gay Concerns[22] has been working since 1980 to counteract heterosexist language. Their recommendations include the following:

Non-sexist language enables men and women to feel equally included as part of the audience.

© Jean L F./Shutterstock.com

- Use examples of people with various sexual orientations in situations assumed as heterosexual domains (such as parenting and athletic prowess).
- Include gay men, lesbians, and bisexuals in discussions of issues unrelated to sexual behavior (to show that homosexuality is not solely concerned with sex).
- Use terms that include different sexual orientations (e.g., "spouses and partners invited" instead of inviting "men and their wives" or "women and their husbands").

Avoiding heterosexist language makes a difference. Health professionals on college campuses recommend inclusive language so students of all sexual orientations can feel more comfortable discussing health issues and get appropriate treatment.[23] A study of college students found that they were more willing to confide in and return to psychological counselors who used non-heterosexist language.[24] The students also rated the counselors who used inclusive language as more competent and willing to listen.

Racially and Culturally Biased Language. Hopefully, we rarely encounter overtly racist language, but race-based language bias does occur more often. Language itself is not simply neutral, as another quick trip to the thesaurus proves. The synonyms for "white" have overwhelmingly positive connotations. These words include: *fair, pure, spotless, immaculate, virtuous, innocent, undefiled.* Turning to synonyms for "black," we discover much more sinister terms, such as: *shady, gloomy, dismal, dirty, murky, menacing, evil, wicked.* Going beyond the thesaurus, consider the unpleasantly large variety of insulting terms specifically reserved as references to non-whites, especially African Americans. Now try to think of insulting terms that refer only to whites. When we speak a language whose vocabulary makes it easier to insult certain groups of people, we should take special care to choose terms wisely.[25]

One other way language becomes biased is through cultural, gender, or racial **markers**. These markers introduce group identifiers that have no direct relevance to the communication at hand.

Examples (Biased Markers with Replacements in Brackets)

- Gender and sex-role markers: male nurse [nurse], woman doctor [doctor or physician], actress [actor or performer], waitress [server or waitstaff], male maid [housekeeper or custodian], female athlete [athlete]
- Sexual orientation markers: gay Marine [Marine], lesbian model [model]
- Racial and cultural markers: black physicist [physicist], white welfare recipient [welfare recipient], Chinese basketball player [basketball player]

The easiest remedy for markers is simply to eliminate such designations. Occasionally, some group identification deserves mention as relevant. For example, someone might want to distinguish between a specific Chinese basketball player and a Korean teammate. A survey might specify the number of males who are nurses, but it would not be appropriate to call all men in the profession "male nurses." Markers become problematic because they call attention to a group's presence as noteworthy, odd, or uncomfortable. Markers perpetuate stereotyped roles for various groups.

That's Debatable: Gender and Language

Much research has noted differences between the ways men and women use language. Some of these findings appear below. What explanations can you offer that would clarify the reasons for each finding? How do these findings compare with your own experiences and observations? How might you challenge the claims of these researchers? Compare your explanations with other students in your class. Which explanations have more plausibility and why? Finally, consult the research cited in this chapter and find out what the researchers say about their own findings.

- Female speakers tend to be more "attentive to emotional concerns" while males tend to be more focused on themselves and on the present.[26(p128)]
- There is no consistent, reliable evidence that women generally talk more than men. Overall, the amount of talk depends on the situation, with neither males nor females consistently monopolizing conversations.[27,28]
- Same-sex pairs and groups tend to interrupt each other equally often, yet men interrupt women far more than women interrupt men.[29,30,31]
- Women use more tentative language than men in public.[32]

PIES Virtue 3: Expressive Language Use

The more your language has force and sounds fresh, the more expressive it becomes. Presentations and conversations often sound dull because they contain flat language that fails to convey a sense of action or excitement. The third virtue deals with recognizing and improving expressiveness.

Choose Vivid, Active Words

Expressive language invites listeners to participate in creating meaning with the speaker. Audiences will gravitate more to lively language, words that embody actions that they can visualize. The technique for injecting this liveliness into language is **active voice**—using verbs that convey definite movements, events, or processes. To quickly convert communication to more active voice, replace all forms of the verb "to be" (am, is are, was, were, be, being, been) with more definite, action-oriented terms. The new version generally will say more with fewer words, as the following examples illustrate.

Examples (Passive Voice)

1. It is evident that Bluto was frightened by the movie that was featured on television last night. I am amazed that he was not hospitalized.
2. Lekethia's windshield was broken by a rock. Afterward, she was questioned by the police.

Examples (Active Voice)

1. Evidently the featured movie on television last night frightened Bluto. Amazingly, he escaped hospitalization.
2. A rock smashed Lekethia's windshield. Afterward, the police interrogated her.

Immediately, you see that active voice can save a lot of words, conserving time by making communication more concise. More active verbs can generate more vivid descriptions that allow the listeners to envision what you describe.

The basic guideline for increasing expressiveness is: Describe, don't just label! Often speech lacks liveliness because speakers settle for simply labeling an action, observation, or emotion without helping listeners feel the vibrancy of the experience. Let's begin with some rather dull descriptions.

1. She is happy with her job.
2. They are afraid of the scary snake.

Not too interesting, are they? These simple labels for emotions accomplish little because they fail to provide a clear image of what actually happened. Vivid language paints specific images in the audience's mind. The descriptions give no sense of what the people experienced or how they behaved while feeling these emotions. Now let's redo these examples, more fully engaging the senses of the audience.

1. She stays late at her office, as if lingering on a romantic date. Her job is her passion. Her heart leaps when she thinks of what she might accomplish tomorrow.
2. Their throats tightened, choking screams they desperately tried to vocalize. The snake slid closer, forked tongue flicking toward their faces while deadly venom dripped from razor-sharp fangs.

Sensory language transports listeners into the midst of the situation. The more you can engage the senses of the audience—sight, sound, smell, taste, touch—the more expressive you will become. Good storytellers (remember the ghost stories that terrified you as a child?) impress audiences with vivid language that places the audience in the story. You can do the same.

Recognize Language Intensity

Language intensity refers to how much terms vary from neutral, non-evaluative descriptions. Intensity describes the valence of language (whether it generates positive or negative connotations) and how far terminology departs from neutrality.[33,34] Think of language intensity as a scale of connotation ranging from strongly negative to strongly positive, as illustrated in Figure 3.4.

Language intensity is always relative; it deals with the relationship between the available choices for terminology. Sometimes there may be no clear choices

FIGURE 3.4 Language Intensity.

Generally, language intensity describes how far language varies from neutral terms.

strongly negative   neutral   strongly positive

Language intensity can be described more specifically by labeling the strength of connotations.

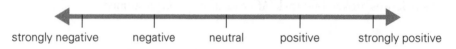

strongly negative   negative   neutral   positive   strongly positive

Using language intensity, we can construct lists that show the relative intensity of terms, ranging from most negative to most positive. We can place specific terms along the language intensity scale to see how they compare.

Examples (terms listed from most negative to most positive):
- illegal alien/undocumented immigrant/guest worker
- terrorist/insurgent/combatant/freedom fighter
- stench/odor/smell/scent/aroma/bouquet

for totally neutral, absolutely positive, or entirely negative terms. As a speaker, ask yourself what kind of emotional reaction you want your choice of terms to generate. As a listener, evaluate whether a speaker's language intensity might reveal hidden biases or attempts to manipulate the audience's emotions. For example, describing undocumented laborers from Mexico as "illegal aliens" might lead to angry calls for fences and troops at the border, while referring to the same people as "guest workers" sounds like a friendly invitation.

You can increase language intensity by adjusting two qualities: emotion and specificity.[35] Highly emotional language rates as more intense, and it can generate audience interest because of its vividness. More specific language makes the concept clearer to listeners so it becomes easier to remember. Vague terminology and euphemisms tend to reduce language intensity, while graphic and precise terms increase it.[35]

Language intensity has several uses for speakers and listeners. During conflict, the language intensity level of participants can signal how aggressive or hostile they feel, and it can reveal their emotional condition.[36] Higher intensity e-mail messages are more likely to generate responses.[37] Intensity is not always a blessing. The more intense language becomes, the more extreme the speaker's position appears. Overall, intensity tends to exert the most influence for (a) respected speakers on (b) controversial topics (c) when the audience is weighing arguments that oppose the speaker's position.[37]

Avoid Clichés

Suppose your supervisor at work begins a motivational meeting with these words:

I know we've all been down in the dumps because sales haven't exactly been going through the roof with all of this dog-eat-dog competition. Well, the buck stops here. I'm ready to bend over backwards and keep my nose to the grindstone to help our company. We're all in this together, since a house divided against itself cannot stand. It's time to get profits into the black again. So let's throw caution to the wind. Run new ideas up the flagpole—the more the merrier. The ball is in your court now. Give it the old college try, and remember: We're number one!

What did your supervisor say in this feeble attempt at motivational speaking? Absolutely nothing! The speaker has strung together a series of **clichés**, phrases so familiar that they have become trite and lost their expressive force. The word comes from the French verb *clicher*, meaning "to stereotype." A cliché operates as a stereotype does, since it triggers familiar, reflex-like responses based on minimal reflection. Clichés, like stereotypes, minimize thoughtful discussion. Instead of stimulating conversation, clichés stifle it. After all, how would you respond to the supervisor's motivational speech or to any of the following phrases?

- An emotional roller-coaster
- 110 percent effort
- This person needs no introduction
- Once upon a time
- Not my cup of tea
- Why can't we all just get along?
- No love lost between them
- The rest is history

An international poll rated the five most annoying clichés in the English language.[38] The winners (or, more accurately, losers) included:

- At the end of the day
- At this moment in time
- With all due respect

What's the problem here? "The trouble with relying on clichés is that they make prose sound stale".[39(p99)] Fresh ideas lose their vitality when clothed in tired terms that everyone has heard repeatedly. The effect of clichés goes beyond mere annoyance. As the number of clichés increases, the audience's interest in the topic decreases, as does their belief in the speaker's concern about the topic.[11] If a speaker resorts only to worn-out phrases, it appears that little effort went into searching for original ideas. Clichés also require no interpretive skill, since they offer automatic, mindless catch phrases. Researchers recommend: "If a speaker's goal is to promote mindfulness and concentration among audience members, such expressions should be avoided".[11(p264)] The more you rely on stale phrasing, the more likely your listeners will tune out. Be careful, however, not to reject all conventional ways of speaking. Originality earns praise as long as it does not violate social norms.[40] You could avoid cliché answers in a job interview by shouting obscenities, but this "creative" response would end your chance of getting hired.

PIES Virtue 4: Sensitive Language Use

Sensitive language use refers to recognizing how language connects with directness, power, and change. To maximize your effectiveness as a speaker, you should become familiar with how to craft language that will adjust to the appropriate level of directness, convey power, and adapt to change.

Sensitivity to Directness

The amount of **directness** in language affects how others react to what we say. The more direct the language, the fewer the options for response. Commands qualify as the most direct language, since they offer no options other than obedience. "Open the window" does not call for discussion. Less direct language provides more possibilities. Note how the following example of *more direct*

↑ "Give me a Gutbuster Burger."
"One Gutbuster Burger, please."
"I want a Gutbuster Burger."
"I would like a Gutbuster Burger."
"May I have a Gutbuster Burger?"
"Could I trouble you for a Gutbuster
↓ Burger, if you don't mind?"

less direct

placing an order for a hamburger at a restaurant illustrates varying amounts of directness.

As language becomes more indirect, it also becomes more tactful, polite, or evasive. Direct language comes in handy when you want quick response. Commands and orders work best in situations when time is limited, and their effectiveness depends on the speaker having the status to issue direct instructions.

Preferred levels of directness vary according to culture and situation. Some Americans, for example, may find Germans very direct—to the point that Americans, accustomed to a more indirect approach, describe straightforward German conversational style as "unfriendly".[41] When refusing a request from a supervisor at work, more traditional Japanese customarily find indirect ways to decline without overtly saying "no," which might demonstrate rudeness or a poor work ethic.[42] Careful examination of directness, however, shows that no culture as a whole is *always* more or less direct. We must recognize the "danger of making generalizations about the communication style of a language or culture as if one style (e.g., direct vs. indirect) is used unilaterally regardless of situation, gender, age, and status".[43(p52)] Instead, each culture adapts the level of directness to the particular communication situation. For example, a long tradition of research classifies Arab culture as highly indirect, but closer observation shows that Arabs and non-Arab Americans refuse requests with approximately equal directness.[43]

Directness plays an important role in teaching. Teacher trainees and student teachers, who may still lack authority in the classroom, benefit from making direct statements such as imperatives (such as "Read Chapter 5 by Friday"). Several considerations support directness in the classroom[44]:

- Directness is not impolite as long as the request is designed to help the students.
- Directness adds to the teacher's perceived authority because it sounds decisive.
- It clarifies the standards for student behavior and work.
- Direct language saves time because it issues clear requests without extended ex-planation and discussion.

If you hear complaints that an instructor "isn't clear," you might find the solution lies in a more direct communication style.

Status plays a big role in acceptable levels of directness, with direct language more common from higher status communicators. For example, Japanese workers are more likely than Americans to issue direct refusals to invitations from people of lower status.[45] On the other hand, when you address someone with higher status, more indirect language would show respect. Be careful, however, not to become so indirect that requests or instructions get lost in evasive language. Suppose you said, "Excuse me, but I wonder if you would mind—if it isn't too much trouble—please, could you spare a moment to send the pepper over here when you get the chance? Thanks." We might finish our meal before I finally realize you wanted me to "pass the pepper."

Sensitivity to Power

The way we use language shapes whether we come across to others as powerful and confident or as helpless and incompetent. Several language patterns can convey an image of powerlessness: hesitations, hedges (sometimes called qualifiers), intensifiers, disclaimers, and tag questions. Hesitations include verbalizations that interrupt the smooth flow of speech: "um," "uh," "like," "you know," and other fillers. We will discuss them in the next chapter when we cover vocal mannerisms. Our focus here will be on the other forms of powerless language.

Tech Talk: Directness and E-mail

E-mail allows us to communicate quickly and sometimes thoughtlessly. The ease and speed of creating electronic messages generates an abbreviated style far more direct than we would use in polite face-to-face communication. Here are a few tips to keep directness from becoming abruptness.

- Remember your manners. If issuing instructions, a simple "please" or "thank you" can make your communication seem less like a direct order.
- Save important e-mails as drafts, then go back and reread them before sending. You might find that you need to finesse your phrasing to make the message more indirect.
- More directness increases the sense of urgency and authority of communication. Do you have a level of authority that corresponds to the directness of your message?
- Less directness increases the politeness of messages, but decreases their force. How well can you summarize what the receiver should do after reading your message?

American audiences generally consider speakers who use a "high-power speech style"—few hesitations, hedges, intensifiers, disclaimers, and tag questions—more competent and attractive.[46] By introducing comments or sounds irrelevant to the message, powerless language can distract listeners and give the impression that the speaker lacks competence or confidence. These language habits can have an especially negative effect on perceptions of female speakers, since women historically have been stereotyped as indecisive.[47,48] Studies have found that men consider women who communicate with more tentative, low-power language more likable but less competent and less intelligent than more powerful female speakers.[49] Powerless language habits actually can negate positive features of a speaker or presentation. One study concludes: "So an acknowledged expert with excellent reasons for advocating a position already accepted by an audience may, nevertheless, fail to be persuasive if he or she uses powerless language".[50(p523)] College instructors who use powerless language patterns the first day of class generate negative student evaluations of credibility, organization, and ability to control the course.[47] College students, like other audiences, associate powerful language with high competence and professionalism.

Hedges verbally retreat from claims, introducing limitations such as "sort of," "kind of," "more or less," "just," "I guess," etc. Weak **intensifiers**

such as "surely" and "really" that verbally attempt to emphasize a message's force fall into the same category because they don't actually strengthen meaning. Did the Spice Girls accomplish anything substantive by adding intensifiers when they sang, "Tell me what you want—what you really, really want"? Similarly, saying "not really" sounds far less certain than simply saying "no." I guess I'm just saying that when speakers basically hedge, it's sort of like they kind of can't really make up their mind entirely. That last sentence employed at least six hedges: "I guess" "just," "basically," "sort of," "kind of," and "really." Far from adding emphasis, these hedges soften the claim. In an attempt to avoid harshness, the speaker who hedges sounds indecisive.[48] Frequent hedges or hesitations produce negative audience impressions toward the source, the message, and the persuasiveness of ideas. These reactions hold for speech and writing, and are greatest when the audience is deeply engaged with the topic.[49]

Disclaimers show powerlessness by lowering expectations about the speaker or message. Often a disclaimer implies the speaker's incompetence or the message's triviality. You probably observe disclaimers almost daily in the classroom when students begin a question by saying, "This is probably a stupid question. . . . " Other common disclaimers include phrases such as: "Maybe I'm just silly, but . . . ," "I'm sure you've already answered this . . . ," "Perhaps I wasn't listening. . . . " Communicators might use disclaimers as a way to defer to authority. If you begin by criticizing yourself or your message, you place the listener in a superior position. Disclaimers also might serve to garner approval and reassurance. Upon hearing "This may be a stupid question . . . ," most instructors will praise the questioner and defend the legitimacy of the question.

Disclaimers may convey powerlessness but actually can have more strategic purposes. If someone wants to ask a very difficult question or make a comment that puts the speaker on the spot, the point might begin with a disclaimer. Inserting a disclaimer reassures listeners (in this case, falsely) that the communicator poses no threat and defers to the superior status of others. If a comment begins with a hint that the commentator is incompetent or the remark is trivial, others will not suspect that an insightful or challenging remark is about to follow. The disclaimer might catch listeners off guard, leaving them more surprised at the weighty communication it precedes.

Example (strategic disclaimer): "Maybe I'm not very observant, but did you provide any direct evidence that you actually are the strongest person in the world?"

In this example, the disclaimer also softens the direct challenge a bit, thus serving another strategic purpose.

Tag questions are short additions to sentences that turn the entire statement into a question.

Examples (Tag Questions)

"That was delicious possum stew, wasn't it?"

"It feels very hot in here, don't you think?"

Women generally use tag questions more often than men. These tag questions could serve various strategic purposes. Some researchers interpret them as signs that women are more tentative in public communication, particularly when addressing men. Instead of making direct assertions, they back away from claims, weakening their force.[32] Others interpret tag questions as signs that women are trying to open conversation by stimulating others to respond to questions. It seems that men also increase their use of tag questions when interacting with women, possibly as a way of inviting the women to participate in conversation more.[30] Tag questions, therefore, carry dangers and dividends.

If interpreted as a sign of powerlessness, tag questions seem to apologize for making a statement, almost saying, "Is it okay for me to say this?".[48] When listeners have deep involvement with the topic, tag questions may disrupt message processing by introducing uncertainty.[49] If interpreted as a conversational stimulus, tag questions enhance communication.

Sensitivity to Change and Difference

Times change. So does language, but maybe not quickly or thoroughly enough for what we want to communicate. Often language tricks us into believing that the meaning stays the same simply because the word remains unchanged. We need ways to distinguish one person or event from another even when the words remain the same.

Although we may need to classify things to understand them, we also must recognize experiences and people as individuals. An experience in a relationship with one male does not mean that all future people labeled "male" will treat you the same way. One encounter with a person from a particular culture does not predict your future interactions with other members of that culture. Each experience introduces unique circumstances, so we can tailor our interactions to specific people in the present instead of remaining mired in faulty, outdated assumptions.[50]

By continuously striving for the four verbal virtues that we have discussed, you should be well on your way to becoming a more effective communicator in many different contexts. Remembering to focus on *precision*, *inclusiveness*, *expressiveness*, and *sensitivity* when speaking and listening will not only enhance your language skills but reduce miscommunication, conflict, and relationship obstacles. Figure 3.5 offers suggestions on how to implement the verbal virtues.

YOUR LANGUAGE TOOLKIT

The verbal virtues of PIES establish the overall goals of language use. This section introduces some specific tools that can help enact the verbal virtues. We begin by discussing several forms of **figurative language**, which refers using words in unfamiliar but insightful ways. Figurative devices such as metaphor, simile, personification, and antithesis can add new perspectives to our understanding of a subject. We also explore how sounds can work to your advantage.

FIGURE 3.5 Using the Verbal Virtues.

Verbal Virtue	Tips for Use	Goals for Use
Precision	• Use concrete language • Use euphemisms for politeness, but not at the expense of accuracy • Use multi-valued orientation	• Specify referents for terms to reduce misunderstanding • Avoid embarrassment, honestly reveal connotations • Invite multiple viewpoints
Inclusiveness	• Avoid biased language • Find alternative expressions for biased terms and phrases	• Respect diversity of all potential audiences, not just your immediate listeners • Enable language to account for a wider array of people
Expressiveness	• Use vivid language • Manipulate intensity of language • Avoid clichés	• Increase audience involvement by enabling them to visualize your subject matter • Adjust intensity to desired level of positive or negative connotations • Maintain interest by showing your originality
Sensitivity	• Use appropriate level of directness • Limit behaviors signifying powerless communication • Alter language in response to changing times and circumstances	• Adjust level of firmness to type of relationship and situation • Take full responsibility for what you say • Reduce overgeneralizations and outdated assumptions or terms

HIGHLIGHTS

1. Words are a type of symbol because they represent reality.
2. Referents are the objects or events that words symbolize.
3. Meanings are interpretations based on experience and custom.
4. The relationship between symbols (words) and referents (what they stand for) is arbitrary.
5. Jargon signifies membership in or exclusion from a community of communicators.
6. Meaning includes denotations (literal referents) and connotations (emotional attachments) of words.
7. Oral style differs from written style, so written manuscripts do not translate easily into speeches.
8. The verbal virtue of precision deals with accuracy in language.
   a. Staying low on the ladder of abstraction reduces chances of misunderstanding.
   b. Euphemisms provide pleasant ways to discuss uncomfortable topics, but when they distort reality they qualify as doublespeak.
   c. Two-valued orientation divides the world into total opposites; multi-valued orientation introduces more nuanced classifications.
9. The verbal virtue of inclusiveness connects with all audience members.
   a. Inclusive language connects the audience with the speaker.
   b. Unbiased language avoids excluding or insulting people on the basis of gender, sexual orientation, race, or culture.
10. The verbal virtue of expressiveness enlivens language.
    a. Words that enable listeners to feel action and emotion are more effective than general labels.
    b. The level of language intensity can adjust the impact language has on the audience.
    c. Clichés can damage delivery by relying on worn-out phrases.
11. The verbal virtue of sensitivity includes awareness of the factors that influence language use.
    a. Directness measures how authoritative and decisive we sound.
    b. Powerless language exacts a heavy toll on communication, generally reducing a speaker's perceived effectiveness—but it can have strategic advantages.

ENDNOTES

1. Ketchum, Inc. (2005). *Case study: California Dried Plums Board*. Retrieved January 31, 2005, from http://www.ketchum.com/DisplayWebPage/0,1003,635,00.html

2. Trudgill, P. (1998). The meanings of words should not be allowed to vary or change. In L. Bauer & P. Trudgill (Eds.), *Language myths* (pp. 1–8). London: Penguin.

3. Richards, I. A. (1991). *Richards on rhetoric. I.A. Richards: Selected essays* (1929–1974). (A. E. Berthoff, Ed.). New York & Oxford: Oxford University Press.

4. Wolff, B. (2005, January 30). Bridge. *Kansas City Star*, p. D7.

5. Lutz, W. (1990). *Doublespeak*. New York: Harper Perennial.

6. Lutz, W. (1996). *The new doublespeak*. New York: HarperCollins.

7. McArthur, T. (Ed.). (1992). *The Oxford companion to the English language*. Oxford: Oxford University Press.

8. Tannen, D. (1988). The commingling of orality and literacy in giving a paper at a scholarly conference. *American Speech, 63*, 34–43.

9. Thomas, G. L. (1956). Effect of oral style on intelligibility of speech. *Speech Monographs, 23*, 46–54.

10. McLaurin, P. (1995). An examination of the effect of culture on pro-social messages directed at African-American at-risk youth. *Communication Monographs, 62*, 301–326.

11. McGlone, M. S., Beck, G., & Pfiester, A. (2006). Contamination and camouflage in euphemisms. *Communication Monographs, 73*, 261–282.

12. Slovenko, R. (2005). Commentary: Euphemisms. *Journal of Psychiatry and Law, 33*, 533–548.

13. McGlone, M. S., & Batchelor, J. A. (2003). Looking out for number one: Euphemism and face. *Journal of Communication, 53*, 251–264.

14. Grazian, F. (1997). On euphemisms, gobbledygook and doublespeak. *Public Relations Quarterly, 42*, 21–23.

15. Lutz, W. (2000). Nothing in life is certain except negative patient care outcome and revenue enhancement. *Journal of Adolescent and Adult Literacy, 44*, 230–233.

16. Bosik, M. (2004, Summer). Listening to doublespeak. *Listening Professional, 3*(1), 13, 19.

17. Bush, G. W. (2001, September 20). Address before a joint session of the Congress on the United States response to the terrorist attacks of September 11. *Weekly compilation of Presidential documents* (pp. 1347–1351). Retrieved August 11, 2009, from http://frwebgate3.access.gpo.gov/cgi-bin/PDFgate.cgi?WAISdocID=9954852645+13+2+0&WAISaction=retrieve

18. Artz, N., Munger, J, & Purdy, W. (1999, Fall). Gender issues in advertising language. *Women and Language, 22*(2), 20–26.

19. McConnell, A. R., & Fazio, R. H. (1996). Women as men and people: Effects of gender-marked language. *Personality and Social Psychology Bulletin, 22*, 1004–1013.

20. Madson, L., & Hessling, R. M. (1999). Does alternating between masculine and feminine pronouns eliminate perceived gender bias in text? *Sex Roles, 41*, 559–575.

21. Salter, M. M., Weider-Hatfield, D., & Rubin, D. L. (1983). Generic pronoun use and perceived speaker credibility. *Communication Quarterly, 31*, 180–184.

22. American Psychological Association Committee on Lesbian and Gay Concerns (1991). Avoiding heterosexual bias in language. *American Psychologist, 46*(9), 973–974.

23. McKee, M. B., Hayes, S. F., & Axiotis, I. R. (1994). Challenging heterosexism in college health service delivery. *Journal of American College Health, 42*, 211–216.

24. Dorland, J. M., & Fischer, A. R. (2001). Gay, lesbian, and bisexual individuals' perceptions: An analogue study. *Counseling Psychologist, 29*, 532–547.

25. Purnell, R. B. (1982). Teaching them to curse: A study of certain types of inherent racial bias in language pedagogy and practices. *Phylon, 43*, 231–241.

26. Cotten-Huston, A. L. (1989). Gender communication. In S. S. King (Ed.), *Human communication as a field of study: Selected contemporary views* (pp. 127–134). Albany: State University of New York Press.

27. James, D., & Drakich, J. (1993). Understanding gender differences in amount of talk: A critical review of research. In D. Tannen (Ed.), *Gender and conversational interaction* (pp. 281–312). New York: Oxford University Press.

28. Mehl, M. R., Vazire, S., Ramírez-Esparza, N., Slatcher, R. B., & Pennebaker, J. W. (2007). Are women really more talkative than men? *Science, 317* (5834). Retrieved January 30, 2008, from http://search.ebscohost.com/login.aspx?direct=true&db=psyh&AN=2007-11018-003&site=ehost-live.

29. Brooks, V. R. (1982). Sex differences in student dominance behavior in female and male professors' classrooms. *Sex Roles, 8*, 683–690.

30. McMillen, J. R., Clifton, A. K., McGrath, D., & Gale, W. S. (1977). Women's language: Uncertainty or interpersonal sensitivity and emotionality? *Sex Roles, 3*, 545–560.

31. Zimmerman, D. H., & West, C. (1975). Sex roles, interruptions and silence in conversation. In B. Thorne and N. Henley (Eds.), *Language and sex: Differences and dominance* (pp. 105–129). Rowley, MA: Newbury House.

32. Lakoff, G. (2008). The political mind: Why you can't understand 21st-century American politics with an 18th-century brain. New York: Penguin.

33. Bowers, J. W. (1963). Language intensity, social introversion, and attitude change. *Speech Monographs, 30,* 345–352.

34. Bowers, J. W. (1964). Some correlates of language intensity. *Quarterly Journal of Speech, 50,* 415–420.

35. Hamilton, M. A., & Stewart, B. L. (1993). Extending an information processing model of language intensity effects. *Communication Quarterly, 41,* 231–246.

36. Gayle, B. M., & Preiss, R. W. (1999). Language intensity plus: A methodological approach to validate emotions in conflicts. *Communication Reports, 12,* 43–50.

37. Andersen, P. A., & Blackburn, T. R. (2004). An experimental study of language intensity and response rate in e-mail surveys. *Communication Reports, 17,* 73–82.

38. Plain English Campaign (2004, March 23). At the endof the day . . . we're fed up with clichés. *Press releases.* Retrieved February 2, 2007, from http://www .plainenglish.co.uk/pressreleases2.htm

39. Barzun, J. (1975). *Simple and direct: A rhetoric for writers.* New York: Harper and Row.

40. Burgoon, J. K., Berger, C. R., & Waldron, V. R. (2000). Mindfulness and interpersonal communication. *Journal of Social Issues, 56,* 105–127.

41. House, J. (2006). Communicative styles in English and German. *European Journal of English Studies, 10,* 249–267.

42. Ueda, K. (1974). Sixteen ways to avoid saying "no" in Japan. In J. C. Condon & M. Saito (Eds.), *Intercultural encounters with Japan: Communication—contact and conflict* (pp. 185–192). Tokyo: Simul Press.

43. Nelson, G. L., Batal, M. A., & Bakary, W. E. (2002). Directness vs. indirectness: Egyptian Arabic and US English communication style. *International Journal of Intercultural Relations, 26,* 39–57.

44. Goatly, A. (1995). Directness, indirectness and deference in the language of classroom management: Advice for teacher trainees? *International Review of Applied Linguistics in Language Teaching, 33,* 267–284.

45. Beebe, L. M., Takahashi, T., & Uliss-Weltz, R. (1990). Pragmatic transfer in ESL refusals. In R. Scarcella, E. Andersen, & S. D. Krashen (Eds.), *On the development of communicative competence in a second language* (pp. 55–73). New York: Newbury House.

46. Hosman, L. A., & Siltanen, S. A. (2006). Powerful and powerless language forms: Their consequences for impression formation, attributions of control of self and control of others, cognitive responses, and message memory. *Journal of Language and Social Psychology, 25,* 33–46.

47. Haleta, L. L. (1996). Student perceptions of teachers' use of language: The effects of powerful and powerless language. *Communication Education, 45,* 16–28.

48. Tannen, D. (1986). *That's not what I meant! How conversational style makes or breaks your relationships with others* (1st ed.). New York: William Morrow.

49. Blankenship, K. L., & Holtgraves, T. (2005). The role of different markers of linguistic powerlessness in persuasion. *Journal of Language and Social Psychology, 24,* 3–24.

50. Johnston, P. D. (1993). Success, ghosts, and things. *ETC: A Review of General Semantics, 50,* 168–172.

4

NONVERBAL COMMUNICATION*

If a picture is worth a thousand words, then body movements, spatial management, facial expressions, and other physical communication must be worth millions. This chapter covers the second and third of the "three Vs" of communication noted at the beginning of the previous chapter: visual and vocal. Together these realms encompass **nonverbal communication**. The authors of *Teaching Your Child the Language of Social Success* suggest that we perceive people who violate nonverbal "grammar" as odd or at last socially awkward, and they recommend that children learn nonverbal communication along with grammar in school.[1] The scope of nonverbal communication includes all messages delivered using the body, either by itself (e.g., gestures, facial expression, eye contact), connected with objects (e.g., clothing and physical surroundings), managing space (e.g., physical distance and positioning), or manipulations of the voice. All physical nonverbal behavior (popularly referred to as "body language") is directly observable, so it provides some of the most vivid examples of communication in action. Vocal communication deals primarily with qualities of the voice—how communicators modulate the voice through characteristics such as volume, pitch, and pacing.

First, we will delve into why nonverbal communication is significant. Then we will discuss the major categories of nonverbal communication. Our examination of each category covers the messages sent through this type of communication and practical advice for effective usage. Next, we move to the vocal side, focusing on common difficulties speakers face in developing effective vocal qualities. The chapter ends by offering some cautions and recommendations about interpreting nonverbal behaviors.

WHY NONVERBAL COMMUNICATION?

From the earliest days of communication studies, delivery got a bad rap. The ancient Greeks suspected flashy speakers would try to lure audiences into ignoring reason, tempting them with elegant style to make poor decisions. Aristotle grudgingly covered delivery at the end of his *Rhetoric*, although he admitted it was "not regarded as an elevated subject of inquiry" (1941, §1403b–1404a). An authoritative popular translation of Aristotle's *Rhetoric* deletes 11 entire chapters of material dealing with delivery, leaving the rest of the text intact. Today we worry that speakers might elevate style over substance, leading audiences to ruin by substituting glibness for knowledge. We hear complaints about political demagogues who deliver impressive speeches, but whose actions fall far short of their campaign performances.

* This chapter was written by Roy Schwartzman and Melody Hubbard.

These fears about delivery could have merit, especially if we ignore how presentation style does convey important messages. A starting point may be to consider five main areas in which nonverbal communication functions:

1. Emotional feelings through our face, body, and voice.
2. Interpersonal attitudes through touch, gaze, proximity, voice tone, and facial expressions.
3. Supporting others when they talk by nodding, glancing. and nonverbal vocalization such as laughing.
4. Presenting ourselves to others through our appearance.
5. Applying ritualized nonverbals like signals when greeting someone.[2(p5)]

Each specific nonverbal behavior is known as a **cue**. The term reminds us that nonverbal behaviors trigger (or cue) responses from others, who interpret and return nonverbal behaviors. Nonverbal signals furnish especially strong indicators of attitudes, regardless of whether they accompany words (Koch, 2005).

More specifically, audiences seem to form most of their impressions about communicators from nonverbals (tone of voice and physical appearance) when the communication focuses on feelings and attitudes.[4] Some research estimates that approximately two-thirds of message content is conveyed through nonverbal codes.[5] These findings parallel everyday experience in communication classes. When asked to evaluate sample speeches, student comments overwhelmingly focus on delivery factors such as vocal quality, physical appearance, and body movement. If you had to define what makes a "good" presentation, chances are that most of the qualities you identify would deal with nonverbals.

Mastering nonverbal communication has critical importance for our development as functional humans. Approximately one out of 10 children has severe difficulties expressing and interpreting nonverbal communication, a condition psychologists have named *dyssemia*.[6] These children experience social maladjustment and serious depression if their nonverbal learning does not receive prompt attention. Nonverbal communication plays an important role in our ability to interact with others and integrate into society. Difficulty with interpreting and responding to nonverbal cues has been identified as a key symptom of Asperger syndrome, and it can "make communication and social interaction a nightmare".[7(p67)] Recent research also links nonverbal communication to adult mental health. People who do not display normal levels of nonverbal involvement with others (such as responding to their nonverbal behavior) run high risks of emotional stress that could trigger depression.[8] The inability to synchronize one's own nonverbal behavior to fit with what others are communicating indicates problems forming social connections.

Some evidence shows that more socially outgoing people have more skill in decoding nonverbal behavior.[9] Apparently, the more socially involved people become, the more skill they develop in interpreting nonverbal cues. Here is another advantage to getting more involved in communication: Not only will these interactions help your own communication, but they also could help hone your skills in understanding other people. More experience at interactive communication translates into greater accuracy at "reading" others.

When nonverbal and verbal messages conflict, observers tend to believe the nonverbal cues over the words. In such cases, actions do speak louder than words. This point has been reinforced by crisis communication experts and by interview consultants.[10] Many people believe—accurately or not—that nonverbal cues offer a truer indication of communicator intent, attitude, and emotional state than words because a lot of nonverbals are involuntary. Much modern research on detecting deception deals with interpreting nonverbal behaviors.

Anyone can manipulate his words to say he is calm, but acting calmly under pressure is another matter. Speakers who giggle while telling a serious story or who whisper a supposedly forceful complaint while smiling broadly will undermine their verbal message.[11]

That's Debatable

Some communication researchers contend that heavy usage of social networking media is associated with reduced sensitivity to nonverbal cues.[12] Supposedly, immersion in computer-mediated social networking makes users less aware of the nonverbal messages they send and less fluent in decoding nonverbal cues sent by others. Some organizations try to improve interpersonal awareness by banning all electronic devices from meetings (or classes). Weigh the pros and cons of this policy. How could it help or hinder communication?

Ideally, nonverbal messages should coordinate with verbal messages. This consistency between verbal and nonverbal communication is called **congruence**.[13,14] Contradictory nonverbal and verbal messages prove especially confusing for children, who have trouble resolving the mismatch between visual and verbal messages.[15] The incongruence of verbal and nonverbal communication may understandably cause miscommunication. As a speaker, make absolutely sure the message you *say* matches the message you *show*.

TYPES OF NONVERBAL BEHAVIORS

A word of caution is appropriate as we approach the various types of nonverbal communication. The communication practices and norms discussed below refer to prevailing practices in the United States. Nonverbal customs and expectations can vary dramatically between and within nations and cultures. These variations receive attention later in the chapter. For now, remember that nonverbal cues—like all communication—occur within a cultural context that provides a framework for interpretation. Every culture's nonverbal practices serve their purpose relative to a background of traditions and values.

Kinesics

The broad category of nonverbal behavior called **kinesics** designates any bodily movement, from slight twitches and postural shifts to pacing across the room. Facial expressions, eye movements, and gestures (all of which we will cover later) are types of kinesics. Early research found that effective communicators develop body movements that adapt to the message and situation.[5] Another finding was that communicators tend to adjust to the nonverbal behaviors of others, matching or compensating for body movements and vocal patterns with behaviors of their own. People naturally synchronize their body movements with each other, and obvious disconnects in nonverbal behavior may indicate relational tension.[16]

Examples (High Nonverbal Synchrony)

- Two people smiling and laughing together.
- One person crying while a companion frowns and shakes her head.

Examples (Low Nonverbal Synchrony)

- One person smiles and laughs while a companion scowls.
- One person puts his arm around a companion and whispers in her ear while she frowns, crosses her arms, and avoids eye contact.

Nonverbal synchrony explains why siblings or couples who have been together for many years may begin to show similar nonverbal or vocal patterns. The movie *Twins* (1988) provides several amusing examples of synchrony between unlikely siblings played by Danny DeVito and Arnold Schwarzenegger. If you ever wonder about the importance of synchrony, just ask anyone who plays team sports. Coordinating behaviors among teammates forms the essence of teamwork and ultimately may determine whether a team wins or loses.

Kinesics can enhance communication *if* it coordinates with the verbal content. Instructors often point to wayward kinesics as a common problem in student presentations. Repetitive body movements—such as tapping feet, fidgeting, or bouncing up and down—that are *un*related to the content can reduce the effectiveness of a presentation. Since repetition emphasizes whatever is repeated and audiences place more credence on nonverbal than verbal messages when the two conflict, extraneous body movements may become the focus of audience attention.

Several techniques can help you maintain control over your kinesics. Practice in front of observers who can note whether your body movement assists or distracts from your presentation. It sometimes helps to instruct some observers to focus only on your body movements so they can note as many behaviors as possible. Video recording your practice sessions can prove indispensable for improving kinesics. You might even try watching your presentation on fast forward, which will emphasize unnecessarily extreme or repetitive body movements. If you seem to be dancing on the screen, it might be time to monitor your body movements more carefully.

Sometimes speakers face the challenge of insufficient body movement. To maximize your expressiveness, allow yourself the maximum opportunities possible for gestures and other physical ways of emphasizing your content. Anything you do that restricts your ability to move or gesture can limit your expressiveness. Pay careful attention to videos and observer reports of your own delivery. Watch for the following behaviors that can limit expressive kinesics.

- Holding notes with both hands. Since your hands are occupied holding your notes, they can't do anything else.
- Keeping hands in pockets for long periods of time. An occasional thrust in the pocket is fine (as long as you don't have keys or other noisy items there), but imprisoning your hands in this way makes you appear more timid.
- Clasping hands, especially holding hands behind your back, which eliminates any hand or arm movement.
- Leaning on the podium or leaning back in a chair, which reduces the opportunity for movement and gesturing.

Emblems

The familiar nonverbal signals known as **emblems** coordinate with specific verbal messages. Consider emblems as road signs, since they visually display a verbal message. Examples of common emblems include waving hello or goodbye, holding up a hand to signify "stop," beckoning to someone by curling the index finger, or saluting. Since emblems have established connections with specific concepts, they provide efficient ways of communicating, especially in situations where speaking is impractical (such as amid noisy distractions, beyond shouting distance, or where speaking is inappropriate). For example, a speaker can quiet an audience politely by motioning with her hands for them to stop applauding. Emblems can reinforce verbal messages effectively because they visually confirm words. Audiences recall messages better when emblems accompany words than when listening to words alone.[17] While emblems do not guarantee that people will remember what you say, they do seem to offer more vivid ways for audiences to recall information than simply listening to the words.[18]

Emblems do carry substantial risks because their verbal equivalents depend on the cultural context. Assuming that an emblem carries a universal meaning has caused embarrassment, misunderstanding, and sometimes hostility. Former President George W. Bush's daughter Jenna experienced the fallout of miscommunication through emblems. During her father's second inauguration ceremonies, Jenna flashed the "Hook 'em, Horns" sign popular among University of Texas Longhorns football fans. In this familiar U.S. emblem, Longhorns supporters extend the index and little fingers—an iconic reference to horns on cattle. Photos of the gesture appalled Norwegian audiences. In Norway, the same gesture is a sign for devil worship and cult violence associated with "death metal" musical groups.[19] By the way, the same "horns" gesture in Italy, bringing the hand to the forehead, means someone's spouse or partner is having a sexual affair[19]! As noted in Chapter 1, identical emblems can carry radically different verbal translations depending on the culture.

Affect Displays

Researchers estimate that we have such complex muscles in our face that we can make more than 1,000 different expressions.[20] The face, therefore, qualifies as the most expressive area of the body.[13] **Affect displays** refer to how we communicate basic emotions including anger, joy, and fear, especially through facial expressions.[3] Some people are particularly aware of their own emotions and adept at paying attention to the emotions of others. They can be thought of as "high in affective orientation," using the emotional cues from others as a guide to communicating and making judgments.[21] These people can "read" subtle emotional changes in others and adapt accordingly. For example, a skillful speaker might note the audience's affect displays of impatience (fidgeting, shifting eye contact, etc.) and get to the point more quickly. You also know the opposite, such as the teacher who ignores all signs of boredom and drones on and on. Highly affective people are frequently more conversationally sensitive and appear to feel their own emotions more intensely.[22]

The extent that someone is oriented to the emotions of others varies among individuals and between cultures. When Japanese and American students took an affect orientation test, researchers found that the Japanese students scored lower and that the difference between Japanese males and females was not significant.[23] These differences may reflect cultural variations in valuing overt emotional displays. Overt public expressions of emotions are considered rude in traditional Japanese culture[24].

Affect displays also seem to vary according to gender. One research team found that when confronted with a distressed person, men more often chose to perform a task for the person (such as getting a glass of water), although the

Deprived of facial expressions or eye contact, we run greater risk of misinterpretation.

© pjcross/Shutterstock.com

task was unrelated to the emotional issue, while women responded more directly to the person's emotions.[25] Many studies have found that women tend to judge emotional messages from nonverbal cues more accurately than men.[26]

How can you use affect displays to improve your communication? Affect displays are especially prone to mismatch with verbal messages. The classic example is voicing a complaint or reprimand while smiling,[27] which sends a confusing mixed message. Typical gender socialization doesn't help our affect display abilities,[11,27] since men tend to earn praise for being firm and expressionless ("manly" emotional restraint) while women hear cautions to appear constantly cheerful ("womanly" charm). These gender-based stereotypes restrict emotional expressiveness by unnecessarily confining the emotional range of men and women. Check the congruence of your affect displays with your verbal message. Also consider whether your emotional expressions are *proportionate* to your message.

Think of your face as a canvas where you can paint a portrait of your emotions. Try reading an emotionally charged passage from a poem or story, checking your facial expressions in a mirror. How well does your face set the mood for what you are reading? When your audience correctly identifies the emotion you were trying to convey, you have succeeded in *showing* what your words only say. Showing *and* telling almost always accomplishes more than just telling.

Eye Contact

Eye contact may be the most studied and noticeable form of nonverbal behavior. Many people believe that eyes indeed are "the mirrors of the soul" because so much weight is placed on messages the eyes convey. The Eagles sang, "You can't hide your lyin' eyes." Avid poker players sometimes wear dark glasses, fearing their eyes might convey their true emotions and betray a bluff. Eye contact carries powerful messages.

Eye contact has been identified consistently as a highly influential area of body language. When judging the emotions of a speaker, audiences tend to focus on the eyes and mouth.[28] Eye contact establishes and maintains a bond with the audience, making them feel included. Most communicators expect direct eye contact, as we might recall from parents or siblings who kept demanding, "Look at me when I'm talking to you!" We all know how frustrating it is to converse with someone who does not acknowledge us with eye contact. Many people with autism do not establish or maintain regular eye contact with others, and this nonverbal behavior unfortunately impedes their social skills.[28]

Eye contact has connections with intimacy. The idea that lovers stare into each other's eyes has become a cliché. Generally, the more frequently we make eye contact with someone, the more intimate that person assumes the relationship to be. Frequent glancing at someone in a social setting often gets interpreted as an invitation to begin a conversation or perhaps initiate a relationship. Duration of eye contact carries high emotional impact; holding a gaze quickly stimulates a reaction. We tend to maintain a long gaze only if the situation has reached a point of great intensity, either positively or negatively.

Examples (Positive Gaze)

- The "lover's stare" when two people "can't take their eyes off each other"
- Gawking in awe at a celebrity

Examples (Negative Gaze)

- "Rubbernecking" to keep watching a grotesque situation such as an automobile accident or injury
- Glaring at someone to indicate anger

Be careful when trying to interpret eye contact, since it may signify adoration ("I ogled at his marvelous beauty") or abhorrence ("I stared at her in disbelief after she insulted me").

Observers strongly associate eye contact with honesty. Supposedly, insufficient or inconsistent eye contact signifies deception. We call liars "shifty-eyed"; we demand forthrightness by saying, "Look me straight in the eye and tell me." Actually, eye contact does *not* accurately diagnose deception or truth; nevertheless, people continue to *believe* that direct eye contact signifies honesty.[29] This belief, although unwarranted, has persisted for ages. The best tactic for speakers is to adapt to audience expectations. Don't risk observers labeling you as dishonest or not taking you seriously because of deficient eye contact. However misguided the assumptions about eye contact may be, they do exist and persist. Even when their interpretive frameworks are misguided, audiences still may use them; communicators must recognize these tendencies.[30] Effective communicators take the realities of audiences into account.

Eye contact also can function as a challenge. Basically, the longer and more direct your eye contact with someone, the closer the relationship will seem—to a point. When the chairperson of a meeting maintains a high level of eye contact while speaking, this behavior signals the position of power over the committee through "visual dominance behavior".[31] In this sense, eye contact signifies dominance; taken to extremes, it can count as aggression. Consider how you would feel if your professor started at you and only you throughout an entire class. The discomfort you would experience demonstrates the potential for sustained eye contact to intimidate or threaten others. In the film *Schindler's List* (1993), the concentration camp inmates avoided making eye contact with the guards. Instead, the prisoners looked down to signal subservience (at least from the guards' perspective) and avoided potentially violent confrontations. More eye contact is not necessarily better. Since excessive eye contact can disrupt communication, you should maintain direct eye contact for a few seconds, then shift slightly to looking at other audience members or (if in a dyad) to other facial features before returning to meeting a person's eyes again.[27]

With so much riding on effective eye contact, you probably want to maximize its impact.

Proxemics

Proxemics refers to the physical space we maintain between others and ourselves. Anthropologist Edward T. Hall[32,33] describes four distances we employ to communicate different messages. Figure 4.1 illustrates these distances. We generally think of **intimate distance** (touching to 18 inches) as appropriate to more private encounters. Intimate distances tend to be reserved for interactions among close companions such as close friends, lovers, or family. A basic principle of proxemics is that closer physical distance conveys closer emotional distance. The more personally you address someone, the closer your physical distance can become. Be careful when communicating at intimate distances. Because the sensory cues from other communicators—their appearance, smell, sound, and possibly touch—are so intense at such a short distance, messages can get intensified as well.[33] Actors realize that a close-up camera shot makes

FIGURE 4.1 Levels of Proxemics Prevalent in the United States.

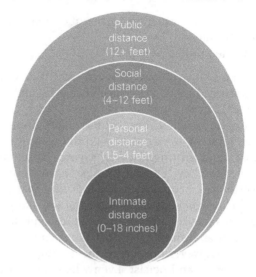

even the smallest facial nuance dramatically apparent. Remember that intimate distances also heighten your nonverbal impact on others. In cultures where people greet each other by quickly kissing each cheek, as in Mexico and much of Latin America, they must necessarily enter intimate space. Cultural norms differ among nations and regions, so interpret and respond to these nonverbal messages relative to where they are used.

Personal distance—measured at about 18 inches to 4 feet—roughly corresponds to the "bubble of space" each person tends to maintain, a space one does not expect others to violate. Suppose you are alone in an elevator. It stops and someone else (a stranger) gets on. Where will you stand? Each of you will stand as far apart from the other as physically possible, probably jammed against a wall to preserve personal distance—especially since the average elevator car offers barely the space to keep this distance. You also will avert your eyes, looking at the ceiling, your shoes, the elevator buttons—anything to keep from entering the other person's visual space as well. In the United States, personal distance serves another function. Americans are not especially touch-oriented, so personal distance allows for a handshake but preserves enough space to minimize opportunities to touch conversational partners.

You experience **social distance** if you interview for a job and the interviewer invites you to sit across the desk, separating you by 4 to 12 feet. Your manager, supervisor, or professor may purposely position furniture to maintain this physical distance, creating a more formal environment. Salespeople are often taught to come out from behind their desk to reduce this formality to avoid appearing patronizing, a message that could destroy a potential sale.

Public distance typifies a speaking situation where the speaker stands on stage and the audience sits in chairs at least 12 to 25 feet away. Many large lecture rooms on college campuses preserve public distance by positioning chairs several feet away from the podium. As the distance between communicators grows, the formality of the interaction tends to increase. The more space between speaker and audience, the less interactive the communication will become. Proxemics works in three dimensions, so a raised platform can create a sense of public distance even in a relatively small area.

Our expectations regarding distance are always tied to context. When we are examined by a physician or are having our hair cut, for example, we don't interpret this as a violation of our intimate space. A speaker who leaves the podium to walk through the audience may be perceived as warm and caring. During a concert, some singers leave the stage and perform in the midst of the audience to convey intimacy with their fans.

Proxemic practices are quite culturally specific.[32] For example, an American from the rural Midwest who travels to South Korea on business will find that appropriate distance norms are different to Koreans. The American may feel threatened if a Korean enters her personal distance zone when Korean norms interpret standing closer to someone as showing caring and personal interest. The customary interpersonal distance in Latino and southern European countries is about half the norm for Americans.[34]

Skillful communicators can use proxemics strategically to make favorable impressions. **Expectancy violations theory** discusses the effects of proxemics that do not obey customary rules.[35] If the audience has positive feelings for the speaker, then moving closer to the audience (encroaching on personal space) generates more favorable reactions. This result applies to communicators seen as credible, high status, likable, or attractive. We want to be closer to people we like and respect. If, however, the audience views the speaker negatively, the proxemic violation intensifies the negative reaction.

Proxemics plays such an important role that people often engage in **territorial behaviors** by physically marking a space as their own. Territoriality establishes an area where a person or group can claim dominance, physically marking where others should not enter.[36] Different types of territorial markers serve various functions.[37]

Boundary markers show where territories begin and end. Areas designated as "authorized personnel only" distinguish spatial privileges that accrue to individuals or groups. Street gangs might mark their territory with graffiti to warn rival gangs to stay off their "turf".[38] Boundary markers may create a more secure sense of "owning" a space. One study found that people whose houses had clear boundary markers such as fences or walls lived in these dwellings longer than people whose property lines were less clearly defined[36].

Central markers lay claim to a space. Examples include placing your notebook on a desk you want to occupy in a classroom or the "reserved" sign on tables at a restaurant. At a Hawaiian luau I attended, the host told guests to reserve their seats at the table by placing a lei on the place setting while they went to a buffet line.

Ear markers (named after the practice of marking or tagging cattle) identify a space or item as your own. Clothing and cars may sport monograms or other personalized features that allow people to claim these objects as theirs. Large wooden or stone monuments with the family name stand in the front yards of some houses. The entire field of branding is dedicated to finding the best way to identity products; examples include university mascots and the uniforms of sports teams. Used by groups, ear markers such as uniforms can increase unity. Used by manufacturers, effective ear markers can maintain brand loyalty.

Touching Behaviors

The power of touch was recognized long before it was formally studied. Touching, also known as **haptics**, carries strong connotations. Use it carefully. Not only do different cultures have different uses and preferences, but individuals differ drastically in their comfort with touching or being touched. Differences in touching behavior have proven especially difficult adaptations for communicators who shift to a different cultural environment.[9] Some general patterns in haptic patterns do emerge, although plenty of exceptions arise depending on specific communication situations. High-touch cultures are more common in warmer climates, while lower touch preferences more frequently occur in cooler climates.[39] High-touch cultures also tend to value open expressions of emotion. Figure 4.2 lists some examples of how touch preferences vary culturally and geographically.

Touching has several major communicative functions. First, let's explore touch and intimacy. People consistently connect touching to expression of interpersonal interest.[30] When not done aggressively (such as shoving), touch tends to convey a desire to draw closer to someone. A complex ritual of touching surrounds courtship, with placement and duration of touch indicating increasing intimacy. Whether romantic or not, touch draws people closer. Touching has many positive effects. A long-practiced religious tradition practices healing by "laying on of hands," believing that direct physical contact transmits God's healing powers. A more modern, secular therapy, known as therapeutic touch, uses touch to sense energy fields and supposedly send healing energy to an ailing patient.[40] Appropriate, caring touch—hugs, caresses, and other demonstrations of affection—has proven critically important for child development from infancy onward.[41] Even as adults, we often "need a hug" to alleviate emotional distress. The very term we use to discuss deep emotion—feeling "touched"—refers to haptics. Touch offers many productive possibilities for communicators. If the audience feels comfortable communicating at an intimate distance, a speaker can immediately establish a personal connection by a light touch. In interpersonal settings, comforting touch demonstrates an emotional bond, providing a physical indication of connection. Touch also carries risks. Frequent or prolonged touching can communicate intense intimacy, an impression that might not fit the relationship or situation.

Touch has some practical purposes as well. Some touch performs necessary social functions, such as tapping someone on the shoulder as a way of attracting attention, a physician manipulating a patient's body in an examination, or a hair stylist turning a client's head.[42] Another form of touch surfaces in ritual behaviors such as greetings that involve handshakes or holding hands during group prayer. In these contexts, touching makes social interactions run more smoothly.

Touch also has associations with power. The privilege of initiating touch accompanies positions of authority or status.[42,43] For example, a cleric blesses people by placing hands on them. A parent rubs the head of a young child as a sign of affection. In either case, what social reactions or consequences would result if the congregant or the child initiated the same behavior?

Adaptors are repetitive, usually unintentional touching behaviors that satisfy a physical or emotional need. Some adaptors may arise as uncontrolled kinesics that provide outlets for nervous energy: "biting, licking the

FIGURE 4.2 Levels of Touch Preference.

Examples of Low Touch	Examples of High Touch
German, East Asian, Scandinavian cultures	Latin and Arab cultures

In lower touch settings, touch is more likely to be interpreted as intrusive or undesirable. In higher touch environments, touch is often expected or invited. Customary forms of greeting reflect these differences.

Culture	Customary Greeting	Level of Contact
East Asian (Japan, China, Korea, etc.)	Bow	No touch
United States	Handshake	Moderate touch
Persian and Arab (Iran, Saudi Arabia, Iraq, etc.)	Embrace, kiss on cheek	High touch

Source: Derived from Andersen & Wang.[39]

lips, playing with hair, picking with fingers, scratching, holding oneself, tapping hand movement, rubbing, or massaging".[44(p23)] Adaptors have been classified according to what someone touches.[20,45] **Self-adaptors** appear to satisfy some physical need, such as scratching an arm. One of my students scratched his arm throughout an entire speech. Clearly, he did not have a chronic itch; he wasn't sure what to do with his hands. **Alter-adaptors** involve touch as a reaction to other people, such as picking lint off someone's clothing or crossing arms as a defensive response to encroachment on personal space. **Object-adaptors** manipulate something in the environment: stroking the rim of a wine glass, clicking a pen, doodling on a sheet of paper, text messaging, drumming fingers on a table, playing with keys or coins in one's pocket.

An entire family of adaptors, known as **preening** or **self-grooming behaviors**, conveys excessive concern about appearance. These mannerisms rob presentations of impact because, instead of gesturing for emphasis, the presenter fiddles with his own body or clothing. Preening behaviors include adjusting clothing, rearranging hair, and touching jewelry or other accessories. Aside from revealing nervousness, such cues also send a message that the speaker's focus lies with himself instead of with the audience.

All adaptors share some features. They distract from verbal content because they coordinate with nothing the speaker says.[11] Adaptors also signify nervousness and discomfort. The more adaptors communicators display, the more apprehensive they feel.[46] Adaptors have substantial effects on perceptions of speakers. Conversational partners rate communicators who display a lot of self-touching behaviors as less effective than those who perform fewer self-adaptors.[47] Self-adaptors often indicate nervousness or lack of confidence, which leads observers to perceive incompetence or poor preparation. Observers also connect adaptors with deception, assuming that the lack of bodily control shows tension from trying to conceal lies.[48] Fidgety speakers, therefore, might get labeled not simply as nervous but as liars.

Regulators

Communicators use **regulators** "to manage the 'traffic' of language interactions".[49] Regulators consist of actions that govern turn-taking, starting, stopping, and the pace of communication. Sometimes a regulator can be a vocalized sound, such as a periodic "uh-huh" or "I see" over the telephone that signals the other person to keep talking. Effectively used, regulators reduce interruptions because people know whose turn it is to speak. On some two-way communication devices such as walkie-talkies, a tone sounds when one communicator has finished speaking. The tone serves as a regulator, signaling one person is ready for the other to speak. Regulators can extend and encourage communication or do exactly the reverse.

Examples of Regulators that Encourage Communication

direct eye contact, nodding the head, smiling, leaning toward the speaker, vocalized responses ("hmmm," "amen," etc.), pausing to let others speak

Examples of Regulators that Restrict Communication

lack of eye contact, no facial expression or response, clearing the throat (as permission to interrupt or a hint to stop talking), yawning, checking a clock or watch, increasing volume to "talk over" others, checking incoming messages on a cell phone

Speakers especially need to note regulators and respond accordingly by expanding or constricting their communication.

Regulators also govern communication closure. If you ever had a guest that lingered too long, refusing to take hints to leave, you have witnessed failure to process regulators. Regulators, like other forms of communication, rely on timing for appropriateness. Notice how often students in classes begin finalizing movements such as gathering their belongings, closing their notebooks, and zipping their backpacks several minutes before class actually ends? That's a regulator, although a rather rude and annoying one. Many of my Arabic students have told me that such behavior would not normally be performed or tolerated in their cultural tradition, where the instructor customarily initiates closure.

Several speech situations call for effective regulators. In public speeches, questions to the audience—especially in the introduction—fall flat without a sufficient pause to permit answers or reflective thought. In group settings, invitations to participate often take the form of direct eye contact and pauses that leave an opening for comments. In interviews, the cue for the other person to speak usually takes the form of a brief pause, maintenance of direct eye contact, raising the eyebrows and widening the eyes, or phrasing a remark to assure clear closure. For example, you might conclude an answer by saying something like: "So that's how I would approach the issue in your question." Skillful use of regulators can encourage others to extend or condense their remarks; however, ultimately it will all depend on how regulators are "read."

Artifacts

Every human creation that is not part of the body itself comprises the wide range of nonverbals known as **artifacts**. Examples of artifacts include clothing, accessories (such as jewelry, briefcases, etc.), furnishings and décor in a home or office, and the vehicles people drive. These objects act as extensions of the people connected with them,[50] so the person can remain utterly silent while the artifacts send loud messages by their mere presence (or absence). Artifacts generate some of the most entertaining observations in communication. What do lawn decorations tell us about the residents of a home? How does the design of an office convey messages about how the organization views employees and clients? What sorts of clothing impress you about someone's social status, and which clothing cues identify someone as sleazy? What does the presence of certain products (e.g., Starbuck's coffee vs. convenience store coffee) suggest about a person or the communication environment?

Clothing can carry many messages, and it is one of the easiest artifacts to observe—and manipulate. *Dress for Success* author John T. Molloy[51(p1)] recommended: "*Let research choose your clothing,*" since clothes, like any other artifact, can be examined more systematically than simply by appealing to personal taste. Be careful when inferring the messages of clothing, since clothes transmit images of how people may want to appear—not necessarily the reality of their character.

Successful use of artifacts largely depends on their consistency with the social environment. Select artifacts that portray you as a member of the community in which you will operate. Many professionals display their credentials in their offices—as diplomas, licenses, awards, or certificates—to reinforce their credibility. Check the walls of your physician's, dentist's, mechanic's, or professor's offices for these artifacts. Display of medals is standard practice in the military; the medals are artifacts that show accomplishments.

The message of consistency, even conformity, with social norms comes through strongly in recommendations of clothing for business settings.[51-53]

Observe the artifacts of others who are already in the environments where you plan to communicate. How do they dress? How are they groomed? Beware of generalizing, since individual organizations may have very different customs. For instance, faculty in some university departments may dress quite formally while other departments have far more casual dress codes. These practices may not generalize to other universities. If you will deliver a speech, consider how your clothing and other artifacts blend with your topic and the formality of the situation. Dress strategically to reinforce your message, not simply to make a fashion statement.

Artifacts can prove tricky to interpret. Although we know *that* they communicate, *what* they communicate might not be clear. The images artifacts convey might not match reality. For example, am I really impoverished or do I just want to cultivate an aura of grunge with my sloppy appearance? Another example: Am I truly a wealthy, fashion-conscious celebrity or do I merely want to look that way with my borrowed designer suits and rented Ferrari? Finally, should you conclude someone is an avid sports fan simply because she wears the local team's gear, stacks issues of *Sports Illustrated* all over her office, and displays sports memorabilia on the wall?

THE VOCAL DIMENSION: PARALANGUAGE

To understand the difference between what you say and how you say it, try saying the following sentence aloud, each time emphasizing the word in italics.

1. *Chicken* soup is Jewish penicillin.
2. Chicken *soup* is Jewish penicillin.
3. Chicken soup *is* Jewish penicillin.
4. Chicken soup is *Jewish* penicillin.
5. Chicken soup is Jewish *penicillin*.

In each case, the same words acquire totally different significance. It all depends on where you place the vocal stress. Notice how drastically the sense of the sentence changes:

1. Chicken, not matzo ball or borscht
2. But not chicken pot pie
3. What? You doubt me?
4. As opposed to Christian or Muslim, for example
5. Focus on the medicinal value

Whenever we concentrate on how words are spoken rather than on the words themselves, we deal with **paralanguage**. The nuances of how we say words convey our moods and attitudes. Paralanguage controls the pacing, affects perceptions of speaker likability and competence, and plays a huge part in determining whether an audience will greet a speaker's words with enthusiasm, dread, or indifference. The voice is one of the most flexible and controllable instruments a speaker has. You can adjust your vocal quality in all sorts of ways to fit your objectives and the demands of the situation. A more challenging, but equally important, task is to become more proficient in judging the emotional content conveyed by other people's paralanguage. During interviews and other interpersonal situations, **mirroring** a conversational partner's paralanguage can increase comfort levels.[54] This mirroring involves matching the emotional tone of someone else's paralanguage, not merely mimicking exactly what the person does. For example, if a friend greets you with ecstatic, high-pitched shouts of joy about winning the lottery, you naturally would respond with a similar reaction instead of with a subdued whisper.

Pitch

Vocal **pitch** describes how high or low the voice registers on a musical scale or, more technically, the sound wave frequency of one's voice. High-pitched speaking voices seem to generate negative reactions because audiences often connect high pitch to childishness and lack of authority.[27,49,55] High pitch also is associated with nervousness and possibly deception, since vocal pitch tends to rise when a speaker feels agitated or self-conscious. Listen carefully, for example, to broadcasters and performers such as Oprah Winfrey, Barbara Walters, and Katie Couric. These women perform with rather low-pitched voices. Very high pitch would invite audiences to label them as girlish and frivolous—exactly the negative perceptions women have worked so hard to overcome.[55]

Maintaining exactly the same pitch along with not varying other vocal qualities results in the dreaded **monotone**. Intuitively, students equate a "boring" presentation with lack of vocal variation: same pitch, same volume, same speed. The problems with a monotone extend far beyond boredom. Since vocal expression cues the audience on how to react, an expressionless voice gives no indication of the emotional weight the words carry. No emotion from the speaker means no reaction from the audience. A monotone also signals lack of speaker involvement with the topic, which in turn generates audience disinterest.

Beware of the vocal pattern known as **uptalking**. In uptalking, speakers unintentionally raise their vocal pitch as they reach the end of sentences. Ordinarily this raised pitch at the end of sentences signals a question in the English language. For example, notice what your voice does when you say the following: "I'm going to give a speech?" Uptalking appears most commonly among young women. Some researchers believe this pattern reflects a desire for approval by appearing to ask permission rather than make an assertion, but the reason for uptalking remains a puzzle.[56]

The problem arises when that rising pitch transfers to remarks not meant as questions. Since listeners are accustomed to identifying rising pitch with questions, they will interpret every remark made with such a speech pattern as an interrogative. Uptalking makes speakers seem more uncertain and hesitant, as if they constantly are asking listeners questions. Uptalkers come across as insecure because they sound tentative.[57] To correct uptalking, record your own voice, especially when practicing a speech. Ask listeners to identify instances of uptalking so you know when to avoid it. Furthermore, try consciously lowering your vocal pitch as you approach the end of declarative sentences. That way, you'll sound more assertive and confident, saving the rising pitch for the times that you intend to ask questions.

Vocalized Fillers

This, like, section, you know, like, deals, sort of, with, like, the little, uh you know, words or, like, um, phrases, that, you know, speakers, like, kind of, insert, like, sort of in the middle of, ah, sentences. Frustrated trying to read that last sentence? Welcome to the world of **vocalized fillers** or **segregates**, repetitive words or phrases that speakers sometimes insert randomly throughout speech. These insertions have no relationship to message content, do not occur at strategically planned times, and can make audiences very uncomfortable. Vocal segregates may arise to avoid uncomfortable pauses. These fillers have no meaning in themselves but prevent silence: "uh," "um," "you know," "like," "well," "man," "er," "ah," and other vocalizations. They do keep speech moving but interrupt the flow of thought. If used too frequently, repetition of segregates can become the main thing the audience remembers. Imagine all that hard work you did preparing for a presentation and the only message the audience walks away with is "uh."

Vocal segregates could arise from several factors, including stress (fear of having nothing to say) or genuine uncertainty about what to say. They do have a clear effect on audiences. Whether accurate or not, audiences judge speakers who use lots of vocal segregates as unskilled, possibly incompetent, and inarticulate. Stylistically, excessive vocalized fillers disrupt the flow of speech, making it sound choppy.

You can monitor vocal segregates by recording yourself. If you're worried about a particular filler, just count the number of times you repeat it. In each practice session, consciously try to reduce the number of times you say that word, phrase, or sound. Set targets of the maximum number of times you can say the filler and gradually decrease that number for the next rehearsal each time you reach your goal.

Speech Rate

Introductory speech texts generally estimate "normal" speech rates at 120–180 words per minute, but observations of actual conversations and public speech across the United States find an average rate of 193 words per minute.[56] The rate of speech does not seem to vary consistently by gender or region.

Speech delivered at a slightly more rapid rate than normal leaves positive impressions. Recall from Chapter 3 that we can listen to speech rates far more rapid than most people can talk. Audiences rate quicker speakers as more competent and more socially attractive than speakers who deliver at slower than average rates.[59] This finding makes sense in light of how we connect competence and speed in everyday language. We label smart people as "quick," "quick-witted," "quick on the uptake," or "quick-thinking." We call their less intelligent counterparts "slow," "slow-witted," or "sluggish."

Rapid delivery does reduce the time available for listeners to weigh arguments. More rapid speech might not allow sufficient time for audiences to evaluate the quality of ideas, and the sheer speed of delivery might raise suspicions about a "fast talker" trying to slip information past the listeners.[60]

Speakers do not have to speak much slower than normal to achieve clarity. Clear speech is possible at normal and higher rates as long as the speaker distinguishes sounds carefully[61]—a point we cover in the next section. Of course, rapid speech has limits. Benefits dwindle and then actually reverse if delivery causes more speech errors and reduces comprehensibility. There are situations that would favor slower speech rates, such as speaking to an audience who is not as fluent in your language.

How do you optimize your rate of speech? Your speech must sound natural—reasonably conversational—to listeners. Extremely rapid or slow delivery can distract from content. As we noted in Chapter 2: Record your practice sessions, then play them back to yourself and others to judge whether you need to adjust your rate of delivery. Use rate of speech as a way to indicate emotional intensity. A dramatic shift in speed quickly draws the audience's attention. Cruise control might work well in cars, but not in speech. Let your rate of speed signal your level of excitement and intensity.

Speech Patterns

The clarity of what we say depends on how clearly we speak the sounds of our language. **Articulation** deals with how we say individual sounds within

FIGURE 4.3 Common Articulation Errors.

Correct Sound	Sound Actually Produced
S (super)	Th
W (wire)	L or R
Th (with)	F or T
Y (yellow)	L
R (rabbit)	W (as demonstrated by Elmer Fudd in the Bugs Bunny cartoons)

words. Clear articulation allows listeners to determine quickly the words you are saying, allowing your audience to focus on your message rather than puzzling over what you are trying to convey. Some common articulation errors appear in Figure 4.3. Recurrent articulation problems will confuse audiences, just as repeated misspellings or fuzzy print can disorient readers.

Persistent articulation errors are no laughing matter. Audiences easily can mistake the words you mean to say, and unfortunately many listeners may falsely assume that poor articulation equals poor understanding of your topic. Not all articulation problems are simply errors. You may have a physical condition that inhibits making certain sounds. If you suspect that this is the case, consider discussing treatment options with a qualified speech pathologist. These professionals work with their clients to address challenging vocal conditions.

Enunciation involves how we say words in context, the pronunciation patterns produced by combinations of words or syllables. When audiences complain that a speaker suffers from "mush mouth" or "slurs words," they refer to enunciation: clarity of each word in its entirety. If you ever try to decipher the lyrics of some popular songs, you understand the frustration of poor enunciation. The words seem to run together in an incomprehensible blob, and you must search for the lyrics online or remain content with catching a few scattered words.

In public presentations, careful enunciation communicates polish, effective preparation, and professionalism. Being able to enunciate all portions of a word distinctly will enable deaf and hard of hearing audiences to speech read accurately.[62] Proper enunciation is challenging. In the film version of *My Fair Lady* (1964), the sloppy street talk of Eliza Doolittle suffers from chronically poor articulation and enunciation. The famous song "The Rain in Spain (Falls Mainly on the Plain)" is simply a musical version of an enunciation exercise. But the overly precise diction of Professor Henry Higgins in the film comes across as snobbish and condescending. Effective enunciation falls between these extremes.

Speech instructors have proposed many enunciation exercises, including the following:

- reading aloud while holding a pencil or other non-toxic object in your mouth
- opening your mouth as wide as possible while exaggerating every vocal sound
- reciting tongue twisters repeatedly without errors

It would be a good idea to monitor the clarity of your speech patterns to improve articulation and enunciation. Sometimes articulation or enunciation problems (such as those listed in Figure 4.4) can subside if you simply reduce your speed of delivery.

The realm of **pronunciation** refers to whether the way we say words conforms to accepted proper usage. A current dictionary will list preferred pronunciations for words. Figure 4.5 lists some of the 100 most commonly

FIGURE 4.4 Common Enunciation Errors.

Correct	Actually Said
Going to	Gonna
What are you	Whatcha
-ing suffix	-in
Give me	Gimme
What did you get	Whadjagit
What's that, What's up	Wazzat, Wazzup
Meet you	Meetcha

Other enunciation errors include dropping or substituting sounds or syllables, especially in longer words. Example: difficulty ⟶ difkuhty.

FIGURE 4.5 Some of the 100 Most Commonly Mispronounced Words.

across	especially	prescription
ask	fiscal	probably
athlete, athletic	foliage	pronunciation
barbed wire	height	realtor
business	library	relevant
drown	miniature	spay, spayed
duct tape	moot	supposedly
escape	nuclear	tenet
espresso	nuptial	Tijuana
et cetera	ostensibly	utmost

mispronounced words as identified by.[63] Compare your pronunciations to those listed in the dictionary. Proper pronunciation not only improves your image as an educated person, but it also preserves the fine distinctions between words that can affect meanings.

A **dialect** is a pronunciation pattern of a geographic region or ethnic group. Typical pronunciation patterns differ in various areas of the United States, although not everyone in a geographic area necessarily shares the same dialect. Discussions of dialect often get tied up in issues of power and cultural dominance: Which dialect is "better" than others? Answer: All dialects are effective as long as they enable people to communicate effectively. Remember that effective communication requires listeners and speakers to adapt to each other. A dialect becomes problematic only when it inhibits understanding what the speaker is saying. Effective communication depends on listener adaptation as well as speaker clarity. With so many different cultures interacting, it might be time for us all to adjust our ears to the many different dialects that we will encounter. A few points about dialects help us keep proper perspective.[43,64,65]

- Dialects do not correlate with intelligence or other abilities.
- There is no such thing as a "pure" language with no dialect whatsoever (although everyone seems to think his own dialect is "normal" and that everyone else has an accent).
- Often the speech of socially disadvantaged groups is labeled "inferior" by more powerful groups when the dialects simply differ.

Volume

One of the most frequent comments instructors of introductory speech courses make is: "Speak up!" The volume of ordinary conversation will not suffice for public speaking. Always check the acoustics of the room where you will deliver a presentation—including rooms where you will be in an interview or conduct a group meeting. Every room has its own sound qualities, but novice speakers usually underestimate how loudly they must speak for the words to carry throughout a room.

Volume matters for other reasons. Varying volume is one way you can call attention to an important point. Think of adjusting your own volume as a sort of verbal highlighter. Just as you would highlight important portions of a text, you can emphasize important points in a speech by saying them louder or softer. Increasing volume usually makes speakers seem more authoritative and dynamic. We don't usually think of a committed, enthusiastic speaker as someone who whispers a presentation. Decreasing volume, however, can add drama. If you lower your voice a bit, the audience must become more attentive to your words.

Skilled speakers have mastered vocal **modulation**, the ability to vary vocal qualities (especially volume) to maximize emotional effect. We know when modulation becomes problematic. Consider people in a restaurant or other public area who talk on their cell phones as if shouting to someone standing across the street. These social misfits have failed to modulate their voices from what suits a public distance to the more appropriate volume for intimate or personal space. Cell phones are not megaphones.

Tech Talk: E-modulation

In electronic communication, sending a message types in ALL CAPS (all capital letters) qualifies as "screaming" and is deemed inappropriate for polite online conversation. The primitive emoticons (literally, icons of emotional states) such as ☺ don't seem to carry much impact anymore, as they are so overused. It also becomes tough to decipher minimal messages, such as the abbreviated snippets we send and receive in text messages. What recommendations do you have for showing the emotional content of online or text messages? Must we settle for online communication as an emotionally impoverished medium?

Silence Speaks

Absence of speech can have substantial impact. Before examining some communicative roles of silence, let's address the question of whether men or women talk more. Apparently, the amount of talk has more to do with perceived comfort in a communication environment than with gender roles or biological sex. Men tend to interrupt more and speak longer than women. Overall, "women tend to talk more with close friends and family, when women are in the majority, and also when they are explicitly invited to talk (in an interview, for example)".[66(p47)] So the generalizations about men or women "talking too much" are too simplistic.

While words can convey a message, so can silence. Silence often causes discomfort. Americans prefer speech to silence and feel great pressure to keep conversation going by saying something.[67] We already noted how this treatment of silence as an absence or void may generate vocalized segregates. This negative silence becomes apparent in phone conversations, when silence usually elicits a comment such as, "Hello? Are you still there?" We also know the irritation of awkward silences, such as the times when new acquaintances find they have little to say to each other and fumble for topics of conversation.

Silence can punish. Sometimes silence results from communication breakdown or avoidance. If we give someone "the silent treatment," we deliberately withhold communication. This tactic poses serious problems, since refusal to interact reduces the opportunity to negotiate a solution to the crisis.

Silence can censor. Refusal to speak about certain topics renders them taboo, removing them from conversation. This type of silence protects from sensitive topics and avoids embarrassment or offense. Silence also may prevent coping with difficult topics. In the novel (and film) *Prince of Tides*, a family's silence about its traumas that include beatings and rapes leaves one character suicidal and mentally disturbed. Her brother is able to begin healing for the family only after psychotherapy sessions where he discusses their tragedies.

Silence can communicate respect. In elementary school, my teachers used to say, "Silence is golden," since it showed willingness to listen. During funerals, quiet reigns as mourners "pay their respects," usually without words except for eulogies that honor the deceased. Speakers—and instructors—dislike students carrying on their own conversations during a speech because it shows disrespect to the speaker. You can show how much you value someone else when you defer to that person as the speaker and do not interrupt.

Silence can signify thoughtfulness and emotional depth. The familiar saying "Still waters run deep" and the desirability of the "strong, silent type" reflect a popular connection between silence and serious contemplation. In religious services, the times reserved for "silent prayer" allow worshippers to communicate deeply and directly with the higher power. Silent meditation deepens contact with inward spirit. Parents often recommend that children take a "time out" to quietly reflect and regroup.

Silence can add drama. A well-chosen "dramatic pause" adds intensity to whatever follows. Watch the Academy Awards ceremony and notice when your anticipation builds to a crescendo: during the pause between the announcement of the nominees and the pronouncement of the winner. Consider adding a few dramatic silences to your own presentations. When you want the audience to place great weight on the next thing you say, pause for just a couple of beats. The dramatic pause is powerful, so use it sparingly.

Finally, whether true or not, silence can indicate agreement. **Spiral of silence theory** holds that people are more likely to remain silent if they believe their opinion is in the minority. The pressure to keep silent intensifies if one fears possible rejection, reprisal, or ridicule from expressing an opinion that varies from the majority. It remains unclear whether spiral of silence holds for non-Western cultures.[68] The theory stresses that minority opinions need to be aired for democracy to flourish, reminding reticent communicators to speak up.[69]

INTERPRETING NONVERBAL BEHAVIORS

Nonverbal behaviors are notorious for generating misunderstandings. One root of nonverbal miscommunication lies in assuming our own customs and meanings hold true universally. This "projected similarity"[34(p51)] mistakenly treats the most familiar nonverbal patterns—one's own—as the norm. Nonverbal communication is easy to observe, but challenging to interpret. Everyone remains susceptible to communication breakdowns. "Nonverbal behavior is notoriously ambiguous in meaning," so even very astute observers should exercise caution in deciding an action's ultimate meaning or underlying motive.[70(p388)]

Adapting to Differences

Meanings of nonverbal cues depend on the cultural context of the source and the interpreter. Consider how nonverbal cues operate within the communicator's cultural customs. In Latino cultures, puckering the lips in a certain direction is a subtle way of pointing, extending the lips to indicate "over there".[34] Many Americans would treat this behavior in their own cultural terms as a romantic overture. Placing nonverbal communication in its cultural context becomes critical when trying to negotiate with people from different cultures, since incorrect interpretations can stall agreements.[71] Anyone planning to interact with other cultures extensively or study abroad would benefit from discussing nonverbal customs with natives of the other cultures. Many commercial and governmental organizations conduct intercultural training seminars to acclimate people to new contexts. For example, Americans traveling to Saudi Arabia in Operation Desert Storm learned not to cross their legs unthinkingly. In Arabic cultures, showing someone the sole of your shoe (the dirtiest item of clothing) is considered an insult. Orientation to this nonverbal cue was part of the official military briefing before many troops went overseas. Take a minute to consider the nonverbal codes you are accustomed to using. Which of these do you think are universally understood and which might be bound by cultural or social context?

Men and women also exhibit some differences in nonverbal communication, although overall the variations are not large. Women generally outperform men in decoding nonverbal messages, facial recognition, and nonverbal emotional expression.[30] Women also tend to give and receive more eye contact, convey more facial expressions, and maintain closer proxemics than males.[72]

Despite extensive research, it remains un-clear exactly what causes sex-based patterns in nonverbal communication.[26] Researchers have suggested variables such as genetics, social status, cultural forces, upbringing, and sex roles as explanations for these differences. Such uncertainty warns us not to generalize about certain nonverbal behaviors being exclusively "masculine" or "feminine," since a lot more could influence communication than whether a man or woman performs a nonverbal act. The same precaution holds for jumping to conclusions about sexual orientation based on an individual's nonverbal behaviors or mannerisms.

Observe Nonverbal Cues in Context

The more nonverbal signals you find pointing to a meaning, the more reliable your interpretation will be. For instance, if a person crosses her arms, that might signal defensiveness. But if she crosses her arms, avoids eye contact, shifts her torso away from you, and crosses her legs tightly, you have much better data for concluding that she feels defensive. Each of these cues can indicate defensiveness, but the theme of defensiveness running through four different cues gives better evidence about her mood. Try to find consistent patterns in nonverbal behaviors. Consider each nonverbal cue as a word in a language. Just as you would not want to judge an entire book based on a single word, avoid reading too much into a single cue. Clusters of nonverbals provide the equivalent of sentences that provide more reliable messages than individual cues.[14]

Nonverbal cues can be ambiguous; *"no position, expression, or movement ever carries meaning in and of itself"*.[5(p45)] Meanings are in people, not in gestures or other individual behaviors. The exact same nonverbal cue in one situation can mean something totally different when observed in another setting. Nonverbal cues acquire meaning only within the overall communication process where they occur.[5] For example, if you make an obscene gesture to your best friend it may signify your close bond. But if you make the same obscene gesture to an unfamiliar police officer, you won't get the same friendly response. So, the same gesture can be fine or get you fined.

Nonverbal Communication and Sexual Harassment

Undesired or uninvited nonverbal behavior has serious consequences. Whether someone interprets your conduct as appropriate or as sexually motivated also has a lot to do with your nonverbal behavior. If you look at discussions of sexual harassment, you will find that many signs of sexual harassment are nonverbal. The United States Army[73(sec 7-5a)] defines nonverbal sexual harassment quite explicitly:

> Examples of nonverbal sexual harassment include staring at someone (that is, "undressing someone with one's eyes"), blowing kisses, winking, or licking one's lips in a suggestive manner. Nonverbal sexual harassment also includes printed material (for example, displaying sexually oriented pictures or cartoons); using sexually oriented screen savers on one's computer; or sending sexually oriented notes, letters, faxes or e-mail.

The U.S. Marine Corps[74(p0207H-4)] has used the following criteria:

> Nonverbal Sexual Harassment: Like verbal behaviors, nonverbal behaviors that constitute sexual harassment take on many forms. Some examples are:

- Paying unwanted attention to someone by staring at his or her body.
- Displaying sexually suggestive visuals (centerfolds, calendars, cartoons, etc.).
- Ashtrays, coffee cups, figurines, and other items depicting sexual parts of the anatomy through actuality or innuendo.
- Sexually oriented entertainment in organizations, base facilities, or officially sanctioned functions.
- Making sexually suggestive gestures with hands or through body movement (blowing kisses, licking lips, winking, lowering pants, raising skirt, etc.).

Examine those lists carefully. The armed forces, like many other organizations, identify physical behaviors than can violate sexual harassment policies. Everyone needs to exercise great care in performing and interpreting nonverbal behaviors.

Morality Matters

Find the official sexual harassment policy of your educational institution or workplace. How clearly does it define when nonverbal behavior becomes sexual harassment? What sorts of difficulties arise when designating specific nonverbal behaviors as harassment?

Accurately Interpreting Nonverbal Cues

By now you might be asking how you ever could "read" someone's nonverbal behavior accurately. No magic formulas exist, but careful observation can reduce the chances of nonverbal communication breakdowns. A few hints can increase your accuracy in interpreting nonverbal cues.

- *Consider intent.* Nonverbal signals may be intentional or unintentional. Compare a wink intended to signify sexual interest versus a nervous tic that closes one eye. Try to determine whether a nonverbal cue is habitual. For example, if someone repeatedly touches you while speaking, does that count as a sexual advance, or is it part of the person's customary way of communicating to everyone? Aside from accidental habits, deliberate manipulation also poses an interpretive risk, as we noticed with artifacts. Ask yourself what the communicator might gain by displaying certain patterns of nonverbal behaviors. This question might distinguish image management from genuine expression.

- *Recognize that cues can evolve.* Accepted meanings of nonverbal behaviors can change over time. During and shortly after World War II, almost anyone in the world would recognize two extended fingers as the "V for Victory" sign. In the 1960s, however, the same cue acquired almost the opposite meaning: the "peace" sign, a protest against the Vietnam war. To a young American child, on the other hand, this nonverbal cue would have one obvious meaning: the number two.

- *Focus on clusters of cues over time.* The longer you observe someone's nonverbal communication patterns, the more you get a sense of how the cues operate for that person. Many studies of deception now try to establish a baseline level of nonverbal behavior that constitutes a person's norm. After establishing behavioral norms, significant variations from the person's ordinary cues might qualify as signs of tension or concealment. Multiple cues also offer better grounds for drawing conclusions. More reliable interpretations arise from noticing groups of cues that point to similar interpretations.

HIGHLIGHTS

1. Nonverbal communication includes visual and vocal dimensions.
2. Although early communication theorists paid little heed to delivery, nonverbal communication conveys vital emotional and cognitive messages. Effective nonverbal expression and interpretation is important for healthy human development.
3. Nonverbal behaviors tend to be trusted more than verbal messages, so congruence between words and actions is necessary.
4. Kinesics, the broad realm of all bodily movement, should coordinate with verbal content for emphasis and clarity.
5. Emblems signify specific, culturally established messages—but their interpretation varies widely across cultures.
6. Iconic gestures, such as two fingers making a cross, physically resemble what they signify.
7. Illustrators enact what they designate, such as outstretched arms to show large size.
8. Affect displays convey emotion, notably through facial expression. Ability to decode as well as express emotions can enhance communication, although the degree of overt emotional expression varies across cultures.
9. Eye contact is a powerful communication device that can express intimacy or aggression. Lack of eye contact commonly gets mistakenly associated with deception.
10. Proxemics is the use of physical space. Intimate, personal, social, and public distance require different communication behaviors. Generally, the closer the distance the closer the perceived relationship will be. Proxemics display noteworthy cultural variations.
11. Territorial behaviors include marking physical space to establish areas of dominance. Boundary markers set the beginning and end of territory, central markers reserve space, and ear markers personalize space.
12. Touching, or haptics, can strengthen interpersonal bonds, but it also has instrumental functions (e.g., gaining attention) and reflects social power structures.

13. Adaptors are repetitive touches that fulfill a personal need. Adaptors can involve touch of self, others, or objects.
14. Regulators control the flow of communication.
15. Artifacts consist of items that a communicator can manipulate to create an impression.
16. Paralanguage deals with how we say things rather than what we say.
17. Pitch is how high or low a voice falls on a musical scale.
18. Vocalized fillers, or segregates, are repetitive interruptions in the flow of speech.
19. The rate of speech can be monitored and adjusted to find a comfortable speed that maximized comprehension.
20. Speakers can modulate, or strategically change, speech patterns to adjust to audiences and situations. Clear articulation (individual sounds) and enunciation (sounds in the context of other sounds) as well as controlling one's volume are essential for effective communication.
21. Although pronunciation should match linguistic norms, no dialect is automatically superior or inferior.
22. Silence has many communicative functions and can be used constructively or destructively.
23. Accurate interpretation of nonverbal cues requires observation over time, understanding when cues are intentional, and recognizing the ambiguity of messages.

ENDNOTES

1. Duke, M. P., Nowicki, S., & Martin, E. A. (1996). *Teaching your child the language of social success.* Atlanta: Peachtree.

2. Argyle, M. (1988). *Bodily communication* (2nd ed.). London: Methuen.

3. Koch, S. C. (2005). Evaluative affect display toward male and female leaders of task-oriented groups. *Small Group Research, 36,* 678–703.

4. Mehrabian, A. (1981). *Silent messages: Implicit communication of emotions and attitudes.* Belmont, CA: Wadsworth.

5. Birdwhistell, R. (1970). *Kinesics and context: Essays on body motion communication.* Philadelphia: University of Pennsylvania Press.

6. Munsey, C. (2006, September). More than words. *Monitor on Psychology, 37*(8), 36–37.

7. Aston, M. (2003). Aspergers in love: Couple relationships and family affairs. London: Jessica Kingsley.

8. Bos, E. H., Bouhuys, A. L., Geerts, E., van Os., T. W. D. P., & Ormel, J. (2007). Stressful life events as a link between problems in nonverbal communication and recurrence of depression. *Journal of Affective Disorders, 97,* 161–169.

9. Albert, R. D., & Ha, I. A. (2004). Latino/Anglo-American differences in attributions to situations involving touch and silence. *International Journal of Intercultural Relations, 28,* 253–280.

10. Raudsepp, E. (2002, December 5). Body-language tactics that sway interviewers. *Wall Street Journal CareerJournal.com.* Retrieved December 24, 2004, from http://www.careerjournal.com/jobhunting/interviewing/20021205-raudsepp.html.

11. Stone, J., & Bachner, J. (1977). *Speaking up: A book for every woman who wants to speak effectively.* New York: McGraw-Hill.

12. Bauerlein, M. (2009, September 4). Why Gen-Y Johnny can't read nonverbal cues. *Wall Street Journal,* p. W15. Retrieved March 1, 2010, from http://

online.wsj.com/article/SB10001424052970203863204574348493483201758
.html#articleTabs%3Darticle

13. McKay, M., Davis, M., & Fanning, P. (1983). *How to communicate.* New York: MJF Books.

14. Nierenberg, G. I., & Calero, H. H. (1993). *How to read a person like a book.* New York: Barnes and Noble.

15. Lightfoot, C., & Bullock, M. (1990). Interpreting contradictory communications: Age and context effects. *Developmental Psychology, 26,* 830–836.

16. Hall, E. T. (1977). *Beyond culture.* Garden City, NY: Doubleday Anchor.

17. Woodall, W. G., & Folger, J. P. (1981). Encoding specificity and nonverbal cue context: An expansion of episodic memory research. *Communication Monographs, 48,* 39–53.

18. Woodall, W. G., & Folger, J. P. (1985). Nonverbal cue context and episodic memory: On the availability and endurance of nonverbal behaviors as retrieval cues. *Communication Monographs, 52,* 319–333.

19. Dansby, A. (2005, January 22). Norway reads something sinister in "Hook 'em" sign. *Houston Chronicle,* p. A1.

20. Ekman, P. (1999). Emotional and conversational nonverbal signals. In L. S. Messing & R. Campbell (Eds.), *Gesture, speech, and sign* (pp. 44–55). Oxford, UK: Oxford University Press.

21. Booth-Butterfield, M., & Booth-Butterfield, S. (1990). Conceptualizing affect as information in communication production. *Human Communication Research, 16,* 451–476.

22. Booth-Butterfield, M. (1992). *Interpersonal communication in the classroom.* Edina, MN: Burgess International Group.

23. Frymier, A., Ishii, S., & Klopf, D. (1990). Affect orientation: Japanese compared to Americans. *Communication Research Reports, 7,* 63–66.

24. Salzmann, Z. (1998). *Language, culture and society* (2nd ed.). Boulder, CO: Westview.

25. Dolin, D. J., & Booth-Butterfield, M. (1993). Reach out and touch someone: Analysis of nonverbal comforting responses. *Communication Quarterly, 41,* 383–393.

26. Hall, J. A., Murphy, N. A., & Mast, M. S. (2006). Recall of nonverbal cues: Exploring a new definition of interpersonal sensitivity. *Journal of Nonverbal Behavior, 30,* 141–155.

27. Phelps, S., & Austin, N. (2002). *The assertive woman* (4th ed.). Atascadero, CA: Impact.

28. Adolphs, R. (2006). Perception and emotion: How we recognize facial expressions. *Current Directions in Psychological Science, 15,* 222–226.

29. Levine, T. R., Asada, K. J. K., & Park, H. S. (2006). The lying chicken and the gaze avoidant egg: Eye contact, deception, and causal order. *Southern Communication Journal, 71,* 401–411.

30. Fichten, C. S., Tagalakis, V., Judd, D., Wright, J., & Amsel, R. (1992). Verbal and nonverbal communication cues in daily conversations and dating. *Journal of Social Psychology, 132,* 751–769.

31. Exline, R. V., Ellyson, S. L., & Long, B. (1975). Visual behavior as an aspect of power role relations. In P. Pliner, L. Krames, & T. Alloway (Eds.), *Nonverbal communication of aggression* (pp. 21–52). New York: Plenum.

32. Hall, E. T, (1959). *The silent language.* Garden City, NY: Doubleday.

33. Hall, E. T. (1966). *The hidden dimension.* Garden City, NY: Doubleday.

34. Cruz, W. (2001, October). Differences in nonverbal communication styles between cultures: The Latino-Anglo perspective. *Leadership and Management in Engineering, 1*(4), 51–53.

35. Burgoon, J. K., & Hoobler, G. D. (2002). Nonverbal signals. In M. L. Knapp & J. A. Daly (Eds.), *Handbook of interpersonal communication* (3rd ed.; pp. 240–299). Thousand Oaks, CA: Sage.

36. Fischer, G.-N. (1997). *Individuals and environment: A psychological approach to workspace* (R. Atkin-Etienne, Trans.). Berlin: Walter de Gruyter.

37. Goffman, E. (1971). *Relations in public: Microstudies of the public order.* New York: Harper Colophon.

38. Ley, D., & Cybriwsky, R. (1974). Urban graffiti as territorial markers. *Annals of the Association of American Geographers, 64,* 491–505.

39. Andersen, P. A., & Wang, H. (2006). Unraveling cultural cues: Dimensions of nonverbal communication across cultures. In L. A. Samovar, R. E. Porter, & E. R. McDaniel (Eds.), *Intercultural communication: A reader* (11th ed.; pp. 250–265). Belmont, CA: Thomson Wadsworth.

40. Pesmen, C. (2006). *Uncommon cures for everyday ailments.* Stamford, CT: Bottom Line Books.

41. Carlson, F. M. (2005). Significance of touch in young children's lives. *Young Children: Journal of the National Association for the Education of Young Children, 60*(4), 79–85.

42. Major, B. (1981). Gender patterns in touching behavior. In C. Mayo & N. M. Henley (Eds.), *Gender and nonverbal behavior* (pp. 15–37). New York: Springer-Verlag.

43. Henley, N. M. (1977). *Body politics: Power, sex, and nonverbal communication.* Englewood Cliffs, NJ: Prentice-Hall.

44. Hill, C. E., & Stephany, A. (1990). Relation of nonverbal behavior to client reactions. *Journal of Counseling Psychology, 37,* 22–26.

45. Ekman, P., & Friesen, W. V. (1969). The repertoire of nonverbal behavior: Categories, origins, usage, and coding. *Semiotica, 1,* 49–98.

46. Jordan-Jackson, F. F., & Davis, K. A. (2005). Men talk: An exploratory study of communication patterns and communication apprehension of black and white males. *Journal of Men's Studies, 13,* 347–367.

47. Ishikawa, H., Hashimoto, H., Kinoshita, M., Fujimori, S., Shimizu, T., & Yano, E. (2006). Evaluating medical students' non-verbal communication during the objective structured clinical examination. *Medical Education, 40,* 1180–1187.

48. O'Hair, H. D., Cody, M. J., & McLaughlin, M. L. (1981). Prepared lies, spontaneous lies, Machiavellianism, and nonverbal communication. *Human Communication Research, 7,* 325–339.

49. Elgin, S. H. (1987). *The last word on the gentle art of verbal self-defense.* New York: Prentice Hall.

50. Fiol, C. M., & O'Connor, E. J. (2006). Stuff matters: Artifacts, social identity, and legitimacy in the U.S. medical profession. In A. Rafaeli & M. G. Pratt (Eds.), *Artifacts and organizations: Beyond mere symbolism* (pp. 241–258). Mahwah, NJ: Lawrence Erlbaum.

51. Molloy, J. T. (1975). *Dress for success.* New York: P. H. Wyden.

52. Molloy, J. T. (1988). *John T. Molloy's new dress for success.* New York: Grand Central Publishing.

53. Molloy, J. T. (1996). *New women's dress for success.* New York: Warner.

54. Sandoval, V. A., & Adams, S. H. (2001, August). Subtle skills for building rapport. *FBI Law Enforcement Bulletin, 70*(8), 1–5.

55. Glass, L. (1987). *Talk to win*. New York: Perigee.

56. Stockwell, P. (2002). *Sociolinguistics: A resource book for students*. London: Routledge.

57. Mandell, T. (1996). *Power schmoozing: The new etiquette for social and business success*. New York: McGraw-Hill.

58. Ray, G. B., & Zahn, C. J. (1990). Regional speech rates in the United States: A preliminary analysis. *Communication Research Reports, 7,* 34–37.

59. Feldstein, S., Dohm, F-A., & Crown, C. I. (2001). Gender and speech rate in the perception of competence and social attractiveness. *Journal of Social Psychology, 141,* 785–806.

60. Smith, S. M., & Shaffer, D. R. (1995). Speed of speech and persuasion: Evidence for multiple effects. *Personality and Social Psychology Bulletin, 21,* 1051–1060.

61. Krause, J. C., & Braida, L. D. (2002). Investigating alternative forms of clear speech: The effects of speaking rate and speaking mode on intelligibility. *Journal of the Acoustical Society of America, 112,* 2165–2172.

62. McManus, J. A. (2002). *How to write and deliver effective speeches* (4th rev. ed.). Lawrenceville, NJ: Thomson/Arco.

63. yourDictionary.com (2003). *100 most often mispronounced words and phrases in English*. Retrieved August 30, 2009, from http://www.yourdictionary.com/library/mispron.html

64. Esling, J. H. (1998). Everyone has an accent except me. In L. Bauer & P. Trudgill (Eds.), *Language myths* (pp. 169-175). London: Penguin.

65. Preston, D. R. (1998). They speak really bad English down south and in New York City. In L. Bauer & P. Trudgill (Eds.), *Language myths* (pp.139–149). London: Penguin.

66. Holmes, J. (1998). Women talk too much. In L. Bauer & P. Trudgill (Eds.), *Language myths* (pp. 41–49). London: Penguin.

67. McLaughlin, M. L., & Michael J. Cody, M. J. (1982). Awkward silences: Behavioral antecedents and consequences of the conversational lapse. *Human Communication Research, 8,* 299–316.

68. Scheufele, D. A., & Moy, P. (2000). Twenty-five years of the spiral of silence: A conceptual review and empirical outlook. *International Journal of Public Opinion Research, 12,* 3–28.

69. Noelle-Neumann, E. (1993). *The spiral of silence: Public opinion—our social skin*. Chicago: University of Chicago Press.

70. Hall, J. A. (2006). Nonverbal behavior, status, and gender: How do we understand their relations? *Psychology of Women Quarterly, 30,* 384–391.

71. Ngai, P. B.-Y. (2000). Nonverbal communicative behavior in intercultural negotiations: Insights and applications based on findings from Ethiopia, Tanzania, Hong Kong, and the China mainland. *World Communication, 29*(4), 5–35.

72. Hall, J. A. (1984). *Nonverbal sex differences*. Baltimore: Johns Hopkins University Press.

73. U.S. Army. (2008, March 18). *AR 600-20. Prevention of sexual harassment*. Retrieved August 30, 2009, from http://www.armyg1.army.mil/eo/docs/Chapter%207%20Sexual%20Harassment.pdf

74. U.S. Marine Corps. (1999, January). *Marine Corps University corporals noncommissioned officers program. CPL 0207*. Retrieved April 6, 2005, from http://www.tecom.usmc.mil/utm/SEXUAL%20HARASSMENT-FRATERNIZATION%20CPLS%20COURSE.PDF

Chapter 4
Nonverbal research rule violation assignment

The student should select two nonverbal rules to violate and then analyze some of the effects of breaking each rule. This exercise is to help the student become more aware of nonverbal behaviors and the effect these behaviors have on people near them. The analysis should be 1–2 pages long, typed and double-spaced, with 1″ margins, a font no larger than 12. The analysis should include the following information:

- Describe your experience
- State the norm/rule in our society for this nonverbal behavior. For example, it's normal in our society to allow plenty of personal space when conversing with another person
- State what happens if you follow the rule
- State what happens if you violate this rule
- State any exceptions to this rule
- Write a 4–5 sentence summary of what you learned through this assignment

Here are a few rule violations to consider, but you are not limited to:

1. Seat yourself next to the person and begin studying in the library (or another appropriate place) at a table where only one person is seated and the other seats are vacant.
2. Talk to another person and stare directly at the person without dropping your gaze.
3. Carry on a conversation with an acquaintance or stranger approximately 1 foot away from them. If the person moves, adjust your position so you continue to be 1 foot apart.
4. During the course of a conversation talk much louder than the other person.
5. Carry on a conversation with an acquaintance. Avoid eye contact completely.
6. Carry on a conversation with an acquaintance or stranger. During the conversation, lightly touch the person on the arm, hand, shoulder or knee.
7. Talk on your cell phone in an inappropriate environment (please, not at the movies!)
8. Be late for an appointment or meeting.
9. Dress inappropriately.

You are welcome to choose a safe violation of your choice.

OR

Record two nonverbal violations against you.

OR

Record one violation you did and one done against you.

THEN

Write a 4–5 sentence summary of what you learned doing this assignment.

Ultimately, you want to get at and report your subjects' reactions to your breaking the rules/norms. Have fun with this assignment. Remember: you are in control, you know what's happening. **Proceed with caution!!! If you feel threatened, back off immediately!** Afterwards, you may wish to debrief your "subjects."

INTERPERSONAL COMMUNICATION*

There's a good reason solitary confinement qualifies as the most severe punishment for any prisoner. Restricted from interacting with anyone, the prisoner's very soul withers. Volumes of scholarship and, unfortunately, a continuing supply of human tragedies testify to the human need for relationships. But there's a catch. Just because we associate with others doesn't mean we have a relationship with them. We can feel isolated and alone even amid a teeming multitude if we don't reach out to others and they, in turn, reach out to us.[1] Simply having relationships doesn't suffice—they must be healthy and fulfilling. If that sounds challenging, you understand why we included this chapter.

When most people hear the word "relationship," they immediately think of romantic couples. That perspective is far too narrow. First, we should recall that (at least in this book) we concentrate on interpersonal relationships because they involve mutual communication among people. Other types of relationships do not involve this kind of human-to-human communication. My relationships with my cats, my computer, my country, my spiritual connections, and many others are not interpersonal because they do not center on person-to-person interaction. Interpersonal relationships come in many flavors besides the romantic, including family, professional, neighborly, friendly, and of course your relationship with yourself. In this chapter, we concentrate on the conduct of *all* types of relationships involving people: how they operate, how they malfunction, how to keep them healthy and fulfilling for everyone involved. So when we refer to "relationships," we mean interpersonal relationships unless we state otherwise.

We begin the chapter by clarifying what interpersonal relationships are and why we work at understanding them. The next major section highlights the process of how we reveal personal information to each other. The third portion of the chapter traces the course of relationship development, pausing at each stage to probe how it operates. Finally, we move to the key components in building fulfilling relationships, troubleshooting potential threats to relationships along the way.

*This chapter was written by Roy Schwartzman, Jessica Delk McCall, and Ruthann Fox-Hines.

INTERPERSONAL RELATIONSHIPS: WHAT AND WHY?

In Chapter 1, we explored the definition of interpersonal communication. Because we live embedded in networks of relationships, our participation in relationships is unavoidable. The matter that concerns us is not whether to have relationships—because inevitably we will continue having them—but how to conduct them.

Getting Acquainted with Relationships

First, we should clear up a few misunderstanding about relationships. Relationships might be unavoidable, but they don't simply happen and run their course automatically. Unfortunately, we form a lot of misguided ideas about relationships from how they get idealized or demonized by movies, television, books, and even our own family and friends. Without having a deeper concept of how relationships operate, we risk plunging into the wrong relationships with the wrong people at the wrong time.

Relationships Carry Risks

Relationships involve risk. That risk increases as the relationship gets closer. As we get closer to someone, we increase our vulnerability. The more we know about each other, the greater the risk. All that personal information could be used against us in an argument, or confidential information might be leaked in breaches of trust. But if we don't take the risks, we can't enjoy the benefits. The flip side of the risk factor is that relationships also call for courage. A genuine, fulfilling connection with someone else requires the courage to open yourself to that person. It also calls for the courage to face the fact that relationships can change people and people can change relationships. Having a functional relationship means that we understand its changing nature: It can ebb and flow, blossom and wither, escalate and stagnate.

Relationships Are Dynamic

You'll notice that we keep talking about having a relationship or engaging in a relationship instead of being in a relationship. That terminology is deliberate. Relationships are dynamic. Remember when we discovered in Chapter 1 that communication is a process? That point deserves added emphasis with relationships. Think of a relationship as a continual crafting, a re-creation of the bond between people. We must be able to adjust our patterns of interaction to fit the changing nature of the relationship. For example, if an aging parent suffers from Alzheimer's disease, the children need to adjust the ways they relate to the parent. In many cases, the relationship reverses: The children as caretakers assume the role of parents, while the biological parent becomes more childlike. Although still a parent–child relationship, it cannot remain exactly the same as it was before the onset of the illness. Relationships demand adaptations from the participants to sustain the connection. A healthy relationship responds to changes in the relational environment, such as alterations in life situations (health, values, work conditions, finances, etc.) of the partners, the passage of time, and external influences (impact of families, friends, geography, etc.). A relationship that fails to change amid these changing circumstances is like a stiff tree in a tornado: It might be firmly rooted, but if it cannot bend, it's liable to break.

Relationships Require Effort

Interpersonal encounters simply happen; we have to *make* relationships happen. Just as a plant needs water and sunlight to grow, a relationship requires contributions from all the partners to flourish. We are constantly in the process of influencing our relationships. Even if we think we are doing nothing, we are indeed acting (perhaps by not acknowledging the relationship partner) in ways that affect the relationship. Examine any reputable guide to lasting relationships and one recurrent theme emerges: Relationships demand work. That's why you often hear the words "commitment" and "relationship" keeping close company. It isn't enough to be committed to the relationship. The commitment must be to do things that will nurture the relationship.

Relationships Involve Mutual Obligations

Trick question: Who bears the responsibility for a relationship going well? Answer (as you probably guessed): everyone. A relationship cannot succeed (that is, satisfy everyone involved) if only one person does all the work to keep it going. Eventually, the workhorse gets frustrated or burns out, and then the relationship reaches a crisis point. Relationships do require shared effort, although not always in the same proportion all the time. For example, I wasn't a highly interactive relational partner while writing this book. Many evenings were spent at the computer instead of at social activities that would have involved my companion and me. Some of my professional relationships had to be placed on hold as well, since I was absent from meetings and collegial activities. These shifts in relationship input can work as long as they wind up treating everyone involved fairly in the long run—and as long as these intentions were communicated clearly. In my case, the relational partners understand that my temporary withdrawal from some interpersonal activities now will obligate me to contribute more later. Relationships work by working out these kinds of tradeoffs and balancing acts.

Relationships Are Unique

Because every individual is unique, every relationship is also unique. While it is fairly easy to see that our romantic relationships are different from our work relationships, we should also recognize that each work relationship is an individual entity. There is no single, specific pattern or format that a particular relationship must follow. This diversity might explain why giving relationship advice is so tricky. You can only speak from your experience, and your relationship is different from the relationship you are attempting to evaluate.

When discussing uniqueness, we should also recognize that relationships begin for different reasons. Typically, any relationship that begins because an individual just happens to be in your life is considered a **relationship of circumstance**. Think about some of the relationships that you have developed with classmates. Did you strategically decide to begin this relationship or did it evolve because two people happened to be in the same class? Family relationships are often circumstantial as well. We didn't choose our biological parents. Sometimes, however, relationships begin because we seek them and develop them intentionally. This type of relationship is known as a **relationship of choice**.

Think about your relationships. Can you easily classify them as either a relationship of circumstance or a relationship of choice? Some relationships are much easier to classify, others are a bit more complex. Let's imagine that you have a strong relationship with one of your professors from your first semester in college. While the relationship certainly began as a relationship of circumstance (you signed up for the class and the professor was assigned), you then found that you had a lot in common with your professor. You intentionally sought out this professor for other classes, conversations, and career advice. What was originally a relationship of circumstance developed into a relationship of choice. Relationships may move from one category to another over time. Furthermore, we may communicate differently in relationships of choice than we do in relationships of circumstance. What differences do you notice in your communication patterns within your circumstantial and your chosen relationships?

Model Relationships

A good way to begin getting grounded in relationships is to find a way to counteract all the misleading propaganda about relationships that clogs the airwaves and the bookstores. The remedy is simple, yet rarely utilized. Search carefully for real people—not stories in celebrity magazines or fairy tales—yes, people close at hand, who embody models of the kind of relationship you seek. So, depending on the relationship you want to enter or improve, go out and find a positive role model. For romantic relationships, seek a long-term (measured in many years, not weeks) couple that you admire. For professional relationships, look for co-workers who have been close colleagues for a long time, or perhaps a client and provider who have stuck together. Families work the same way: Find a happy family. Whatever the relationship, discuss with your role model what makes his or her relationship work—and remember to get more than one side of the story. For instance, a happy marriage results from things both the spouses do, so make sure you get information from both of them.

Once you find relationship role models, observe their behaviors and ask them questions about what makes their relationship successful. We aren't talking about a formal interview here, but an ongoing process of mentoring. Keep in touch with your role models over the long haul; you probably will need to consult them throughout the stages of your own relationships. You also might find it prudent to select more than one role model. After all, relationships change and you might need to find new role models if your original choices no longer qualify (e.g., if their relationship ends or if they lose contact with you).

Two cautionary points: First, when selecting relationship role models, don't idealize the relationships that you find. All relationships have flaws; no family quite matches the perfect Huxtables on *The Cosby Show*. Instead of searching for the flawless relationship (you won't find it), seek people who work through their relational challenges effectively. Second, remember that all relationships are unique. While we can certainly identify model relationships, we must remember that what works in another relationship might not transfer to your relationship.

When we start a new job, our training for the technical tasks seems endless. We get formal hands-on training, a probationary period, a training manual, a successful employee to shadow, and a formal grievance process. But in the most important emotional areas of our life—our relationships—we're just supposed to dive in and hope for the best. What we recommend here is that you construct a continuing education program in relationships for yourself.

Relationships and Support Systems

A critically important reason to build relationships is to establish a network of support systems. Note the plural here: "support systems," not the singular "support system" or "support person." True support serves various functions and needs to include a variety of people.[2] It is very self-defeating to pick out one person—a spouse, a best friend, a therapist—and expect that individual to be your support in all situations no matter what. Someone should always "be there for you," but it doesn't have to be (and probably shouldn't be) the same person in every case. Just as a skillful speaker adapts to different audiences, we need to adapt our support systems to different circumstances and needs. Relationships can build at least five different types of support systems.[3]

- *Emotional support.* People who will allow us our feelings and do not tell us to feel something different; people we trust to accept us, let us feel and be; people who will listen to us; people who will be there to share sorrows, fears, frustrations, joys. Note: "people" not one person.
- *Technical support.* People who will listen to our ideas, who will encourage us in our professional areas. These people need to be in the same, or very close to, the field we are in, and they have to be people we trust.
- *Emotional challenge.* People who can stretch us in the emotional areas, who can help us go beyond the immediate feelings to understanding and change; people who can ask the right questions, who can help us gain new perspectives.
- *Technical challenge.* People who can stretch us professionally, make suggestions, offer constructive criticism, ask the right questions, gain new insights, perspectives. These people need to be in our area of expertise (or something closely related).
- *Social validation.* People who, in the different areas of our lives, hold values similar to ours and who have had similar experiences; people who help us realize we are not "crazy," people who help us feel not alone or like a reindeer at the equator.

In each case, we should identify people, not just one person. Why? First, the same person may not always be physically or emotionally available to offer support. We need back-ups. Second, constantly leaning on the same person for support can emotionally drain the other person. This overreliance could lead to burnout and reluctance or inability to provide further support.

THE SELF-DISCLOSURE PROCESS

Self-disclosure, revealing personal information to others, forms an important part of relationships. Before examining two ways of understanding self-disclosure, let's take a closer look at what self-disclosure involves. First, self-disclosure can be voluntary or involuntary. With voluntary self-disclosure, one chooses to share information. Voluntary self-disclosure represents a typical part of relationship development. As people gain more comfort with each other, they choose to share more about themselves. Involuntary self-disclosure usually spells trouble because the person has lost control over when, how, or how much he or she reveals. Involuntary self-disclosure might arise nonverbally when you say "I'm just fine" while trembling and sobbing. Your behavior discloses your distress.

Self-disclosure also reveals information, which means it must be something previously unknown to the other person. Telling something that is obvious or common knowledge does not qualify as self-disclosure. For example, it would not count as self-disclosure to tell you, "I'm alive," as that would be pretty obvious if I were talking. For information to qualify as self-disclosure, it also must be revealed to someone else. That is the interpersonal side of self-disclosure: It presumes an audience, someone to disclose to. That audience might be a best friend or, in the case of a public blog, anyone in the world with a computer.

The Johari Window

The **Johari window**, shown in Figure 5.1, is a popular way of illustrating the role self-disclosure plays in interpersonal relationships.[4] The open self comprises everything you and others know about you. This quadrant describes the area of public presentation and self-disclosure. Some parts of the open self are obvious, such as your physical appearance, while others are known through deliberate self-disclosure, such as sharing information that you were adopted as a child. The blind self consists of everything that other people know about you but that you don't know. A classic example of the blind self is someone asserting "My breath smells just fine to me" while co-workers hold their noses. All of our unconscious vocal and nonverbal habits that others notice (while we remain oblivious) qualify as part of the blind self. The hidden self is the realm of secrets: things we know about ourselves but are invisible to others. Some people diagnosed with a terminal disease decide to keep it as part of the hidden self, telling no one until the symptoms become apparent. The unknown self, known neither to you nor to others, consists of things that are unrealized or undeveloped. These aspects of the unknown self can be all sorts of things you and others never recognized, such as an unsuspected aptitude for math or discovering your true cultural heritage for the first time.

The four panes of the Johari window are not static; each expands or shrinks with changing circumstances and relationship behaviors. Someone in a top secret job at the FBI inflates the hidden self with the accumulation of more confidential information. For homosexuals, "coming out of the closet" describes the shift of confidential sexual orientation (hidden self) to public awareness (open self). Your blind self should shrink in this communication course as your classmates and instructor observe your public presentation skills and suggest improvements you had not considered before. (Example: "I never knew I sounded like that.") The unknown self also gets smaller through psychotherapy, which brings deep-seated but unrealized thoughts and feelings to the surface. In effect, psychotherapy shifts content from the unknown self toward the open self.

Generally, we can expect the amount of self-disclosure to increase as a relationship becomes closer. Plugged into the Johari window, this development means that as the relationship matures, the open quadrant expands. For most Americans, a major component of relationship development involves expanding the open quadrant—a point that also applies to leaders who want maximize trust throughout an organization.[11] This tendency has been confirmed

FIGURE 5.1 The Johari Window.

	known to self	not known to self
known to others	**open self** What you freely present in public *(public facts, observable characteristics)*	**blind self** What others know about you, but you don't realize *(habits that annoy others without your knowledge, unconscious mannerisms)*
not known to others	**hidden self** Personal secrets *(fantasies, unspoken love, shameful past)*	**unknown self** Unconscious, unexpressed parts of your identity *(repressed memories, unrealized potential, latent talents)*

The Johari window acquired its name from its creators: Joseph [Jo] Luft and Harry [Hari] Ingham.

FIGURE 5.2 Observed Cultural Variations in Self-Disclosure Patterns.

Nationality	Disclosure Patterns
American	Generally prefer high self-disclosure across wide ranges of topics in friendships and romantic relationships
Korean	Disclose at levels comparable to Americans, but less likely to reciprocate self-disclosure on the same topic[5]
Argentinian	Very high in self-disclosure, even higher than Americans[6]
Finnish	Lower willingness to communicate than Americans[7]
German	Disclose less than Americans, especially early in relationships[8]
Japanese	Lower self-disclosure levels than Americans across relationships types;[9] in online relationships build intimacy through self-disclosure (like Americans), but unlike Americans do not associate self-disclosure with trust[10]

While the patterns represent customary preferences, they describe tendencies that may not hold for every individual within the stated cultural tradition or nation. What confirmations or exceptions to these findings have you observed? What might explain these results?

in Korean as well as American relationships.[12] Some interesting cultural differences do emerge re-garding self-disclosure. These differences are listed in Figure 5.2.

Social Penetration

Social penetration theory notes that as relationships become closer, the partners reveal more information to each other.[13] This communication pattern is depicted in Figure 5.3. As a relationship deepens, the nature as well as the amount of disclosure changes.[14] We can consider two aspects self-disclosed information: breadth (the variety of information) and depth (how personal the information is). Early in relationships, participants are cautious and obey social rules of propriety between acquaintances. They are more likely to reveal information that is not very deep (superficial) and limited in scope. In the early stages of relationships, people especially withhold expression of negative emotions, presumably for fear that this disclosure might endanger the relationship's development.[15] As intimacy increases, negative emotions (and information in general) emerge more openly as the partners feel more comfortable expressing a fuller range of feelings. As you might guess, the depth and breadth of information they reveal will likely increase as the relationship develops and becomes more intimate. This increasingly personal self-disclosure builds closeness in a relationship.[16] When you say, "I can tell my best friend anything," you are speaking the language of social penetration.

FIGURE 5.3 Social Penetration in Relationships.

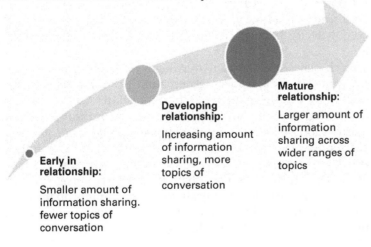

Mature relationship:

Larger amount of information sharing across wider ranges of topics

Developing relationship:

Increasing amount of information sharing, more topics of conversation

Early in relationship:

Smaller amount of information sharing, fewer topics of conversation

Advantages of Self-Disclosure

Self-disclosure can generate self-knowledge. Self-disclosure—in the Johari window's terms, letting others "see" us—can add to our own self-understanding and contribute toward our ability to operate more authentically in the world. By sharing information about ourselves, we can discover new insights about our own personality, background, and connections with others.

Self-disclosure furnishes a way to cope with relational uncertainty. By sharing personal information, a communicator invites the relationship to move to a more intimate level.[17] So self-disclosure can connect people more closely, intensifying a relationship. "I hardly know you" often precedes refusals for more personal contact. After self-disclosure, that phrase becomes rarer.

Self-disclosure relieves burdens of keeping things to ourselves. Instead of bottling up information inside us, self-disclosure provides an outlet. Every child knows the agony of trying to keep secrets hidden. Self-disclosure releases that emotional straitjacket by allowing us to share what we know about ourselves.

Self-disclosure opens communication channels. Unless other people know us, they might not even be able to recognize us as potential friends or collaborators. A model for self-disclosure's opening of channels is psychotherapy sessions, where clients disclose personal information to a therapist so they can understand how to cope with personal challenges. As another example, you might self-disclose your religious beliefs or home town to link with others who share these characteristics.

Self-disclosure also can put others at ease and increase the genuineness of interpersonal interactions. If others know something about you beyond the surface, they are more likely to let you know more of who they really are.

Self-disclosure counteracts loneliness. The need for self-disclosure in order to build connections with others is based on extensive research showing that having strong and healthy relationships is mentally and physically more healthy than isolation.[18] Health professionals note: "Strong interpersonal relationships and support networks reduce the risk of many [health] problems.… In contrast, social isolation has been identified as a heart disease risk factor".[19(p3)] Self-disclosure relieves loneliness by literally sharing part of yourself with others.

Limitations of Self-Disclosure

As indicated above, self-disclosure is usually beneficial; however, it is important to be discerning in how much and to whom we disclose. Self-disclosure is a powerful device in relationships. As with any powerful device, use it carefully.

Too much self-disclosure can overwhelm others. If you give a certain amount of yourself, the unspoken expectation is that the other person will self-disclose in return. This pattern of returning self-disclosure from someone else with self-disclosure of your own is known as **reciprocal self-disclosure**. But if you share too much at the outset, you may scare many people away. The situation resembles playing poker. If you put too much money in the pot to begin with, many players will fold; if you want them to stay in the game, you gradually up the ante. If you do not share anything of yourself, people begin to wonder what you are hiding and begin to mistrust simply on the grounds of assuming negative hidden information. Gradual sharing of self is usually the best approach if you wish to build relationships.

Gender differences might influence the degree of reciprocal self-disclosure. Women engage in more self-disclosure than men. In heterosexual couples, men also may tend to restrict their self-disclosure to women as a way to exercise power,[20] perhaps under the impression that "what you don't know can't hurt me."

Too much self-disclosure also can make you vulnerable to people who take advantage of this information. They might misuse the information by spreading it beyond the context in which it was shared. This is why all reputable process groups in counseling practice a basic rule of confidentiality, which the leader vigorously protects.

Self-disclosure tends to be most beneficial when the information is connected to the immediate conversational context.[21] For example, a teacher in a Spanish class who discusses her experience studying abroad in Spain could improve student interest. Consider when disclosure might actually bring the conversation or relationship to a deeper and more desirable level. The following *true* examples (with names changed, of course) illustrate inappropriate self-disclosure.

- When Brandi first introduces herself to her classmates, she explains in vivid detail her experience of being gang raped.
- During his first day on the job as a new faculty member, Raul casually encounters another faculty member at the photocopy machine in the department office. While copies are running, Raul discloses that he is homosexual.
- The first day of his Communication Theory class, Dilip tells the instructor and the rest of the class how much he detests another professor in the department.

Do you see why these examples of self-disclosure show poor discretion? More intimacy is not always better. In each case, the information might have been helpful, but no relational foundation had been laid to justify the disclosure at that time. The communication environment also may not have been conducive for private conversations. Because the relationship had not yet assured mutual trust, the disclosure was risky. Would confidentiality be kept? Would the other person reciprocate by disclosing also? What would be the consequences of the revelation? Not everyone will interpret self-disclosure as a sign of increasing closeness, friendship, and a desire to connect.[22] Before disclosing, weigh the risks and benefits of sharing intimate information. To practice **selective self-disclosure**, decide how much personal information fits properly within the constraints of the communication environment. Instead of "baring your soul" or "spilling your guts" indiscriminately, weigh how much disclosure should occur at a given point in the relationship.

Self-disclosure is a matter of degree. "To disclose or not to disclose" is not the question, but how much to disclose and to whom definitely are the questions to ask. Think of appropriate self-disclosure as choosing what to wear in the presence of certain people. In our lives, there are usually a few ultra-trustworthy individuals with whom we can actually be emotionally "naked." At the other end of the spectrum, there are those very untrustworthy people that call for you to wear a full suit of armor. And then there are all sorts of possibilities in between: bathing suit with those you generally trust close to 100 percent, those with whom it's wise to have a full three-piece suit and an overcoat, those with whom you can throw on a robe, and those who still call for a suit but you may be able to loosen your tie. Think of the whole spectrum of wardrobe as a metaphor for the whole spectrum from very trustworthy people to very untrustworthy ones. It is absolutely foolish to wander around emotionally "naked." It is equally silly and exhausting to clomp around in a full suit of armor. Gradually disclosing who you are, your likes, dislikes, hopes, desires, fears, life experiences—good and bad—and observing how others respond to and treat your self-disclosure (with respect or laughed at, valued or misused) is the way to develop accurate choices of "wardrobe": how much to self-disclose at the time, in that situation, with that particular individual or individuals.

Relationship Maintenance and Repair

Movement along the relationship staircase need not occur at a uniform pace or order. Some stages proceed quickly. Others creep along slowly. Different sorts of people and relationships move at different speeds. One person's preferred pace might not match someone else's. The warning "You're moving too fast" indicates a premature attempt to move to the next relationship stage. Sometimes relationships skip steps entirely or reduce them to momentary pauses along the staircase. Some relationships (such as those based on "love at first sight") zoom through experimentation and intensification and accelerate toward bonding. Other relationships spiral downward toward termination without preliminary steps such as circumscribing or stagnating. Occasionally an especially volatile relationship might hop all over the staircase according to the ups and downs the partners experience. The staircase of stages shows overall patterns that relationships tend to exhibit, although the movement does not have to be as linear as the stages show.[23]

Relationships don't always move. Although the staircase shows how far relationships can proceed (or how far they can fall), relational partners may spend a lot of their time stabilizing their relationship at a specific level. No law says every relationship must move to the next stage or that it should move at all. Some roommates stabilize their relationship at the avoidance stage, living separate lives in the same dwelling. Stupendous starts and tension-filled terminations of relationships can grab attention. "Yet across the history of a long-term relationship most of the time is spent in its maintenance and repair".[24]

Relationships, like cars and houses, require maintenance. Relationship **maintenance** describes the effort needed to keep the relationship functioning at a desired level. Relationships that are not maintained tend to worsen.[25] Maintenance does not mean the relationship will go to a different stage, but it is designed to increase the probability that the relationship will continue. Maintenance most commonly nourishes the bonding stage, reinforcing the bond and preventing slippage into differentiation. Although we might focus more on beginnings and endings, maintenance occupies the majority of time spent in relationships.[26]

Consider what you have done recently to maintain the important relationships in your life. What more could you do to nourish them? Undergraduate students identified the following maintenance behaviors (among others) across several different kinds of relationships:[27]

- Expressing positive attitudes and behaviors about the relationship.
- Open sharing of information, especially self-disclosure and confronting problems together.
- Reassuring each other.
- Sharing tasks (dividing up work).
- Doing things together.
- Humor (laughing together).

A relationship maintenance strategy you might consider implementing immediately is simply staying in touch. Text messaging, e-mailing, and social networking make it easier to stay connected even when you can't make a phone call or write a letter. One or more of these behaviors might become part of your relationship maintenance toolkit.

Just as we can maintain relationships, we can repair them. Of course, if we don't want to participate in a relationship, we might simply jump down the staircase, step on termination, and exit. These exits are easy at the initiation stage, but become more difficult and painful in the more advanced stages of becoming closer. At any step on the journey downstairs, we can choose **repair** options by trying to restore the relationship to bring the partners closer. Professional therapy, intervention from a friend, third-party arbitration, or mutual reconciliation represent a few different repair strategies that could improve the course of a relationship. Repair strategies don't suddenly make a relationship perfect, they only attempt to move the relationship in a positive direction. Repair becomes more difficult as the relationship progresses through the stages of de-escalation. So we don't leave Zippy and Skippy on a tragic note, let's revisit them as they try to repair their romance.

> Skippy: "I'm really sorry. I never should have bought all of those video games without asking. I knew we needed to save money for school."
>
> Zippy: "That was pretty bad. But I went a bit too far when I sold your favorite video games on eBay to get back at you."
>
> Skippy: "I probably played those games too much anyway."
>
> [Both laugh.]

Nothing magical has happened between Skippy and Zippy, but if they continue in this direction, they may be able to repair the relationship—if both of them want to. Skippy and Zippy approach repair by confronting a central conflict directly, not assigning blame, and depersonalizing the issue by laughing about it. Laughing together and opening up to each other qualify as relational maintenance strategies. Will the marriage recover? Hard to tell. But Skippy and Zippy have taken some action instead of sitting back as spectators and helplessly watching the relationship dissolve.

Gender Communication

Deborah Tannen wrote about gender communication in "You Just Don't Understand: Women and Men in Conversation" discussing general differences between how women and men use communication to get their ideas, wants, and plans across to another. Here are some of the ideas that she discussed.

Much of Tannen's work focuses on symmetry between men and women. A frequent generalization is that men focus on solving problems or establishing status while women focus on building relationships. So if a man starts a conversation with a woman he may assume that she knows he needs help or wants advice (although men might not readily seek advice), while the woman may assume that he is trying to build a relationship with her. Right from the start the conversation is at cross purposes. A health issue she gives is an example. A woman may speak to her husband about her condition expecting sympathy and support while he may respond with ways to help her feel comfortable and find the best way to approach the condition. The woman may feel emotionally unsupported. "Eve wanted the gift of understanding, but Mark gave her the gift of advice" (50).

Tannen refers to these different ways of talking as rapport-talk and report-talk. She describes rapport-talk as "a way of establishing connections and negotiating relationships" (77). Women like to find ways they are alike and compare experiences, looking for connections. With report-talk, however, men talk about their knowledge and skills, like to be center stage, and to feel independent (77). "Girls are not accustomed to jockeying for status in an obvious way; they are more concerned that they be liked" (44). So while women are building connections, men are more aware of who has a higher status and control. Often when women complain about husbands who don't share intimate details about their work it's because the men feel that the relationship itself is intimate and they don't need to work to increase intimacy.

If relationships are inherently hierarchical (62) then this asymmetry in goals and expectations is understandable. Tannen even refers to gender communication as "cross-cultural conversation" (42). "Instead of different dialects, it has been said they speak different genderlects" (42). While women seek interdependence, men are focusing on independence and freedom of action (39).

This difference affects listening styles as well. Women generally offer frequent vocal support – "yes," "uh-uh" – that to men is an interruption. Men's silence is often viewed by women as not listening. Men also consider the listener to be subordinate and may not listen (139). This attitude may be exhibited even in body language. Research showed that when instructed to talk, girls will sit face to face while boys sit side by side and are less likely to look at each other (269). Sometimes the boys' seeming non-attention appears that they are not engaged, but when asked about the conversation show they were totally engaged.

There are differences in attitudes about conflict as well. Often women view conflict or any disagreement as "a threat to connection and to be avoided at all costs" (150). "But to many men, conflict is the necessary means by which status is negotiated, so it is to be accepted and may even be sought, embraced, and enjoyed" (150). In fact, it can be regarded as a way to connect (150). Men also expect that if someone has something to say they will say it, and actually prefer that even if it means that there will be disagreement. "Friendship among men often has a large element of friendly aggression, which women are likely to mistake for the real thing" (150).

Many of these conversation differences were found in research done with young children and exhibited by elementary school-aged boys and girls and sometimes even among younger children. Tannen also refers to cultural differences found in children as well as adults, especially in "friendly aggression" talk from women.

Tannen encourages us all to be flexible in our expectations and attitudes toward others (187). In spite of the many differences she refers to, they aren't insurmountable, as seen in many successful relationships between people who have found ways to work through, around, or in spite of the challenges. She quotes Alice Walker who wrote in "The Temple of My Familiar" that "really what we're looking for is someone to be able to hear us" (48).

Tannen, Deborah. "You Just Don't Understand: Women and Men in Conversation." New York: William Morrow, 1990.

RELATIONSHIP DRIVERS

The final portion of this chapter covers several concepts crucial to building and maintaining relationships that are genuine and bring out the best in the participants. While no formula guarantees any relationship's success, the ingredients in the following discussion detail important influences on any relationship. By recognizing and addressing these influences, you will enter into relationships more prepared to help them succeed.

Relational Dialectics

Earlier in this chapter we noted that relationships take work, but work on exactly what? A smoothly functioning relationship doesn't simply coast on cruise control. **Relational dialectics** points out that every relationship constantly reconciles conflicting forces. The dialectic consists of the ongoing attempt to cope with these contradictory impulses. If not addressed properly,

FIGURE 5.4 Dialectical Tensions in Relationships.

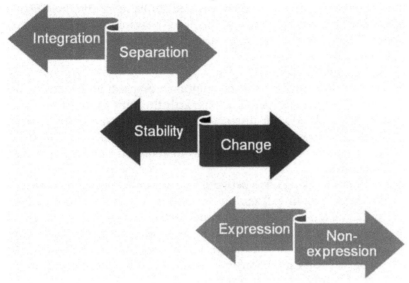

Partners in relationships engage in ongoing efforts to reconcile these opposing forces.

these opposing tendencies pull the relationship apart. According to,[28] three major pairs of opposing forces influence relationships: integration/separation, stability/change, and expression/non-expression. Figure 5.4 illustrates these dialectical pairs. Both of the opposing tendencies in each pair always infuse relationships. So our task in relationships becomes working out ways to balance the conflicting forces.

Let's examine these tensions. Integration/separation arises as the tug between identifying one's self as connected with another person or as an individual. In romantic relationships, this tension may surface as a question over whether two people consider themselves "a couple." Someone seeking integration may lean toward linking with the other person, favoring moving in together and merging all possessions, including joint bank accounts. Separation might pull this couple apart if the other person prefers classification as "me" instead of "us," with the separate homes and belongings that entails.

The stability/change dialectic represents the pull of the past against the push toward the future. Should the relationship go in a new direction or should it stay on the same course? Many situations can trigger this dialectical tension, such as a family's main breadwinner getting a job offer that requires relocation. The family must weigh the familiarity and security of the status quo against the uncertainty and potential rewards of the move.

Expression/non-expression deals with different tendencies for overt communication—not simply whether to communicate but how much to communicate, how often, how overtly, and with whom. Different cultural approaches to self-disclosure might result in clashing views of what information should remain private.

These dialectics affect each person within a relationship as well as the relationship itself. Regardless of age, every child feels an internal tension between integration and separation. Part of every child wants autonomy: "I want to do things myself!" But part of the child also craves comfortable integration into the family: "I want my mommy!" Here are more examples of how these dialectics play out in relationships.

Example (integration/separation): family outings vs. "doing your own thing"
Example (stability/change): traditional vs. unconventional gender roles
Example (expression/non-expression): overt vs. subdued expressions of love

So, how do we reconcile the conflicting forces of relational dialectics? Apparently, the presence of these contradictions does not affect relationship satisfaction, but the way they are managed plays a role in the relationship's success.[29] Some ways relational partners can manage dialectical tensions include the following techniques.[28-30]

- *Denial.* Choosing one side over another, pretending the tension does not exist. Example: Always following exactly the same routine for a date, which indulges stability, but disregards change. This strategy invites problems, since the opposing force still exists and exerts its pull. Denial ignores the source of tension and does nothing to address the underlying cause of relational stress.
- *Alternation.* Taking turns between the two opposing forces so each one gets privileged over time. Example: Weekdays are the usual routine (stability), while weekends are times to try new activities together (change).
- *Segmentation.* Reserving certain areas or topics for each of the opposing needs. Example: Minimum public expressions of affection in front of strangers (non-expression) but frequent displays of affection in the presence of family members (expression).
- *Neutralizing.* Explaining or disqualifying a pull toward one pole so it no longer poses a threat. Example: "I want to be alone a lot [separation] because I'm depressed about not getting the job, but bear with me because I still want to continue our friendship [integration]."
- *Balancing.* Finding a compromise between the two opposing forces by fulfilling each of them partially. Example: Instead of always going to dinner and a movie, maintain the dinner tradition (stability), but vary the other activity (change).
- *Reframing.* Maintaining a dynamic tension between the opposed forces, but creatively affirming it as something positive. Example: Partners in a long-distance relationship might communicate often via e-mail, Facebook, Twitter, text messaging, and phone calls, treating this variety of contacts as an opportunity to connect in more ways (instead of as an inferior alternative to face-to-face interaction).

The same management technique may not work every time, so partners should prepare to experiment with the methods that produce the greatest relational harmony.

Your Relationship Balance Sheet

Inevitably you will ask questions about whether and when a relationship should begin, continue, escalate, change, or end. These questions become more frequent and urgent when a relationship verges on moving to another stage. Wouldn't it be great if we had some sort of relationship balance sheet that tallied the profits and losses, risks and benefits, and then calculated where to go in the relationship?

Proponents of **social exchange theory** contend that we determine the value of a relationship by weighing its rewards against its drawbacks. You employ a social exchange theory approach when you say things such as: "This relationship isn't worth the effort," "I need to get more out of this relationship," or "You owe me for helping you last week." Social exchange theory treats any relationship as a balance between costs and benefits: Participants try to minimize costs and maximize benefits.[31] As long as the rewards of a relationship remain satisfactory for each participant, the relationship continues. In this view, relationships are continuous bargaining processes, with each participant giving, withholding, and receiving rewards. By the social exchange standard, a

FIGURE 5.5 The Social Exchange Theory Approach to Relationships.

relationship achieves stability when each partner considers the costs and benefits to be fairly distributed.[32] Fair distribution of rewards reminds us that all relationships do carry some costs. The "all rewards, no costs" relationship is as much a fantasy as the risk-free investment.

The fundamental question becomes: How do we calculate rewards? Exactly what counts as a reward will vary with each person. Each person has a **comparison level** that affects a relationship's perceived value.[31] The comparison level consists of the experiences and expectations that shape what qualifies as a satisfying relationship.[33] Your comparison level includes factors such as:

- Your prior experience with similar kinds of relationships.
- Your family's and culture's expectations.
- What you feel you deserve in a relationship.
- What you feel you can get from a relationship.
- What you consider most important in a relationship.

When a relationship exceeds your expectations based on these factors, you assess the relationship as having positive overall value.[34]

While helpful, social exchange theory also raises some concerns. It says little about the ethical side of relationships.[35] Strict application of social exchange theory implies that relationships operate more on the basis of cold calculation of pleasure and pain, with little discussion of self-sacrifice or the innate value of people aside from the rewards they can generate. A more humane side of social exchange theory includes recognizing that relationships require meeting obligations and keeping promises in order to maximize gains.[36] Sometimes the justification for a relationship may be less what we can get than what we can give. Figure 5.5 illustrates the basic concept of social exchange theory.

Confirmation and Disconfirmation

Confirmation behaviors play an essential role in relationships. Confirmation describes all the actions that allow another person to feel accepted, appreciated, and valued as a unique individual. **Disconfirmation** encompasses the actions that do the opposite: reduce someone's status as a genuine, significant human being. "Confirmation is viewed as the pivotal feature of all human interaction, a process that shapes a person's identity and causes one to feel accepted and endorsed. . . . Many researchers feel that confirmation of an individual's self-image is perhaps the most significant factor ensuring mental development and stability".[37] If we consistently encounter disconfirmation from a relational partner, not only do we experience dissatisfaction with the relationship, but we suffer serious damage to our self-esteem.

Confirmation and disconfirmation can infuse relationships in many ways aside from overt affection or personal insults. Confirmation validates a person as worthy of attention and response, while disconfirmation indicates someone is unworthy as a participant in communication.[38] A sample of confirming and disconfirming communication behaviors appears in Figure 5.6.

FIGURE 5.6 Confirming and Disconfirming Communication Behaviors.

Confirming Communication	Disconfirming Communication
Recognizing the other person fully (complete attention: direct eye contact, no iPod earbuds or other distractions, direct greeting)	Ignoring the other person
Direct responses	Dismissive comments ("Whatever.")
Valuing the person even if disagreeing with his or her ideas ("I respect the strength of your convictions, although I disagree with your point.")	Personal ridicule ("That's a stupid question.")
Respecting the other person's choice to engage in conversation	Changing the subject rather than responding
Remaining focused on the topic	Offering irrelevant comments
Acknowledging the other person's feelings or messages ("I hear the sadness in your voice.")	Denying legitimacy of the other's feelings or messages ("You have no right to feel angry," "Oh, get over it.")
Personal mode of address (calling the person by name)	Impersonal mode of address ("Hey, you!")

Rarely would a single confirming or disconfirming act make or break a relationship. The degree of relational fulfillment depends on the overall assessment of confirmation throughout the entire course of the relationship.[38] Relationships also operate along degrees of confirmation instead of totally confirming or disconfirming.[39] We need to notice the pattern of confirming and disconfirming behaviors, striving to enable others to feel valued and validated.

Assertiveness: An Essential Skill

One of the most important communication skills for improving our satisfaction with ourselves and with our relationships is **assertiveness**. It involves standing up for your own rights without stepping on the rights of others.[40] Assertiveness is both an attitude and a set of behaviors. The attitude is one of self-respect and respect for others in terms of respecting personal and interpersonal rights. The behaviors are verbal and nonverbal actions based on this attitude of mutual respect. The behaviors enable a person to express directly, stand up for, and protect his or her rights without denying others those same rights. An added aspect of assertiveness that arises out of the self-respect component is the willingness to take responsibility for one's feelings, needs, priorities, expectations, and relational approaches—not blaming others and not manipulating others through ambiguous or misleading communication.

What are these rights we've been talking about? We are talking about personal rights, such as the right to your feelings; the right to control of your time, money, property, energy, ambitions, etc.; and the right to have needs, desires, and hopes, likes, and dislikes. We are talking about the interpersonal rights of expressing feelings and needs, hopes and dreams, likes and dislikes. We are talking about being able to protect our priorities in regard to our time, money, property, energy, ambitions, and to resist pressure to set our own needs aside.

For example, I have the right to ask you to help me wash my car. You have the right to tell me that you have other things to do. If I am assertive, I will ask for help *and* be willing to hear a "no." If you are assertive, you will hear my request *and* be able to say "no" if that is your true answer.

What are the verbal and nonverbal behaviors involved? In general, the behaviors and words fit the following formula, where R = respect and S = specifics:[41]

Communicate *respect for other(s)*: tone of voice, facial expressions, body posture and selection of wording that will not push the other person away.

 Communicate *respect for self*: nonverbal expressions of immediacy, of confidence plus making "I" statements. "When such and such happens, I feel. . . ." "I need time to think about my answer to your request."

 Communicate personal responsibility by communicating about SPECIFICS—not generalities. "On Saturday I need help washing my car; would you help me?" versus "Would you do me a favor on Saturday?" "I'm sorry but I'm busy Saturday and I *cannot* help you" (specificity—clear "no") versus "Well, I'm kind of busy on Saturday" (hoping the person making the request will get the hint and let you off the hook).

Assertiveness and Aggressiveness

When we communicate assertively, we share our thoughts and feelings honestly, taking responsibility for our own behaviors, attitudes, and reactions while respecting the thoughts and feelings of others and ourselves. Assertiveness contrasts with **aggressiveness**. Aggressive communication shows disrespect for others by attacking their self-esteem. Aggressiveness personalizes matters, making the other person feel inferior and insignificant. Any conflict can turn ugly if someone criticizes the other person instead of focusing on the other person's ideas or behaviors. Typically, an aggressive communicator resorts to personal attacks, insults, or put-downs.

Assertive communication is effective because it protects the other person's self-esteem. An assertive communicator can state things quite firmly but preserves the other person's dignity. If someone attacks you, whether the attack is verbal or physical, your immediate reaction is self-defense. But if you don't fear that someone will attack you as a person, then you can engage in vigorous debate without the risk of ridicule.

Consider how you would react if your supervisor said, "You're a lazy, worthless, incompetent moron." You might launch your own barrage of insults, probably sneering and shouting your own verbal abuse in return. Put yourself in the place of the supervisor. If you were the supervisor, how would you make your message assertive but not aggressive? Answer: Focus on the performance of the employee. State your points as factual statements instead of accusations. In distinguishing the person from the behavior, remember: "Your efforts ought to be directed at solving s substantive problem, not 'taking care of' a difficult person".[42(p193)] You might explain the situation and your reaction: "The records you worked on yesterday were filed incorrectly. These kinds of errors make us look bad when the auditors request information and we can't find it." The assertive version avoids personal attacks, and it offers specific information that can open discussion. Figure 5.7 illustrates the difference between assertive and aggressive responses to the same situation.

Assertive and aggressive communication aren't the only options. **Passive communication** signals compliance—or apathy. Sometimes in the desire to be liked or to seem "easy going," we simply agree to what others suggest or command. Rather than shoulder the responsibility of getting involved or having the courage to express an opinion, we go with the flow. Passivity can come in handy, such as when you must avoid a conflict. But a pattern of passive communication, such as silent consent or never saying "no," reduces you to a

FIGURE 5.7 Assertive versus Aggressive Communication.

In this situation...	The assertive communicator would...	The aggressive communicator would...
A patient has waited more than an hour for a dental appointment and begins yelling at you, the receptionist.	Acknowledge the person's feelings and take action: "I understand your frustration. Let me see what's causing the delay and when the dentist can see you."	Shout in return, offering no concrete solution: "You have no right to yell at me. Now sit down and wait your turn!"
Your comments in a staff meeting are ignored.	Ask politely for feedback: "Could I get some input about my ideas so I know whether I'm going in the right direction?"	Make an angry comment about how your co-workers are self-centered and rude.

doormat that others can step on at will. As someone who never objects, a passive communicator becomes easy prey for manipulators.

The **passive-aggressive** communicator appears pleasantly compliant and agreeable, but expresses aggression in deceitful, backhanded, or manipulative ways. Because passive-aggression hides anger, a passive-aggressive person might go to great lengths to mask that anger, resorting to concealment or exploiting others.[43] A prime example of passive-aggressive behavior is gossiping about people behind their back, which avoids confronting someone directly (passive) while attacking them verbally (aggressive).

Learning to Be More Assertive

An important step in becoming more assertive is to take responsibility for yourself and your actions. Recognize how many times you blame external conditions for what happens to you.[44] Example: Look at your past relationships and why they ended. Explain the reason in one sentence. Does the sentence start with "I"? If not, see if you can change it so that it does. Instead of "He didn't understand me," try "I seem to choose men who do not understand me" or "I couldn't seem to make myself understood." Include active verbs instead of using language that casts you only as a victim. Instead of "I am destined to have nasty supervisors at work," try "I keep having per-sonality clashes with my supervisors." These I-statements make you a full participant in the relationship, recognizing that you always contribute something to a relationship's prosperity or poverty. I-statements don't assign blame, but instead distribute responsibility more fairly among the relationship partners.[42]

Children always seem to know what they feel: sad, happy, angry. Thus they can more easily and honestly express themselves. It takes only a split second to ask yourself: "What am I feeling right now?" If we would do this before starting any kind of communication with a relational partner, we would save a lot of wasted energy and misdirected emotion.[44] Assertiveness requires us to tune into our emotions. Take time to listen within, to be aware and responsible for your own feelings. Do not use this time to set up your "arguments" that you want to "win." Use the time to really listen to yourself and to consider how best to express the feelings you are becoming aware of. The word "best" is used in terms of getting your feelings across—not in the sense of how well put or how good they will sound. Assertiveness thrives in a spirit of openness for expression of feelings. Relational partners should agree to be as open as possible to encourage assertive communication. If only one partner shares deeply, that partner often develops negative feelings of having to carry the relationship alone.

Try to share the awareness of self that you developed while tuning into your feelings. Avoid intellectualizing ("As Freud stated..."), generalization

("I'm sort of unhappy with our relationship"), labels ("We have a co-dependent relationship"), and accusations ("The problem with you is…"). Stay in the first person as much as possible ("I," "me," "my") because you can speak with authority about your own feelings and perspective. Own your feelings and your perceptions—as viewpoints, not as the ultimate truth.

Development of an assertive attitude can be approached by focusing on the word "respect," and then working, perhaps with a therapist, on the blocks to self-respect or respect for others. Also, in basic learning theory "feelings follow doing," so if you work on learning the skills of assertive behavior, you should begin to "feel" more assertive.

Assertive behaviors can be learned as any skill is learned because they are simply a set of personal and interpersonal skills—by guided practice. Working with other people on practicing these interpersonal skills is the best way to hone them. Start with small, simple things. Begin by making an assertive request to a friend instead of trying immediately to accomplish a monumental task such as "I'll fix my relationship with my mother."

Recognizing Perception Errors

Some recurrent communication patterns can threaten relationships, so it pays to note what they are before they pose a problem. In Chapter 9 we dealt with overattribution, the tendency to explain all of someone's behaviors and orientations as resulting from only a few characteristics. A related problem can plague relationships. **Fundamental attribution error** assumes the causes of behavior lie within someone's internal character rather than in particular situations.[45] In relationships, fundamental attribution error would lead someone to believe his or her partner acts a certain way "because that's the way men are" or "it's in her nature to be disagreeable." This kind of thinking is an error because it ignores the situational factors that might cause people to behave in particular ways. If all relational behaviors stem from an inaccessible, invariant "nature," "essence," or "character," then little hope remains for productive change.

Within any relationship, we need to recognize that some people will prefer to act in their self-interest. **Self-serving bias** describes the tendency to claim personal responsibility when things go well and blame others when problems arise. For example, partners working in online groups assign to other group members the blame for failures while taking minimal responsibility themselves.[46] Self-serving bias can affect relationships because it identifies how easily one partner can take the credit when things go well and dish out blame when things go poorly. Self-serving bias defies the basic principle that everyone in a relationship shoulders some responsibility for its maintenance and development. Excessive self-serving bias creates a relational environment like an unfair coin toss: "Heads, I win; tails, you lose." Some consistent gender differences emerge with self-serving bias.[47] Men seem to demonstrate self-serving bias more than women, possibly because men have been socially conditioned to expect success while women have been taught to distribute credit to others. Interestingly, this gender difference is less observable in closer relationships.

Talking It Out

Have you ever assumed that you should just store your relational concerns and bring them up at a later date? I know I have. The downside is that my partner is bombarded with a laundry list of problems I have been "saving" for just the right moment to dump them all out at once. **Gunnysacking**, or storing up past

Gunnysacking stores up old relationship grievances only to unleash them later when they can do more damage.

© Anke van Wyk/Shutterstock .com

grievances and then retrieving them later when trying to solve a problem, carries serious risks. Digging up the past and never letting go of negative experiences can permanently keep linking a relationship to its worst moments. Don't ignore the past, since we always can learn from it. Gunnysacking, however, simply keeps repeating the past, airing the same complaints, reliving the low points, and recycling criticisms. Gunnysacking can distract from issues in the present. It creates a relational climate that inhibits open conversation for fear of dredging up the past.

Gunnysacking steers us to a positive recommendation: Be able to share honestly what is happening when it happens. Staying in the here and now is not easy, but try to note how many times you dwell on the past or allow it to cloud the present. Think about how often you look to the future and ignore the present. Before sharing anything together, be able to say to yourself, "I am here now." Be able to tell your partner what you are really feeling. Communicating your fantasies or your façades isn't really communicating—although it may provide useful information if you are aware that they are fantasies and façades. Be aware and be able to share your awareness honestly.

Metacommunication, or communication that discusses communication, can help diagnose and deal with potential trouble spots. In metacommunication the participants step back from the relationship and make observations about it. You can use metacommunication to diagnose and address communication problems. Examples: "We need to talk about the way we display affection for each other." "It's time we considered how we gossip in front of the new employees." On more neutral or optimistic notes, metacommunication can invite joint participation in relationship-building or call attention to desirable behaviors. Examples: "Let's update our dating habits." "I appreciate the way you acknowledge me during the board meetings."

Metacommunication provides a powerful tool for maintaining, improving, or repairing relationships, but it does have disadvantages. Too much metacommunication might give the appearance of undue concern or alarm about the relationship. Just as constantly asking "Do I look OK?" probably means you don't think you look OK, frequent status reports about the relationship raise some suspicion that you might be worried. An attempt at metacommunication might encounter remarks such as: "Why can't you just be in a relationship instead of having to talk about it so much?" Metacommunication also presumes a certain degree of commitment to examining the relationship critically. Not everyone will be eager to examine his or her own conduct in a relationship.

Emotional Intelligence

Unlike the intellectual intelligence supposedly measured by IQ (intelligence quotient) test scores, **emotional intelligence** deals with the ability to read your own and other people's feelings and respond to them appropriately. Emotional intelligence (often called EI) covers the realm of "people" skills that include the ability to get along with others, be attuned to their needs and desires, and care about them as human beings. In addition, EI encompasses understanding and appropriately enacting your own emotions. Since emotional intelligence can be improved, we will discuss ways to enhance your ability to read and respond to emotions. Developing greater insight about your own emotions has important benefits. "This is because intrapersonal EI (related to understanding emotions in oneself and emotion regulation) should promote stress management and adaptive coping".[48] Interpersonally, EI can improve your ability to form social networks and avoid negative peer pressure.[49] Overall, EI can assist with developing healthy methods of expressing emotions rather than lashing out at others or feeling emotionally overwhelmed.[50]

The interpersonal side of EI involves developing greater **empathy**, which we defined in Chapter 2 as the ability to understand a situation from someone else's viewpoint. EI, however, adds the intrapersonal dimension of reading and adapting to your own emotions. Let's begin with interpersonal EI.

Interpersonal Emotional Intelligence

Raising your EI involves listening to *how* something is communicated, not just *what* someone says. As people cultivate their interpersonal EI, they become more perceptive of subtle vocal and nonverbal qualities that might indicate sarcasm, fear, disappointment, anger, or other feelings. To develop greater sensitivity to vocal and physical indicators of emotion, try taking the same sentence, such as "You are doing a wonderful job," and say the sentence aloud repeatedly. Use exactly the same words, but each time try to convey a different emotion by tone of voice and facial expressions. Pay careful attention to the vocal inflections you use and how you look when expressing the sentence with anger, sarcasm, surprise, admiration, and other emotions. If you practice this exercise with a partner, both of you can improve your "people-reading" skills by trying to guess the emotion the other person is communicating.

Consider the following case study related to EI. An elderly patient's wife has been in the emergency room waiting area for more than an hour while her husband has been treated. She begins to sob and moans, "Sixty years of marriage and we've never been apart more than a day. What are they doing to him? Where is my husband?" You are a nurse on duty and hear her. Unfortunately, you have no idea where the gentleman is or what procedures are being performed. What should you do?

Whenever you encounter someone having a difficult experience, *avoid* saying, "I know just how you feel." You probably do not know exactly how the person feels unless you had exactly the same personal history and underwent the identical experience. In this case, first remember the value of honesty. You don't know how the woman feels, so don't claim that you do. You also currently lack access to the information she wants, so don't offer potentially false reassurances such as "I'm sure he's fine and nothing is wrong." The best reaction would be to give her an opportunity to air her concerns. You do know how frightening uncertainty can be, so acknowledge her fear: "I know it's awful to be away from someone you love. But you're not alone—I'm here for you." If it is within your authority, offer to check on the patient's status so you can at least let the spouse know what is happening. Sometimes an emotionally intelligent response simply means being there for another person, validating his or her feelings instead of forming opinions and drawing conclusions.

Intrapersonal Emotional Intelligence

EI is not just another trendy, "touchy-feely" idea likely to vanish soon. The level of EI can predict how people will fare throughout life. In a famous experiment known as the marshmallow test,[51] a group of 4-year-old children were asked to wait until someone returned from running an errand. The children who waited the 15–20 minutes would receive a reward of two marshmallows. The children who could not wait would get only one marshmallow right away. Essentially the study focused on the effect of controlling immediate impulses and delaying gratification. The study followed up with the same children when they were graduating from high school. The results were astounding.

The children who waited for the two marshmallows were better students, with 13 percent higher SAT scores and more positive evaluations from parents than their one-marshmallow counterparts. The children who delayed gratification at age 4 were, a dozen or more years later, more assertive, better adjusted, more socially functional, better organized, better at performing under pressure, more self-confident, and more persistent than those who settled for one marshmallow. The lesson: Controlling impulses has big payoffs.[52]

Before proceeding, answer the following questions:

- Do you often blurt out things without thinking?
- Do other people consider you hot-headed or accuse you of overreacting?
- Do you often say things off the cuff that you regret later?
- Do you insist on seeing immediate results?
- Do other people often tell you to calm down or keep quiet?
- Do you interrupt people to offer advice or instructions?
- Do you feel impatient while other people are talking, feeling as if you must express yourself now or burst?

The more you answered "yes" to questions such as these, the more you may need to develop EI to harness your emotions. Note the term here: harness, not stifle or squelch your emotions. EI doesn't call for inhibiting your feelings. It suggests knowing what they are and making conscious decisions about expressing, not expressing, goals of expressing, and modes of expressing those feelings. Each of the questions deals with a behavior characteristic of people who have trouble regulating their emotions and allowing others to express their feelings fully.[53] Self-control plays a major role in emotional intelligence. Again, we are not talking about self-censorship but how and when to express feelings. Intra-personal EI helps in managing one's own emotions. Research on domestic violence reveals that "deficits in emotional intelligence are related to propensity for abusiveness in batterers and the general population".[54(p265)] Overall, emotional intelligence consists of managing one's own emotions, understanding other people's feelings, and offering appropriate responses.

Relationships Through Electronic Channels

Thanks to social networking technology, our relationship connections can extend to more people and we can make quicker, more frequent contact. Instead of simply displaying information as a tradition web page does, social networking enables users to interact with each other and influence the content of web-based material. Computer-mediated communication or CMC (including e-mail and instant messaging) as well as other electronic tools such as cell phones (including text messaging) have certainly changed the way we interact, but they have not eliminated many foundational considerations of relating interpersonally.

The traditional models of relationship stages were developed as ways to describe face-to-face interactions. Some concern has emerged, however, that "the social patterns for modeling relationship behavior have been disrupted".[55(p737)] If social networking makes us less aware of ways to cultivate trust and gradually build a relationship's intimacy, then our relationship skills may suffer. We still need to distinguish types of relationships, which will require tools more nuanced than simply calling everyone a "friend." How many of actor Ashton Kutcher's more than one million followers on Twitter actually qualify as his reliable, trustworthy friends?

Social networking tools can work well for adding dimensions to existing relationships and for finding some information about people you might consider interacting with.[56] Various technological tools can augment face-to-face relationships, but they might not provide suitable alternatives to direct interaction. Typically, "relationships that develop online are not likely to result in greater intimacy than the levels experienced by individuals in their face-to-face relationships".[57(p760)] That doesn't mean you should scrap your electronic devices and live in the Stone Age. Technological tools can augment relationships—but only if used wisely. Let's apply our communication knowledge to electronic interactions.

One study of social networking sites and uncertainty reduction found that individuals use all three types of information-seeking strategies (passive, active, and interactive) to reduce uncertainty and seek information about others online; however, the active strategy is used the least.[58] This makes sense when we think about how we use the passive strategy (we look at other people's profiles and most recent activity), and we also use the interactive strategy (we chat and send messages), but we don't generally use other people's profiles to find out information about our friends. What other concepts do you believe still apply when developing and maintaining relationships via social networking sites?

While social networking sites, e-mail, and texting can certainly present problems in relationships due to the lack of nonverbal cues and possibilities of deception, we can use techniques to promote interpersonal relationships instead of the impersonal exchanges typically associated with mediated communication.[59] First, let's consider how to evoke immediacy. The fact that someone responds to a message at all increases immediacy. How many times have you sent a message and never heard back? How does the lack of reply affect your assessment of the other person's competence or caring? You might assign credibility differently if you specifically asked for a reply and did not get one. Other immediacy strategies that are effective in face-to-face situations can help in electronic communication as well. These mediated immediacy behaviors include using personal examples, addressing receivers by first name, careful use of humor, appropriate self-disclosure, and individualizing your messages (almost everyone quickly deletes a mass e-mail "form letter"). Other strategies to increase perception of immediacy include using of **emoticons** (symbols that convey emotional states or moods), varying the color or font of your messages, not typing in all capital letters, using an informal "friendly" tone, avoiding flaming (hostile personal insults), and keeping your messages brief.[59]

Morality Matters

Much concern has arisen about the dangers of online relationships. Teachers worry that adolescents are not prepared to handle the potentials for abuse that lurk when developing relationships online.[60] Occasional horror stories of cyberstalkers warn us that the Internet can make deception easier and escalate relationships too quickly. Working with classmates, develop a set of suggested guidelines for appropriate online conduct when using social networking sites (such as sites for finding friends, dating, and sharing interests). How closely do your guidelines for proper online relationship conduct resemble your principles for proper in-person relationships?

E-mail, social networking sites, and other forms of CMC often offer at least one advantage when developing relationships. That advantage is time. When using these channels, the sender (and receiver) are given time and the opportunity to plan responses to others—you can truly think through what you would like to say and how you would like to say it.[61] When considering the importance of confirmation, displaying assertiveness, and many other factors we have previously discussed, extra time could be useful in managing relationships. If you have ever received an e-mail (or Facebook message for that matter) that caught you off guard, or was more than a simple request, you probably took a little time to think through exactly how you wanted to respond. Taking a bit of time to craft your message—instead of hastily firing off a possibly offensive reply—displays emotional intelligence. Your extra effort can create a response more properly adapted to the person and situation, and it could save the relationship from unnecessary anguish.

Our discussion of electronic channels must also consider the role of texting. Many people would likely agree that relationships would be "lacking" something without the ability to text. Research does show that "text messages are being used to commence, advance, maintain, or otherwise influence interpersonal relationships"; approximately half of text messages are used for relationship maintenance.[62(p698)] Many people perceive texting "as a private and direct communication channel" since texting allows you to separate yourself from those in your immediate physical context.[62(p703)] If you have felt that others around you should not hear your conversation and you still wanted to connect with your relational partner, you probably chose to send a text.

Text messages might seem private, but their content can find its way to public forums such as Web pages and social networking sites. Recent cases of **sexting**, or sending explicit sexual images electronically, have led to serious legal and personal consequences. Unauthorized posting or distribution of this content has triggered criminal prosecutions, lawsuits, physical attacks, and lasting emotional pain.[63] The sexting scandals teach two lessons: (1) Don't assume any form of electronic communication will always remain private. (2) Consider the consequences of "going public" with someone else's private information.

As we have learned throughout this chapter, interpersonal relationships require continuous effort regardless of whether they are developed face-to-face or via an electronic channel. This chapter has provided you with a foundational understanding of what to look for when developing healthy relationships.

CONFLICT AND NEGOTIATION

When was the last time you saw a reality TV show or movie that included at least one conflict scene? You probably did not need to think too hard to recall several examples. It seems that many of us are drawn to these conflicts and we can't wait to see who will be yelling and cursing in the next episode of our favorite reality show or who finally "wins" the "fight" on any number of TV dramas.

Why are we so interested in conflict? A few reasons explain our focus on conflict.[64] First, war and violence have been prevalent during the twentieth and twenty-first centuries. From World War I to more recent wars in Iraq and Afghanistan, conflict has been a part of our present and past. Second, there is great concern about scarcity of our planet's resources. This crisis not only evokes strong feelings and emotions, but it also promotes competition and fear. Third, diversity increasingly surrounds us in our workplaces, homes, schools, and communities. While this diversity carries enormous benefits, differing opinions and lifestyles raise the potential for conflict.

In addition to world trends, the mediaframes our views and understanding of conflict. From TV to video games, we have created a world that appears to be full of conflict and competition.[65] Because of all of these factors, we often see "social and political life as saturated with difference and dissension".[64(p3)]

While we may be drawn to and surrounded by conflict, we often recognize this conflict as "difficult, complex, and frequently mismanaged".[66(p3)] Despite the fact that conflict and competition can be frightening, it is unavoidable. In fact, some scholars suggest that it is not only inevitable but also necessary in human relationships.[66] Conflict can cause damage, but we must separate violent attacks from productive disagreements. In work groups, for example, "while relationship conflicts based on personality clashes and interpersonal dislike are detrimental to group functioning, task conflicts based on disagreements regarding the specific task content are beneficial in many situations".[67(p287)]

This inevitability of conflict explains why this chapter talks about "managing" instead of "eliminating" conflict. The choices we make concerning conflict management will undoubtedly affect our personal relationships and the greater society. The way we handle conflict can prove helpful or harmful to our relationships. This is why we must reflect on our individual experiences with conflict and work to develop effective strategies for managing conflict—even recognizing it as positive and constructive.

You might be asking yourself: "What is this thing called conflict that is so prevalent and what causes it?" or "Can't I just pretend I don't know something that I think might cause a conflict between me and a friend?" In the next few sections, we will address these questions and more.

What Is Conflict?

So, you and a friend are talking about your differing religious beliefs, or you and your parents are brainstorming different gifts that you might like to receive for your birthday. Are these examples of conflict? Probably not, although if the conversations escalate and both parties in the conversation begin to argue over competing views, it could become a conflict. **Conflict** can be defined as "an expressed struggle between at least two interdependent parties who perceive incompatible goals, scarce rewards, and interference from the other party in achieving their goals".[68(p201)] This definition recognizes that two people must be aware of the problem for conflict to occur, and it emphasizes the interconnectedness of both people. We can understand conflict as "a difference that matters".[69(p11)] This definition allows us to focuses on the difference of opinions and beliefs that we often openly see during a conflict.

Now that we know what conflict is, we need to break it down a little further. You probably know from experience that conflict can be extremely destructive to a relationship. This **destructive conflict** usually "results in a worse situation and sometimes, harm to the participants".[66(p4)] But another type of conflict might actually enhance a relationship. This type of healthy, or **productive conflict**, allows people involved to move "toward resolution" and protects the "psychological and relational health of the participants".[66(p4)] Productive

FIGURE 5.8 Four Ways to Seek Productive Conflict.

Suggestion	Example
1. Ask deep questions about conflict experiences.	Why are we fighting? What are my beliefs and goals? What are the key negotiation principles I should remember? NOT: What's wrong with you?
2. Learn from your own and other people's conflicts.	I will focus on understanding this and not brush it under the rug or save it until later.
3. Make understanding conflicts a priority.	What has happened in the past that may have started this pattern? What happens with me during conflict?
4. Manage conflicts by continuously examining and inquiring.	How might forgiveness change our relationship? How might I manage my communication skills to prevent this from happening in the future?

conflict may benefit the relationship and the people in it in several ways: (1) Conflict can create energy and motivation; (2) conflict can bring out different viewpoints and increase creativity; and (3) conflict can help people understand the argument and themselves as communicators.[70]

So, what is required if we seek to have and manage productive conflict in our lives? Four suggestions can help you to continuously seek productive conflict and reduce destructive conflict.[66] Figure 5.8 identifies these suggestions and provides an example of self-talk that might be helpful in achieving this.

Seeking productive conflict will not be a one-time event, nor is it something that you can do without hard work. As you notice from the previous suggestions, we should be asking deep questions about the nature of the conflict, prioritizing conflict and concerns, continuously learning, and continuously examining and inquiring about conflict and how it can best be managed. You will want to pay attention to your own needs and tendencies as well as those of your relational partners. This takes time and commitment—and of course, effective communication!

Hopefully, you have chosen to invest the effort required for productive conflict; however, if it were as simple as choosing one type over another, we certainly would not be spending so much time studying this material. As with conversations, actually managing conflict in the moment is extremely difficult. We are often so emotionally invested and care so much that we forget that the other person is a human being and we use hurtful words, react inappropriately, and make the situation much worse than it originally was. The next section is designed to give you a few pointers for managing conflict and a strong foundation for understanding what is happening in that difficult moment.

How Can Conflict Be Managed?

Before we consider how to manage conflict, it will be important for us to openly recognize the misconceptions that often make conflict even worse. The follow examples illustrate common myths concerning communication and conflict:[71]

- Myth: "If I communicate more, I will clarify everything."
- Myth: "I don't care what people say, there is an easy solution."
- Myth: "I'll just change what I am doing and it should fix everything."
- Myth: "If everything seems peaceful, that must mean there is no conflict."

Many of us have thought or said the previous myths. We need to consider why each of points is in fact a myth.[66]

- First, as we noted in Chapter 1, "communication concerns quality, not quantity." The type of communication matters more than the amount of communication. Therefore, more communication is not always better and in fact sometimes makes conflicts worse.
- Second, conflicts are often deeply rooted in historical patterns and cultural beliefs. Even when we understand a conflict and work toward an agreement, the conflict does not always disappear. Furthermore, it takes time and hard work to move through many conflicts. Even with hard work, there are still times when you may need to "agree to disagree."
- Third, initially conflicts need to be understood. The understanding should always come before the action. Simply changing behavior will likely not address the root of the problem.
- Fourth, people often choose to avoid conflict or continue to be peaceful around one another even if there is a problem. This is why we must continue to utilize dialogue throughout relationships.

Now we know that we shouldn't handle conflict based on our assumptions and societal myths. The question becomes: How should we handle conflict? We will now focus on foundational conflict management styles, influential factors, and suggested ways to negotiate a conflict.

Conflict Management Styles

Now that we have a foundation for seeking productive conflict, let's consider five conflict management styles.[72] Each style is associated with its degree of cooperativeness or assertiveness and its concern for self or others. Figure 5.9 contains a breakdown of each style. We can use these management styles to improve our understanding of how we individually tend to handle conflict situations.[66] While we may tend to prefer a particular conflict management style, it is also important to remain flexible when choosing a style to address a specific situation.[73] Being an effective communicator often requires you to use different styles of conflict management. As you consider each of the following styles, try to determine which style of conflict you use most frequently, but also consider which styles you might use in specific situations.

Let's imagine that you and your best friend have just discovered that both of you are attracted to the same person—we'll name the object of your affection Jordan. You really like Jordan and think there is potential for a relationship, but you also now know that your best friend feels the same way about Jordan. Both of you want to date Jordan. This has caused a lot of tension. Your friend suggests that the two of you talk. Assuming that Jordan likes both of you, what should you do? This will all depend on the style of conflict management that you choose. Let's look at the options.

Avoiding: You could choose a style that is not assertive or cooperative. Avoiding can be described as trying to ignore the fact that there is a problem. It is the most passive style of conflict management. You might say to yourself, "I'll just pretend that I don't know, and we will just let it blow over." You might choose to simply not respond to the request for conversation, or you may try to delay the conversation. Both of these strategies would suggest that you are avoiding the conflict. The pro of utilizing this style might be that you

FIGURE 5.9 Styles of Conflict Management.

Sources: Folger, Poole, & Stutman;[73] Rahim, Antonioni, & Psenicka (2001).[74]

can sidestep confrontation for the moment, but of course the con is that you are also eliminating the chance of working this out. Avoiding conflict is commonly recognized as a no-win style, and as you can see, it reflects low concern for your own needs or the needs of other people.

Accommodating: Your second style option is not assertive, but it is highly cooperative. Accommodating involves going along with what others want, just to appease them and keep everything conflict free. You might agree to the meeting and tell your friend, "I'll just let you date Jordan, you deserve this opportunity more than I do." If you don't openly give in to what your friend wants, you may find yourself continuously apologizing or excessively using disclaimers. Any of these strategies may be used to manage conflict through accommodation. The pro of accommodating might be that you make your friend happy, but the con is that you completely abandon your own needs and desires. Accommodating is commonly known as a lose-win style. It allows your friend to reap all the benefits, but you leave empty-handed.

Competing: Your third option is very assertive, but not very cooperative. Competing can be described as looking to achieve your own goals. If you choose to compete, you will likely agree to the meeting and try to use power, status, or force to convey your ideas. If you think or say something like, "We'll see who wins Jordan over," you are likely competing. The pro of competing might be that you get want you want, but the con is that you may hurt or silence others in doing so. Competing is commonly known as a win-lose style. It allows you to gain, but at someone else's expense.

Compromising: Your fourth option is moderately assertive and moderately cooperative. Compromising can be described as giving something to get something in return. If you choose to compromise, you might continuously restate your desires and summarize your friend's ideas. You might make statements like, "If you are willing to let me go out with Jordan on Friday, then I will let you go out with Jordan on Saturday." The pro of compromising is that both parties have some of their needs and desires met, and it is a quick way to come to a decision. Conversely, the con is that both parties have some needs and desires that remain unmet. For this reason, compromising is commonly known as a lose-lose style. Everybody sacrifices something in the process.

Collaborating: Your final option is highly assertive and highly cooperative. Collaborating can be described as seeking a mutually agreeable solution. You may find yourself deeply exploring a disagreement to see each other's perspectives and then openly sharing all concerns and desires in hopes that the underlying issues can be discovered and an appropriate solution can be implemented. Suppose as a result of dialogue with your friend, you find that one of you wants Jordan as a date to a specific formal occasion while the other is interested in pursuing an ongoing romance. By sharing the rationales behind your attraction for Jordan, you can help each other. You might encourage Jordan to accompany your friend to the formal event, and during that event your friend could note how eligible you might be for longer-term companionship. The pro of collaborating is that everyone is validated and consensus is reached. The con of collaborating is the time and effort required. If managed effectively, collaborating is commonly known as a win-win style. All par-ties have their needs met.

So, it is time to choose your style. Figure 5.10 summarizes the five styles. Which approach do you normally use? Do you use this style in all situations? Let's consider a few more factors that may affect or confirm—or challenge—your decisions.

FIGURE 5.10 Comparison of Conflict Management Styles.

Style	Approach	Explanation	Advantages	Drawbacks
Collaborating	Win/win	Seeks mutually beneficial outcomes, inclusive toward others; cooperative partnership	High level of buy-in from all participants; usually yields mutually satisfying outcomes	Time-consuming; requires mutual trust (rare and challenging to develop); requires willingness to share power
Competing	Win/lose	Zero-sum mentality: benefits to one party must come at the expense of others; style often involves dominating or coercing others	Maximizes personal benefits; can motivate high performance to "defeat" competitors	Encourages cutthroat practices; sets up conflict as antagonistic
Accommodating	Lose/win	Voluntary surrender; giving in to someone else	Maximizes generosity toward others; effective as showing obedience	May be seen as weakness; minimizes chance of personal gain; presumes other party is correct
Compromising	Lose/lose	Each party sacrifices something in order to gain something else; "give a little to get a little"	Does not insist on total "victory" for satisfactory outcome; highly flexible as each party can adjust what it gives/gets	All parties may remain dis-satisfied; all parties must be willing to sacrifice; high degree of compromise may equal capitulation (e.g., appeasement of Hitler prior to WWII)
Avoiding	Don't play	Refusal to acknowledge or address conflict	Prevents pain and time expenditure of working through conflict	Fails to address root causes of conflict; unaddressed conflict can smolder and intensify

Source: Covey (1989).

ENDNOTES

1. Riesman, D., Glazer, N., & Denney, R. (1970). *The lonely crowd: A study of the changing American characte*r (Abridged ed.). New Haven: Yale University Press.

2. Spira, M. (2006). Mapping your future—A proactive approach to aging. *Journal of Gerontological Social Work, 47*(1/2), 71–87.

3. Pines, A. M., & Aronson, E. (1981). *Burnout: From tedium to personal growth.* New York: Free Press.

4. Luft, J. (1970). *Group processes: An introduction to group dynamics* (2nd ed.). Palo Alto, CA: National Press Books.

5. Won-Doornink, M. J. (1985). Self-disclosure and reciprocity in conversation: A cross-national study. *Social Psychology Quarterly, 48,* 97–107.

6. Horenstein, V. D.-P., & Downey, J. L. (2003). A cross-cultural investigation of self-disclosure. *North American Journal of Psychology, 5,* 373–386.

7. Sallinen-Kuparinen, A., McCroskey, J. C., & Richmond, V. P. (1991). Willingness to communicate, communication apprehension, introversion, and self-reported communication competence: Finnish and American comparisons. *Communication Research Reports, 8,* 55–64.

8. Plog, S. C. (1965). The disclosure of self in the United States and Germany. *Journal of Social Psychology, 65,* 193–205.

9. Kito, M. (2005). Self-disclosure in romantic relationships and friendships among American and Japanese college students. *Journal of Social Psychology, 145,* 127–140.

10. Yum, Y.-O., & Hara, K. (2005). Computer-mediated relationship development: A cross-cultural comparison. *Journal of Computer-Mediated Communication, 11,* 133–152.

11. Little, L. (2005, March). Leadership communication and the Johari window. *Administrator, 24*(3), 4.

12. Won-Doornink, M. J. (1979). On getting to know you: The association between the stage of a relationship and reciprocity of self-disclosure. *Journal of Experimental Social Psychology, 15,* 229–241.

13. Altman, I., & Taylor, D. (1973). *Social penetration: The development of interpersonal relationships.* New York: Holt.

14. Dunleavy, K., & Booth-Butterfield, M. (2009). Idio-matic communication in the stages of coming together and falling apart. *Communication Quarterly, 57*(4), 416–432.

15. Aune, K. S., Buller, D. B., & Aune, R. K. (1996). Display rule development in romantic relationships: Emotion management and perceived appropriateness of emotions across relationship stages. *Human Communication Research, 23,* 115–145.

16. Samter, W. (2003). Friendship interaction skills across the life-span. In J. O. Greene & B. R. Burleson (Eds.), *Handbook of communication and social interaction skills* (pp. 637–684). Mahwah, NJ: Lawrence Erlbaum Associates.

17. Parrott, R., Lemieux, R., Harris, T., & Foreman, L. (1997). Interfacing interpersonal and mediated communication: Use of active and strategic self-disclosure in personal ads. *Southern Communication Journal, 62,* 319–332.

18. Stokes, J. P. (1987). The relation of loneliness and self-disclosure. In V. J. Derlega & J. H. Berg (Eds.), *Self-disclosure: Theory, research, and therapy* (pp. 175–202). New York: Plenum.

19. Mars vs. Venus: The gender gap in health (2010, January). *Harvard Men's Health Watch, 14*(6), 1–5.

20. Henley, N., & Freeman, J. (1995). The sexual politics of interpersonal behavior. In J. Freeman (Ed.), *Women: A feminist perspective* (5th ed.). Palo Alto, CA: Mayfield. Retrieved March 28, 2010, from http://www.jofreeman.com/womensociety/personal.htm

21. Lanutti, P. J., & Strauman, E. C. (2006). Classroom communication: The influence of instructor self-disclosure on student evaluation. *Communication Quarterly, 54,* 89–99.

22. Abell, J., Locke, A., Condor, S., Gibson, S., & Stevenson, C. (2006). Trying similarity, doing difference: The role of interviewer self-disclosure in interview talk with young people. *Qualitative Research, 6,* 221–244.

23. Knapp, M. L., & Vangelisti, A. L. (2005). *Interpersonal communication and human relationships* (5th ed.). Boston: Allyn and Bacon.

24. Dindia, K., & Baxter, L. A. (1987). Strategies for maintaining and repairing marital relationships. *Journal of Social and Personal Relationships, 4,* 143–158.

25. Punyanunt-Carter, N. M. (2006). Evaluating the effects of attachment styles on relationship maintenance behaviors in father-daughter relationships. *Family Journal, 14,* 135–143.

26. Dindia, K. (2003). Definitions and perspectives on relational maintenance communication. In D. J. Canary & M. Dainton (Eds.), *Maintaining relationships through communication: Relational, contextual, and cultural variables* (pp. 1–30). Mahwah, NJ: Lawrence Erlbaum Associates.

27. Canary, D. J., Stafford, L., Hause, K. S., & Wallace, L. A. (1993). An inductive analysis of relational maintenance strategies: Comparisons among lovers, relatives, friends, and others. *Communication Research Reports, 10,* 5–14.

28. Baxter, L. A., & Montgomery, B. M. (1996). *Relating: Dialogues and dialectics.* New York: Guilford Press.

29. Baxter, L. A. (1990). Dialectical contradictions in relationship development. *Journal of Social and Personal Relationships, 7,* 69–88.

30. Montgomery, B. M., & Baxter, L. A. (1998). *Dialectical approaches to studying personal relationships.* Mahwah, NJ: Lawrence Erlbaum Associates.

32. Stuart, R. B. (1980). *Helping couples change: A social learning approach to marital therapy.* New York: Guilford Press.

33. Sabatelli, R. M., & Shehan, C. L. (2004). Exchange and resource theories. In P. Boss, W. J. Doherty, R. LaRossa, W. Schumm, & S. K. Steinmetz (Eds.), *Sourcebook of family theories and methods: A contextual approach* (pp. 385–411). New York: Springer.

34. Sabatelli, R. M. (1984). The marital comparison level index: A measure for assessing outcomes relative to expectations. *Journal of Marriage and the Family, 46,* 651–662.

35. McDonagh, E. L. (1982). Social exchange and moral development: Dimensions of self, self-image, and identity. *Human Relations, 35,* 659–673.

36. Stafford, L. (2008). Social exchange theories. In L. A. Baxter & D. O. Braithwaite (Eds.), *Engaging theories in interpersonal communication: Multiple perspectives* (pp. 377–389). Thousand Oaks, CA: Sage.

37. Turner, J. S. (1996). *Encyclopedia of relationships across the lifespan.* Westport, CT: Greenwood Press.

38. Dailey, R. M. (2006). Confirmation in parent-adolescent relationships and adolescent openness: Toward extending confirmation theory. *Communication Monographs, 73,* 434–458.

39. Wood, J. T. (2006). *Communication in our lives* (4th ed.). Belmont, CA: Thomson Wadsworth.

40. Davis, M., Eshelman, E. R., & McKay, M. (2008). *The relaxation and stress reduction workbook* (6th ed.). Oakland, CA: New Harbinger Publications.

41. Fox-Hines, R. (1992). Being assertive—not passive or aggressive. In J. N. Gardner & A. J. Jewler (Eds.), *Your college experience* (pp. 295–305). Belmont, CA: Wadsworth.

42. Alberti, R., & Emmons, M. (2001). *Your perfect right: Assertiveness and equality in your life and relationships* (8th ed.). Atascadero, CA: Impact Publishers.

43. Oberlin, L. H., & Murphy, T. (2005). *Overcoming passive-aggression: How to stop hidden anger from spoiling your relationships, career and happiness.* New York: Marlowe.

44. Gilles, J. (1974). *My needs, your needs, our needs.* New York: Doubleday.

45. Jones, E. E., & Harris, V. A. (1967). The attribution of attitudes. *Journal of Experimental Social Psychology, 3,* 1–24.

46. Walther, J. B., & Bazarova, N. N. (2007). Misattribution in virtual groups: The effects of member distribution on self-serving bias and partner blame. *Human Communication Research, 33,* 1–26.

47. Sedikides, C., Campbell, W. K., Reeder, G. D., & Elliot, A. J. (1998). The self-serving bias in relational context. *Journal of Personality and Social Psychology, 74,* 378–386.

48. Austin, E. J., & Saklofske, D. H. (2010). Introduction to the special issue. *Australian Journal of Psychology, 62*(1), 1–4.

49. Hogan, M. J., Parker, J. D. A., Wiener, J., Watters, C., Wood, L. M., & Oke, A. (2010). Academic success in adolescence: Relationships among verbal IQ, social support and emotional intelligence. *Australian Journal of Psychology, 62*(1), 30–41.

50. Downey, L. A., Johnston, P. J., Hansen, K., Birney, J., & Stough, C. (2010). Investigating the mediating effects of emotional intelligence and coping on problem behaviours in adolescents. *Australian Journal of Psychology, 62*(1), 20–29.

51. Goleman, D. (1995). *Emotional intelligence.* New York: Bantam.

52. Mischel, W., Shoda, Y., & Rodriguez, L. M. (1989). Delay of gratification in children. *Science, 244,* 933–938.

53. Mayer, J. D., & Salovey, P. (1997). What is emotional intelligence? In P. Salovey & D. Sluyter (Eds.), *Emotional development and emotional intelligence: Implications for educators* (pp. 3–31). New York: Basic Books.

54. Winters, J., Clift, R. J. W., & Dutton, D. G. (2004). An exploratory study of emotional intelligence and domestic abuse. *Journal of Family Violence, 19*, 255–267.

55. Barnes, S. (2009). Relationship networking: Society and education. *Journal of Computer-Mediated Communication, 14*(3), 735–742.

56. Subrahmanyam, K., & Greenfield, P. (2008). Online communication and adolescent relationships. *The Future of Children, 18*(1), 119–146.

57. Scott, V., Mottarella, K., & Lavooy, M. (2006). Does virtual intimacy exist? A brief exploration into reported levels of intimacy in online relationships. *CyberPsychology and Behavior, 9*(6), 759–761.

58. Antheunis, M. L., Valkenburg, P. M., & Peter, J. (2010). Getting acquainted through social network sites: Testing a model of online uncertainty reduction and social attraction. *Computers in Human Behavior, 26*(1), 100–109.

59. Waldeck, J., Kearney, P., & Plax, T. (2001). Teacher e-mail message strategies and students' willingness to communicate online. *Journal of Applied Research, 29*, 54–70.

60. Chou, C., & Peng, H. (2007). Net-friends: Adolescents' attitudes and experiences vs. teachers' concerns. *Computers in Human Behavior, 23*, 2394–2413.

61. Shonbeck, K. (2006). Thoughts on CMC by an e-mailer, IMer, blog reader, and Facebooker. In K. M. Galvin & P. J. Cooper (Eds.), *Making connections: Readings in relational communication* (4th ed.; pp. 372–378). Los Angeles: Roxbury.

62. Pettigrew, J. (2009). Text messaging and connectedness within close interpersonal relationships. *Marriage and Family Review, 45*, 697–715.

63. Chalfen, R. (2009). 'It's only a picture': Sexting, 'smutty' snapshots and felony charges. *Visual Studies, 24*(3), 258–268.

64. Melchin, K. & Picard, C. (2008). *Transforming conflict through insight.* Toronto: University of Toronto Press.

65. Brigg, M. (2008). *The new politics of conflict resolution: Responding to difference.* New York: Palgrave Macmillan.

66. Kellett, P. M., & Dalton, D. G. (2001). *Managing conflict in a negotiated world: A narrative approach to achieving dialogue and change.* Thousand Oaks, CA: Sage.

67. Jehn, K., Chadwick, C., & Thatcher, S. (1997). To agree or not to agree: The effects of value congruence, individual demographic dissimilarity, and conflict on workgroup outcomes. *International Journal of Conflict Management, 8*(4), 287–305.

68. Hocker, J. L., & Wilmot, W. W. (2006) Collaborative negotiation. In K. Galvin & P. Cooper (Eds.), *Making connections* (4th ed.; pp. 201–208). Los Angeles: Roxbury.

69. LeBaron, M. (2003). *Bridging cultural conflicts: A new approach for a changing world.* San Francisco, CA: Jossey-Bass.

70. Walton, R. E. (1987). *Managing conflict: Interpersonal dialogue and third-party roles* (2nd ed.). Reading, MA: Addison-Wesley.

71. James, J. (1996). *Thinking in the future tense: Leadership skills for a new age.* New York: Simon & Schuster.

72. Kilmann, R. H., & Thomas, K. W. (1975). Interpersonal conflict handling behavior as reflections of Jungian personality dimensions. *Psychological Reports, 37*, 971–980.

73. Folger, J. P., Poole, M. S., & Stutman, R. K. (2005). *Working through conflict: Strategies for relationships, groups, and organizations* (5th ed.). New York: HarperCollins.

74. Rahim, M., Antonioni, D., & Psenicka, C. (2001). A structural equations model of leader power, subordinates' styles of handling conflict, and job performance. *International Journal of Conflict Management, 12*(3), 191–211.

75. Covey, S. R. (1989). *The seven habits of highly effective people: Restoring the character ethic.* New York: Simon and Schuster.

Chapter 5
Interpersonal Paper

You will write a paper about some ideas/principles that you found interesting or helpful or useful in the past few weeks and share with me how they have helped your communication. Here are the instructions.

- Choose three interpersonal principles from Chapters 1-7 in the textbook
- One principle MUST reflect the experience working in your groups and explain the significance it had in the group interaction
- To support each point relate experiences you have had using these with friends, coworkers, family
- You may also use definitions from a credible source for support or interviews (personal or telephone) with family or friends that should be cited
- In the first paragraph (the introduction) make an attention-gaining statement and list the three principles to be discussed in the paper
- In the paragraphs in the body (there should be 3 – one for each principle), the first sentence should mention the principle to be discussed in that paragraph followed by support for that principle with specific personal examples, definitions, descriptions, etc.
- In the final paragraph restate the three principles, then make a strong concluding statement.
- Spelling errors and incorrect grammar will affect the grade
- Be sure to cite your sources within the paper. At least three sources must be cited as Works Cited in MLA style on a separate Works Cited page
- Wikipedia or Wikidictionary are not acceptable sources to use
- The paper should be typed with 1″ margins on all sides, a font no larger than 12 and double-spaced.
- You may reference the textbook more than once, but have 2 additional sources as well.

When ready to turn in the assignment, your paper should:
- Be double spaced
- Be free of spelling errors
- Have sources cited within the text
- Include a Works Cited on a separate page but stapled to the paper
- Have 1″ margins
- Have a 12 font
- Be stapled

GROUP COMMUNICATION

INTRODUCTION

"I hate group work!"

This statement is often heard when college students are told they will be working in groups to complete projects. The same sentiment is expressed across offices and at work sites every day. "Why can't I just do this project myself?" Dissatisfaction with working in groups is so common that the term *grouphate* was coined to describe the negative attitude toward group work.[1] If people hate working in groups so much, then why are groups so often used? The answer to the question is fairly simple: Groups outperform individuals most of the time, and groups are capable of taking on more complex tasks. In fact, many employers are willing to pay the added expense of operating a group to take advantage of a group's ability to creatively solve problems and to make high-quality decisions.

For most of us, our first exposure to groups was as early as elementary school. Perhaps we were asked to collaborate with other students to complete an in-class activity or to play on a sports team. These early exposures to groups provide us with our first instructions about how to play nicely with others, how to share, and how to get along. The collaborative learning process continues through college, where the skills being taught are more complex (e.g., conflict management, patience, and negotiation skills) and the stakes are much higher (e.g., grades in our major, grades influencing the next school we attend, financial aid, and our future professions). The stakes continue to rise in our careers. Our ability to work effectively with others affects our salaries, our upward mobility, and even our job security.

Television has capitalized on just how difficult it is to work with others, which is evidenced by the number of popular group-based reality shows. Although the subject of these shows is not directly related to the process of building an effective group or team, they do require participants to work within the framework of a group to achieve goals. For instance, teams are formed on one show to achieve business goals such as marketing and selling a product. Each group member is judged by his or her individual contribution, approaches to group collaboration, and decision making throughout the process. The selling point of such shows is not only the completion of the task at hand but also the relationships among group members. There is something enjoyable about watching how group members balance their own goals with the group goals, manage conflicts, and how they are able to succeed, or fail, under such circumstances.

Why do groups have an advantage when it comes to problem solving?
© 2008, JupiterImages Corporation.

The way we respond to groups, the roles we play, the understanding we bring to them, and the communication skills we use (or fail to use) combine to influence our group experience. Earlier in this book, we discussed the importance of using communication skills to exercise our democratic rights. Effective group communication skills allow us to foster a free flow and thorough discussion of ideas critical in a democracy. Controversial issues discussed in the context of a group can move from divisive arguments to productive dialogues when the proper skills are employed.

The purpose of this activity is for you to reflect on this particular group experience when reading about the skills necessary to effectively work in and manage groups. Use this experience as a reference point while reading this chapter and participating in class activities.

Take a Closer Look

Working in a Group
Think of the last group in which you worked.

- What was the purpose of the group?
- Was the group voluntary or mandatory?
- What was the best part of the group experience?
- What was the worst part of the group experience?
- If you could repeat the group experience, what would you have done differently?

How do individual strengths combine to make a group successful?
© 2008, JupiterImages Corporation.

WHAT IS THE NATURE OF SMALL GROUPS?

Stated simply, a **small group** is a collection of people who work together either voluntarily or involuntarily to achieve a goal or solve a problem. But a small group is actually a complex social and communication phenomenon, so let's expand our definition. If we examine how other scholars have looked at small groups, we can gain some additional insight.

Keyton tells us that a small group is three or more people who work together interdependently on an agreed-upon activity or goal.[2] Forsyth says that a group is made up of "interdependent individuals who influence each other through social interaction."[3]

Wallace et al. suggest that a small group is an interdependent collection of persons engaged in a structured, cooperative, often (but not always) face-to-face, goal-oriented communication; each aware of their own and others' participation in the group; and each getting some satisfaction from participating in the activities of the group.[4]

Finally, Beebe and Masterson define a small group as a "group of people who share a common purpose or goal, who feel a sense of belonging to the group, and who exert influence on one another."[5]

As we look at these definitions, let's focus on the important issues:

Goal Orientation

The small groups being discussed in this chapter are created to solve problems or make decisions. As such, they are driven by a focus on some goal to be achieved. The more clearly this goal is defined, the more likely the group will be able to find a solution to the problem or make a quality decision. Group goals provide focus and direction for small groups.

Size Matters

A small group consists of at least three or more members. When there are fewer than three members, the communication is dyadic. When the third member is added to the mix, things begin to change. With three or more members, it is possible for factions to form and for subgroups of members to exchange information that is not available to the whole group. Adding more members to the group can be positive because it means that the group will have more points of view to consider when making a decision.

There is a limit, however, to the size of an effective problem-solving small group. What that specific limit is depends, to a large extent, on the individual personalities in the group, the context in which the group is operating, and the nature of the task or problem the group is trying to solve. A group is too large when every member cannot directly communicate with every other member. If you can't carry on a group conversation, then the group members cannot be interdependent. Although there is no definitive upper limit, groups larger than twelve seem to have troubles with interdependence, cohesion, and mutual influence.

Interdependence

The product of a small group is greater than the sum of its parts because of the communication interaction and the **interdependence** of its members. People draw energy, motivation, and ideas from each other, and they take advantage of one another's talents and expertise. Members combine their talents and resources, which gives them the ability to solve more complex problems than they could as individuals working alone. As a result of interdependence, groups have the potential to make better decisions than individuals.

Collection of People

A small group is not just an assembly of individuals, but a dynamic combination of people working together to accomplish some common goal. This shared goal and communication among the members are the major elements that separate groups from random collections of people, and it is responsible for the ability of groups to solve problems. For example, a group of people standing on a street corner waiting on a bus to arrive is a collection of people, but they aren't focused on some common goal. They aren't doing anything but waiting on a bus. They just happen to be doing it in the same place. However, these same people could *become* a small group if they decided to design a bus shelter to make their wait more comfortable or if they tried to figure out a better route so the buses would run on time.

A collection of people isn't necessarily a small group.
© 2008, JupiterImages Corporation.

Structure

Even though they might sometimes appear to be chaotic, small groups have structure. Some of the structure is fairly common across nearly every group, like there are usually leaders and there are usually followers. Some structures, however, only emerge in certain groups, and the compositions of those structures depend on the nature of the group task and the individual characteristics of the group members. After the group has been together for a while, these structures become more stable, but they are rarely static. Groups tend to negotiate and then continually renegotiate roles, expectations, cohesiveness, the group identity, the way conflict is managed, and many other structural elements.

WHAT ARE THE BENEFITS OF GROUPS?

<table><tr><td>

Take a Closer Look

The Pervasiveness of Groups in Your Life
Take time to think about all the groups in which you are currently involved.

- Which groups are voluntary?
- Which groups are involuntary?
- What did you hope or need to accomplish in each group?
- What function did each group serve in your life?

</td></tr></table>

Understanding groups is a bit easier if you understand some of the properties or characteristics that are common to most small groups. Some of these properties are positive and help groups' productivity, and some are not so positive and present a challenge to a group's ability to accomplish its goals. Let's look at the more positive properties first.

Synergy

Synergy usually occurs in situations in which people with a variety of talents and skills cooperate. **Synergy** suggests that the end product of a group's efforts is superior to the product of the individuals working independently. In essence, the sum is greater than the total of its parts. If we were to examine this in terms of a math equation, then the comparison would look something like this:

The sum of the group's efforts
$2 + 2 = 7$

The sum of individual efforts
$2 + 2 = 4$

The consequences of a synergistic system can be seen in the group product. A simple and easy way to think of it might be when a light bulb blows out in a very high ceiling. One person working alone is not tall enough to replace it, but two people working together could do it. If one person stood on the shoulders of the other, the goal can be accomplished! In terms of the kind of groups we are concerned with, here's another way to consider synergy. Say you were taking a marketing class and one of your assignments was to market a new line of cell phones to fellow college students. The synergy perspective argues that if you and three others were sent off to complete the task individually, you would not come up with a campaign as comprehensive, innovative, or effective as those who were collaborating in a group. Some of the explanation for this phenomenon can be found in the other properties of small groups.

Pooling Talent

Groups allow members to pool their talents, combining the strengths of each group member. Instead of just depending on the knowledge and skills of a single member, a group can take advantage of the knowledge and skills of all its members. This means that groups tend to have better collective memories, a variety of expertise, diversity of strengths (and weaknesses), a variety of perspectives (which is essential to group decision making), and more creativity.

Brainstorming

When working with others, ideas are developed further. **Brainstorming** is a free flow of ideas from all participants, and the process can spark initial ideas into new directions and solutions. This process helps to open the group up to original perspectives and ideas with a thinking-outside-the-box mentality. Brainstorming can be a powerful tool for creative decision making, but it can also *fail* to be effective if all the members don't participate or cooperate or if the rules for brainstorming aren't followed. Brainstorming will be discussed in a later chapter as a tool for generating a wide variety of solutions to problems.

Complexity

Small groups of people working together are *complex*. This means that a number of individual and independent people have become interdependent and are interacting together in many ways to accomplish some mutually agreed upon goal.[6] If you think of all the ways that individuals are different from each other, and then you think of five individuals working together in a group, the possible combinations of behaviors, conflicts, and outcomes challenges the imagination!

Complexity explains why groups of experts are commissioned to solve societal problems, make policy, and to analyze disasters and tragedies. We see this in the form of national think tanks, political or organizational committees, and commissions. This property of groups allows them to provide more thorough, more creative, and high-quality decisions.

Self-Organization

Groups have a strong tendency to organize themselves. As we will explore in this chapter, groups experience phases or stages of development with no guidance from rules or outside sources. Sometimes this kind of organization works very well and allows groups to achieve their goals. But sometimes the organization that emerges does not allow the group to be productive. In these cases (and often when the nature of the problem to be solved demands it), many groups choose to follow established decision-making procedures.

Adaptivity

Complex, self-organizing systems are *adaptive*.[7] This means that small groups interact with their environments or situations and change or reorganize themselves as needed to be able to accomplish their goals. They have the ability to learn from their experiences and to make appropriate changes in their behaviors or problem-solving strategies. This property allows groups to stay on course or focused even when they face distraction, conflicts, or other difficulties that might otherwise prevent goal achievement.

Dynamic

Small groups do not stand still; they are always moving and changing. They are often unpredictable, messy, and strongly inclined toward disorder. You could even think of it as a goal-oriented, living system that just happens to be made up of other goal-oriented living systems. Successful small groups are able to overcome all the messiness and even take advantage of it by bringing it into a kind of balance that allows goals to be achieved.

Norms

A product of group interaction is a shared standard of acceptable behavior. **Norms** *are shared guidelines for beliefs and behavior.*[8] Norms develop as groups reach implicit agreement that certain behaviors are appropriate and other behaviors are inappropriate. Although there will be some deviance within each group, *norms help establish the group identity* and they are have considerable influence on the behavior of the group members.

Cohesiveness

When a group is cohesive, individual group members feel a connection or attraction to each other. They are motivated by the attraction to each other and by their attraction to the task. Members feel a sense of bonding and they experience a feeling of trust and interdependence. This is important to the group's productivity, as those who have a strong sense of cohesion are generally more productive. It is not clear if high cohesion causes high productivity or if high productivity causes high cohesion. Whatever the case, the two appear to be strongly related. When cohesion gets too high, however, there is a strong potential for **groupthink** to exist, and this condition can prevent groups from making quality decisions.

Take a Closer Look

Group Cohesion

Thinking about one of the groups you listed at the beginning of this chapter, reflect on the following:

- On a scale from 1 to 10, how cohesive was the group? (10 = most cohesive)
- Why did you assign this score to the group?
- How was cohesion built in the group?
- What opportunities were missed to build cohesion?
- If you could change one thing the group did, what would you change?

Companies are aware of the value of group cohesiveness and actively promote cohesion among their employees. Some companies send entire departments to volunteer together, not only to help the community, but also to give those employees an opportunity to bond. Other companies have been known to fund beach parties and picnics for their employees.

WHAT ARE THE DRAWBACKS OF GROUPS?

We have discussed the more positive properties of groups; however, groups also have some properties that present significant challenges to group success.

Time Consuming

Groups can be time consuming. There are many factors that cause groups to be more time consuming than individuals working alone. Groups begin with organizing schedules. We are all familiar with the scheduling nightmare of trying to get a group of people with varying work, volunteer, family, and school schedules to meet. Solving logistics problems with five or six people can be more difficult than completing the task itself. In a later chapter we will discuss ways we can preschedule meetings and use computer meeting space to help us with this challenge.

In general, while group decisions often take up more "person-hours," the overall time for a group decision is usually less than an individual working alone. For example, a five-member group might work on a problem for ten hours. If you do the math, you will see that the total time equals fifty hours. The same problem might take an individual thirty hours. If you are employer who has to pay all these people, you can quickly appreciate this difference! There are two important differences, however. One is that the group solved the problem more quickly in real time (i.e., 10 hours vs. 30

hours), but it cost more. The other difference is that the group is more likely to produce a higher-quality solution than the individual working alone. An employer (who needed this problem solved) will have to make a judgment as to whether the difference in solution quality is worth the difference in price.

Difficult Members

Difficult group members can also prove to be a time drain. They come in many forms and use a variety of strategies that cause the group to stall. Their behavior distracts the group from time spent on task. Cooperative group members may need to complete work not completed by a difficult group member, to mediate aggressive behavior, and to talk through unsupported objections. The group may find that the time required to finish the task is greatly extended. This will be explored in more depth in our discussion of conflict.

Require a Balance of Task and Social Dimensions

Fostering the social dimensions in groups leads to cohesion and is good for a group as it works to accomplish its task, in moderation. Take, for example, the situation of Samantha, a straight-A student majoring in sociology. When Samantha attended the first meeting of her Sociology 101 group, she found herself incredibly frustrated. After a two-hour meeting, the group had only achieved one thing: deciding on a topic for the project. The meeting was held at a convenient location near the college. When she arrived, she found group members eating pizza, talking about instructors, and debating recent films they had seen. It was not until the last ten minutes of the meeting that the group decided to chat about the project. When they were finally engaged in meaningful discussion, some group members needed to leave, ending the discussion before it really started. Samantha, who had turned down an extra shift at work to attend the meeting, was more frustrated than ever. What happened here?

This example shows a group that is building cohesion without moderation. This group needs self-discipline or a leader who allows time for building cohesion but also keeps the members focused on the task at hand. A balance of both task and social dimensions is necessary. It is critical that we learn how to be tolerant of the social time groups need, yet still balance it with appropriate task time. In Samantha's case, the group was imbalanced and spent far too much time on the social dimension.

Samantha could have done one of two things to address the situation. First, as soon as she realized the group was taking too much time to socialize, she could have talked to the group leader to request the meeting get started. Second, if the group had no specific or appointed leader, Samantha could have taken control by asking the group members to focus on the task at hand with her for the next hour. She could have softened this request by reminding them that those who were able to stay longer could socialize a bit more after the meeting.

Groupthink

Mentioned earlier, the term *groupthink* refers to a phenomenon that very often results in a flawed decision made by groups whose cohesiveness becomes so

What Is Groupthink?

Making a good decision requires that groups *completely* execute the DMP or what-ever quality decision-making strategy that they decide to use. To the extent that you *do not* study the problem, make a thorough search and evaluation of alternatives, de-liberate about commitment, and collect feedback during the implementation stage, you have made a **defective decision**. Another cause of flawed decision making is *groupthink,* which is associated with an incomplete search and evaluation of alterna-tives, as well as some factors concerning the relationship among group members.

Groupthink is the tendency of group members to avoid conflict and to express agreement with their group even when a proposed solution has not been adequately investigated or critically analyzed. Groupthink manifests itself in strong pressure to conform to the will of the group and motivates members to avoid disagreements with the proposal, and to avoid questioning weak evidence or unsupported arguments. An alternative is selected by the group, or by the group leader, and all the members "fall in line" behind the alternative.

We stated in an earlier chapter that conflict should be encouraged and not avoided when making decisions in a group. The clash of diverse ideas is one of the primary strengths of small groups, and it is absolutely essential to quality decision making. Although it is true that too much conflict can stifle a group's ability to be creative and productive, too little task-related conflict usually results in defective or flawed decisions.

In some *highly-cohesive* groups, the motivation to maintain the relationships in the group can be more important than the necessity of making quality decisions. This is especially true if the group is caught up in defensive avoidance (where the hope of finding a satisfactory solution is low). In this case, group members strongly support a decision proposal with very little searching or deliberation.

Groups with powerful leaders seem to be especially susceptible to groupthink. Members do not want to disagree with the leader. Instead, all members express enthusiastic agreement.

Determining If My Group Is Experiencing Groupthink

How do we know when a group's cohesiveness has shifted from something that helps the group make better decisions to something that causes a group to make defective decisions? Janis[18] found eight symptoms of groupthink.

1. *Illusion of invulnerability.* This is a collective view that the group is incapable of making bad decisions. The group has unwarranted confidence and supports high-risk deci-sions and behaviors.
2. *Belief in inherent group morality.* Group members do not challenge the ethical con-sequences of a decision or of the group's actions.
3. *Collective rationalization.* Group members discuss reasons why their decision is the best course of action while discounting op-posing evidence and warnings. These warn-ings might influence group members to reconsider their assumptions.
4. *Out-group stereotypes.* Group members view any opponents to be inferior by stereotyping them as weak, misinformed, or unqualified to challenge their decisions.

How do you avoid groupthink?
© 2008, JupiterImages Corporation.

5. *Self-censorship.* Individual concerns are not voiced for fear of rejection, ridicule, or embarrassment by the group. As such, members play down the importance of their own doubts about the chosen course of action.

6. *Illusion of unanimity.* Group members truly believe all individuals agree with the decision, even when they have not made attempts to examine the situation from multiple perspectives. There is a belief that silence indicates consent or approval.

7. *Direct pressure on dissenters.* Members are pressured to agree. This may come in the form of direct threats (e.g., loss of job or position) or indirect pressure (e.g., hints of rejection). Dissent is *not* expected from members loyal to the group.

8. *Self-appointed mindguards.* Individuals perform the function of protecting group members from information that does not support the decision.

These symptoms strongly relate to some high-profile poor decisions that have affected public opinion, resulted in lost jobs, and even cost lives. In February 2003, the Space Shuttle *Columbia* exploded over Texas while reentering the atmosphere. All seven crew members died. NASA was criticized for giving in to pressure to keep the space program funded by pitting shuttle flights and the associated risks against political and economic pressure to keep the program visible to hold the public's interest.[19]

The structure of NASA's organization set the stage for groupthink to occur. NASA provided bonuses to independent contractors for on-time delivery. This resulted in an unwillingness to discuss problems or to raise flags that might slow a project. Additionally, investigators found the *Columbia* mission management team was unwilling to say anything potentially negative about the mission and failed to investigate suggestions that the foam insulation could cause serious damage to the spacecraft, which was later found to be the cause of the accident. The transcripts from the investigation show evidence of a team that was both isolated and isolating. The NASA middle managers in the mission evaluation room, where engineering issues during flight are resolved, were found to be reluctant to raise issues of importance. It was concluded that there was pressure to overestimate the success of the shuttle, and there was a culture of management that rationalized risks against political and economic factors. This indicates that the disaster could have been prevented.[20]

Another example of groupthink occurred during the 2004 presidential election year. At that time, CBS news aired a story critical of presidential candidate George W. Bush's military record. The report was later found to be incorrect. Many were at a loss to explain how this could happen in such a reputable news organization. The subsequent investigation revealed that those in charge of checking facts and ultimately authorizing such a report suffered from many symptoms of groupthink.

Preventing Groupthink

So how do we prevent this from happening in our own decision making? Janis has suggested strategies for avoiding groupthink:[21]

- *Assign a devil's advocate.* Give a group member license to pick apart the group's decision. Ask the devil's advocate to examine the decision from an opponent's point of view and have fun with tearing it apart. Ask

The structure of NASA's organization has resulted in instances of groupthink.
© 2008, JupiterImages Corporation.

(Continued)

the other group members to think about the ques-   tions raised by the devil's advocate and discuss them as a group.

- *Leader should avoid stating a position.* Individuals tend to conform to a strong group leader's position. This makes sense if the leader, for example, is also your boss. Who wants to disagree with the person who controls decisions about your future promotion, future raises, hiring and firing? Thus, the leader, whether the boss or not, should refrain from stating his or her position until all other group members have shared. This is meant to help free the decision from bias.
- *Hire an unbiased outside expert to evaluate the decision.* Companies often use outside experts to help them understand the impact of a decision or to assure them that a proposed course of action will, indeed, be the best. This is also true of companies who hire research firms to conduct focus groups with employees to better understand the impact of their policies from their employee's perspectives, or educational institutions who hire researchers to interview students enrolled in special programs or majors.
- *Split the group.* Another strategy is to split the group into two or more sub-groups, with the each subgroup working to solve the problem. The solutions are then brought forward for evaluation and selection by the group as a whole. This is comparable to Donald Trump's reality TV show *The Apprentice.* In this show, competing teams work on business-related tasks and bring forward their ideas to the "boardroom," where Trump and his executives decide which approach is the best.
- *Encourage questioning and challenge others.* There are many ways we can encourage questioning and respectfully challenge each other's ideas. We can set up a climate where all questions are welcomed and appreciated. This is not accomplished by simply making the statement, "There's no such thing as a stupid question;" rather, it is accomplished by the manner in which the question is received and responded to. To respond with understanding, appreciation, and encouragement is to send the message to the group as a whole that constructive criticism is an acceptable practice.

strong they stop challenging each other's ideas. Political mistakes have been attributed to groupthink such as the Bay of Pigs invasion, the Watergate cover-up,[9] the space shuttle *Challenger* disaster, and the 2003 space shuttle *Columbia* disaster.[10] This disadvantage to groups will be discussed in more depth in Chapter 11.

GROUP DEVELOPMENT: HOW DO COLLECTIONS OF PEOPLE TURN INTO GROUPS?

Educational psychologist Bruce Tuckman studied group behavior in the 1960s and identified five stages that groups progress through before reaching a point of maximum productivity.[11] An understanding of these stages can help us better manage our own group experiences. Before reading through these stages, take a moment to reflect on the group you described in the beginning of this chapter. Use your memory of that group experience to see whether the group followed Tuckman's stages.

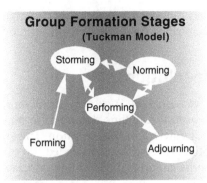

Group Formation Stages
(Tuckman Model)

Storming

Norming

Performing

Forming

Adjourning

Forming (Orientation)

This initial stage of a group's experience is characterized by a high uncertainty level. Group members are typically quiet and uncomfortable as they attempt to understand the group's goals, member personalities, and overall dynamics. There is an absence of norms of behavior and an absence of clearly defined roles, so there is a lot of uncertainty about how to behave and what to say. The **forming stage** is characterized by group members: (1) attempting to orient themselves, (2) testing each other and the group boundaries, and (3) creating dependence on the group leader or other group members for support during this uncomfortable time. The most important job for the group in this stage is to orient itself to itself.[12] The tension is reduced as members get to know each other better and roles begin to be defined.

Storming (Conflict)

The **storming stage** occurs as a result of interpersonal struggles and polarization inherent in responding to the task at hand. This is where different ideas often compete for consideration, and group members share and challenge each other's ideas. This tension is also a response to struggles for authority and the direction taken by the group that occurs between leaders and the rest of the group. This stage requires active leadership while the group works out its most important dimensions: goals, roles, relationships, likely barriers, and support mechanisms. But as soon as patterns of authority and communication become fairly stable, the conflict is reduced. Until this time, however, the group can be a very active and stormy place! As you might guess, forming and storming are very time consuming, making up about three-fourths the length of Tuckman's five-step process.[13]

Norming (Structure)

The **norming stage** happens when group cohesion develops, new standards evolve, and new roles are adopted. The group members have become more unified and more organized. A structure is put into place that enables the group to complete the task at hand.[14] The end results of this stage are that roles are clarified and accepted, a team feeling develops, and information is freely shared among group members.[15] At this stage, members try to make decisions by consensus. Hare says that this is when the group becomes cohesive.[16]

Performing (Work)

It is during the **performing stage** that most of the productive work is accomplished. Group roles become flexible and functional, and group energy is channeled into the task.[17] People are getting their jobs done properly, on time, and in coordinated

What happens during the storming stage?

sequence.[18] Research has demonstrated that this is the point of development, later in the group's life, at which most groups are most productive.[19]

Adjourning (Dissolution)

The **adjourning stage** was added by Tuckman, in collaboration with Mary Ann Jensen,[20] and takes us beyond the time that a group remains productive and functional. This phase involves group dissolution. The group has achieved its goals, solved the problem, or is no longer needed. Roles are abandoned, and participants often experience mourning feelings associated with the loss of a relationship.[21] Care should be taken at this stage because several members of this group could very well become members of another group. Failure to properly handle this stage could jeopardize the success of future groups.

GROUP CULTURE: WHY ARE ALL GROUPS DIFFERENT?

Robert Bales found that members of groups cooperate not only to accomplish some task, but also to create a group culture.[22] Through communication with each other over time, a collective personality and a unique group point of view emerge from the interaction.[23] The emerging culture is based on the values and experiences of all the group members, and it expresses a set of values, behavioral standards, and an identity that influence the way the group members make decisions, respond to each other, and interpret information.

For example, a local water utility was receiving comments about a small group of maintenance technicians who installed and repaired fire hydrants in the city. The comments were all very positive and they came from citizens, the fire department, and from supervisors in other city departments. The members of this group made it their goal to make each repair quickly, neatly, and with a high standard of quality. This kind of group culture was not typical of other work groups in the city. The other groups did generally good work, but the standards of this group were much higher than the norm.

How did this happen? All the members of the group were formerly members of other city work groups and shared general the culture of the city utility. This group found that it actually took less time, but only a little more effort and focus, to do a high-quality job. In addition, the members of the group found that they were getting satisfaction from doing good work! So, in addition to getting a paycheck, they felt good about what they did and they were motivated to come to work and spend the day with the group.

This culture began to develop one day when the group installed a fire hydrant. In addition to the ubiquitous yellow fire plug that we see next to the street, there is always a four- or five-foot pipe reaching below to the main water line. Replacing a hydrant means digging a hole down to the water line, disconnecting the hydrant, and then connecting a new hydrant to the line. When they first started working together, whenever they discovered a hydrant that needed to be replaced, they would call the city office and ask for heavy equipment to be dispatched to dig the hole. The usually had to wait up to two hours for the equipment to arrive and then wait for the hole to be dug. In addition, the use of the equipment made quite a mess in people's yards that was difficult to repair.

One day the crew found a hydrant that required replacement, so they called the city and they were told all the equipment was busy and could not be dispatched. So the crew got out their shovels and began to dig. They were surprised to learn that it took the four of them very little time to dig the hole, and they also discovered that they could do it more neatly than when the heavy equipment was used. They did such a great job that day that the lady whose yard they were digging in brought them cookies and then called the city supervisor to report how happy she was with the quality of the work and the care that was taken by the crew. This experience was only the beginning for this group, who found other high-quality ways to approach their jobs and gained a great deal of satisfaction from working together.

You might think this is a silly example, but the fire departments that depended on the hydrants to work properly when needed and the citizens who retained neat lawns would disagree with you. The city also found that this group made their repairs at lower cost than all the other maintenance crews. They didn't do anything to change the world, but because a culture of quality work evolved in this group, it turned into a true high-performance team.[24]

All groups develop their own unique cultures. Fraternities and sororities, clubs, social groups, and work groups each negotiate their own unique view of reality. The rules that govern your interaction with other group members, your interpretation of events, and the meaning you give to messages and behaviors differ from group to group. The culture of the group provides the frame of reference that tells members how to behave and how to interpret others' behavior.

WHAT SHOULD MY ROLE BE IN SMALL GROUPS?

Your specific roles in small groups will very likely be different as you become a member of different groups and as those groups attempt to accomplish different tasks. You and other members in your groups will adapt your behaviors and problems-solving strategies to these different situations. Considerable research has identified typical roles that appear in most groups, and they have been categorized as **task roles**, **group maintenance roles**, and **individual-centered** (also referred to as disruptive or egocentric) **roles.**

Keep in mind that you can often fulfill more than one role when working in groups, and that the roles you play may change, depending on the group and the group task.

Functional Roles in Small Groups

Earlier we discussed the fact that there are both task and social dimensions to groups. Similarly, the informal roles we play work to fulfill the tasks or the maintenance of our groups. Informal roles differ from formal

Take a Closer Look

What Kind of Group Member Are You?
One of the critical factors determining your success as a communicator is the ability to monitor and reflect on your own behavior. It is through this process that you can discover communication behaviors and skills that can be improved.

To help you do this, think of the last group you worked in and consider the following:

- What do you believe to be your greatest strength as a group member?
- What was your most significant contribution to the group's goal?
- What do you believe to be your greatest weakness as a group member?
- What two aspects of your participation in groups would you like to improve?

roles like chairperson, secretary, or sergeant-at-arms because they are not appointed or elected. Informal roles often result from an individual member's personality, knowledge, or talents, or they arise from the problem-solving context itself. Task roles contribute to the group's productivity and are concerned with moving the group toward achieving its goals. Maintenance roles strengthen the group's social and emotional structure and contribute to the group's cohesion. They have a more indirect impact on group productivity than task roles, but are still necessary for group success at making high-quality decisions. Benne & Sheats concluded that for a group to survive and for it to make quality decisions, it must focus on accomplishing its task and it must maintain relationships among the group members.[25] Table 6.1 illustrates a selection of the task and maintenance roles.

Not all group roles contribute to building cohesiveness and solving problems. There are individuals who fulfill *individual-centered*[26] or *disruptive* group roles.[27] This type of role distracts the group or blocks the group from moving forward toward goal or task completion. Individuals exhibiting these roles harm the group's productivity, cohesiveness, and harmony.

Group members who play individual-centered roles might be doing so consciously or unconsciously. Although it is possible that they are trying to prevent the group from accomplishing its goals, it is likely that they just have some strong personal needs to be fulfilled and they use the group to get attention, recognition, or help with their problems. Whatever the cause, the effect is interference with group problem solving. Table 6.2 identifies some specific individual-centered roles.[28]

What role does the man at the end of the table play?
© 2008, JupiterImages Corporation.

TABLE 6.1	Selected Group Task and Maintenance Roles
Task Roles	**Maintenance Roles**
Initiator-contributor: Makes suggestions, considers new ways to look at group problem.	*Compromiser:* Tries to find agreements among conflicting points of view. Could change own position to help mediate conflict.
Information seeker: Focused on finding the facts; asks questions.	*Follower:* Serves as audience for the group; goes along with the other members.
Opinion seeker: Looks for expressions of attitudes and opinions of group members.	*Gatekeeper/expediter:* Tries to encourage participation from all group members.
Information giver: The expert of the group. Provides information based on experience.	*Encourager:* Gives positive feedback to others. The encouragement results in an increase in group members' self-esteem, excitement to complete the task at hand, and confidence.
Coordinator: Finds connections in suggestions and possible solutions; pulls information together into a coherent whole.	*Standard setter:* Expresses or begins discussion of standards for evaluating the group process or decisions.
Procedural technician: This person volunteers to complete tasks, help others, takes notes, distributes information, and takes on additional work.	*Harmonizer:* Always willing to listen. Group members often seek this person out to help soothe nerves, mediate interpersonal conflicts, or solve problems not group-related.
The organizer: This person helps to keep the group organized via scheduling, mapping out courses of action, coordinating efforts, etc.	*Observer/commentator:* Calls attention to the group's positive and negative characteristics and advocates change when necessary.

Source: Benne and Sheats, 1948.

TABLE 6.2	Individual-Centered Roles
Aggressor: Communicates disapproval of ideas, attitudes, and opinions of other group members. Attacks the group and other members.	
Blocker: Takes advantage of opportunities to oppose group plans or procedures. Says he or she wants no part of the group. Expresses negativity.	
Dominator: Manipulates group members and situations; Creates defensiveness with certainty and superiority.	
Self-confessor: Wants to talk about his or her own feelings that are unrelated to the group goal.	
Help seeker: Seems insecure and confused; asks for personal advice.	
Recognition Seeker: Self promoter; wants attention or praise for himself or herself.	
Playboy/girl: No interest in being involved in the group; detached; interested in having a good time.	
Special interest pleader: Separates self from the group; identifies strongly with another group or interest.	

Source: Benne and Sheats.[25]

Disruptive Roles in Small Groups

Mudrack and Farrell identified **disruptive group roles** that are similar in type and function to the individual-centered roles mentioned above.[29] The following roles fit the disruptive definition, and we suggest some communication strategies to help counteract them.

How is this man's role disruptive to the group?
© 2008, JupiterImages Corporation.

The Nonparticipant

This is a passive group member characterized by not participating in group activities, consistently missing group meetings, and not completing individual group work. When he does attend a group meeting, he either arrives late or leaves early. There could be many reasons why an individual may be a nonparticipant. Some people are very shy. Their intent may be to be an active group member, only they simply cannot overcome their communication apprehension to the point where they speak up. Others just might not care, do not feel connected to the group, or are bitter toward the group for some reason.

Strategy. Regardless of the cause, a constructive way to approach nonparticipants is with encouragement.

- Gently invite them to participate.
- Ask for their opinions, ideas, and help.
- Notice when they do not attend meetings.
- Try to avoid assuming that their behavior is intentional. Rather, give them the benefit of the doubt and make a strong effort to include them.

The Bulldozer

This person takes control of the group without paying much attention to the desires, opinions, or ideas of others. A bulldozer monopolizes conversations, imposes courses of action, and discourages the participation of others. Individuals might bulldoze as a result of (1) a past experience in which they were not listened to or heard, (2) a lack of awareness of *bulldozing*, or (3) a desire to be the group's leader, but without the knowledge of how to approach the role constructively.

Strategy. One way to respond to bulldozers is with an intentional description of group norms. To prevent them from monopolizing the group, set up expectations for balanced participation, such as asking every group member to contribute at least one idea at each group meeting or by using an agenda to impose time limits on any one individual's *floor time.*

The Controller

This group member wants to make all of the decisions for the group. He or she appears to have a self-perception of superiority above the other group members and a belief that his or her ideas and plans are the best. An individual may feel a need to control the group due to insecurity, fear, or hunger for power. Whatever the reason, it is important to avoid making assumptions and to approach this behavior positively.

You can use communication strategies to balance the power in the group. This may be achieved in a variety of ways: by rotating group roles, by assigning tasks by pulling names from a hat, or by creating a meeting agenda. Whichever approach is used, first try to understand the reason for the disruptive communication choices and then do your best to respond in a way that helps the group to continue moving toward its goal.

The Gossiper

Although some gossip is inevitable in all groups, it becomes a problem when it hurts the feelings of others or undermines the group's goal achievement. An individual may do this to get back at a group member in retaliation, to be popular, to control the group, or to intentionally sabotage the group.

Strategy. Group members should work to create a climate of trust and mutual support when the group is in the early stages of formation. This can be done through increased social time (hosting a barbeque at one of the group member's houses, for example) or by utilizing team-building activities such as paper airplane contests, working through puzzles together, or volunteering to help with a campus club drive.

To respond to the gossiper, constructively confront the person. Discuss not necessarily the content of the gossip, but more importantly, the reason for it. Many times dissatisfaction is expressed in a passive-aggressive fashion. After confronting the group member, use the collaborating conflict management style (see the Interpersonal Communication chapter for additional information about conflict management styles) to unearth the real problem and work toward finding a mutually satisfactory solution.

The Social Loafer

This is one of the most troublesome of group members. The social loafer is an individual who loves working in groups because it means a *free ride* for the project's duration. The loafer does not complete assignments, is generally unreliable, and often submits inferior work. A loafer is often perceived to be someone who simply does not care, is not skilled, is lazy, or is a low achiever. However, some loafers are not lazy at all; rather, they loaf because they can. Other group members allow them to loaf by completing work for them that they do not finish.[30]

Strategy. This is a good time to practice your leadership skills. Most individuals will work when there is motivation to do so. It is important that the loafer feel valued and that his or her contributions are needed and are important. It is critical that other group members *do not* complete the work for them, as this only allows loafers to continue in that role. Instead, loafers can be mentored by being paired with another group member who is willing to

Some gossip is inevitable in a group, but it can become a problem.
© 2008, JupiterImages Corporation.

mentor. In extreme cases, you can resort to the **group contract** (explained later in this chapter).

Coping with Disruptive Members

There are a number of strategies we may use to respond to disruptive or egocentric members. In addition to those already mentioned, we have included some strategies for coping with more generalized types of egocentric and disruptive behaviors.

Feedback Sessions

A feedback session is the act of communicating to the disruptive group member how his behavior is affecting the group. Many students who have experienced trouble working in their groups go to their instructor for help. When asked if they have discussed the issue with the troublesome group member, the usual answer is that they have not. Before approaching a supervisor, manager, or teacher, group members should first try to solve the situation using *feedback*.

Negative or corrective feedback is not always easy to give to others. If you are not careful about the manner in which the feedback is given, then relationships could be damaged. However, when used effectively, it is one of the most powerful communication tools available. The feedback process involves the following:

How could he convey his disappointment constructively?
© 2008, JupiterImages Corporation.

1. *Describe the problem as clearly, neutrally, and specifically as possible.* (See discussion on group decision making for a discussion of description versus evaluation.) Point out the similar interests you have with the group member, such as earning a good grade on the assignment or the satisfaction of a job well-done.
2. *Resist the temptation to place blame.* Instead try to take a *mutual problem approach* in which you use language such as, "How can *we* work to remedy this situation?" The use of *we* shows a sense of mutual responsibility and commitment to solving the problem as a team.
3. *Take ownership of your feelings and avoid blaming or attacking the disruptive member.* This can be achieved by using "I" messages instead of "you" messages.
4. *Stick to one issue at a time.* Bringing up more than one concern complicates the discussion and makes resolution more difficult.
5. *Do not gang up on the disruptive person with the other group members.* Those receiving the feedback need to be sent the message that it is fair, unbiased, and that your goal is *not to criticize*, but to work together to solve the problem.

Perception Checking

Imagine the following situation:

> You are in Athens, Greece, on vacation and decide to go to the flea market, the *plaka*, to buy some souvenirs. You find yourself in a negotiation with a merchant for an item. As you keep insisting on a price, the merchant nods his head from left to right and says "ne." You interpret this as a rejection, are disappointed, and are ready to leave when he interjects and keeps repeating the same phrase "ne, ne." You perceive his behavior to mean "no."

Before leaving the market and missing out on an opportunity to buy a great souvenir, it would be a good time to use some perception checking. You find a translator and go through the perception checking process as follows:

1. *Describe* the behavior: "I am trying to buy this item from the merchant over there. When I offered him a price, he nodded his head from left to right and said 'ne.'"

2. *Interpret* the behavior: "I thought he did not want to negotiate. However, he kept at me. I am not sure whether I have misunderstood his rejection or if I have offended him in some way."
3. *Ask:* "Can you tell me what is going on?"

Through this perception checking and with the translator's help, you find that "ne" means "yes" and his headshaking is, in fact, a sign of confirmation.

You do not need to be in a foreign country to experience misunderstandings like this. When group members communicate with each other, differences in perception occur often. Try using the three-step perception-checking process when you suspect that your perception may be inaccurate.

Utilize a Group Contract

Since we often do not know if we are going to encounter disruptive group members until we are in the middle of a group task, it is wise to use some preemptive strategies to handle problems before they arise. This can be done by writing up a group agreement, or contract, that outlines group norms and consequences for breaking them. Although the contract is usually a preemptive tactic, group members will still misbehave and problems will still come up. So you could draw up a contract even when your group is fairly mature. The contract is something a group should resort to only when all communication attempts fail.

Group contracts should have these elements:

- All group members are involved in the writing of the contract.
- Responsibilities and behaviors expected of all members are clearly defined.
- Consequences for misbehavior behavior are clearly specified.
- All group members sign the contract and receive a copy.

Group Deliberation

Many kinds of groups have a specific task they must perform, and this mission may actually be the reason for the group's existence. Any group that assembles to complete a specific task and render a decision is traditionally called a **problem-solving group**. Unfortunately, the conventional terminology is somewhat narrow. Problem-solving groups may not simply convene because something is wrong. The task may involve improving or building upon something already successful, or it may seize an opportunity and make the most of a positive situation. Consider problem solving in the broad sense of a mathematical problem: solving a puzzle and justifying the solution. Contrast this sense of problem with a **complaint**, which expresses dissatisfaction with a problem but offers no productive solution.

Regardless of the specific task, all so-called problem-solving groups *render reasoned decisions* to complete their work. This feature clearly distinguishes problem-solving groups from support groups, for example, which need not take specific actions to function. Problem-solving groups plan and act systematically to recommend courses of action. By contrast, we can (and often do) get meaningful support from others without them advising us how to act. Purely social groups also lack this action orientation. If asked what they do with their groups of friends, most people would answer simply "hang out," proving that any decisions are far less important than the fact of being together.

Just as in solving mathematical problems, arriving at the answer isn't enough—you must show your work. In other words, you must show you understand the process of reaching a solution. With groups, you must understand and practice the method for reaching decisions. The rest of this chapter guides you through that process.

Group decision making is quite common, and it may or may not involve the entire group in making a formal presentation. Group members interact with each other to reach an outcome. After the decision is made, it may be presented by an individual or by a group. The actual decision-making process is separate from the presentation to an audience beyond the group. A jury renders a verdict, and then the verdict is announced. A fundraising committee discusses the alternatives, and then presents them to the entire organization for a vote. Coaches devise a game plan, then they present that plan to the players.

If a group is charged with making a decision, their decision is only as good as the method they use to reach it. If the process of deciding is disorganized, full of personal animosity, or has no clear objective, the decision itself probably will be poor. The consequences of poor decisions can be devastating. A sloppily formulated verdict of a jury could unjustly condemn someone to prison or death. A fundraising committee could lead an organization to bankruptcy. Inadequate preparation for crucial sports games could spell the end of a coach's contract or the demise of the entire team.

Despite the variety of decisions groups can make, the basic process of decision making has remained relatively constant for the past century. In 1910 the philosopher and educational theorist John Dewey[31] explained the five steps that he considered crucial in all logical thought. With minor changes, the same system Dewey elaborated is used as a basis for decision-making seminars conducted by major corporations throughout the world. Dewey outlined several steps that have become the accepted gospel for solving problems. These steps have been revised and expanded a bit to make them more applicable to situations you will encounter.

Step 1. Define the Problem or Issue

First, the group must agree that an issue or need exists. Just because a group has been assembled to find a solution does not mean that the problem is real. Sometimes a few people might mistakenly perceive a problem where none actually exists. For an issue to be genuine, there must be widespread agreement that the situation should be addressed at all.

Once a need is recognized, the group must determine its nature. The definition of the problematic issue must be specific and factual. Do not assign blame for problems. At this stage, the group's task is purely descriptive. Several questions can keep the group's attention focused on description. The group might consider the following lines of inquiry:

- When and did the issue first arise? How did it happen?
- Is it a problem, an opportunity for improvement, or some other type of challenge?
- What is its history? When does it improve or get worse?
- Who does this problem affect? How are they affected?
- Who has an interest in solving or not solving the problem?
- What is the significance of this problem? How severe is it? How widespread is it? What are its effects?
- When must the problem be solved? Is there an absolute or target deadline? (Just establish the time frame now, since the actual solutions and their implementation schedule will be handled later.)
- What other information is needed to understand the problem? What more does the group need to know before it can proceed?

(Continued)

FIGURE 6.1 Outcomes of step 1 in problem solving.

Step 1, Outcome A	Step 1, Outcome B
– Employee morale stinks.	– Employees don't want to work on weekends.
	– Employees want longer lunchtimes.
– Our history professor is awful.	– The history professor does not keep scheduled appointments with students.
	– No woman has passed any of this professor's courses in ten years.

Answering such questions should yield exact specifications of the problem. Notice the difference between the pairs of outcomes listed in Figure 6.1.

The outcomes in column A might show that a problem exists, but they fail to find the cause or symptoms of the problem. They remain vague and very subjective. Different people will define "stinks" and "awful" in different ways, so their assessments of the problem will vary. The outcomes in column B offer exact sites where the problems lie. By explaining the nature of the problem very narrowly, the group can address the roots of those difficulties.

The outcome of the first step should be a precise, factual description of the situation the group faces. Going into the second step, the entire group should agree on exactly what the problem is. Decision making should not proceed until the group reaches consensus on defining the problem. You might find the first step to be time-consuming and tedious. Typically, a group will spend most of its time on defining the problem. Effort at this stage, however, pays off. Without a clear and specific identification of the problem, no proposed solution can be entirely effective.

Troubleshooting Step 1: Too often, groups zoom through step 1 only to find much later that a poorly defined problem has led to vague or ineffective solutions. You can't solve what you don't know. *Research* the nature of the issues. Who says the issue or problem is what you think it is? Are there several issues that need to be addressed instead of just one?

Step 2. Establish Criteria for Solutions

Before diving right into considering solutions, the group needs to decide the ground rules that govern acceptable solutions. The guidelines enable the group to determine the best solutions later (Step 4). Typically, several considerations might apply when setting the boundaries for acceptable solutions. Depending on the task at hand, a group might emphasize some of these factors more than others.

The list in Figure 6.2 is only representative of the criteria a group may choose. In addressing its task, each group must devise its own criteria, and those criteria may look very different from the items listed here. The group should determine which criteria are required and which are desired. Required criteria are standards that any potential solution absolutely must meet. Desired criteria are those that the group

FIGURE 6.2 Sample decision criteria.

Stakeholders

- Who should the solutions take into account? Do some people or organizations deserve more benefits than others?

Precedent

- Should the solutions be things that have been tried before (so there is a track record for evaluation), or does the group want totally new ideas (to encourage originality but at the risk of untested solutions)?

Time Frame

- How long should solutions take to implement? What is a reasonable time frame?

Logistics

- What financial resources will be available? Will solutions have to operate within a budget?
- What personnel will be available? Where and how will personnel be acquired?

Constraints

- Are certain alternatives automatically ruled out? What sorts of solutions are off limits and why? Specify any relevant constraints on resources and options.

prefers a solution meet, but that permit some compromise. For example, a required criterion might be that the solution must be fully implemented within three years. A desired criterion might be that a solution could be put into place within one year.

Troubleshooting Step 2: This step is often overlooked or not taken seriously because groups may not appreciate its importance. Step 2 establishes ground rules for which of the proposed solutions should be kept or discarded later in the process. This step also provides the basis for evaluating solutions. For example, you might discard a solution because it does not meet budget criteria. Be careful not to jump ahead with suggesting possible solutions yet—that will come in the next step. At this point, you should just focus on what the potential solutions should or should not do.

Step 3. Identify Solutions

After the group defines the problem and establishes criteria, it can consider potential solutions. This step involves generating as many ways of coping with the problem as possible. At this stage, the group should concentrate on producing ideas. Quantity should be the goal. The quality of these ideas will be discussed in the next step.

Groups often prove especially adept at generating ideas for solving problems. It is a common and serious mistake to try to identify solutions individually. Working collectively, you should be able to generate more suggestions, formulate more original ideas, uncover errors that you or others made, offer and receive encouragement if you run short of ideas, and escape from "conditioned thinking" that restricts your repertoire of solutions.[32(pp84-85)] Even if no one person generates many suggestions, group members can stimulate each other's creativity by making connections between ideas and using someone else's input as a springboard for more proposals.

Brainstorming to Find Solutions

One specific way that groups can produce innovative ideas is through **brainstorming**. The objective of brainstorming is to generate in a criticism-free environment as many ideas as possible. Many methods of brainstorming exist, but here are some suggestions to make your brainstorming sessions effective.

Solicit input from each group member. Group members should offer ideas freely, without feeling pressure to contribute. The brainstorming session should allow everyone some opportunity to contribute. Quiet members might require verbal encouragement from the rest of the group. Group members should feel they are being invited, not forced, to participate.[33] All ideas should be accepted without fear of judgment. Invite group members to be creative, crazy, and outlandish in their ideas—sometimes these "strange" ideas end up being the best.

A designated person records all ideas. Record every idea. Since the list of ideas will be narrowed and evaluated later, do not limit the range of contributions. Sometimes ideas that seem irrelevant or impractical can serve as springboards for other actions or concepts later. The ideas should be listed so that all group members can refer to them. A chalkboard, whiteboard, or flipchart comes in handy here. Having everyone's input ready at hand frees participants from having to remember everything that has been said. When the suggestions are available for examination and review, previously unnoticed relationships among them may arise, stimulating more input.

Accept ideas at face value. Brainstorming generates ideas, but does *not* weed out or alter ideas. That process occurs later, after brainstorming is complete.

(Continued)

Circulate a list of ideas generated. As quickly after the meeting as possible, all group members should receive a complete list of the ideas the group generated. Timing is important, because the list should be received while the ideas are fresh in everyone's mind. Individuals might think of new suggestions while they review the list. Make sure all proposed solutions were recorded. At this point, duplicate ideas are deleted and the group might organize the suggestions so they can be examined easily.

Tips for Identifying Solutions

Brainstorming is easily mistaken for haphazard and cursory invention of ideas. That characterization applies only to poorly conducted brainstorming sessions. For brainstorming to be effective, it should conform to the following guidelines.

- Brainstorm more than once. You can't always expect brilliant ideas to emerge from just one attempt. Several sessions might be necessary to generate enough proposals to proceed to Step 4.
- Invite diversity. Varying the mix of participants will supply fresh ideas. If a group has worked together a long time, the participants might need new input to escape from a rut of the same old suggestions.
- Keep your brainstorming sessions short. Take a break from brainstorming when no one has any more suggestions or when input gets repetitive.
- Divert your attention between brainstorming sessions. If you keep racking your brain for solutions to a problem, you tend to repeat the same patterns of thought. Diversion can give you fresh insight when you resume the decision-making process. After escaping from the issue at hand for a while, "we can then see it in a fresh light, and new ideas arise".[32(p88)] Our friends (and my great-grandmother) may have been right when they recommended that we reconsider solving a problem "after getting a good night's sleep."

As the group assembles its list of possible solutions, remember to include an option that always remains, even if only as a default: maintaining the status quo by doing nothing. This option serves two purposes: (1) It provides a benchmark for comparison to other solutions so you can definitely decide whether other options actually improve on the current situation. (2) It reminds the group that even though the status quo might not be maintained in its entirety, some components of the present system could be incorporated into the group's preferred solution.

Troubleshooting Step 3: In step 3, discussion sometimes slips ahead into the evaluation stage (step 4). The next step (Evaluate Solutions) allows you to critique the suggested plans, so save your judgments of solutions until then. The important priority now is to generate a large number of potential solutions. One way to generate more and better solutions is to combine or divide proposals that have been suggested, creating new combinations of ideas.

Step 4. Evaluate Solutions

When the group is satisfied that it has proposed as many solutions as possible (not just "good" solutions), evaluation begins. Organization of the suggestions will allow the group to see how ideas cluster or differ. When discussing the merits and drawbacks of each idea, record the results so everyone can refer to them. The designated recorder should list the strengths and weaknesses of each suggestion so that the options can be compared easily. One method for doing this is the simple chart that Benjamin Franklin used when he had to make a difficult decision. He would list each option, and then list the advantages and disadvantages in separate columns. Figure 6.3 shows an example of a balance sheet like the ones Franklin used.

The group must go beyond merely counting the advantages and disadvantages—look at the *impact* of the pros and cons. The crucial questions in the evaluation step for each proposed option are:

- Do the advantages outweigh the disadvantages?
- Which options carry the greatest benefits with the least drawbacks?

To make these determinations, the group can subject each option to the following kinds of questions. These questions are designed to reveal the pros and cons of suggested solutions.

1. What are the short-term and long-term benefits?
2. What are the short-term and long-term drawbacks?
3. What are the intangible costs (time, effort) as well as the financial costs?
4. When will the costs and benefits be realized?
5. Which parts of the problem are solved by this proposal?
6. Which parts of the problem remain after this proposal is implemented?
7. Where have similar proposals been tried? How have they worked in those situations?
8. How will others outside the group react to the proposal? How readily will they endorse the option?

The preceding list offers suggestions for stimulating group evaluations of solutions. You may find that your group devises its own set of questions as the decision-making process continues. Regardless of the questions you use, make sure that you evaluate each option fairly and carefully.

To examine proposals impartially and rigorously, all group members must concentrate on evaluating the ideas instead of whoever proposes or supports them. Discussion should remain issue-centered, not people-centered. Personalized criticisms can cause discord within the group and prevent participants from reaching decisions. The leader and other group members can prevent animosity in at least two ways. First, discussion could focus first on a proposal's advantages and *then* on its disadvantages.[34] Such an organizational pattern prevents participants from too hastily criticizing an option. Second, participants should depersonalize the options by separating the person from their proposal.[35] Whenever the group discusses a suggestion, participants need not mention who thought of the idea. Comments then focus on the idea itself, not on the person who offered it.

The fourth step in decision making should end with one or more solutions that the group endorses. The endorsement need not be unqualified support, but the group as a whole should be convinced that its proposed solutions represent the best available options.

Troubleshooting Step 4: Don't settle for vaguely labeling proposed solutions as "good" or "bad." If you completed step 2 carefully, you already constructed a basis

FIGURE 6.3 Balance sheet to evaluate proposed solutions.

	Advantages	Disadvantages
Proposed Solution 1	1. 2. 3.	1. 2. 3. 4. 5.
Proposed Solution 2	1. 2. 3. 4.	1. 2. 3.

(Continued)

for evaluating the solutions in step 4. Refer to your criteria in step 2 for elements that might play a role in your evaluation of solutions: feasibility (including cost, personnel, and time to implement), impact on stakeholders, moral concerns, etc. The ability to see both the pros and cons of solutions allows the group to anticipate and correct any problems with implementing a solution.

Step 5. Select the Best Solution(s)

Now it's decision time. A very important aspect of choosing solutions is to set up and follow through with a specific method for making decisions. The group must—read that again: MUST—explicitly employ a method for reaching decisions. Everyone in the group should understand the group's method of decision making. Votes should be taken when needed and recorded in case questions arise later. Some of the more common methods of reaching decisions are:

Consensus: For a solution to be selected, all group members must agree. Although it sounds ideal, consensus may prove difficult or impossible to reach. Furthermore, false consensus might arise due to groupthink. Group members may simply agree because they don't want to dissent (and not because they endorse the solution).

Majority Rule: The group votes on solutions and selects the solution(s) with the most votes. Some groups establish rules for a "super majority," such as three-fourths of group members, to assure more support for final decisions. For example, the U.S. Congress can override a presidential veto only with a two-thirds or greater majority vote. Majority rule is useful when differences of opinion remain. The main problem is that the minority gets left out unless they present a **minority report**, which explains dissenting views.[36] Whenever the U.S. Supreme Court renders a verdict that is not unanimous, justices will issue majority and dissenting opinions to justify their decisions.

Authoritarian Rule: A person decides on behalf of the entire group. Often people assume this method means that a leader does all the work and everyone else shuts up. Definitely not. All the steps in the deliberative method remain intact. Authoritarian rule simply means that one person shoulders responsibility for rendering the decision, taking into account the ideas and opinions of other group members. The authoritarian approach sometimes works well in online groups when it becomes impractical to get everyone to participate or render a decision. This method also saves time because disagreements among group members don't delay decisions. Although efficient, authoritarianism can leave group members feeling excluded from final outcomes that don't "belong" to the entire group. For this method to work well, the person making the decision must be highly competent, allow others to participate in the deliberative process, and take responsibility for the ultimate decision. Other group members contribute to the process, but one person generates the ultimate outcome. For example, academic departments and committees recommend professors for hire, but the chief academic officer makes the actual academic appointment.

Troubleshooting Step 5. Too often, group members simply express individual opinions about solutions and consider that a decision. There needs to be some indication of how the group arrives at its selection of solutions. If using an authoritarian system, clearly establish who is responsible. For majority votes, decide on the minimum number of members who need to participate. A "majority" vote of 3-1 with three more people not voting does not constitute a genuine majority. To avoid false consensus, each participant should justify the choice of a solution. What rationale can you offer for choosing one option as opposed to others? This justification of decisions reduces chances of passive agreement.

Step 6. Implement and Test Solution(s)

The final stage is most often overlooked or given inadequate attention by student problem-solving groups in this course. Work does not end when a solution has been selected. Your group now has reached the stage for putting proposals into practice. In deciding how to implement what the group has endorsed, consider these issues:

- Who is responsible for implementation? Mustthe person (or people) who supervises implementation also monitor outcomes?
- When will implementation occur? When should it begin? When should it be completed?
- How long will adoption of the plan take? Will the solution be adopted all at once or will it be phased in?
- What resources are required for the solution to take effect? What are the minimum resources needed? What resources would be most desirable?

Typically, a solution goes into effect according to a timetable that allows people who are affected to anticipate change. When Congress passes a law, the new regulation usually takes effect after a sufficient time elapses for people to be notified of the change.

Sometimes a group will find that an excellent option encounters insurmountable problems in the implementation phase. For example, a clothing company may decide to increase the price of shirts it manufactures to cover the increased cost of raw materials. If customers refuse to pay the higher cost or if retailers refuse to change the prices of the shirts, the solution cannot take effect. In cases where the desired option cannot take effect, the group must return to Step 4 and evaluate other possible solutions.

Throughout the implementation process and afterwards, the group must monitor the progress of its solution. You probably are saying: "But our solution hasn't gone into effect yet!" Exactly. Successful group deliberation includes predicting possible outcomes of solutions so you can prevent setbacks. For example, a food manufacturer doesn't simply stop as soon as a new product hits the market. The manufacturer has developed detailed plans to measure success and anticipate ways to improve. Essentially, the testing part of step 6 requires answering a simple but vital question: How would you know whether the solution worked? Phrased another way: How do you define success? You need to look at where similar solutions have succeeded or failed, using this research as a basis for predicting what your solution will accomplish. Most important, in this step you need to determine how you will know whether the group's solution(s) will work and how you will monitor progress.

To decide whether the solution actually works, the group should answer the following kinds of questions:

- What are identifiable or measurable ways to identify success? Here the group should refer back to the criteria for evaluating solutions (step 2).
- When will the effects be realized?
- How often should the solution be monitored and assessed?
- Who ultimately determines whether the solution has succeeded?
- What alternatives exist if this solution fails?

Preparing answers to the final question involves the group in **contingency planning**. Whenever solutions are implemented, some back-up solutions should be prepared just in case the preferred solution does not work. Contingency planning is common in military operations. Commanders devise a first choice for a military campaign. If that choice proves unsuccessful, they resort to their second choice, a plan that would not have the same disadvantages. Contingency plans allow groups to implement new solutions quickly in case of an emergency without having to go through the entire decision-making process from the beginning.

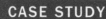

CASE STUDY

What Would You Do?

You have been asked to help out in a freshman class at the local high school. You are responsible for organizing student work groups (teams), introducing the student's group assignment, and monitoring the students as they discuss their approach to the task. Most students in this class are hardworking, motivated, and ambitious. However, there are a few class members who are known to engage in loafing and troublemaking.

You consider your options:

1. Mixing them into the group with the students who are hardworking, knowing that those students will more than likely do the work for them.
2. Speaking with them ahead of time to ask them to be "good" to their group members.
3. Group all the loafers and troublemakers together to work as a team, taking the risk that they will either meet the challenge or fail miserably.

What Would You Do?

A teacher faced this very challenge while teaching high school. She did not want to burden the hardworking students with the loafers and troublemakers. She did not think it would be fair to the dedicated, hardworking students. This was especially true given the fact that these disruptive students had already been talked to about their behavior, only to have it continue. She opted for the third choice and put them in a group together.

Through this experience, she learned a great deal about these types of troublesome group members who knew they were loafers and troublemakers and responded to the teacher's decision with attitudes reflecting, "How can you put us all together? We will fail." Ironically, they did not fail. As a matter of fact, it was with this project that the teacher was able to get them to work the hardest. They rose to the occasion and completed the task; it met all the requirements, was submitted on time, and helped participants feel better about themselves and the class.

From *Communication: Principles of Tradition and Change* by Wallace et al. Copyright © 2008 by Kendall Hunt Publishing Company. Reprinted by permission.

ENDNOTES

1. S. Sorensen, "Grouphate," paper presented at the International Communication Association, Minneapolis, Minnesota, 1981.

2. J. Keyton, *Communicating in Groups: Building Relationships for Group Effectiveness* (New York: Oxford University Press, 2006).

3. D. Forsyth, *Group Dynamics.* (Belmont, CA: Wadsworth, 1999).

4. S. Wallace, L. Yoder, L. Hungenberg and C. Horvath, *Creating Competent Communication: Small Groups* (Dubuque: Kendall/Hunt, 2006).

5. S. Beebe and J. Masterson, *Communicating in Small Groups: Principles and Practices.* 8th ed. (Boston: Allyn and Bacon, 2006), p. 4.

6. M. Waldrop, *Complexity: The Emerging Science at the Edge of Order and Chaos* (New York: Simon & Schuster, 1992).

7. Ibid.

8. S. Kiesler, *Interpersonal Processes in Groups and Organizations* (Arlington Heights, IL: Harlan-Davidson, 1978).

9. R. Cline, "Small Group Dynamics and the Watergate Coverup: A Case Study in Groupthink," paper presented at the annual meeting of the Eastern Communication Association, Ocean City, MD, April 27–30, 1983.

10. J. Schwartz and M. L. Wald, " 'Groupthink' Is 30 Years Old, and Still Going Strong," *New York Times*, March 9, 2003, p. 5.

11. B. W. Tuckman, "Developmental Sequence in Small Groups," *Psychological Bulletin* 63 (1965): 384–399. Also B. W. Tuckman and M. A. Jensen, "Stages of Small Group Development Revisited," *Group and Organizational Studies* 2 (1977): 419–427.

12. H. Robbins and M. Finley, *The New Why Teams Work: What Goes Wrong and How to Make It Right* (California: Berrett-Koehler Publishers, 2000).

13. Ibid.

14. B. W. Tuckman (1965).

15. Robbins and Finley.

16. A. P. Hare, *Handbook of Small Group Research* (New York: The Free Press, 1976).

17. B. W. Tuckman (1965).

18. Robbins and Finley.

19. R. F. Bales and F. Strodtbeck, "Phases in Group Problem Solving," *Journal of Abnormal and Social Psychology* 46 (1951): 485–495. Also, A. P. Hare and D. Nevah, "Conformity and Creativity: Camp David, 1978." *Small Group Behavior* 17 (1986): 243–268.

20. Tuckman and Jensen.

21. Ibid.

22. R. Bales. *Personality and Interpersonal Behavior.* (New York: Holt, Rinehart, and Winston, 1970).

23. E. Bormann, Fantasy and Rhetorical Vision: The Rhetorical Criticism of Social Reality. *Quarterly Journal of Speech*, 58 (1970): 306–407.

24. J. R. Katzenback and D. Smith, *The Wisdom of Teams: Creating the High Performance Organization* (New York: Harper Business, 1993).

25. K. Benne and P. Sheats, "Functional Roles of Group Members," *Journal of Social Issues*, 4 (1948): 41–49.

26. Ibid.

27. P. E. Mudrack and G. M. Farrell, "An Examination of Functional Role Behavior and Its Consequences for Individuals in Group Settings," *Small Group Behavior*, 26 (1995): 542–571.

28. Benne and Sheats.

29. Mudrack and Farrell.

30. D. R. Comer, "A Model of Social Loafing in Real Work Groups," *Human Relations* 48 (1995): 647–667. K. Williams, S. Harkins and B. Latane, "Identifiability as a Deterrent of Social Loafing: Two Cheering Experiments," *Journal of Personality and Social Psychology*, 40 (1981): 303–311.

31. Dewey, J. (1991). *How we think.* Buffalo, NY: Prometheus. (Original work published 1910)

32. Beveridge, W. I. B. (1957). *The art of scientific investigation*. New York: Vintage.

33. Foss, S. K., & Griffi n, C. L. (1995). Beyond persuasion: A proposal for an invitational rhetoric. *Communication Monographs, 62,* 2–18.

34. Osborn, M., & Osborn, S. (2000). *Public speaking* (5th ed.). Boston: Houghton Mifflin.

35. Schwartzman, R. The winning student: Dividends from gaming. *Communication and Theater Association of Minnesota Journal* 21(1994):107–112.

36. Robbins, H., & Finley, M. (1995). *Why teams don't work*. Princeton, NJ: Peterson's/Pacesetter.

LEADERSHIP

INTRODUCTION

How can my group manage itself to be productive and make quality decisions? That's a very hard question! One way to get some insight is to learn the group objectives. Even if you have the best group staffed with very bright and highly motivated members, most groups still need some help. You will have to find ways to help the group coordinate all its efforts, as well as help the members remain civil with each other. After all, the groups we are talking about are challenged with complex problems requiring information gathering, analysis, debate, and commitment. All that activity needs to be coordinated to keep the group on track. The members will require occasional motivation and, perhaps, even some discipline. In addition, because this process is rarely completed overnight, the potential for conflict is very high. It's natural for people to become irritated with each other and argue, especially when they spend a lot of time together. We're people; it's what we do! We have to find ways to keep that conflict under control and to use it to help our groups make the best decisions.

To help answer all these questions, this chapter addresses three separate but related topics: leadership, power, and conflict.

Groups are challenged with complex problems requiring a coordinated work approach.

© Zsolt Nyulaszi/Shutterstock.com

How does a leader motivate others in the group?
© 2008, JupiterImages Corporation.

In a give-and-take relationship, followers allow themselves to be influenced by the leader.
© Yuri Arcurs/Shutterstock.com

ARE POWER AND LEADERSHIP THE SAME THING?

Leadership is the ability to influence the behavior of others. A leader is someone who can use interpersonal *influence* to move people to action. A person exercising leadership uses persuasion to motivate people to action. **Power,** by contrast, is the ability to *control* the behavior of others.[1] Power can be based on legitimate authority or position, access to information, or access and control of desired resources.

The use of power and the use of influence are not the same thing. It is possible to use one without using the other. For example, a group member in a leadership role could be very successful at motivating other members to complete tasks in the effort to accomplish the group goal, but that leader could have no source of power. Conversely, a group member with some form of power (control over desired resources, for example), might be able to control the behavior of other group members, but he or she might not be personally persuasive or motivating.[2]

In reality, many leaders likely use a combination of influence and power to accomplish tasks with groups of people. Good leaders try not to rely on power to motivate people, because a reliance on power damages the motivation and creativity of group members, and it results in flawed decisions and inferior products.

Leadership and power will be treated separately because they are different, but the discussion will emphasize the relationship between the two concepts.

WHAT IS THE ROLE OF LEADERSHIP?

Forsyth says that leadership is a specialized form of social interaction. It is a "reciprocal, transactional, and sometimes transformational process in which cooperative individuals are permitted to influence and motivate others to promote the attainment of group and individual goals."[3] Let's look at the parts.

Reciprocal suggests that leadership is an ongoing process and is defined by the leader, the group members, and the particular situation that the group happens to be experiencing. There is a give-and-take relationship between the leader and the members in which the followers allow themselves to be influenced by the leader. There is no leadership without followers.[4]

Leaders and group members work together in a *transactional* process "exchanging their time, energies, and skills to increase their joint rewards."[5] The leader specifies what follower behaviors are needed to solve the problem and how the group's or followers' needs would be satisfied as a result.[6]

Transformational means that leaders can communicate a group vision that members find appealing. This vision motivates and empowers followers to become leaders themselves and influence the outcomes of group tasks. The leader's task is to make the vision clear to the followers. It asks them to make the group goals perhaps more important than their own individual goals.

As we mentioned earlier, leadership is really a *cooperative* process that uses persuasion instead of power and control. Members with the most influence usually emerge as leaders over time, and they are followed by the other members of the group. Remember that we are talking about the member with the most influence, and not *necessarily* the person who was appointed or elected leader of the group. Finally, leadership should function to help the group to adapt to changing circumstances and remain focused on *accomplishing goals*. Leadership helps to provide the direction that moves the group toward its objectives.

Influence of a Leader

Leadership is not "built in" to particular people who possess certain personality characteristics. That is, people are not born or destined to be leaders or followers. Instead of leadership being determined by a set of personality traits, we suggest that it depends more on experience and skills that can be learned and developed. Leadership is given or attributed to a person by others in the group. Even though we have suggested that personality characteristics or traits do not determine who has the ability to lead others, personal qualities do seem to affect *perceptions* of leadership.[7]

If your group does have an appointed leader, it doesn't necessarily mean that he or she will be the most influential person in the group. Leadership is not the sole possession of *the* leader. Many members of the group could provide leadership in different areas or at different times as the group progresses through a task. For example, if your group is working on a project related to the responsible use of energy resources, and even though you might not be *the* leader, you could be influential in decision making because you know a lot about the issue, because you are interested in energy policies, or because you belong to an active energy conservation organization. Whenever you influence the course the group takes, or when you help move the group toward the accomplishment of its goals, you have provided *leadership*.

How can you emerge as a leader within your group?
© kristian sekulic/Shutterstock.com

Take a Closer Look

A study by Geier reports that a process of elimination of contenders for leadership takes place in the initial meetings of any group. If you want to contribute to the goals of the group and become a leader, take these steps[8]:

1. *Be informed:* Being uninformed is seen as a negative characteristic that eliminates most contenders.
2. *Participate:* Groups typically judge quiet members as nonparticipative and unsuitable for leadership.
3. *Be flexible:* Try to remain open to new ideas or methods, especially when your ideas or methods are in conflict with group norms or goals, and be willing to compromise.
4. *Encourage:* Encourage other members to participate; don't try to make all the decisions yourself or dominate the discussion.

Task and Maintenance Leadership

Task roles are oriented toward helping the group accomplish its goals, while maintenance roles are focused on the social and relational issues that arise whenever people work together.

Consistent with this model, **task leaders** are those group members who help the group with organization and advancement toward making a decision of completing a job. They are sometimes perceived as the leader of the group, but they can also be group members who are influential in a particular situation. Task leaders often *emerge* from the interaction of the group over time, but they could also be appointed or elected by the members. The presence of effective task leadership results in the group spending more time on task and staying focused on specific topics. Groups with leaders have longer attention spans than groups without leaders.

Maintenance leaders focus on relational issues, the development of an open and supportive climate, motivation of members, and conflict management. This type of leader also emerges from the interaction of the group. This function is far more than a cruise director sort of position. Maintenance leaders are critical to quality decision making because they mediate differences of opinion and interpersonal conflicts, maintain a high set of standards for group behavior and contributions, and encourage the participation of all the group members.

Both task and maintenance functions are essential to groups interested in making important decisions or completing complex tasks. Keep in mind these important functions of leaders as you consider the three perspectives on leadership presented in the next section.

Leadership Styles

The **styles approach** to leadership is focused on the behaviors of the leader. McGregor tells us that the behavior of a leader is based on assumptions that he or she makes about the members of the group.[9] These assumptions are divided into two groups, Theory X and Theory Y, which were designed to show leaders two ends of a continuum of leadership possibilities.

Theory X Assumptions

- People don't like to work and require the control of a leader.
- People do not like responsibility and they will resist it.
- People are not creative problem solvers.
- People are motivated by lower level needs such as security, food, and money.

Theory Y Assumptions

- People like to work; it comes as naturally as play to them.
- People are capable of self-direction.
- People are attracted to self-control and responsibility.
- People are creative and imaginative in problem solving and like to make decisions.
- People are motivated by higher-level needs such as recognition and self-actualization.

Theory Y assumes that people are creative and imaginative in problem solving.
© Andresr/Shutterstock.com

The practical application of these assumptions can be seen in the leadership styles: autocratic, laissez-faire, and democratic.[10] Autocratic and democratic leadership capture the ends of the continuum, and those will be the primary focus of our illustration.

The Autocratic Leader

The **autocratic leader** follows the Theory X assumptions most closely and creates an authoritative atmosphere that is based on direction and control. This type of leader does not solicit follower feedback. Instead, he or she makes the decisions and supervises followers to make sure the task is being accomplished. Members do not communicate much with each other. Instead, they communicate mostly with the leader, and communication is mostly task-related questions. There is very little discussion. An example of autocratic leadership can often be found in military organizations and on the shop floor in factories geared for high-volume production.

The autocratic style normally results in high efficiency and a high quantity of work, but it is low on cohesiveness, creativity, and member satisfaction. Lewin found that groups with autocratic leaders had the highest incidents of aggressive activity and exhibited the most productivity, but only when closely supervised.[11] Additionally, employees who had low needs for independence and were authoritarian performed best under autocratic supervision.[12]

What does the autocratic style of leadership accomplish?
© Dmitriy Shironosov/Shutterstock.com

The Laissez-Faire Leader

The **laissez-faire leader** is one who takes a hands-off approach to leadership and provides very little direction to those being led. This leader seems to be a nonleader, because he or she does so little to guide the group. He or she abdicates responsibility, delays decisions, gives no feedback, and makes little effort to help followers satisfy their needs. There is no exchange with followers or any attempt to help them grow.[13] This is rarely an effective style.

The Democratic Leader

The **democratic leader** adopts the Theory Y assumptions and creates an atmosphere of member integration, self-control, and participatory decision making; the input of subordinates is encouraged and is used to make decisions. This type of leadership is most effective with groups who have some knowledge about how to complete the task at hand and are fairly motivated to do so. Followers tend to be motivated by higher-level needs such as self-esteem and job satisfaction. In this case, a leader who is too authoritative will only serve to inhibit the group's creative processes.

The democratic leader facilitates group discussion and participation in the decision-making process. In Lewin's study, groups with democratic leaders had the highest levels of individual satisfaction and functioned in the most positive and orderly fashion.[14] Likewise, employees with a high need for independence and who are not authoritarian performed best under a democratic supervisor.[15]

Why are democratic conditions better when searching for a creative solution?
© Dmitriy Shironosov/Shutterstock.com

The strength of the styles approach is its focus on leader behaviors and assumptions made by leaders about followers. Some styles would only be effective in particular situations. For example, the autocratic style should be useful in a factory type setting where work is repetitive and high quantity is expected. By contrast, a group trying to find a creative solution to a complex problem would probably perform better in a democratic condition. The situation, the task, and the composition of the group members will determine what style will produce the best outcomes.

How does a leader effectively analyze the group?
© Tomasz Trojanowski/Shutterstock.com

Situational Leadership

Situational leadership assumes that a leader's effectiveness is contingent, or dependent, upon how well the leader's style fits the context.[16] The situational leadership model by Hersey, Blanchard and Johnson argues that leadership effectiveness is built on a combination of task-based and relationship-based behaviors of the leader.[17] The composition of the group will determine what leadership approach will work best. People in leadership positions should first analyze the group, and then implement one of a variety of leadership styles designed to address the situation.

The primary factors that leaders look for are the ability of members to complete a particular task and their motivation to do so. As we discussed earlier, groups function on two levels: a task level (which is focused on goal achievement) and a relationship level (which is focused on maintaining the group as a unit and motivating members). As such, after situational leaders examine the abilities and motivation levels of followers, they must determine what combination of task and relationship leadership behaviors will work for the group in this situation. Hersey, Blanchard, and Johnson have outlined four leadership styles that consider these issues: telling, selling, participating, and delegating.[18]

1. *Telling.* A high-task and low-relationship approach is used when group members have low levels of ability and low motivation. Groups that are not motivated to perform a task need and expect the leader to be direct in telling them what they should do. Communication is one-way and the leader decides what should be done and how. This leader typically uses a clear, confident, and directive communication style.

2. *Selling.* A high-task and high-relationship approach is used when the members have low levels of ability but high motivation to complete the task. The leader is comparable to a salesperson and works to gain acceptance of a particular course of action by explaining why it is the right or best one to take. The communication used by this leader offers emotional support, and it is motivational, encouraging, and, at times, stern.

3. *Participating.* A low-task and high-relationship approach is used when the members have high levels of ability but low motivation to complete the task. The leader and the group work together to determine what should be done, how, and when. It is similar to the democratic style mentioned earlier. It requires the leader to be less directive, more supportive, and to include the members in decision making. The leader utilizes an open communication style conducive to facilitating discussion, sharing ideas, and encouraging input.

4. *Delegating.* A low-task and low-relationship approach is used when the members have high levels of ability, as well as high levels of motivation to complete the task. This group needs very little guidance or motivation. The leader outlines what needs to be accomplished and the group gets the job done its own way and at its own pace. This requires the leader to use feedback as well as clear communication that fosters a supportive climate, while still maintaining a sense of his or her role as a facilitator. The leader demonstrates confidence in the group by delegating more responsibilities.

The strength of the situational approach to leadership is its focus on member assessment and thinking through what and why a particular leadership approach should be used. For example, we may be more authoritative when a quick response is due and more facilitative when we are working with a mature group and have the time for facilitation. In addition, individuals from high context and collectivistic cultures may not ever use an authoritative (i.e., telling) style, as this approach would cause both leaders and followers to lose face. Please see the cultural discussion later in this chapter.

Transformational Leadership

A **transformational leader** is someone who possesses the charisma necessary to motivate followers and evoke change. Transformational leaders have charisma and vision, provide intellectual stimulation, and inspire their followers:

- They stimulate interest among colleagues and followers to view their work from new perspectives.
- They generate an awareness or a vision of the mission for the group.
- They develop colleagues and followers to higher levels of ability and potential.
- They motivate colleagues and followers to look beyond their own interests toward those that will benefit the group.[19]

Transformational leaders are visionary and inspire followers to achieve higher goals. Lee Iacocca, a transformational leader, joined the Chrysler Corporation in 1978 when the company was on the verge of bankruptcy. From 1979 to 1986, Iacocca was able to turn the company around and make it profitable. Stephen Sharf, who was the head of manufacturing for Chrysler when Lee Iacocca took over, attributed the Chrysler transformation to Iacocca's leadership style. Iacocca is described as someone who knew what he was doing, someone who was well liked, and a person who took charge. Sharf states: "His tremendous self-confidence radiated to whomever he talked to—workers, suppliers, banks, and the government. He was articulate and a motivator. There was no doubt in his mind that he could turn Chrysler around and people began to believe he really could."[20] Iacocca was a transformational leader and a visionary who was able to share that vision with others and transform Chrysler's way of doing business. Lee Iacocca is still regarded as a folk hero because of his leadership and achievements at Chrysler.[21]

Other examples of transformational leaders include John Kennedy, Sam Walton, Steve Jobs, Abraham Lincoln, and Franklin D. Roosevelt.

As with the other leadership approaches mentioned in this chapter, there are some weaknesses of transformational leadership. One is the possibility that passion and confidence may be mistaken for truth and reality. Additionally, the energy these leaders exert can become unrelenting and exhausting because the followers and leaders of this type tend to see the big picture at the expense of the details. However, this approach helps us to understand why some leaders are more successful than other leaders. They can empower individual members to perform beyond their own expectations. This kind of motivation can create strong group identity and often changes the culture of entire organizations.

How to Destroy a Group
Understanding What Not to Do

In order to improve our communication skills, understanding what *not to do* is important. Communication scholar D. M. Hall jokingly suggests eight ways in which a group member should not behave in groups:

1. Never prepare in advance; speak spontaneously. It keeps things on a superficial level.
2. Always take your responsibility lightly. This reduces your anxiety level and increases the frustration levels of others.
3. Never try to understand the group's purposes. This guarantees you'll accomplish nothing.
4. Always do the lion's share of the talking. None of the others have good ideas anyway.
5. Never give credit; hog it all for yourself. The rest love a braggart.
6. Always speak of your many years of experience. This compensates for your lack of ability.
7. Never tell anyone how to do it, else you may lose your prestige and position.
8. Always encourage the formation of cliques. The group can't last long when they begin to fight among themselves.

Have you engaged in any one of these communication behaviors? If so, what can you do to avoid doing so in the future?

Source: Written by D. M. Hall, summarized by Murk.[22]

Good leaders always adapt their approach as the group changes.
© Yuri Arcurs/Shutterstock.com

You don't need to be born with certain personality traits to be a good leader. You can rise to leadership if you take the time to develop the skills and gain experience. Hackman and Johnson tell us that skill development is a continuous, life-long process. The moment you think you have "arrived" as a leader, the progress stops.[23]

From the discussion of leadership styles and types in this chapter, you should learn that a single leadership type will not always be successful. There is no absolute or formula that will be perfect in every situation. To be a successful leader, you should be able to analyze the task, the context of the task, and the group of people who will be making the decision or working on the task. When you have completed that analysis, you should gain some insight into what kind of leadership approach will be most useful in that situation. However, you should not get comfortable! Groups mature, motivation levels change, and the nature of the task could vary as you move toward completion. You should always pay attention to these changes and be ready to adapt and to alter your leadership approach as needed to best achieve your group's goals.

WHAT IS THE ROLE OF POWER?

At the beginning of this chapter, we defined *power* as the ability to *control* the behavior of others.[24] As you read before, power can be based on legitimate authority or a person's position in an organization, access to information, and access to or control of desired resources. It is possible to use power without being influential (i.e., exhibiting leadership), and it is possible to be influential without using power. The best situation exists when leadership and power are combined: the influential leader who uses power at the appropriate times and in moderation can be very successful at helping groups accomplish goals.

French and Raven identified five foundations of power that are typically used in small groups:

1. Legitimate power
2. Coercive power
3. Reward power
4. Expert power
5. Referent power

This section looks more closely at these five power sources, plus one more—interpersonal linkage.

Legitimate Power

Legitimate power exists as a function of someone's position in an organization. Followers defer to the *authority* carried by the position regardless of who occupies the position. Respect for the individual in the position of legitimate power is not required for control. The higher the position in the organization, the more legitimate power a person typically has. An example of the amount of influence and psychological effects legitimate power can have over an individual can be found in the studies of Stanley Milgram.[25] This series of studies found that people would obey legitimate power even when it conflicted with what they believed to be the right thing to do. The best condition exists when the person holding the legitimate power in the organization is also respected by the subordinates. In this condition, the power can be used to direct activities rather than to control group members.

Coercive Power

Coercive power could also be called power to punish. Members follow leaders with coercive power because they want to avoid reprimand or punishment. Followers allow themselves to be controlled in order to avoid the punishments or sanction that could be associated with the failure to comply. Such punishments could include criticism, social ostracism, poor performance appraisals, reprimands, undesirable work assignments, or dismissal.

Coercive power ends when the power holder is no longer able to inflict punishment. Unless it is necessary, it is a good idea to avoid the use of this type of power because it is uncomfortable for most people and it can have a negative effect on the motivation and creativity of group members.

Is using coercive power an effective way to lead?
© Jaimie Duplass/Shutterstock.com

Reward Power

Reward power is just the opposite of coercive power. Where coercive power threatens to punish (or remove access to some desired resource) for noncompliance, reward power offers access to some desired resource as payment for compliance. The primary motivation of the follower is to comply with the leader to get the reward. Your teacher could reward you with bonus points for coming to class on a very cold day, or your boss could give you a bonus for completing a project on time or under the budget. Other rewards at your workplace could include pay increases, recognition, interesting job assignments, or promotions.

Like coercive power, this individual's power ends when he or she is no longer able to provide rewards. Individuals with only reward and not coercive power promise fewer rewards than someone who has both coercive and reward power. Likewise, those who possessed coercive power without reward power were more likely to invoke coercive power more frequently.

These first three power bases can be considered as what Porter and his colleagues termed *position power*, which includes power that is granted as a result of a person's position in an organization rather than by the unique characteristics of the individual.[26] Position-based power is an impersonal source of power. It is also granted to those who have supervisory positions.

The last two bases of power identified by French and Raven[27] and one identified by Hocker and Wilmot are forms of personal power.[28] Unlike position power, these are granted based on individual knowledge, skills, or personality. These power bases often transfer from role to role and are used by either supervisors or subordinates.[29]

Expert Power

A person with **expert power** is able to assist the group in reaching its goals because of his or her expertise on a given topic. Group members comply because they don't have the knowledge to complete the task without help. Followers perceive that the expert has the knowledge to achieve the group's goals. This person can easily lose power if his or her knowledge base is needed for just one subject and if the knowledge is no longer needed or desired.

Referent Power

Referent power is based on the personal liking or respect that one person has for another. The person with referent power is influential because others respect or admire the way he or she does a job or if the power holder possesses personal qualities that others would like to emulate. When people admire you and want to be liked or admired by you, they are often willing to be influenced. You could say that people who have referent power have charisma. As long as followers feel connected with this leader, he or she will exert referent power. If, for some reason, followers' perceptions are altered, then this leader's power is diminished.[30]

Interpersonal Linkages

In addition to the five bases of power identified by French and Raven,[31] Hocker and Wilmot identified a power base that comes from the power holder's access to people who control desired resources.[32] The **interpersonal linkage** is power based on who you know and what resources those people control. If your group needs information from a government agency, for example, and you happen to know somebody at that government agency who can get the information for you, then that can be a source of influence. You don't have access to the information, but you know somebody who does!

Power bases give us insight into the reasons that some leaders are effective. Power can be based on one's position in a company, as we see with legitimate, coercive, and reward power. Power such as expert, personal linkage, and referent can be based on one's individual qualities. Any group member

A person with referent power is influential because others respect or admire the way he/she works.

© Yuri Arcurs/Shutterstock.com

can have this kind of power, and it is dependent on the context and task facing the group. When you possess this kind of power, it is essential that you are ethical with its use. You should be aware of the unethical use of power and question it when it comes in direct conflict with your moral and ethical standards.

DOES MY GROUP HAVE TO HAVE CONFLICT?

Just as you can count on the sun coming up in the morning, you can count on the presence of conflict in small groups. Whenever you get two or more people together who are trying to do something, there will be conflict! Even though many of us are quite similar, we still have individual differences that make us unique. We see the world around us in our own unique ways. When we come together as a small group, those individual differences are going to clash to create misunderstandings and disagreements. Conflict!

Conflict involves disagreement over task and procedural issues, over personality and affective issues, and over competitive tensions among group members. It can arise from differences of opinion, incompatible personalities, and even from geographical and cultural differences.

Conflict is inevitable in small groups. It is not something that you can avoid. But don't walk away from this discussion with the idea that conflict is always a bad thing. Conflict is a central and essential element for groups trying to solve complex problems. As we mentioned in the previous chapter, one of the primary reasons that groups make better decisions than individuals working alone is the multiple perspectives that group members bring to the table. It is when these perspectives conflict that new ideas, points of view, and solutions are created. This is group synergy in action!

Conflict related to the problem challenging a small group is central to the group's success, but it has a darker side. Conflicts based on personality clashes or competitive group members can be a distraction to groups, prevent the group from thoroughly completing the decision-making plan, and even threaten the existence of the group. However, personality-related conflicts can serve a maintenance function. Members of even friendly and cohesive groups get upset with each other now and then. Conflict provides those members with an outlet for hostile feelings, and it can facilitate a close examination of relationships. The bottom line is that if conflict is properly managed, it can be productive on both the task and relationship levels.

As you might have guessed by now, we will be discussing two kinds of conflict: conflict *intrinsic* to the task and conflict *extrinsic* to the task.

How is group conflict a *good* thing?
© Diana Lundin/Shutterstock.com

Intrinsic Conflict

Intrinsic conflict usually centers on disagreements related to the task facing the group. Intrinsic conflict can take two forms. It can be *substantive conflict,* which involves issues directly related to the content of the decision being made. It is unrelated to personal tensions that might exist between group members. Substantive conflict helps groups achieve their goals. Intrinsic conflict can also be *procedural*, which involves group policies and methods of solving problems. Members could disagree, for example, on what is the best way for reaching agreement.[33] Some members might favor voting, for example, while other members believe that all decisions made by the group should have the complete agreement of all members. To prevent procedural issues from taking too much time, some groups adopt explicit policies that specify member responsibilities and decision making processes.[34] Some groups even adopt standard policies such as *Robert's Rules of Order*.[35] You can see an application of *Robert's Rules of Order* in the section on "Running a Meeting" in the appendix of this textbook.

Young, et al. provide us with a comparison of three standard procedures for reaching decisions: voting, compromise, and consensus.[36] If your group gets stuck deciding how to decide, consider adopting of these procedures as your standard policy. Before you choose one, however, carefully look at the strengths and weaknesses of each procedure. We have ranked them good, better, and best, but all decision making experts might not agree with our assessment.

If your group gets stuck on substantive or procedural differences, then you should consider adopting a policy that will help you resolve or manage them. If intrinsic conflict is not managed well, it distracts from the group working on the task. In addition, it could get out of control and lead to extrinsic conflict.

Standard Procedures for Reaching Decisions

- *Good: Voting.* Voting is quick and it solves the problem efficiently, but it creates a majority and a minority. The majority gets everything it wants, so its members are satisfied and committed to carrying out the decision. The minority gets nothing that it wants, so the commitment level of its members is often low, which results in a lack of motivation to follow through with implementation.
- *Better: Compromise.* In this situation, the members made trade-offs to make the decision. All of the members get some of what they want, and all of the members have to give up something to gain the agreement of the group. The resulting level of commitment is only moderate from all members, so follow through on decision implementation could be weakened. Compromise is not as quickly accomplished as voting.
- *Best: Consensus.* Consensus implies unanimous agreement of all members. Because all the members are satisfied and take ownership of the outcome, commitment to the decision is high and all are motivated to follow through on implementation. Consensus could take a very long time with complex issues. You should also beware that a consensus decision, because it has to please all the members to gain agreement, might not always be the most creative or best decision.

The decision-making plan (DMP) described in Chapter 11 is a comprehensive procedure designed to help you understand and solve complex decisions. The three strategies just described will be very useful as your group navigates its way through the DMP procedure.

Extrinsic Conflict

When most people think of conflict, they are probably thinking of **extrinsic conflict**. This kind of conflict is related to the personalities and relationships between members. It can arise when you *just don't like* another group member, or when some basic incompatibility exists between members that cause tension.

There are multiple causes of extrinsic conflict:

- Recall that group communication implies interdependence among the people. When the communication becomes less interdependent and more competitive, the potential for conflict is high. Group members who are committed to the group's goals (creative solution to the problem facing the group) are at odds with members who are more committed to their own individual goals (promotion, money, job recognition).
- The use of power such as threats and punishments and the poor application of legitimate power by leaders or other members can lead to extrinsic conflict.
- Extrinsic conflict can arise when individuals do not understand the reasons for the behaviors of others. If the reasons are not understood, then the behaviors can easily be misinterpreted and lead to resentment. For example, geographic diversity and cultural differences are often a source of conflict.[37] These will be described in the next section.
- Extrinsic conflict often arises from the ways the members communicate with each other. Sometimes it is not *what* you say but *how* you say it that creates the problem. If communication makes another member defensive, then extrinsic conflict becomes more likely. The final section of this chapter looks at communication that can create defensive climates and strategies that can help you avoid conflict.
- Extrinsic conflict can arise because you just don't like another group member. Maybe he or she reminds you of the kid who broke your pencil in kindergarten or the bully who beat you up. If it's all inside your head, then here's some friendly advice: *It's time to be an adult and let go of it!* If, however, the other person feels the same way about you, you should handle the problem in private. If you and the other member can't resolve these differences, try to agree on a strategy for at least managing your relationship while you are working with the group. If you can both commit to the goals of the group, petty differences can be put aside and maybe you can share a friendly, professional relationship.

As stated before, extrinsic conflict can serve a useful maintenance function. However, unmanaged extrinsic conflict often causes harm to a group. If unmanaged, even minor extrinsic conflicts can turn into major problems. Conflicts that go unresolved or unmanaged generally do not go away. They can "explode," and the group cannot go about the business of making decisions because it is caught up in destructive conflict.

Whatever the kind of conflict that arises in your group, the key to making it work for you is **conflict management**. Some strategies you can use for managing extrinsic conflict include the following.

1. *Do everything you can to encourage cooperation among group members.* Look for opportunities to agree whenever possible. Small agreements can eventually lead to larger agreements and cooperation.
2. *Try to encourage participation of all members.* Approach reticent or shy members in a nonthreatening way and ask for their opinions. Listen to their answers. When they realize that other members listen to them, participation will increase.
3. *Be honest about your intentions.* Don't play games or try to manipulate other members.
4. *Maintain a supportive climate.* Look at the final section of this chapter and be able to recognize the difference between defensive and supportive climates. If the climate in your groups becomes defensive, use some of

---

Example: Countering Extrinsic Conflict

A group member complains, "Steve is always late for our meetings. He says we meet too far from his house. That really burns me up. Let's throw him out of the group!"

Problem: Extrinsic conflict leads to low member satisfaction, a lack of agreement, the loss of the cooperative climate, low productivity, and even the disintegration of the group. What do you do when you see escalating extrinsic conflict?

Strategy: Individual group members can successfully counteract extrinsic conflict by turning disruptive acts (that would normally escalate the conflict) into constructive contributions.[38] This helps defuse the situation and refocus the attention of each member to the task at hand. You could turn that expression of anger into a constructive suggestion by saying, "Let's meet at *Steve's* house. That way, he can't be late! Besides, we can watch the game on his HDTV and his refrigerator is always full of food!"

---

the strategies suggested to move toward a more supportive, cooperative atmosphere.

5. *Keep the group goals as a priority.* They should take precedence over the individual goals of members.

How has the "digital age" changed the way we do business?
© Yuri Arcurs/Shutterstock.com

HOW CAN CULTURAL DIFFERENCES LEAD TO EXTRINSIC CONFLICT?

Cultural influences have a profound effect on decision quality and the overall decision-making process. Chances are, you have already worked in a group made up of people from a variety of cultural and ethnic backgrounds. If not, get ready! The world is becoming increasingly *flat*. This means that collaboration and competition for jobs is open to people from all over the world, not just those who live near you or even in your country! Instantaneous communication technology in the "digital age" is shaping the way we manage our lives and do business, and that business is increasingly conducted with others around the globe.[39] Because diverse groups are more likely to experience extrinsic conflict than homogeneous groups, we will briefly examine some of the cultural dimensions that affect groups.[40]

If you are aware of the cultural influences on others, and if you are aware of your own cultural influences and biases, you will be better able to adapt to new situations when they present themselves. Instead of moving directly to an extrinsic conflict situation, you should be willing to understand (and possibly explain to others in the group) that the source of your differences is culture related and perhaps not a fundamental interpersonal disagreement.

Geert Hofstede used the term *cultural dimensions* to refer to the common elements or the key issues of a culture that can be studied and analyzed in meaningful ways.[41] Hofstede's value orientations are used to test and understand culture's influence in today's digital world. Some of these dimensions can be directly applied to the small-group context.[42]

Individualism/Collectivism

In **individualistic cultures**, people are taught personal autonomy, privacy, self-realization, individual initiative, independence, individual decision making, and an understanding of personal identity as the sum of an individual's personal and unique attributes.[43] People from individualistic cultures are taught that their needs and interests are just as important, if not more important, than the needs and interests of others. Some examples of individualistic societies are Australia, Great Britain, Canada, and the United States.[44]

Group members from individualistic cultures are most comfortable working on projects alone and have a tendency to do all the work or none at all. This is not because they are uncooperative or difficult. Rather, it is because they are not socialized to collaborate like those from collectivistic cultures. For individualists, the group experience can be exceedingly frustrating. When an individualist approaches group projects and collaboration with a collectivistic mindset, he or she may find that to put group goals before personal goals is not necessarily a losing position.

Collectivism characterizes a culture in which people, from birth, are integrated into strong, cohesive in-groups.[45] Collectivistic cultures emphasize emotional dependence on groups and organizations, less personal privacy, and the belief that group decisions are superior to individual decisions.[46] They believe in interdependence, an understanding of personal identity as knowing one's place within the group, and concern about the needs and interests of others.

Collectivistic cultures include China, Hong Kong, India, Japan, Pakistan, and Taiwan.[47] Group members from collectivistic cultures experience less frustration when working with group members who also have collectivistic tendencies. This is largely due to the practice they have had collaborating with their own families, friends, and colleagues. Their frustration with groups is more likely experienced when they are collaborating with people who approach group work as individualists.

Group members from individualistic cultures are most comfortable working on projects alone.
© 2008, JupiterImages Corporation.

High Power Distance/Low Power Distance

Power distance is the extent to which the less powerful members of organizations and institutions accept and expect that power is distributed unequally.[48] Individuals from low power-distance cultures believe that inequality in society should be minimized, that all individuals should have equal rights, that power should be used legitimately, and that powerful people should try to look less powerful than they are. Individuals from high power-distance cultures stress coercive and referent power and believe that power holders are entitled to privileges, and that powerful people should try to look as powerful as possible.

Participating effectively in small groups may be more challenging for group members from high power-distance cultures. Likewise, decision-making processes and approaches to conflict resolution are likely to be influenced by the group's power distance level. For instance, conflict management in teams with a low power-distance factor is based on principles of negotiation and cooperation, while in high power-distance teams, conflict is resolved primarily by the power holder.[49] On the one hand, those who come from low power-distance cultures think that group decisions should be made by consensus, should have shared leadership, and that role responsibilities should be based on expertise. On the other hand, people from high power-distance cultures use voting, expect leaders to lead, and are uncomfortable in teams where they are asked to take on more autonomy and responsibility.[50]

Uncertainty Avoidance

Uncertainty avoidance refers to the extent to which risk and ambiguity are acceptable conditions. Hofstede suggests that it is the extent to which the members of a culture feel threatened by uncertain or unknown situations.[51] This is one of the cultural dimensions most problematic for groups.[52] Group members from high uncertainty avoidance cultures interact based on a need for rules, suppression of deviant ideas and behavior, and resistance to innovation. They are motivated by security, esteem, and belongingness. Some countries with high uncertainty-avoidance cultures are Greece, Portugal, Guatemala, Uruguay, and Japan. Low uncertainty-avoidance cultures include the United States, Sweden, Jamaica, Singapore, and Hong Kong.[53]

Group members from low uncertainty-avoidance cultures are more tolerant of different opinions, prefer as few rules as possible, are more calm and contemplative, and they are not expected to express emotions. They are better able to function within a group that is less structured. Such groups are characterized by loose deadlines, undefined roles, few rules, and a high tolerance for innovation and "outside-of-the-box" thinking. Understanding the uncertainty avoidance tendencies of members can help groups structure a productive decision-making environment. Such an environment would provide a balance of structure for those high in uncertainty avoidance. They would still maintain a spirit of innovation and encourage unique approaches to decision making for those who are low in uncertainty avoidance.

High Context/Low Context

Hall divided cultures into high and low context according to their ways of communicating.[54] A **high-context culture** uses communication in which most of the information is either in the physical context or internalized in the person. To understand high-context communication, one should consider the content of the messages and the context together. Context is the situation, background, or environment connected to an event, a location, or an individual.[55] Very little is explicitly stated. High-context communication is typically indirect, ambiguous, harmonious, reserved, and understated.[56] A **low-context culture** is just the opposite. The majority of information is stated explicitly. Low-context communication is direct, precise, dramatic, open, and based on feelings or true intentions.

When interacting with people who are from a high-context culture, using communication that is too direct can result in embarrassment or even anger. Likewise, when interacting with someone from a low-context culture, using communication that is indirect or implied can result in confusion and frustration because it is perceived that the communicator does not say what he or she means. For instance, if a North American supervisor is unsatisfied with a subordinate's sales proposal, the response will probably be explicit and direct: "I can't accept this proposal as submitted, so come up with some better ideas." A Korean supervisor, in the same situation, might say, "While I have the highest regard for your abilities, I regret to inform you that I am not completely satisfied with this proposal. I must ask that you reflect further and submit additional ideas on how to develop this sales program."[57] The message is essentially the same, but as you can see, the approach is different.

High Context Cultures
Japan
Arab Countries
Greece
Spain
Italy
England
France
North America
Scandinavian Countries
German-speaking Countries

Low Context Cultures

Source: Hall & Hall (1990) Understanding Cultural Differences

In addition to personal and ideational differences that normally exist between people, multicultural groups have a high potential for intrinsic conflict based on their different points of view. The potential for extrinsic conflict is even higher, considering the number of potential misunderstandings and interpersonal transgressions resulting from the clash of cultural expectations. An awareness of different cultural expectations will help keep nonproductive conflict to a minimum and promote the level of communication, understanding, and cooperation necessary for making creative decisions.

HOW IS COMMUNICATION A SOURCE OF EXTRINSIC CONFLICT?

A frequent source of extrinsic conflict is communication itself. Sometimes it's not what people say that creates the problem but the way they say it.

Control/Problem Orientation

Most of us need to feel we have some control over our lives. So we respond to control with *psychological reactance*.[58] In response to feeling controlled, we do the opposite of what we are told to do. Communication typical of **control strategies** includes statements such as, "You need to be more considerate," "You must stop procrastinating," and "You have to listen to me." Statements like these create psychological reactance and lead to defensiveness, which leads to extrinsic conflict. Gibb says that hidden in attempts to control is the assumption by the controlling person that the other is somehow inadequate.[59] Wouldn't that make *you* feel defensive?

Using a **problem orientation** allows others an equal contribution to the discussion and decision making. It sends the relational message that the other's position, opinions, and concerns are important. When you take a problem orientation approach to interacting with others, they are likely to be more committed to the resolution of the problem. Just as individuals may respond with psychological reactance when feeling controlled, individuals who feel they have a voice in decision making are more likely to commit to the decision's implementation. Statements that illustrate a problem orientation include, "We are in this together," "What can we do to solve this problem?" and "What do you think?"

Defensive versus Supportive Behaviors

Defensive and supportive climates can be created and maintained with communication behaviors

Defensive Behaviors
1. Control strategies
2. Superiority
3. Evaluation
4. Neutrality
5. Strategy
6. Certainty

Supportive Behaviors
1. Problem orientation
2. Equality
3. Description
4. Empathy
5. Spontaneity
6. Provisionalism

Take a Closer Look

Sometimes when your group has a competitive environment or spirit, it means that there is a lack of compatibility between group goals and the goals of individual members. What should you do?

Try this: Create a cooperative climate!

Instead of allowing the competitive attitudes of group members to become more intense and inhibit cooperation in the group, try to find something on which all members can agree. Even if the members don't go along with you, discovering these opportunities to agree should push the group climate toward the more cooperative end of the continuum. Agreement tends to be reinforcing in that, before too long, others in the group will begin to "pay back" your agreement with their cooperation. Over time, the environment of your group should become more cooperative.[60]

Communicating equality involves treating others with respect and valuing their opinions.
© Répási Lajos Attila/Shutterstock.com

Superiority/Equality

Communicating **superiority** creates defensiveness by demonstrating that we perceive ourselves to be better than others, and that quickly leads to extrinsic conflict. Superiority is characterized by comments such as, "You do not know what you are doing," and, "I have had more experience with this type of situation; I will handle it." This sends the relational message that the other's opinion is not worthy, his expertise is not valued, or that he is not important.

Equality, by contrast, involves treating others with respect and valuing their thoughts and opinions, regardless of their knowledge about the topic, their status, age, or position. People who *appear* to be of lower status or position are capable of having profound insights. Communication illustrating equality would be, "What do you think?" and, "I never thought of it that way; let's explore this idea together further."

Evaluation/Description

If a communicator appears to be evaluating you, either through tone of voice, expression, or message content, you will likely go into a protection mode. This kind of communication is often perceived as an attack on a person's self-esteem. The person feeling attacked then focuses energy on defense, which draws his or her focus from the problem to be solved. When communicating with others, you should first *describe* before forming evaluations. This is not to say that you cannot evaluate behavior, but before jumping to conclusions, you should demonstrate that you are attempting to understand. Through description, you may create a more supportive climate. To be descriptive is to be factual without offering an opinion.

If you look at the descriptions provided in the box, can you say with certainty that the behaviors indicate rudeness, pushiness, or unfairness? Based on the behaviors described, there *may* be other possible interpretations. Could Kate have not realized she bumped into someone? Or did she softly say she was sorry but was not heard? Could Tom have had an urgent message? Could Stacey have valid reasons for her decision that were, indeed, fair? The answers to these questions are, *maybe*. We cannot be entirely sure without more information. The point is we need to be descriptive if we want to avoid extrinsic conflict by creating a defensive climate.

Take a Closer Look

| Kate is rude. | Tom is pushy. | Stacey is unfair. |

Each of these statements is an evaluation. Now, if we were to take the time to describe the behavior that made us conclude that Kate is rude, Tom is pushy, and Stacey is unfair, we might come up with the following descriptive statements:

- Kate bumped into me without acknowledging it. She didn't say she was sorry or excuse herself.
- Tom kept phoning me after I told him I was too busy to talk.
- Stacey didn't give me the opportunity to work on the marketing project.

Neutrality/Empathy

One of the best ways to devalue someone is to respond in a way that communicates a lack of caring. **Neutrality** communicates that you simply do not care about the person or what he or she is saying. Using the supportive strategy of **empathy** means approaching a discussion with the intent to understand the other person's position from his or her point of view. This is not to be confused with sympathy, or responding with how we would feel in a particular situation. To be empathic is to express genuine interest in hearing what others have to say; it is one of the most confirming communication forms. Some examples of empathic responses are, "Kate, you must feel very upset by your layoff," and, "Stacey, I can only imagine how you must feel right now." To respond with neutrality, you might use responses like, "It doesn't matter to me," and, "Whatever you want."

If you want to create and maintain a supportive climate in your group, practice responding in ways that demonstrate that you care and understand.

Strategy versus Spontaneity

To use **strategy** is to communicate that you have a hidden agenda. There is something motivating your communication that is not initially revealed to others. You try to manipulate others in the effort to gain some advantage. Have you ever had someone ask you, "What are your plans Friday night?" And you respond with, "I am free. Do you want to do something?" only to hear, "Oh good, can you babysit?" Somehow, this approach asking us to babysit feels like a trick. Another stereotypical example is the feeling when you walk into a sales presentation. You suspect that everything from the first handshake to the free dinner is carefully scripted to get you to buy something. Your defenses are activated and you begin to interpret everything that is said to you as part of a sneaky plot to buy that time-share in an exotic resort area. Strategic communication is revealed when you feel that people are flattering you for their own personal gain, or using self-disclosure to get you to reciprocate.

Spontaneity is characterized by honesty, directness, and good faith. It is saying: "I really need a babysitter Friday night; if you are free I would greatly appreciate your help." In a spontaneity condition, you probably won't be as suspicious of others and you will take things they say at face value. If they attempt to shake your hand, you can be sure it's an invitation to friendship and nothing else. When you get into the defensive mode, it is easy to misinterpret and start looking for hidden meanings in things that people say.

Certainty versus Provisionalism

People who communicate **certainty** seem to know all the answers. There is nothing they don't know, and they are quite sure about it. We tend to see this dogmatic individual as needing to be right and "wanting to win an argument rather than solve a problem."[61] This behavior communicates to others a lack of interest in their position on an issue. The defensiveness that is created by certainty can be countered by provisionalism. **Provisionalism** means trying to explore issues, look for solutions, and consider the points of view of other group members.

Research tells us that supportive climates not only produce happier and more satisfied group members, but that groups with predominately supportive climates are more productive.[62] When the climate becomes defensive, group members become distracted by the suspicion that they are being manipulated or attacked, the potential for destructive extrinsic conflict is high, messages are consistently misinterpreted, and the group loses sight of the problem to be solved. All the assumptions that we make about groups making better decisions are based on the broad assumption that the members are fully engaged in the solution of the problem. When the attention of the group is distracted from that problem-solving goal, defective decisions will be the result.

ENDNOTES

1. D. Ellis and B. A. Fisher, *Small Group Decision Making: Communication and the Group Process*, 4th ed. (New York: McGraw-Hill, 1994). Also J. French and B. Raven, "The Bases of Social Power," in Group Dynamics: Research and Theory, ed. D. Cartwright and A. Zander, (New York: Harper and Row, 1968).

2. E. P. Hollander, "Leadership and Power," in *The Handbook of Social Psychology*, 3rd ed., ed. G. Lindzey and E. Aronson (New York: Random House, 1985), 485–537.

3. D. Forsyth, *Group Dynamics*, 3rd ed. (Belmont, CA: Wadsworth, 1999): p. 343.

4. J. Barrow "The Variables of Leadership: A Review and Conceptual Framework," *Academy of Management Review* 2(1997): 231–251. Also E. P. Hollander, and L. R. Offermann, "Power and Leadership in Organizations: Relationships in Transition," *American Psychologist* 45 (1990): 179–189.

5. Forsyth, p. 364.

6. B. M. Bass, (1985). *Leadership and Performance beyond Expectations* (New York: Free Press, 1985).

7. M. Hackman and C. Johnson, *Leadership: A Communication Perspective* (Prospect Heights, IL: Waveland Press, 2000). Also D. Kenny and S. Zaccaro, "An Estimate of Variance Due to Traits in Leadership," *Journal of Applied Psychology* 48 (1983): 327–335; and R. Lord, C. De Vader, and G. Alliger, "A Meta-analysis of the Relation between Personality Traits and Leadership Perceptions: An Application of Validity Generalization Procedures," *Journal of Applied Psychology* 71 (1986): 402–410.

8. Geier (1967). "A Trait Approach to the Study of Leadership in Small Groups," *Journal of Communication* 17 (1967): 316–323.

9. D. McGregor, *The Human Side of Enterprise* (New York: McGraw-Hill, 1960).

10. K. Lewin, R. Lippit, and R. K. White, "Patterns of Aggressive Behavior in Experimentally Created Social Climates," *Journal of Social Psychology* 10 (1939): 271–301.

11. Ibid.

12. V. H. Vroom, *Some Personality Determinants of the Effects of Participation* (Englewood Cliffs, N.J.: Prentice Hall, 1960). Also W. W. Haythorn, A. Couch, D. Haefner, P. Langham, and L. Carter, "The Effects of Varying Combinations of Authoritarian and Equalitarian Leaders and Followers," *Journal of Abnormal and Social Psychology* 53 (1956): 210–219.

13. Peter G. Northouse, *Leadership Theory and Practice*, 2nd ed. (Thousand Oaks, CA: Sage, 2001).

14. Lewin, Lippit, and White.

15. Vroom; also Haythorn et al.

16. Northouse.

17. P. Hersey, K. Blanchard, and D. Johnson, *Management of Organizational Behavior: Leading Human Resources*, 8th ed. (Upper Saddle River, NJ: Prentice-Hall, 2000).

18. Ibid.

19. B. M. Bass and B. J. Avolio, *Through Transformational Leadership* (Thousand Oaks, CA: Sage, 1994).

20. S. Sharf, "Lee Iacocca as I Knew Him; He Was Certainly the Right Man at the Right Time," *Ward's Auto World* (May 1, 1996).

21. J. Smith, "Lutz for Chairman? His Leap from Ford Fuels Talk about Iacocca Succession," *Ward's Auto World* (July 1, 1986).

22. P. J. Murk, "Effective Group Dynamics: Theories and Practices," paper presented at the International Adult Education Conference of the American Association for Adult and Continuing Education, Nashville, TN, 1994.

23. Hackman and Johnson, p. 358.

24. Ellis and Fisher; French and Raven.

25. S. Milgram, "Behavioral Study of Obedience," *Journal of Abnormal and Social Psychology* 67 (4) (1963): 471–478.

26. L. W. Porter, A. Harold, and R. Allen (eds). *Organizational Influence Processes* 2nd ed. (New York: M. E. Sharpe, 2003).

27. French and Raven.

28. Hocker, J., and Wilmot, W. *Interpersonal Conflict*, 3rd ed. (Dubuque: Brown, 1991).

29. Porter et al.

30. Ibid.

31. French and Raven.

32. Hocker and Wilmot.

33. Forsyth.

34. C. Houle, *Governing Boards: Their Nature and Nurture* (San Francisco: Josey-Bass, 1989).

35. H. M. Robert, *Robert's Rules of Order, Revised Edition* (New York: Morrow, 1971).

36. Young et al.

37. R. Moreland, J. Levine, and M. Wingert, "Creating the ideal work group: Composition effects at work," in *Understanding Group Behavior: Small Group Processes and Interpersonal Relations,* ed. J. Levine and M. Wingert (Mahwah, NJ: Erlbaum, 1996).

38. D. Gouran, Principles of counteractive influence in decision-making and problem-solving groups," in *Small Group Communication: A Reader,* ed. R. Cathcart and L. Samover (Dubuque: Brown, 1992), 221–235.

39. T. L. Friedman, *The World Is Flat* (New York: Farrar, Straus and Giroux, 2005).

40. Moreland et al.

41. G. Hofstede, *Cultures and Organizations: Software of the Mind* (London: McGraw-Hill, 1991).

42. E. Würtz, "A Cross-cultural Analysis of Websites from High-context Cultures and Low-context Cultures," *Journal of Computer-Mediated Communication* 11(1)(2005), http://jcmc.indiana.edu/vol11/issue1/wuertz.html (accessed May 28, 2007).

43. A. F. E. Darwish and G. L. Huber, "Individualism vs. Collectivism in Different Cultures: A Cross-cultural Study," *Intercultural Education* 14 (1) (2003): 47–57.

44. A. Baron and R. Byrne, *Social Psychology* (Boston: Allyn and Bacon, 1997).

45. G. Hofstede and H. M. Bond, "Hofstede's Culture Dimensions: An Independent Validation using Rokeach's Value Survey," *Journal of Cross-Cultural Psychology* 15 (4) (1984): 417–433.

46. Darwish and Huber, pp. 47–57.

47. Baron and Byrne.

48. G. Hofstede, *Culture's Consequences: Comparing Values, Behaviors, Institutions, and Organizations across Nations* (Thousand Oaks, CA: Sage Publications, 2001). Also M. Mulder, *The Daily Power Game* (Leiden, Netherlands: Martinus Nijhoff, 1977); and Hofstede.

49. M. Deutsch, *The Resolution of Conflict: Constructive and Destructive Processes* (New Haven, CT: Yale University Press, 1973).

50. T. M. Paulus, B. Bichelmeyer, L. Malopinsky, M. Pereira, and P. Rastogi, "Power Distance and Group Dynamics of an International Project Team: A Case Study," *Teaching in Higher Education* 10 (1) (2005): 1–14.

51. Hofstede.

52. S. Van Hook, "Cross-cultural Variances in Team Effectiveness: The Eastern European Experience," http://wwmr.us/teams.htm (accessed Febuary 4, 2007).

53. Hofstede.

54. E. T. Hall, *Beyond Culture* (New York: Anchor Press/Doubleday, 1976).

55. Würtz.

56. W. B. Gudykunst, Y. Matsumoto, S. Ting-Toomey, T. Nishida, K. Kim, and S. Heyman, "The Influence of Cultural Individualism-collectivism, Self-construals, and Individual Values on Communication Styles across Cultures," *Human Communication Research* 22 (4) (1996): 510–543.

57. Y. Choe, "Intercultural conflict patterns and intercultural training implications for Koreans," Paper presented at the 16th Biennial World Communication Association Conference, Cantabria, Spain, 2001.

58. S. S. Brehm and J. W. Brehm, *Psychological Reactance: A Theory of Freedom and Control* (New York: Academic Press, 1981).

59. J. Gibb, "Defensive Communication" *Journal of Communication* 11 (1961): 141–148.

60. Gouran.

61. Gibb, p. 79.

62. C. Tandy, "Assessing the Functions of Supportive Messages," *Communication Research* 19 (1992): 175–192.

INTERVIEWING

WHAT IS INTERVIEWING?

Most of us have participated in interviews in either a casual or formal setting, so you probably have a decent idea of what is and what is not an interview. You probably know already that an interview is a *form of interpersonal communication* or conversation, so let's begin there.

Although it is true that all interviews are conversations, you should recognize that *all conversations are not interviews!* The ways in which conversations and interviews differ will help us get a handle on exactly how we should view an interview.

Two Parties

All interviews have two parties: interview*er* and an interview*ee*. More than two people could be participating in the event, but there will still be those two parties. For example, a group of reporters could be questioning the producers of the latest reality show, *Excessive and Unnecessary Ear Alteration,* about the rumor that the program could be turned into a full-length feature film. The group of curious reporters makes up one of the parties: the interviewer. The group of *EUEA* producers is the second party: the interviewee. Keep your fingers crossed that *this* movie never makes it to the theaters!

Questions and Answers

The primary structure of this kind of conversation centers on asking and answering questions. The kind of questions and sequence of questions that are asked are largely determined by the type of interview and goals for that interview. Types of questions and organization of questions will be discussed shortly.

Goals

Both parties in an interview have deliberate and specific goals they wish to accomplish with this event. Typical interview goals include gathering information, giving information, seeking employment, seeking employees, making a sale or creating an impression, helping self or others, evaluating employee performance, and assessment of self or another. The more precise or detailed you can be in determining your goals for an interview, the more clearly you can plan and organize your role in the process. Interview goals provide the purpose of the interview, determine the kinds of questions that will be asked,

When you think of an interview, does a group of pushy reporters automatically come to mind?
© Milos Jokic/Shutterstock.com

Clear and precise goals are as important for a successful interview as they are in other situations.
© David Lee/Shutterstock.com

and, to some extent, affect the structure of the interaction.[1] If the goals of the interview are ambiguous or not well thought out, one or both of the parties will leave the interview unsatisfied.[2]

Awareness

All the people involved should know that they are participating in an interview. They should understand that this is not a casual conversation and that they are guided by their own goals for the interview.

Exchange of Roles

While roles of the parties remain constant, each participant engages in a brisk exchange of speaking and listening roles. Both parties in an interview ask as well as answer questions. There is no formula for determining who talks more in a particular context, but it depends on the type of interview (see following section), the goals of the individual parties for the interview, and the conversational styles of the participants.

A common view of an employment interview, for example, is that the employer (interviewer) asks all or most of the questions and the applicant (interviewee) provides all or most of the answers. This might be true in a **screening interview,** in which the employer is attempting to determine the qualifications of the applicant for the specific job being offered. However, in later interviews, the interviewee could be asking more questions to better understand the nature of the specific position and the nature of the company. The applicant wants to know if he or she would like to work for this particular company. In this situation, the interviewer (employer) will likely do more talking to provide the necessary information to the applicant.

In a **counseling** or **helping interview,** a psychologist (interviewer) might ask some questions of the interviewee to determine the kind of problem he or she is experiencing, but then the counselor might do more of the talking to give advice to the interviewee about how to try to solve the problem. In other kinds of counseling interviews, the psychologist could determine that the best way to provide help is to ask questions for the purpose of gently guiding the interviewee to talk about his or her problems. In this case, the interviewer would ask a few questions while the interviewee does all or most of the talking.

WHAT TYPES OF QUESTIONS ARE USED IN INTERVIEWS?

As you already know, all interviews are structured around the asking and answering of questions. Although questions and answers might be viewed as a limitation on the interaction in an interview, there is a wide variety of question types that allow considerable flexibility in the kinds of conversations that you can hold. This section will explore a variety of types of questions and their uses.

Primary and Secondary Questions

A **primary question** is used to introduce topics or new areas of discussion. A primary question is easy to identify because it can stand alone, out of any kind of context, and yet it can still make perfect sense. Here are some examples of primary questions:

- Where did you attend high school?
- What is your opinion of the "designated hitter" rule in baseball?
- For what company have you been working the past two years?

A **secondary question** (or probing question) usually does not make much sense if asked outside of a particular context. This question is used to encourage an interviewee to keep talking, to provide additional or more focused information, or to clarify an answer. If an interviewee doesn't answer a question to the satisfaction of the interviewer, the interviewer can follow up the primary question with a secondary question. Secondary questions can be preplanned and written into your interview plan, or they can just spontaneously emerge during the course of the interview. Some examples of secondary questions that might be used to expand or probe responses to primary questions include the following:

- What classes did you think were the most interesting? (preplanned follow-up)
- Why? What was interesting to you about biology? (spontaneous follow-up)
- Do you think every player should play both offense and defense? (preplanned)
- What's so special about pitchers? (spontaneous)
- Which of those jobs did you like best? (preplanned)
- What was so unusual about that job? (spontaneous)
- Is there anything else that you would like to say?

To avoid possibly influencing the interviewee's response, make an effort to keep your probing questions as nondirective or neutral as possible. Try not to say (with a shocked or surprised look on your face), "*Why* would you do *that?*" Instead, Willis suggests "Tell me more about that."[3]

In addition to asking an actual question as a secondary or probing question, the interviewer could also simply pause and wait for further response. The pause, combined with a posture and/or facial expression that indicates listening or curiosity can "nudge" an interviewee to provide additional information. It's probably a good idea to list possible probing questions on your interview guide, especially if you anticipate that a question will require some probing to accomplish the information-gathering goals of the interview.

Finally, be careful not to lead the interviewee with your probing questions or suggest an answer. Be as neutral as possible. See the section about biased questions that follows shortly.

Open and Closed Questions

Open Questions

When using an **open question**, the interviewee has a great deal of freedom in how to respond to the question. An open question can request very general or nonspecific information, and there is usually very little direction provided by the interviewer as to the direction of the desired response. Here are some examples of open questions:

- Tell me what happened.
- How do you feel about smart videogames?
- What do you know about internet telephones?

Open questions can be very useful for exploring a topic in depth because the interviewee can talk about nearly any related topic for as long as he or she wants. Open questions also allow the interviewer to discover facts concerning a topic about which he or she knows very little. So this kind of question is good for exploring and investigation of new areas of interest. They can also be used to learn more about an interviewee's perspectives, priorities, and depth of knowledge of a particular topic.

The use of open questions requires that the interviewer be very skilled. The questions can take time to answer and therefore demand excellent listening skills. In addition, because the interviewer provides little direction for the desired response, the interviewee is free to go off in any direction with the answer. Consider this question asked by the interviewer: "What are your feelings about cable TV?" The purpose of the interview might be to discover the opinions of a community about programming on the local cable TV system. But because the question is so broad, the interviewee might seize that opportunity to complain about how the cable installer scared his dog or dug up his yard when laying the cable. It takes a good deal of interviewer skill to acknowledge that undesirable response and then to gently direct the interviewee to discuss programming. Consequently, in addition to discovering information consistent with the goals of the interview, the interview must also *manage* the interaction to keep the conversation on topic.

Finally, open questions are rarely useful for covering a wide range of topics because of the amount of time necessary for the interviewee to respond to each question. If the goal of the interview is not coverage of a small number of topics in depth, but a larger number of topics, a more closed type of question should be used.

Closed Questions

In sharp contrast to an open question, a **closed question** attempts to limit or restrict the response and focus the interviewee on providing only the desired information. Closed questions allow the interviewer to better control the topics covered by the interviewee by requiring more precise and specific answers. Examples of closed questions include the following:

- What is your favorite summertime sport?
- What mode of transportation do you use to commute to work every day?
- In what city would you like to live?

Interviewers can use different types of closed questions to accomplish specific interview goals. In addition to the less restrictive questions, you can also use multiple-choice and dichotomous questions.

Multiple-choice questions restrict the interviewee's response options. Public opinion polls and other types of surveys often use this kind of question. Multiple choice is an example of extremely closed questions. They are more common in survey kinds of interviews, but they are occasionally used in more mainstream types of interviews, especially if several people are being interviewed.

Using multiple-choice questions, interviewers are able to collect very specific pieces of information in a relatively short time. The information collected is fairly uncomplicated and easy to summarize, and the responses from many interviewees can be compared because all the collected data are in the same form. In addition, because the responses are restricted and predetermined, the level of interviewer skill and training does not have to be nearly as high as when using open questions. Interviewees are forced to choose the option provided by the interviewer that best describes their responses to the questions.

Even though the interviewers do not need the highest level of skill to use closed questions, the questions themselves must be written with great care. The questions themselves must be clearly worded, and the response lists should be exhaustive and mutually exclusive.

To be *exhaustive*, a list of responses must include all possible answers that could be given by interviewees. For example, in an interview conducted by an automobile manufacturer to gather customer reactions to a new model, the interviewer asked how long the interviewee had owned the car. The possible answers were 3 months, 6 months, 9 months, or 1 year. What if the interviewee had owned the car for only 5 weeks? What is that person to answer? To make this list exhaustive, the responses could be changed to 3 months or less, 4 to 6 months, 7 to 9 months, 10 to 12 months, and more than 12 months. With this change, all interviewees could find a response appropriate to themselves.

Another strategy for achieving exhaustiveness is to include an "other" response. For example, the question you asked is, "With what political party do you affiliate yourself?" Given the variety of existing political parties, the list of responses could be quite long. And even with a long list, you might not cover all the possibilities. However, to make your list exhaustive, you could include several of the more popular parties, and then include an "other" to provide all interviewees with a response.

The responses for multiple choice questions must also be *mutually exclusive*. That is, an interviewee should be able to find only one applicable choice. When constructing this kind of question, you should examine the list and ask if an individual might realistically choose more than one response. Responding to the political party question, it seems unreasonable to expect that anybody would select more than one of those response categories.

Dichotomous questions restrict responses to one of two possible choices. The responses can be a yes/no answer or various two-option answers.

Although this kind of question is easy to ask, easy to answer, and provides results that are easy to summarize, they provide little depth of understanding or insight because they reveal little information beyond what is specifically asked by the interviewer.

As you have likely concluded, closed questions have strengths and weaknesses. On the strength side, they are easy to write, easy to administer, and easy to analyze and compare. Also, they require a lesser level of skill and training to conduct an interview. They also provide the opportunity to precisely direct the flow of an interview and to gather information about a variety of topics in a fairly short time. On the weakness side, closed questions limit the depth of potential responses because of the restrictive format of the question and possible answers.

The kinds of questions that you use really depend on the goals you have for the interview and how you intend to use the information collected in the interview. If you would like to understand the "soul" of the interviewee and find out what makes him or her tick, then more open questions will allow freedom to follow unexpected directions and to explore in depth. However, if you want to collect a variety of information from a large and diverse group of people, perhaps the more closed questions would work better for you. Of course, it's always possible to mix the kinds of questions to achieve your specific interview goals.

With what political party do you affiliate yourself?
a. Democrat
b. Republican
c. Green
d. Independent
e. Other _____ (please specify)
f. No party affiliation

Dichotomous Questions

- Are you satisfied or dissatisfied with the course you are taking?
- Did you complete the assignment for today's class?
- Do you agree or disagree with the designated hitter rule in baseball?

The kinds of questions you use depend on the goals you have for the interview.
© 2008, JupiterImages Corporation.

Question Hazards and Other Dangers

Biased Questions

Questions phrased in such a way that they would be likely to influence the interviewees' responses are called **biased questions**. You should make every attempt to avoid biased questions, because the responses given do not necessarily represent the true thoughts of the interviewee. Biased questions come in at least two forms: leading questions and loaded questions.

A **leading question** guides the interviewee in the direction of the response preferred by the interviewer or otherwise requires the interviewee to give the socially correct or acceptable response. Leading questions are often used by sales people to persuade customers to buy a product or service.

Leading Questions

- Isn't this a great car?
- Everyone knows that fuels burned by cars and trucks harm the environment and contribute to global warming. Are you in favor of restricting vehicle emissions?
- Aren't golden retrievers fabulous dogs?
- You *actually* listen to talk radio *every day*?
- Most people agree that the governor of the state is doing a great job and should be re-elected. Using the following scale, how would you rate the governor's work in education?

Great Job	Good Job	Neutral	Poor Job	Very Poor Job

Similar to a leading question, a **loaded question** can incite emotional responses, give equally disagreeable response alternatives, or place the interviewee in a paradox where any answer is inappropriate. Loaded questions almost always create a defensive reaction from the interviewee and seldom yield usable information. Fortunately, these questions are rarely used, so be careful that you avoid them.

Loaded Questions

- Have you stopped beating your cat?
- Did you get caught cheating on your girlfriend again?

To fix leading or loaded questions, make sure that your questions are *neutral*. That is, the wording of your questions should suggest no particular response. Remember that you are trying to *discover* information by asking questions. You are not merely trying to get interviewees to say something you want them to say. If you can't decide by proofreading them yourself if your questions are neutral, then you can ask others to read them for you. You can also pretest your questions on a very small number of interviewees. In either case, you can ask the readers if they spotted any biased questions. Here's a re-write of one of the examples:

Fix: Unbiased Question

Which one of the following best represents your opinion of the governor's work in education?

Great Job	Good Job	Neutral	Poor Job	Very Poor Job

Double-Barreled Questions

It's pretty easy to place two questions into one question, so you have to be careful to proofread your questions before you include them in your interview plan. With a **double-barreled question,** you would be asking for a single answer to what might be several questions.

For example, a question might ask: "Are you in favor of increases in cable TV and electricity rates for this community?" The question asks for a yes or no response. However, if you say yes, what exactly is it that you are in favor of? Are you in favor of a rate increase for electricity? Are you in favor of a rate increase for cable TV? Or are you in favor of a rate increase for both electricity and cable TV? If you say no, what do you oppose? What if you support the increase in cable rates but oppose the increase in electricity rates? How can this attitude be expressed with a single yes or no answer? Here are other examples:

Double-Barreled Questions

The United States should get out of the post office business and spend the money on preparing for natural disasters or other emergencies.   YES   NO

Do you support the president's position on the hurricane clean-up and tax relief?   YES   NO

To fix double-barreled questions, carefully proofread your questions with a sharp eye out for two-pronged questions. If you spot one, the best fix is to break it down into separate questions, assuming that your interview goals include all the concepts covered in the original question. Keep the issues separate and clear. Looking at the previous example, you could rewrite the question as two new questions:

Fix: Individual Questions

Do you support the president's position on the hurricane clean-up?   YES   NO

Do you support the president's position on tax reform?   YES   NO

Open-to-Closed Questions

With this question hazard, the interviewer begins with a question, but then follows up very quickly with a much more narrow, closed question. Although the question is originally designed to allow the interviewee some depth and flexibility in the response, the follow-up question severely limits the response, and often reduces it to a simple yes or no. Here's an example of an **open-to-closed question.**

Open-to-Closed Questions

Tell me what it's like to be married. *(then immediately follow with)* Do you guys fight a lot? (or) Do you guys go out a lot? (or) Do you enjoy being married?

Can you please describe the position that you have available? Would I get a vacation? (or) Are there educational benefits? (or) Would I get my own office?

In each case, attempting to take advantage of the benefits of open questions, the interviewer begins by looking for some depth in the response. The goal is to allow the interviewee to provide some personal insight. But before the response can be expressed, the interviewer changes the question and limits the interviewee to a very simple answer.

The cure in this case is less a matter of careful proofreading (that is *still* very important!) but more a matter of careful timing and listening to the interviewee's response. Make sure you give the interviewee enough time to fully answer your original open question. Then, if you still would like more information, use your follow-up or probing questions. Be patient!

HOW DO I PREPARE FOR AN INTERVIEW?

To prepare for an interview, you should have firmly determined what you want to gain from the interview. In addition, you should have a strategy for reaching your objective.

Goals

As you saw in the definition of an interview, at least one of the parties comes into the situation with a specific goal in mind. So before you begin any kind of interview, you need to pause and reflect on your **goals** for the interaction. Just what do you want to get from this interview? Are you looking for advice, information, employment, attitude change, directions, instructions, motivation, or solutions to a problem?

When you have made a general determination of your goals, try to narrow the focus and decide what you want to take with you from this specific conversation. Do you want advice on a career choice? Do you need help with a particular problem in your life or career? Do you want to make the "short list" for an employment position? Are you trying to select a major? The more specific your goals, the better you can plan for the interview.

What do you want to accomplish in the interview? Determine what you want to gain before you participate.
© 2008, JupiterImages Corporation.

Interview Plan

When you have arrived at a decision about what goals you would like to accomplish in your interview, you should develop an interview plan. The **interview plan** outlines your strategy for goal achievement and it includes the topics that should be discussed as well as the sequence and wording of specific questions. The exact format of the plan is directly tied to your interview goals. The format of your plan can range on a continuum from directed to nondirected.

In a *directed* interview, the interviewer controls the areas of discussion and the pace and flow of the conversation. Questions used in this plan are usually more closed, restricting the focus of the interviewee. If you use a *nondirected* plan, you would include more open questions that allow the interviewee some flexibility of response. As a result, in this type of interview, the interviewee tends to exert more control over the flow of the conversation and, to some extent, the topic areas covered.

As mentioned earlier, the specific plan that you choose depends on your goals for the interview. If you don't know a great deal about the topic, and if you would like to explore that topic in depth with a relatively small number of interviewees, then you should select a more nondirected interview plan. With this plan, the interviewer begins by asking open questions to start the conversation and establish a focus. Because the questions and potential subject areas are broad, the interviewee must be prepared to probe responses and to more completely investigate different content areas. The interviewer therefore has to be very skilled to not only *follow* the flow of the conversation but to *adapt* to the different directions the conversation might take. Here are some examples of questions appropriate to this type of interview plan:

- Tell me about yourself.
- What happened?
- How do you feel about life as a college student?

If a completely nondirected question is not necessary, that is, if you would like to guide the interviewee more toward a specific topic area, you can use a more restrictive question. The question supplies a little more direction about the desired response. Take a look at these examples:

- What is the biggest challenge you see to attending college part time while raising a family?
- What is your biggest concern about life after college?

If this form of the question doesn't bring the amount of focus that you want, you can follow up your open question with probing questions to move the interviewee to the topics you wish to discuss:

What is your biggest concern about life after college?

- Probe: getting a job? (getting a better job?)
- Probe: raising a family?
- Probe: finding a satisfying career?
- Probe: making a meaningful contribution to society?

Using a more directed question form allows the interviewer not only to keep the interviewee focused on appropriate topics, but also to restrict the duration of the responses. Pace is important! You do not want to run out of time or energy before you accomplish your interview goals!

The directed interview plan allows the interviewer to exercise more control over responses and the topics covered. If you are interested in gathering a broad range of information about a topic from a fairly large number of interviewees, then the directed interview is the plan you should choose. Common applications for the directed plan include market surveys and opinion polls which typically interview large numbers of people. In addition, employers who conduct screening interviews of large groups of applicants often use a more directed approach. Each interviewee responds to questions that are usually more closed, worded the same way to improve reliability, and asked in the same order. Here are some examples of questions that might be used in a directed interview plan:

What specific questions could you ask a student about her concerns about life after college?
© aceshot1/Shutterstock.com

Directed Interview Questions

- Which member of the City Council do you think should be the next mayor of the city?
- If you could only make one improvement to this proposal, what would it be?

If you want to completely control the range of possible responses, you can use a multiple choice or standardized response question:

- The County should construct four new recreation centers in the next 3 to 5 years.

    Strongly Agree   Agree   Neutral   Disagree   Strongly Disagree

- Which one of the following is your favorite Simpson's character?

    a. Marge
    b. Homer
    c. Bart
    d. Lisa
    e. Maggie
    f. Other

HOW ARE INTERVIEWS STRUCTURED?

An interview has a recognizable structure much like the structure of a public speech or other messages. There are three main parts to an interview: the opening, the body, and the closing.

Opening

The **opening** or introduction is a critical part of the interview, yet it is often neglected during the planning stages. The opening serves at least three functions critical to the success of the interview. The opening should *set the foundation* of the relationship between the parties that will be further developed during the course of the interview. Some interviewing professionals suggest some small talk or even some self disclosure at this point, but that should be decided case-by-case based on the specific individuals involved and the goals of the interview.[4]

The opening should *motivate* the other party to participate fully in the interaction. You can offer a reward, stress the importance of the interview goals, show respect for the other, or use some other motivational strategy. The important idea is to let the other party know that you hope for and would appreciate full participation.

Finally, the opening should *provide an orientation* to the interviewee about what will take place in the interview. The interviewer should talk about the goals of the interview, what procedures will be followed as the interview progresses, approximately how long the interaction might take, and provide details about what is expected of the interviewee. If appropriate to the type of interview, the interviewer should let the interviewee know how the information collected will be used after the interview.

When the opening is complete, you should try to move smoothly into the body of the interview. This transition might be best achieved by asking an open question.[5] This first question should be nonthreatening and fairly easy to answer. The open question should get the interviewee talking and allow an easy movement into the body.

Structure and Function. This progression of ideas begins with how something is structured and then turns to a discussion of its function. If you're asking questions about an organization, you might begin with questions about how a particular department or unit is organized or structured. Then you ask questions about what exactly the department does. If you're trying to understand the structure and function of the U.S. government, you could ask about the three branches of the government and how they are organized, and then you could ask about what each branch does.

Build the Relationship

Relationships between people in interviewing situations develop in much the same way as relationships between people in other contexts. In cases where the parties do not know each other, the communication that occurs initially is fundamentally superficial because it is based on broad generalizations and assumptions made by each party about the other. Miller assumes that all initial interactions are impersonal or noninterpersonal, and that relationships become more interpersonal as they develop.[6]

Miller and Steinberg explain that individuals relate to each other on three levels: cultural, sociological, and psychological.[7] The relationship begins on the cultural level, and progresses through the sociological toward the psychological level. A brief look at these levels should help you understand how relationships can grow and be maintained during an interview.

On the *cultural* level, individuals do not relate to each other as persons, but only as role occupants or generalized members of a culture. The communicators only know as much about each other as they know about any other member of the culture, so uncertainty is high. Communication takes place on a superficial and somewhat formal level and is often made up of small talk. There is little or no disclosure of personal information. When the relationship gets to the *sociological* level, individuals relate to each other as stereotyped members of groups. One person interprets the behavior of the other based on what is known about the group to which that other is believed to belong. Finally, on the *psychological* level, individuals begin to relate to each other not only as members of a culture or group, but also as unique individuals. This level of relationship can be reached after the communicators have experienced one another's behaviors and have exchanged more personal types of information. They get to know each other!

Why is individual uncertainty high on the cultural level?
© 2008, JupiterImages Corporation.

In an interview, the initial relationship is likely to exist at the cultural level, or at best, if you have done a reasonable amount of research on the other party or organization, at the sociological level. Regardless, uncertainty at either level is high, and each party is trying to feel out the other to find out if he or she can be trusted with more personal information. As the parties interact, and if they begin to build trust, then more and more personal disclosure will take place and the relationship can move toward the psychological level. As a relationship moves through these levels toward the psychological, the relationship becomes more interpersonal.

The more interpersonal the relationship between the parties, the more freely information will be exchanged. If you can move the relationship toward the interpersonal end of the relationship continuum, you will more likely be able to achieve your goals for the interview. The bad news is that it will not always be possible to move into a trusting interpersonal relationship within the course of just one interview. Even so, you should make the effort to make the relationship as interpersonal as the situation permits!

While there are many ways to build relationships in an interview, here are three suggestions:

1. *Take a little risk!* Volunteer some personal information. Allow the other party to get to know you more on a more interpersonal level. You would prefer the interviewer remember you as "Sam from Dayton who has applied for the drafting position," rather than "applicant 356-C." If the employment interviewer gets to know something about you as a person, he or she will be more able to remember you and differentiate you from the rest of the candidates.

2. *Try to create a supportive climate!* A supportive climate is one in which neither party feels threatened by the other. A perception of threat creates an atmosphere of defensiveness in which both parties begin to question each others' intentions and suspect manipulation by the other. The result of this is inaccurate interpretation of meanings and intentions, and information will not be freely exchanged in this atmosphere. You will probably never make it to the psychological level!

Tips for Creating a Supportive Climate

To avoid the formation of a defensive climate, follow Gibb's advice[8]:

- Try to use descriptive statements.
- Try *not* to use evaluative statements.
- Try to remain focused on solving the problem.
- Try *not* to give the impression that you want to exert control over the situation.
- Try to maintain a natural, spontaneous, and engaged point of view.
- Try *not* to give others the impression that you are using a strategy to control the situation or to get whatever you want.
- Try to show a sincere concern and interest in the other.
- Try *not* to appear detached and neutral.
- Try to establish and maintain an atmosphere of equality.
- Try *not* to make the other feel inferior.
- Try to keep an open mind!

3. *Be engaged!* It could be that the most significant thing you do to build and maintain a relationship with an interview (or conversational) partner is to be involved in the interaction. Involvement means full participation in the "here and now" of the interaction without being distracted by factors not connected to the communication. This involvement will not only help you achieve your goals for the interview, but it also communicates an interest in the other participants in the conversation. As the other participants discover that you are genuinely interested and involved in what is happening, they will become more motivated and involved as well. So the outcome of your engagement is the increased commitment to the free exchange of information and to the success of the interview! It's all good!

Transition

When you complete the body of the interview, you should make this very clear to the interviewee. You can do this in a straightforward way by simply saying that the time for the interview is over or that you have no more questions. Be sure that interviewee understands that the questioning is completed.

Closing

Much like the opening, the **closing** of an interview is often overlooked while planning, and it often results in the interviewer attempting to simply "wing it." Because they think that there is nothing left to accomplish when the questioning is over, interviewers have a tendency to rush this phase. If the interviewer's only goal is to collect information, once that information is received, he or she might think that the interview is over. Many times the interviewer will just say "thanks!" and leave, giving no consideration to the interviewee or properly closing the interaction. This kind of "nonclosing" leaves interviewees with a poor impression and would not motivate them to cooperate again should the interviewer require more information.

The closing needs to be carefully considered because it also plays a critical role in the interview process: It provides closure, helps to maintain the relationship that was developed during the interview, and can help motivate the interviewee if further cooperation is needed.

How can you tell that this interview is finished?
© Phil Date/Shutterstock.com

As mentioned before, the interviewee should not have to wonder if the interview is over. The interviewer should *provide closure* by being very clear that the conversation is completed. This can be done by summarizing the content of the interview, letting the interviewee know if there is a next step in the interviewing process (such as multiple employment interviews), reminding the interviewee what will be done with the information collected from the conversation, or even through exhibiting some simple verbal or nonverbal leave-taking behavior.

The interviewer should make a strong effort to *maintain the relationship* that has been created and developed during the interview. Try to keep the relationship upbeat and positive, especially if you will be working together with the interviewee after the interview or if you will need further cooperation at a later time. The effort you make to treat the interviewee with respect and maintain that relationship will motivate him or her to cooperate further if needed. The motivation that you provide will also give the interviewee a sense of satisfaction by knowing that the effort and time in the interview was well spent.

ENDNOTES

1. L. Hugenberg, S. Wallace, D. Yoder, and C. Horvath, *Creating Competent Communication*, 4th ed. (Dubuque, IA: Kendall/Hunt, 2005).

2. K. Kacmar, and W. Hochwater, "The Interview as a Communication Event: A Field Examination of Demographic Effects on Interview Outcomes," *Journal of Business Communication* 32 (1995); 207–232; and S. Ralston and R. Brady, "The Relative Influence of Interview Communication Satisfaction on Applicants' Recruitment Interview Decisions," *Journal of Business Communication* 31 (1994); 61–77.

3. G. B. Willis, *Cognitive Interviewing: A Tool for Improving Questionnaire Design* (Thousand Oaks, CA: Sage, 2005).

4. R. Anderson and G. Killenberg, *Interviewing: Speaking, Listening, and Learning for Professional Life* (Mountain View, CA: Mayfield, 1999). Also C. Stewart and W. Cash, *Interviewing: Principles and Practices* (New York: McGraw-Hill, 2003).

5. Stewart and Cash.

6. G. R. Miller, "The Current Status of Theory and Research in Interpersonal Communication," *Human Communication Research*, 4 (1978); 164–178.

7. G. R. Miller and M. Steinberg, "Between People," Palo Alto, CA: SRA (1975).

8. J. Gibb, "Defensive Communication," *Journal of Communication*, 1 (1961), 141–148.

CHAPTER

9

SPEECH PREPARATION

Imagine that you are going to sit in for a late-night talk-show host, and you get to choose your guests. One will be an important politician or social leader, one will be an actor or director, and one will be a musician or writer. These people can be living or dead. Who would you choose, and why? The *why* reveals what is important to you when you consider the draw of these guests. Are you interested in people who have made a difference? Perhaps it is power that lures you. Maybe it is someone's sex appeal or the characters that person has played. There might be something about a singer that compels you. (Think of the voting in shows like *American Idol*. Does the best singer win, or is there something else at work there?) We know that audiences are deeply affected by their perceptions of the person who is delivering the message. They may accept or reject the message based on how well the other dresses, vocally or physically presents ideas, or even some unknown quality involving "likeability." These audience perceptions of believability are known as the speaker's *ethos* or *credibility*.

Credibility is constructed; it is developed, maintained, and changed through communication activity. Keep in mind that credibility is the *impression* of others that are placed on a source, but rather than repeating *perception of credibility*, this chapter will use the simple term. Credibility might be applied to a person, to an organization, or even to a Web site or other media form. In examining credibility, we will consider the qualities that affect credibility, the stages that credibility may progress through, and strategies that you can make use of when attempting to enhance others' perceptions.[1] In addition, we will explore communication apprehension, which limits your ability to be an effective, credible communicator.

WHAT ARE THE QUALITIES OF CREDIBILITY?

In Book Two of his *Rhetoric*, Aristotle investigated the qualities that make up the audience's perception of the speaker's ethos. The first quality, *character*, involves the perceived integrity, sincerity, honesty, or trustworthiness of the communicator. The second, *intelligence*, is based on a perception of the speaker's apparent expertise, competence, or knowledge. The third, *goodwill*, consists of the audience's perception that the speaker has its best interest at heart; the speaker is not communicating just for self-betterment.[2] In contemporary studies, a fourth quality, *charisma*, has been added. Charisma is a sense of power, energy, or attractiveness that draws an audience in.[3]

While a communicator may have strategies that impact these four qualities, it is essential to remember that your believability exists in the audience's minds. We know that these qualities are perceived differently by receivers. Think about someone that you find very attractive; a friend might wonder aloud at your taste. You might think that someone who has many degrees is very smart; your friend might say that this person's foul language shows he is not. Preteens might idolize Paris, Britney, Lindsay, and Nicole (their last names aren't even important); their parents probably wonder why bad behavior is a draw.

In addition, the perception of credibility elements might clash. President Bill Clinton was a Rhodes Scholar; that suggests intelligence. Yet his extramarital affair cast doubt on his character. You might pine for a beautiful member of the opposite sex and find her very charismatic, but you are dismayed as you watch her cut down everyone around her, showing a lack of goodwill. In another vein, who do you believe when selecting what course to take, what restaurant to eat at, where to get your news? How do you make those decisions? Perhaps you follow the media polls that proclaim whose approval ratings are rising or falling, who is the most beautiful, who is the most powerful.[4] Credibility is essential to communicating, and you cannot accurately predict how the audience will perceive you. However, there are some simple techniques that you can consider to enhance audience impressions. Hopefully, you believe in what you are communicating; sincerity shows in the words you choose and the manner in which you speak or write.

Character

Character includes perception of integrity, honor, trust, altruism, and ethics. President Dwight D. Eisenhower said this:

> In order to be a leader a man must have followers. And to have followers, a man must have their confidence. Hence, the supreme quality for a leader is unquestionably integrity. Without it, no real success is possible, no matter whether it is on a section gang, a football field, in an army, or in an office. If a man's associates find him guilty of being phony, if they find that he lacks forthright integrity, he will fail. His teachings and actions must square with each other. The first great need, therefore, is integrity and high purpose.[5]

One strategy to enhance character is to maintain eye contact with your listeners. Think about someone who will not look at you as he speaks; how do you judge his character? Most likely, you feel that he is less than honest or is trying to hide something. Eye contact is an essential feature of delivery, and it can add a dimension to your audience's perception of your honesty. As an example, here's what Synchronics Group, a pre-trial consulting firm recommends:

> Losing eye contact is particularly devastating in the courtroom. A good opposing counsel will pick up on the hesitation and attack the witness with it.
>
> Maintaining a steady eye contact under assault makes your witness look steadfast and invincible in the eyes of the jurors. Jurors often do not understand the questions that are being asked, or the answers that are being offered, during cross-examination. They might miss the substance of the power play, but they are aware of the struggle. And any witness who meets the verbal assaults of opposing counsel without batting an eye communicates self-confidence and authority.[6]

Maintaining steady eye contact makes you look steadfast in the eyes of jurors.
© Tim Pannell/Corbis.

You could also use personal examples that show you have experienced what you are talking about; self-narratives have the power to create credibility. For instance, if your speech is about immigration reform, your credibility will be given added weight if you can relate to the struggles that immigrants go through, either because you came to the United States via immigration, or because you have association with those who have those experiences. Members of the audience may think, "Well, if that's happened to him, I can see how it impacts me." In this way, you will be seen as "practicing what you preach." In one class, a female student revealed that she was a breast cancer survivor. She explained how she had gone through chemo at twenty-one. The young audience's perception of her ethos was much stronger than if she had just said, "You should check for breast cancer," because in this case, it was someone their age who shared her actual experience.

Intelligence

Intelligence is a perception of competence, expertise, and knowledge. Intelligence can be projected by careful preparation, supporting details, and clear language. Your messages (whether they are speeches, group presentations, interviews, or other communication activities) should be supported by research, should provide a variety of believable supporting materials, and should use appropriate language. Other chapters deal with gathering evidence and developing delivery strategies, and later in this chapter you'll think about language, but think of it this way for now. How much do you believe someone when you ask, "Where were you?" and the answer is, "Around." What about someone who argues that you should really see this new movie, "Because it is good."

You need to provide supporting materials that let the audience know that you have a grasp of the facts. Cite the research that you've conducted; if you can include sources that are respected by your listeners, your credibility will be enhanced. Explain your competence or expertise; why should your listeners believe you? Did you experience this topic? Did you investigate it through research? What qualifies you to speak on this subject?

You also need to speak in terms that the audience will immediately grasp, or you need to define your terms so you are speaking at their level. You'll learn some definition techniques when you read about informative speaking, but for now, just remember that your audience will be lost if they're not using a term in the same way as you are. If you think that *criticism* means judging or analyzing, and your audience perceives it to be negative statements, a simple concept can become very confusing.

You can also help the audience's perceptions of your intelligence by skillful delivery, which is covered in its own chapter. We tend to attribute expertise to someone who exudes confidence and competence in speaking or writing. A hesitant vocal or physical delivery may create an impression of someone who is unsure of the facts. Someone who uses instant messaging (IM) to send an important response to a job offer may be seen as not qualified; the IM language and acronyms, designed for the simplistic context, are not appropriate for "more important" communication. Think of delivery as all of the ways you send that message. Is the impact of the message, "I want to break up with you," different if it is sent via text message, e-mail, phone message, through a third party, or in person? Yes, the message is important, but it is safe to assume that the *way* it is delivered will also receive much attention in terms of perceiving your ethos.

Goodwill

Goodwill suggests to the audience that you care for them more than yourself. Goodwill is an aspect that your message should naturally create, because communication centers on strategies that make speaking other-directed. If you have done an adequate context analysis of the audience and occasion, you know what is needed to let the audience know their needs come first.

One specific technique of enhancing the impression of goodwill is to adapt your supporting materials to the audience whenever possible. This means, for example, that statistics should be translated into specific audience terms so they are understandable. If you were trying to convince people to spay or neuter their pets, you need to drive that home. The U.S. Humane Society says that the average number of litters a fertile dog can produce in one year is two. That results in an average number six to ten puppies. In six years, one female dog and her offspring can theoretically produce 67,000 dogs.[7] Imagine translating that number into the members of your audience. How many dogs would they have to adopt to manage that number? How would those numbers look when visually displayed without numerals? You might also use examples to which the audience can relate; find out how many are pet owners, how many have visited a shelter, how many know someone who has gotten a pet but has acted irresponsibly toward that pet because veterinary care costs too much? In addition to adapting your supports, your use of language that reflects the culture and level of the group is essential.

Finally, your use of clear organization, including summaries for listening guidance and specific structure, will also give the audience a sense that you care about their understanding. If you want to see the "anti-goodwill" strategies in action, think about poorly planned meetings, jokes told that have made you uncomfortable, stores where salespeople hover over you (making you think that they are waiting for you to shoplift), or classes where the language is so far over your head that the instructor might as well be speaking in a foreign tongue. Goodwill places an expectation on you: When you communicate, you need to show the audience that you have put them ahead of yourself.

Charisma

But what about **Charisma?** Is it something you are born with? We cannot all be Brad Pitt, Nelson Mandella, Jennifer Lopez, Billy Graham, or Saddam Hussein (and perhaps when you read some of those names, your reaction was, "Those people do not have charisma, as far as I'm concerned.") This element is probably the most difficult to conceptualize and to promote, because it is the most personal, individualized, and fleeting. Max Weber defined someone possessing charisma as "an individual personality set apart from ordinary people and endowed with supernatural, superhuman powers, and heroic qualities. In short part Hero, and part Superman/Superwoman."[8]

If you think about people who have that "something," people you would like to be around because of the energy, life, and personality they possess, your list would probably be very different from someone else's.[9] Your list might include former president Ronald Reagan, country singer Tim McGraw, Quincy Jones, your best friend, your favorite elementary teacher, and the late Reverend Jerry Falwell. Someone else might scoff at all of these choices. Certainly, all of these people are very different from each other, but each has a fascination for you. Although you might not appreciate the positions they took, you might admire something about them. It is difficult to identify exactly what makes a person charismatic, but there appear to be a few strategies that you can try to give your message a feeling of energy, which is an element of charisma. In speaking, you can truly be enthusiastic about your topic. If you are disinterested or bored, it will show in your manner, and your speech will be flat. You can appear dynamic and alive in front of your audience; a person whose delivery is low-keyed, riveted to a manuscript, and hidden behind a lectern will not inspire much personal confidence on your part.

Enthusiasm can be contagious; if you can connect with the audience by showing that you are enthusiastic about your message, it's likely that the audience will take on some of that passion.

Let's sum up the suggestions for a communicator to have input on the audience's impression for credibility. Be prepared. Have a well organized, well-supported message, and be flexible enough to alter it if needed. Be ready to answer questions competently. Use language that is adapted to the audience; you do not want to insult them by talking down, but if you have any doubts about their ability to comprehend what you're saying, then define, describe, and illustrate with examples. If you share group affiliation (because of your age, location, educational or work experiences, cultural background, or organizational membership), be sure to incorporate those affiliations into your message if appropriate by referring to them or using supporting materials which will reinforce them. Persuading another by talking his or her language by "speech, gesture, tonality, order, image, attitude, and idea," is called *identification* by rhetorical theorist Kenneth Burke.[10] In simpler terms, this is called establishing common ground, or *homophily*. If a listener feels that you both share similar backgrounds, attributes, concerns, beliefs, and values, you are more likely to be believed. Infomercials make millions of dollars a year on that premise, despite questionable product claims and late-night direct response marketing.[11]

HOW DOES CREDIBILITY CHANGE?

Because credibility is dynamic, ideas about what constitutes it vary because of era, context, and culture. Martha Stewart's image was the personification of gracious living as portrayed in her magazines and two popular television programs, as the author of several books and hundreds of articles on homemaking, and commercial spokeswoman for K-Mart. In 2001, she was named one of the thirty most powerful women in America, and third most powerful woman in America by *Ladies Home Journal.* However, in 2004, her personal stock trading brought charges of insider trading by the Justice Department and the Securities Exchange Commission. Although she maintained her innocence, in 2004 a jury found Stewart guilty of misleading federal investigators and obstructing an investigation; she eventually served a five-month prison sentence. Since then, Stewart has worked to rebuild her reputation and her "brand."[12] *Time* magazine in 2005 called her a person who shapes our lives, naming Stewart as one of the nation's top 100 "Builders and Titans."[13] In 2007, *Forbes* magazine listed her as one of the twenty richest women in entertainment, despite the fact that she had been forced to step down as CEO from her namesake company, Martha Stewart Living Omnimedia. Stewart's rise and fall is a good example of credibility's dynamic nature.

Are the photos you've posted on the Web ones you'd want a potential employer to see?
© Carsten Reisinger/Shutterstock .com

Our understanding of ethos has evolved over the years. Although the classical Greeks believed that a person's credibility existed only during the communication act, today we recognize that ethos is a complex web of past and present impressions. What you have done before impacts the way an audience accepts your current ideas, and that blend, in turn, affects the impression that they take away from you. As an example, think about your feeling toward a past historical figure such as Franklin D. Roosevelt, Martin Luther King Jr., Betty Ford, Neil Armstrong, or Cesar Chavez. Our knowledge of them is based on what we have gleaned from texts, classes, and perhaps television or movies. Perhaps you have no clear image of them at all. But ask your parents or grandparents about those people and their reactions will probably be quite different. They will probably have strong images of speeches or actions these figures took, stands they made, or ways they looked. Your family members' characterizations of those historical figures' ethos are, therefore, dissimilar to yours.

The stages of credibility demonstrate both how credibility is a personal perception and how it progresses or evolves.[14] Initial credibility is the perception of the source prior to exposure to a message. Simply put, it is your reputation, the images that establish your credibility before the listener encounters you. As a result, initial credibility is built on known accomplishments, positions or roles, and titles. Sometimes, your initial credibility is established by something as simple as an introduction or statement in a program. However, with the growth of social networking sites, initial credibility has been discovered in other ways. Employers have begun to use search engines such as Google or Yahoo! when they conduct background checks. But as reported in the *New York Times*, some recruiters are looking up applicants on social networking sites such as Facebook, MySpace, Xanga, Orkut, and Friendster, where college students often post risqué or teasing photographs and provocative comments about drinking, recreational drug use, and sexual exploits in what some mistakenly believe is relative privacy. When viewed by corporate recruiters or admissions officials at graduate and professional schools, such pages can make students look immature and unprofessional, at best.[15] Warren Buffett, U.S. business executive and CEO of Berkshire Hathaway, noted the importance of reputation when he said, "It takes 20 years to build a reputation and five minutes to ruin it."[16] What the audience knows about you or your organization, or what is revealed to them about you prior to your message, influences their expectations of the communication event and message to come. **Derived credibility** is the believability you produce in your audience's mind as you present the message. It consists of your organization, supporting materials, delivery, and connection that the audience receives as they process the message. You'll focus on elements of derived credibility throughout this text as you learn strategies for creating and adapting all sorts of messages for different contexts. Finally, **terminal credibility** is the cumulative result of initial and derived credibility. It's the image that the audience carries of you at the end of the message, and it usually forms the next round of initial credibility.

All three of these stages are dynamic. You could begin with low initial credibility (the audience doesn't know anything about you, for instance, except that you hold a low title or come from a rival school). As you present your ideas, your well-developed points, sound supporting materials and dynamic delivery combine to give the audience a more positive perspective of you; your derived credibility rises. By the end of your message, the audience is ready to agree to your proposal; terminal credibility is high.

When the final book in the *Harry Potter* series was imminent, people worldwide were buzzing with guesses about its content. *Harry Potter and the Deathly Hallows* enjoyed widespread popularity (initial credibility). That can be demonstrated by some astounding figures: Barnes & Noble expected to presell 1 million copies of the book; Amazon.com received 600,000 orders; and Scholastic Books ordered an initial printing of 12 million books in preparation for the worldwide launch. Prior to the July 21, 2007, installment, the entire Harry Potter series had sold roughly 325 million copies around the world in 64 different languages.[17] When the book was released, most fans and critics gave it positive reviews. Michiko Kakutani, a book critic of the *New York Times*, said that the book gave "good old-fashioned closure: a big-screen, heart-racing, bone-chilling confrontation and an epilogue that clearly lays out people's fates. Getting to the finish line is not seamless—the last part of *Harry Potter and the Deathly*

Hallows, the seventh and final book in the series, has some lumpy passages of exposition and a couple of clunky detours—but the overall conclusion and its determination of the main characters' story lines possess a convincing inevitability that make some of the prepublication speculation seem curiously blinkered in retrospect."[18] Thousands of fans reported staying up all night to read their copies. Derived credibility was nearly uniformly high; the book kept readers on edge, right to the end. And how do you evaluate terminal credibility? Marty Dodge of Blogcritics online magazine summed it up this way:

> *Harry Potter and the Deathly Hallows* is probably not Rowling's best book in the series, and adults might find it to be a bit thin at times. It reads a bit rushed, and there are some spelling errors and plot glitches. But taken as a whole series, Rowling has done something only few other authors like Tolkien have done. She has created a series of books that can be read by child and adult alike and enjoyed in similar but slightly different ways. One just has to wonder if Rowling will be allowed to finish with Potter and what she has planned for her next novel.[19]

As you can see, the high positive anticipation led to continued positive derived credibility, with the final feeling seeming to be satisfaction, relief, and wonder about what's next. You could predict that if author J. K. Rowling chose to write a sequel (or prequel, or spin off), that the book would begin with high initial credibility.

Credibility is a changing factor, based on a number of elements. The only constant is that ethos exists within the mind of the audience, and your listeners or readers attribute character, intelligence, goodwill, and charisma based on their own unique perceptions. Those perceptions can change because of time, context, and message content, and you have a limited means of impacting those perceptions.

The creation of a credible persona is not easy; in fact, it carries some peril with it. When you open yourself up to others by sharing your ideas or values, you are taking a risk. What if others do not agree? What if they find your ideas to be ridiculous or wrong? When you attempt to establish yourself as an authority (in order to persuade), others might think you lack expertise or are trying to come off as a know-it-all. But because credibility is an essential factor in communication, it is worth the risk. There are some pretty simple strategies that you can use to enhance your audience's perception of your credibility. You can use **mystification,** which is the use of special jargon to imply that you have special authority or expertise (but remember, if your audience does not know the meaning of the jargon, you might confuse them). The use of humor can be employed positively: self-deprecating humor (making fun of yourself) is especially successful if you already enjoy high credibility. However, the negative side of humor is that the audience might evaluate your message as a joke rather than an important issue. Showing dispositional similarity (demonstrating similar views) lets the audience identify with your ideas. Citing sources of evidence and using sources that the audience already accepts can add to your credibility. All-in-all, though, the needs of the audience will often override extensive considerations of a persuader's credibility. For example, let's say that you like an instructor because she's entertaining, but your friend might find humor less important because the friend needs to have a clear explanation of technical material. When your friend asks for your opinion (or you do a search on Rate My Professors.com)[20] the impressions given may not meet you friend's needs.

AUDIENCE ANALYSIS AND ADAPTATION

We already know that the audience assumes paramount importance in oral communication. But how do you gain enough knowledge about your audience? Once you gain that knowledge, how do you use it to adapt to the audience? These questions form the basis of the next section.

Know Your Audience: Gathering Data

Several sorts of information about your audience might affect how they react to your presentation. Your task will be to determine which features of the audience have some relevance to you, the situation, the topic, and your approach to the topic.

Types of Audience Data

Demographic information about your audience classifies them into categories based on their characteristics. These characteristics include classifications of identity, such as age, sex, religious affiliation, ethnic group, nationality, native language, race, sexual orientation, hometown, etc. Other demographic data includes membership in organizations such as political parties, interest groups, or sports teams.

Demographic data can prove useful, but you have to know what to do with it. Too many speakers make hasty assumptions about demographics, designating some topics as "for women," "for elderly audiences." Rarely do all members of a demographic group believe or react the same way. Careless audience analysis can lead to **overattribution**, the tendency to explain all of someone's behaviors and orientations as resulting from only a few characteristics. Demographic analysis can trigger a false assumption that people with a certain demographic filter all experience through that one demographic trait. If I refuse to eat a barbecued pork sandwich, is that necessarily because I am Muslim? Not all members of a religion are equally observant of dietary rules. Or could the refusal stem from my demographic as an overweight person? Does someone's affiliation with the Republican political party mean they will adopt the official party stance on every issue? Does membership in the Roman Catholic Church enable you to predict a person's alignment with all the Pope's positions?

Whenever possible, confirm that your audience members share more than superficial similarities. For example, what appears to be the same skin tone, accent, or religion can cloak a wide range of positions. The clear lesson: gather several types of information about your audience before attempting to predict their preferences or reactions.

You also will need **topic-specific information** that identifies the audience's perspective on your subject matter. The audience's level of concern and understanding should influence your choice of what to cover and your approach. Topic-specific data includes:

- Level of interest about the topic area
- Understanding of key terms related to the topic
- Knowledge of recent developments regarding the topic
- Priorities regarding the topic (what they consider most/least important)
- Personal connections to the topic (how it might affect them)
- Familiarity with relevant sources of news about the topic (useful to determine what the audience considers as credible sources)

Based on this information, you can determine more accurately what will generate enthusiastic listening, the amount and type of background information you will need, and the best angle for approaching the topic.

Another type of information, critically important if you want to influence your audience, concerns attitudes, beliefs, and values. **Attitudes** are the feelings people have about specific issues, people, or things. Attitudes always have valence (that is, they are positive or negative) and a degree of intensity. You can't simply have "a bad attitude," the attitude has to be directed toward something specific. Attitudes predispose us to respond in certain ways. For example, if I have a strong attitude in favor of peanut butter, then I will be more likely to choose it for lunch. The direction and strength of your listeners' attitudes will help you understand whether you will have a receptive audience.

Beliefs are the general principles that underlie attitudes. Beliefs imply a level of commitment, and one belief can generate many attitudes. My attitude in support of peanut butter may rely on the belief in its nutritional benefits. Your audience's belief structure can help you predict how they will react to your topic and approach. Beliefs also can influence your choice of main ideas and supporting materials. For example, an audience of fundamentalist Christians will not count evolutionary biologists as credible sources about the earth's development.

Values are priorities that people hold strongly and usually accept as self-evident. Values anchor beliefs and attitudes in a moral foundation. We usually acquire values early in life, and our indoctrination into these values leads us not to question or alter them very readily.[21] The value that guides my choice of peanut butter might be my commitment to family. Since proper nutrition should increase my life span, I select peanut butter to enable me to be alive for my family's sake.

Generally, attitudes are most susceptible to change. Beliefs and values tend to persist over longer periods of time and usually require repeated, sustained efforts to alter. Not only will you need to determine what the audience's attitudes, values, and beliefs are, but you also should examine their extent. What exceptions might the audience allow? You may find that an audience's positions are more complex than you had assumed, so investigate the limits as well as the composition of their commitments. Information on attitudes, beliefs, and values has special importance because it reveals the audience's actual positions and outlooks. You know where the audience stands without having to risk guessing.

Collecting Audience Data

How do you gather this information? Many speakers rely on simple observation, but that is risky and often inaccurate. Merely because someone looks or sounds a certain way does not mean she will conform to your expectations about that sort of person. For example, hearing my Georgia accent might lead you to predict that I like country music and grits. That prediction might be logical, but in my case utterly wrong. I'm a metalhead and jazz fan who suspects grits is a deadly alien life form.

Another type of observation yields more helpful information: Notice how the audience acts and reacts. Observe your audience's behavior to understand them better. What should you observe?

- Which styles of presentations generate the most favorable reactions?
- Which topics generate the most enthusiastic response?
- If your audience members formally introduced themselves, what did they discuss?
- What topics dominate conversation before and after speech events?
- What is your audience doing before or between listening to presentations?

Think of yourself as a communication scientist. Like an anthropologist, you are gathering data from the field—the world of your audience.

Sometimes you won't be able to observe your audience directly. You might speak to a group of people you have never met, or you might address your audience through a video camera. In these cases, gather reports about your audience. Interview people familiar with them, such as the sponsor of an event where you are the keynote speaker. Whenever I guest lecture in another professor's class, I first

(Continued)

get a sense of the student audience by speaking with the professor. The audience also might have a track record that you can research. If addressing a religious congregation, you might ask the cleric about the congregants' favorite sermon topics. If your audience has heard other speakers, find out which speakers and topics were the most successful and why.

Questionnaires provide an excellent source of audience information. You can gather data directly from audience members, focusing on whatever areas you find most helpful: demographics, topic-centered, or attitudes/beliefs/values. You will get the most precise information by providing definite, distinct choices for answers.

<u>**Poor Examples**</u> **(proper answer choices):**

1. Do you like communication studies? Yes/No
2. How old are you?

<u>**Better Examples**</u> **(proper answer choices):**

1. How much do you like communication studies?
   a. Strongly like
   b. Somewhat like
   c. Neutral
   d. Somewhat dislike
   e. Strongly dislike

2. My age is
   a. 18 years old or under.
   b. 19–21 years old.
   c. 22–25 years old.
   d. over 25 years old.

By providing clear options, you can group the responses easily to determine clusters of audience identity, positions, and preferences. If you ask questions that require more elaboration (such as a short answer or essay), the answers might be difficult to categorize but you will get more detailed responses that could reveal unexpected information.

The drawback of questionnaires is that they rely on self-reports. Respondents might lie outright, but they more likely may distort answers unintentionally. When completing a questionnaire, especially in the presence of someone else, respondents may provide answers they think other people want to hear.

The most accurate information about your audience stems from multiple sources—demographic, topic-specific, and attitudinal—that you cross-apply and compare to avoid unwarranted assumptions. You also should rely on a combination of data, observation, and reports.

Adapting to Your Audience

We have reviewed the kinds of information you can obtain about your audience and how to gather that data. But suppose your audience analysis gives you conflicting results. It's likely that your audience, especially in a university setting, will include a diverse group with fairly wide variance in some demographic characteristics, diverse attitudes and beliefs, and unknown or inconsistent past reactions to presentations. Aside from diversity, you might encounter other challenges when adapting to your audience. If your presentation deals with a controversial topic, you could encounter an audience that disagrees with your position. How do you entice them to give you a fair hearing? You also might confront an involuntary audience: People who don't really want to be there, but attend because they must (such as required attendance in a class). What should you do in these situations? Several additional methods are available for dealing with challenging audiences.

Audience Segmentation

One approach to audience adaptation recognizes that you probably can't please all of the people all of the time—or even at any one time. Think about how television dealt with diverse audiences. Channels began to emerge that catered to specific audience demographics and interests. Not only can we view sports channels, but we have channels that specialize in particular sports. You can employ **audience segmentation** in a similar way. Review the information you have gathered about your audience. You should be able to identify clusters of people who have similar characteristics, viewpoints, backgrounds, or experiences. Audience segmentation would instruct you to recognize those clusters and include something in your presentation that would appeal to each group within your audience.

Using audience segmentation allows you to appeal to your entire audience, but in a piecemeal fashion. By the end of the presentation, several (perhaps all) major groups within the audience should have connected with something you have said or done. Imagine, for instance, that you are giving a history of women's volleyball to an audience consisting of fans who support several different teams. To use segmentation, include examples and references to historic moments of each team whose fans are in the audience.

With proper audience adaptation techniques, you gain power to tailor your message to your listeners instead of facing a mysterious mass of onlookers.

© Oshchepkov Dmitry/ Shutterstock.com

Maslow's Hierarchy of Needs

A very different approach to your audience involves connecting with their fundamental needs. Abraham Maslow[22] proposed a hierarchy of needs, which identified the essential requirements for psychological well-being and personal growth. Since these needs affect everyone, they can apply to all sorts of audiences. The needs usually are shown as a triangle, as Figure 9.1 demonstrates.

Physiological needs are the most basic. They determine physical survival at a level necessary to seek fulfillment of any other needs. Once a person can exist from day to day, **safety needs** can apply. Fulfillment of safety needs assures some continuity and ability to plan for the future. One such long-term commitment involves being part

FIGURE 9.1 Maslow's hierarchy of needs.

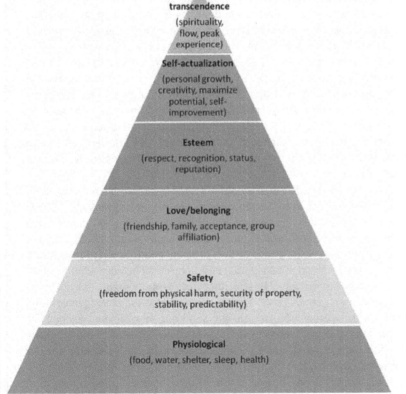

of a relationship, which activates **love and belonging needs**. Love and belonging include the need for long-term, unconditional acceptance from others. When you feel part of a larger whole, you pay attention to your social standing, which implicates **esteem needs**. These esteem needs may explain the human drive for dignity, self-respect, and recognition of each person's individual worth. Some theorists have argued that the drive for recognition applies to entire nations and cultures as well as to individuals.[23] **Self-actualization** becomes active when people feel confident enough about their own existence and social position to expand their horizons. Perhaps the most perfect expression of self-actualization appears in the mission of the starship *Enterprise* in various incarnations of the *Star Trek* television series: "To explore strange new worlds; to seek out new life and new civilizations; to boldly go where no one has gone before."

Maslow suggested the final level of the hierarchy in various later writings and presentations, yet almost every textbook ignores it.[24] **Self-transcendence** recognizes that for some people, losing themselves in fulfilling tasks or in total dedication to an ideal represents the highest achievement.[25] Spiritual enlightenment exemplifies self-transcendence, since the individual lives by serving a higher being rather than by serving one's own needs. A secular version of self-transcendence appears in peak experiences when we feel everything is in total harmony and we are utterly absorbed in an activity we love. At these moments we achieve a sense of flow, equivalent to "being in the zone" for athletes or musical "rapture".[26(p29)]

Self-transcendence adds a vital dimension to the hierarchy of needs. Without self-transcendence, the hierarchy of needs remains very individualistic and perhaps even selfish with its focus on the individual's own actualization, self-esteem, acceptance as an individual, personal safety, and physical needs. What about more collectivist cultures that place highest value on group solidarity? Self-transcendence also recognizes that people might get the most satisfaction from giving to others or devoting themselves to a higher cause than their own development.

You probably can't create self-transcendence in a brief presentation, but you can harness its power. You could invite a contentious audience to set aside their disagreements and devote their energy to a larger cause, such as responding to a disaster. The key to using self-transcendence is to identify a greater purpose that goes beyond the particular agenda of any specific subgroups within the audience. Fortunately, tragedies aren't the only things that can unite a divided or uninterested audience. Celebrations, great works of art, remarkable performances, or the wonders of nature can transport audiences beyond their individual differences. The remarkable life of Emperor penguins in Antarctica, depicted by the documentary *March of the Penguins* (2005), transcends diverse demographics and conflicting beliefs that might splinter an audience. Perhaps you could invoke an important event in the audience's shared history that showed everyone at their best. Highlight reels of sports teams or "great moments in history" features accomplish this purpose.

Each of the lower needs must be satisfied before a person will seek fulfillment of a higher need. For example, people preoccupied with getting enough food to avoid starvation (unmet physiological need) will not show great concern with whether they fit in with a fashionable crowd or receive awards (esteem needs). If you fear you might be a victim of crime (unmet safety need), your top priority is to ensure your security instead of taking up a new hobby (self-actualization).

By now you probably think, "This hierarchy of needs is great, but how can I actually use it in my presentations?" People don't consider something important if they don't need it. A person who isn't hungry won't eat, for example. You can activate Maslow's hierarchy of needs in two ways. Maslow[27] notes that the four lower levels of need (physiological, safety, love and belonging, and esteem) are necessary for basic psychological health. These *deficiency needs* require fulfillment. Psychologically healthy people have met the deficiency needs, so a speaker won't succeed by simply offering another way to meet an already fulfilled need.[27] Given their importance, a speaker could connect with deficiency needs by demonstrating how they are threatened and showing how the presentation helps achieve satisfaction of the needs. Essentially, the presentation offers a way to meet needs that might otherwise go unmet.

Example (safety needs):

Are you looking forward to a delicious dinner this weekend? How would you like to dine on gourmet seafood smothered in a sauce of tar and toxic waste? Thanks to the disastrous April 2010 blowout of British Petroleum's Deepwater Horizon oil rig, we could face the risk of contaminated seafood and a tainted Gulf Coast environment for years to come. Huge volumes of oil have poured into the ocean, and this pollution can work its way up the food chain—to us. How safe is our food supply and our entire planet as we satisfy our ever-increasing hunger for oil? I will propose several measures designed to prevent and deal with oil spills so we may not have to face another such catastrophe.

This example illustrates the risk to safety by referring to a well-known incident and relating it to the audience. The speaker doesn't simply scare the audience, but offers to restore the safety that the audience wants to recover.

Self-actualization and self-transcendence qualify as *growth needs* because their deficiency does not injure psychological health. Growth needs optimize human experience, so a speaker must show the desirability of stretching toward new opportunities. In summary, you can use the hierarchy of needs in two ways:

- For deficiency needs (physiological, safety, love and belonging, esteem), arouse the need by demonstrating how it might be unmet or at risk. Then show how the content of your presentation fulfills the need.
- For growth needs (self-actualization, self-transcendence), provide a rationale for the audience to extend themselves beyond their present condition. Invite the audience to explore possibilities beyond their current state of affairs.

Universal Values

Although we often stress the value of diversity, harmonious human communities rely on shared values. Without some communal commitment to principles, life would degenerate into a chaotic, violent struggle. Some people, such as Mother Teresa, receive universal admiration. Might some values be so widely endorsed that they quality as universal? Some evidence indicates points to an answer of "yes."

Interviews with people around the world yield a remarkably consistent and very small number of values that seem to span various cultures. The Institute for Global Ethics has identified eight such values: love, truthfulness, fairness, freedom, unity, tolerance, responsibility, and respect for life.[28(pp43–44)] When asked about the most important core values in their own community, people around the world respond with similar answers: "honesty, responsibility, respect, fairness, compassion".[28(p43)]

Three decades of research on values throughout dozens of cultures confirms a consistent emphasis on certain priorities. Shalom Schwartz, a leading researcher in the field of universal values, identifies three universal human requirements that underlie all values: individual survival, social interaction, and group welfare.[29] Studies have examined a wide range of languages, ages, political systems, religions, and other demographics, and the same core values emerge consistently.[30] Figure 9.2 lists the values described as universal in these studies.

What do these findings mean for your presentations? If you can tie the content of your presentation to one or more of these universal values, you stand a good chance at connecting with your entire audience. Even when discussing a controversial topic, you should be able to find widespread agreement about the values identified in this section. The more you can show how your presentation encourages or helps to achieve these values, the more you will bridge differences of opinion.

(Continued)

FIGURE 9.2 Universal values.

Values	Examples
Pleasure	Enjoyment, recreation
Achievement	Ambition, advancement, accomplishments
Power	Wealth, social standing, rank
Self-direction	Freedom, curiosity, choice
Stimulation	Excitement, variety
Maturity	Patience, tolerance, wisdom
Benevolence	Generosity, kindness, forgiveness
Security	Maintaining social order, keeping peace
Conformity	Obedience, fulfilling social obligations, minding manners
Tradition	Humility, honoring the past, observing rituals
Spirituality	Inner harmony, connection to a greater being
Universalism	Concern for the greater good, caring about others beyond one's own group

Sources: Derived from Schwartz[29], Schwartz and Bilsky[30], and Feather, Volkmer, and McKee.[31]

WHAT COMMUNICATION GOALS SHOULD I CONSIDER?

When preparing your message, you will have both general and specific goals that you will want to teach through your communication.

General Goals

Communication can be thought of as addressing one of three general goals (or general purposes), each answering the basic question, "Why am I talking about this issue/topic for this specific audience and occasion?" Every communication event, whether it is an interpersonal, small group, interview, or public address situation, requires you to determine your goal. You might be pursuing comprehension (information-giving), influence (persuasion), or emotion or value-sharing (expression). Think of **general goals** as the primary purpose of your communication. Although any communication context or event may have elements of all three, there are fundamental differences that will guide the kind of message you create.

Information Giving

Information giving means communicating data or beliefs in order to develop understanding and awareness. Your goals here should be reception, comprehension, and retention on the part of your audience. Perhaps you have found yourself explaining how you chose your major or the career you are preparing for; that's providing information. When you give someone directions, you are informing by detailing the routes and milestones the person should look for. In the same vein, if you try to explain the problems that exist in a certain

When you are explaining procedures your goal is to inform your audience.
© Diego Cervo/Shutterstock.com

proposal, you are aiming for an understanding of the issues (and not necessarily trying to fix them—at least not yet). All of these primarily involve the goal of information giving.

Persuasion

The goal of **persuasion** is to influence the audience; it is much more complex than information giving, yet it also involves reception, comprehension, and retention. But persuasion adds the dimension of acceptance to its goal. When you persuade, you attempt to influence people to change something about the way they think or behave. If you want your friend to practice safe sex, you might give data about rates of STDs and HIV, but your goal is beyond understanding or knowing those data—you want your friend to make a change in behavior. As another example, think about a job interview you went on. You offered information about your past education and occupational experiences, but you went beyond those details to share why you should be the one hired. There may have been many others competing for that job, but you wanted to convince that employer that you were the one who most fit the company's needs. Finally, when proposing a change in the way a meeting is run, you might explain how past meetings have been ineffective, but additionally, you will suggest a means for altering the meeting protocol. In persuasion, you seek audience change.

Expression

Expression is sometimes called value-sharing or emotional communication. When your goal is expression, you are seeking an outlet to convey your feelings or values to your audience. For our purposes, expression as communication is goal-oriented; when you speak your mind or reflect on some emotion or value, your goal should be to create in the audience the same state of mind. Think about some time when you were angry, and you just needed someone to listen to how you were feeling. In the end, did you only want the person to listen to you, or did you want that person to identify with your emotional state? Did you want that person to suggest some means of relieving that anger? Beyond the interpersonal need to share, there are many special occasions for public address where expression is the goal. Listening to a eulogy at a funeral, we want to reflect on a deceased person's life and the ways he affected our lives. We go to a commencement address to hear about how the graduates have succeeded in their goal and are embarking on a new journey. When giving someone an award, we celebrate in her achievement. None of these is "simply" expressing emotion; in each case, we are attempting to create an emotional communion within the audience.

Your general purpose is naturally constrained by the occasion or context, which we'll consider later in this chapter. A meeting where you are proposing a change in a procedure probably requires persuasion. A commencement would seem to suggest an expressive message. Lecturing in the classroom is supposed to be informative. But these general goals are relative. Is news as informative as it purports to be? How about scientific reports? Are their intentions only to capture audience understanding, or do they have an additional goal of affecting the way the audience acts? When your professor shares information with you, does she choose stories that reflect her personal experience that perhaps are expressions of values or emotions as well?

When considering your general goal, keep in mind the initial question: "Why am I talking about this issue/topic for this particular audience and occasion?" This will guide you. Your general goal must be considered as you begin to construct your message.

What kind of message do you expect to hear from those who speak at a graduation ceremony?
© Stephen Coburn/Shutterstock .com

Specific Goals

A **specific goal** (or specific purpose) answers the question, "Where do I want this audience to be at the end of my message?" You can think about specific goals as being one of three types: adopt, discontinue, or continue.

Adoption

If your goal is for your audience to adopt your message by the end of your speech, *you want them to take on something new.* Examples would be if you want them to grasp some new data, to learn about something they have never heard of, or to take on a position they never considered. In each case, the goal of **adoption**—of taking on a belief that was not considered before—is your target. For example, you might want to persuade the audience to boycott a particular company because of its policy toward migrant workers. The audience is likely not to have a prior position on this issue, and your specific goal for them would be to adopt a negative attitude toward the company and to not buy its products. Or, you might be telling someone about a brand-new product on the market: you are introducing something novel, and at the end of your message, your friend will have acquired new information. To *adopt* does not mean to replace some already-held conception; as a goal, it is the creation of something new.

Discontinue

If you want to *replace* something your audience already believes with something else, you would have the specific end goal of **discontinue:** you want your audience to end one belief (or behavior) and to replace it with another. For instance, say your friend does not like amusement park rides. She says that she is never going to Disney World, because she would not go on the rides. If you told her that at Disney World there are historical and animal exhibits, international restaurants, and a host of nonride activities, she might change her mind about visiting the place, replacing her conception with a new one.

Continuance

As a specific purpose, **continuance** means that you want to supplement, or add on to, what the audience already knows, without denying previous knowledge. Consider a coach who exhorts her lacrosse players to work harder. The athletes already know that practice will improve their game, but hearing motivational phrases or getting new timing goals might present them with greater awareness of what they can achieve. You have experienced continuance all through your academic career as concepts have gotten more and more complex. When you were younger, you might have learned a simplistic view of history, but as you took more courses, you learned more than just names and dates and a simple cause or two: You understood economic, social, political, and philosophical foundations for historical events. Learning about the death of a president not only reviews historical fact; it also supplements those facts with details not known when the events occurred. When faced with an audience that already has some knowledge, continuance means that you have to create added value in your message.

Goal setting is important for a communicator; without clear goals, your message may fail, or your audience might not be able to engage in their own critical thinking. In later chapters, you'll see how these goals can be developed in specific communication contexts. However, you're probably thinking that you do have so much to share, but you need someone to share it with! That is where your audience comes in. You have to know

How does a coach motivate a player to keep trying?
© Scott Milless/Shutterstock.com

who they are and why they're part of the communication event before you can reach your goals. That involves audience analysis and adaptation.

HOW DO I CONSTRUCT THE BODY OF THE MESSAGE?

The body of your message is the "meat" of the content. It's where the audience will learn the most, will be given the most evidence, or will be given arguments to influence them. As a result, it's the most important part of your message, and it should also be the longest. If you structure the main part of the speech first, developing the introduction and conclusion can be made much easier.

Importance of the Main Points

The **main points** are the ideas generated by your specific purpose; they divide your message into manageable units for you to present and your audience to consider. They need to be selected carefully and arranged strategically to meet your purpose. How do you decide what main ideas to consider for inclusion? Your specific purpose provides a simple starting point: it tells the audience what you expect of them. Let's take the earlier example of this informative specific purpose: to create awareness in my audience about the services provided by the American Red Cross. What kinds of questions could you ask yourself to determine how best to develop that awareness? Consider these for a start:

- What is the Red Cross's purpose?
- What is the history of the Red Cross?
- What does the audience already know about the Red Cross?
- Who are the people in my community involved in Red Cross activities?
- Who receives benefits from the Red Cross?
- Is there a difference between the national Red Cross services and local ones?
- Does the Red Cross have divisions?
- How does the Red Cross raise money?

Now, you can see that there is no way you could answer all of these in one speech, considering the time it would take to adequately answer each question. Learning the history of an organization is a speech unto itself. The question about what the audience already knows is answered by your audience analysis; it's possible that you'll find out they've never heard of the Red Cross, so you need to start pretty basic in your speech. You probably also realize that some of these questions don't really relate to your specific purpose, since it's a focus on services provided by the Red Cross. Would it be important to know the difference between the national Red Cross services and local ones? That lets you eliminate several questions, and end up with maybe two or three:

- What is the Red Cross's purpose?
- Who receives benefits from the Red Cross?
- Does the Red Cross have division?

If you inspect these questions, you'll see that even they can be further divided. "Who receives benefits from the Red Cross?" could be split into something like, "How does the Red Cross help meet emergency needs from natural disasters?" and, "How does the Red Cross help meet emergency needs from accidents?" You can carry out this exercise until you feel comfortable with the main points you think are important in order to meet your purpose.

Your speech topic may answer how a volunteer group helps those who've suffered a natural disaster.
© Wendy Kaveney Photography/ Shutterstock.com

Then you can add depth to those main points by including the supporting materials you have gathered.

Generally, the guidelines suggest dividing your specific purpose into between two and four main points; this is enough to be specific and focused and still meet a gamut of time limits. Remember: Your main points must be directly relevant to your specific purpose; if they're not, you either reconsider and refine those points or rethink your specific purpose. In addition, you would like to have a balance among the main points. You don't want to load up most of the information under one point and have the other two be entirely subordinate. If, for instance, you wanted to change your specific purpose to a more in-depth look at the Red Cross overall, you might want to talk about what services it offers, what values it represents, and how it is funded. If you find yourself spending the majority of your time detailing the services the Red Cross offers, then you can go back and restrict your specific purpose. Maybe your specific purpose is better stated as "to learn about the Red Cross organizations' outstanding (or unheralded) services." In that case, your main points could be disaster services, blood services, and health and safety services. If you can create parallel wording in the structure, that can help the progression and retention of ideas. The example about natural disasters and accidents is created in parallel structure. Compare that with two points that say, "The Red Cross gives help in natural disasters" and, "If there's a local emergency the Red Cross is there." Similarly, the three services are easy to create in parallel wording. Once you've settled on some possible main points (they still can be refined), you're ready to decide on their order.

Sequencing Choices

As with the shopping trip scenario, there may be many "right" ways to organize your ideas, deciding what to do first, second, and last. A list of organizational patterns could go on forever, because we arrange our perceptions through our own experiences and needs. However, there are some simple, standard patterns that you can use as you help your audience to take meaning from your message:

- **Chronological order** *structures ideas according to time orientation.* It is used most often when explaining how to do something or how something occurs, since order of activities is critical. An example of chronological order would be an informative speech about the history of the World Wide Web would discuss its evolution from the 1980s to today. You can structure time order from the past to the present or vice versa. A speech on weight clubs in your community could start with the current state of affairs, then move backwards to the origins.
- **Spatial order** *arranges your main points in terms of their place or position.* Think about how sometimes we explain ideas in terms of how they're related to each other by location. Describing how Hurricane Katrina devastated the Gulf Coast could easily move from the impacts in Louisiana to Mississippi to Alabama. Another example would be a speech that identifies the various component pieces connected to create the Web, starting with your home computer. If you wanted to focus on global impacts of some issue and move closer to the audience's immediate context, that would also be spatial order: Uncontrolled pet population growth affects our nation, our state, and our community.
- **Categorical** or **topical order** *is the "natural" or "relevant" organization pattern.* As you think about your main points, they seem to fit best in this way. There is no required order other than what you impose. If you wanted to talk about the three impacts that social networking sites have had on

interpersonal communication in the twenty-first century, what topical order would you use in discussing the ideas of privacy, job search, and politics?

- **Cause-effect order** *is used to show a relationship between a source and its outcomes.* You could also reverse the order and show how some effects can be traced back to their origins. Explaining how an animal became endangered could be shown by the causes of habitat depletion, pesticides, and invasive competing species, for example. The key is that you must be able to demonstrate that such a causal relationship exists.

- **Comparison and contrast** *structures ideas by showing that there is a similarity and/or difference of your topic with something the audience already knows.* You could explain how the changes the Internet has created are similar to the changes brought about by television's introduction, for example. Since your audience has always known television, its early impact may surprise the audience. You may have to decide whether to focus on only the differences or the similarities, or both. This is shown in a topic such as immigration issues of the early twenty-first century are both similar and dissimilar to those of the early twentieth century.

- **Problem-solution order** *structures ideas by pointing out a dilemma and offering (or supporting) its potential remedies.* If you use this structure, you must first demonstrate that a dilemma exists, that it's serious, and that it affects your audience. Then you are able to move into the potential solutions, perhaps even focusing on one resolution. Perhaps you feel that the allocation of special event tickets to currently enrolled students should be changed. The first main point you'd make is the extent of the problem: how ticket allocation is inefficient and how ticket allocation is unfair. You would then suggest a means for resolving this problem: Ticket allocation should be tied to class standing. The problem-solution order is quite common in advertisements. You are exposed to a problem you hadn't been aware of (you are alone and lonely, you have no opportunity to meet potential mates, you have no sense of how to talk to members of the opposite sex). Then, as if by magic, Dating Site X can resolve those issues by helping you to meet hundreds of compatible potential mates in your area, and they'll even coach you in how to fix your communication style.

If you assert that an animal became endangered because of habitat depletion, you need to demonstrate the cause-effect order.
© 2008, JupiterImages Corporation.

Finally, there is **Monroe's motivated sequence,** developed by Professor Alan H. Monroe in the 1930s. This organizational pattern, used mostly in persuasion, combines logic and psychology, because it models the human thinking process and motivates the audience to action. When you read it, you may see it as an extension of the problem-solution order, but it does much more. The motivated sequence consists of five major steps: attention, need, satisfaction, visualization, and action. In the **attention step,** you want to cause the listeners to focus tightly on you and your ideas. This step comes in the introduction of the speech. The next three steps constitute the body. **Need** demonstrates to the audience that a serious problem exists that demands change. Potentially, four elements are covered:

1. *Statement:* a clear, concise statement or description of the problem(s)
2. *Illustration:* one or more detailed supports that picture the need for change
3. *Ramification:* any additional data to show the problem's extent
4. *Pointing:* convincing demonstration of how the need directly affects this group

Remember, in the need step of the body, you try to create in your audience an uncomfortable state that they will want to alter.

Satisfaction proposes a plan of action that will solve the need. Three elements should be covered:

1. *Statement:* Briefly state your plan.
2. *Explanation:* Clarify the details of the plan (who, what, when, where, how much).
3. *Practical experience:* If possible, give an actual example of how this plan has worked effectively elsewhere, or how this belief has been proven correct by others.

The third part of the body (or fourth step of the motivated sequence) is **visualization,** where you picture for the audience what the world will be like if your plan is adopted. This step projects the audience into the future to intensify their desire for change. You may visualize in one of three ways:

1. *Positive method:* Describe conditions as they will be if your advocated action is accepted. Each motive appeal and problem from the *need* step should be answered.
2. *Negative method:* Describe adverse conditions that will prevail in the future if advocated belief/action is not accepted. Describe unpleasant conditions that will result.
3. *Contrast method:* Combine the negative and positive approaches.

It's important to remember that the visualization step must stand the test of reality. The conditions you picture must seem probable. The visualization step should be a logical counterpart to all of the ideas brought up in the need step. Finally, the last step is **action,** where you urge the audience to do a specific, definite act. You want to give them specific information on how to accomplish this action, so that they will know how to commit themselves. One caution: Asking your audience to "think about this" isn't an action! What behavior do you want them to do?

Take a Closer Look

If you have utilized the motivated sequence correctly, the audience will respond in a fashion somewhat like the following:

ATTENTION: Audience response will be, "I want to listen."

NEED: Response will be, "Something ought to be done. I can't live with things the way they are now." Or even, "I didn't know it was so bad. What can I do?"

PLAN: Audience will say, "This plan sounds like it will solve the problem."

VISUALIZATION: Reaction will be "I can see how I'll benefit" or, "Gee, without this solution, things will get worse."

ACTION: "I will do this."

Integrating My Evidence with My Main Points

As you make the selection of your order, you'll begin to arrange your supporting materials. Main points are nothing without the evidence that clarifies them. But how exactly do you organize your evidence within your main points? What if you have a great set of statistics, a quote or two, and an example, all of which support the first main point? What goes first? Sometimes, the answer is based on the same structural choices as the body: you might move chronologically through your evidence, for instance. In some cases, you can use the principles of primacy and recency to guide you. **Primacy** arranges ideas in terms of how convincing they are, moving from most important to least important. The belief is that by putting the most

---

Example: Five Ways to Organize a Speech about HIV/AIDS

Imagine that you plan to present a speech about HIV/AIDS. The speech design will influence the aspect of HIV/AIDS that you will discuss.

Match each of the following five speech designs with their associated purpose statement.

1. Chronological
2. Topical
3. Spatial
4. Logical
5. Compare/contrast

A. To inform the audience about the latest HIV/AIDS treatments
B. To demonstrate for the audience the process of how HIV becomes AIDS
C. To inform the audience about the causes of HIV/AIDS and its effect on the world's population
D. To compare and contrast the magnitude of the HIV/AIDS epidemic in South Africa and India
E. To inform the audience how HIV/AIDS spread, beginning in Africa and moving east

Answers: (A. 2, B. 1, C. 4, D. 5, E. 3.)

---

important first, you will compel the audience to believe what comes after. **Recency** is the opposite; it moves from the least convincing to the strongest. You might use this technique when you have some simple examples that lead naturally to a major example, for instance. With recency, the last thing heard is the one that is best remembered. Finally, you might choose to arrange by **specificity;** you could start with a general illustration and move to a specific one, or vice versa. You could present national statistics, regional ones, and end on local ones.

Because you probably have gathered more supporting materials than you really need, here is when you start to edit. You'll want to use your audience as your guide: What examples, statistics, testimony, narratives, and analogies will help them to achieve meaning? Which ones fit into the time limits you're facing? Are there some that are easier to explain than others? Do some require additional explanation through presentational aids? There is no magic number of supporting materials that any one point should have; that's totally dependent on your purpose, your audience, and your context.

WHAT GOES INTO A COMPELLING INTRODUCTION?

You now know about the structural choices to be selected from as you create the body of your message. You are able to start adding in evidence that augments and clarifies those main points. But sequencing isn't just about creating a pattern for the body. You have to develop the entire package of the message, which also includes a welcoming, compelling introduction and a reinforcing conclusion that establishes psychological closure.

You need to determine which supporting materials you ultimately use for your speech.
© Amihays/Shutterstock.com

The opening remarks made that provide the audience with initial message orientation is the **introduction**. This starting part of your message serves two important purposes: It motivates the audience to listen, and it prepares them to focus on the subject. You can meet these purposes by setting the stage through some strategically considered statements. Remember, you probably won't develop your introduction until you've already put the body of the speech together. Once the latter is done, you can then set up the introduction to reflect what will follow. How do you launch a speech? You do it by gaining attention, revealing the topic, suggesting to the audience a reason to listen, establishing credibility, and previewing the body through an initial summary.

Gaining Attention

You have probably heard the famous maxim, "You never get a second chance to make a first impression." That's certainly true about presenting a message. The first thing you say should capture the audience's attention; if you fail to establish that focus from the start, there's really no need to continue. Think about what captures your interest. Is it something creative? Something unique? Something surprising or unexpected? Popular television shows often begin with a powerful dramatic moment, perhaps the portrayal of a crime or a unforeseen circumstance. This "hook" is used to capture viewers' interest so that they do not switch the channel. This isn't a new idea. In 1947, Elmer Wheeler was one of the best-known salesmen of his time. Among the gems that he shared about initiating a sale were statements like, "Your first 10 words are more important than your next 10,000," and you must "Excite 'em, annoy 'em, or startle 'em, all in the first ten seconds."[32] His advice is good: Use your opening lines to capture your listener so he wants to hear what you have to say. Some popular approaches to capture an audience's attention are as follows:

- *Relate a narrative or anecdote.* Everyone likes to hear a riveting story. This may be accomplished in one of two ways. You could share a narrative, which is a story about someone else. You might share an anecdote, which is a story about yourself. If the story is told with conviction, it can capture the audience's imagination.
- *Create a hypothetical situation.* If you ask the audience to imagine something, they can be transported into a specific place, with accompanying emotions and images. We all like to imagine, but be sure to ask the audience to conceive of something they can realistically picture. Asking an audience composed of eighteen- to twenty-two-year-olds to imagine they are through with college, married with two kids, and contemplating a career change is a bit of a stretch. The audience may struggle to imagine finishing college, let alone anything beyond that. It would be better to ask this audience to image something within the realm of their current life, another reason to analyze your audience. Also, when you let the audience think of themselves in another place, be sure to bring them back to the present and your message. If your speech was about the advantages of taking a cruise and you asked us to see ourselves relaxing on deck, umbrella drink in hand with no cares in the world, we might just decide to stay in that daydream, rather than come back to the present.
- *Ask a series of rhetorical questions.* Rhetorical questions do not require the audience to answer aloud or by a show of hands. The answers are implied or are meant for audience members to think about. This mental participation can be very effective in creating immediate involvement. A speech talking about genocide in Darfur, for instance, could easily begin with the query: Do you know where Darfur is? Are you aware of the mass killings that are being perpetrated there? Do you know when you first heard about the crisis? The pitfall to avoid with this type of attention-getter is

asking a question that is not thought-provoking or that should really have been asked as part of the audience analysis. An example of a question that should have been asked as part of a class survey would be, "How many of you are registered to vote?" It is not a rhetorical question and it certainly is not thought-provoking. A more effective rhetorical question to ask would be: "How many of you have thought about your voting rights being revoked? Would this threat motivate you to exercise those rights?"

- *Startle with some surprising information or statistics.* The Internet has enabled us to gather interesting statistics at the click of a button. Opening a speech with a startling statistic or shocking information can startle the audience into wanting to learn more. For example, you could begin a speech about the dangers of distorted body image with some shocking facts such as these. The average U.S. woman is 5'4" and weighs 140 pounds, whereas the average U.S. model is 5'11" and weighs 117 pounds. Young girls are more afraid of becoming fat than they are of nuclear war, cancer, or losing their parents. The "ideal" woman—portrayed by models, Miss America, Barbie dolls, and screen actresses—is 5'5", weighs 100 pounds, and wears a size 5.[33]

- *Use a thought-provoking quote.* It's not unusual to find an authoritative or memorable statement by someone else that fits into your speech. This can even add to your initial credibility, because that quotation will resonate with what you're about to say. The guiding principle to using such quotes is to be sure they are indeed interesting, related to your topic, and linked to the purpose of your speech. A quote such as, "Experience is a hard teacher because she gives the test first, the lesson afterward. And in the end, it's not the years in your life that count. It's the life in your years," by Abraham Lincoln can be a great way to interest an audience about speeches, ranging from financial planning to pursing a dream career.

- *Use humor.* A funny story, relevant joke, or witty comment can help to relax your audience, and ease any sense of anxiety, especially on subjects where they disagree with your position. But there are some pitfalls to consider with this attention getter. A joke can be offensive in its language or in the way it pokes fun at other groups (e.g., age, gender, ethnicity). If this is the type of joke you would like to share, it is not appropriate and is unethical to use. Also, some witty comments or jokes are grounded in cultural knowledge and a clear understanding of the language in which they were developed. If you are faced with an audience whose members are from diverse cultural backgrounds, you may run the risk of them not "getting" the punch line. Finally, to employ the delivery required to tell a joke well, the speaker must be at ease at the beginning of the speech. For novice speakers, this can be challenging.

- *Share some information counter to the audience's beliefs.* This could be in the form of stating a truth that was typically accepted but recently shown to be false. For example, many people believe senior citizens to be helpless, yet a recent *Los Angeles Times* article revealed that senior citizens are not as vulnerable as we might think. The article titled "U.S. Tourists Kill Mugger, Costa Rica Says," recounts an unfortunate incident in which a man who pulled a .38 caliber revolver on a group of senior citizen tourists was killed when the group jumped on him in self-defense.[34]

- *Refer to the occasion.* Sometimes, you'll be asked to speak at some special event or occasion, such as a holiday, a professional conference, or even graduation. It's appropriate to say something like, "I'm honored to be part of this celebration with you," and then continue with a reference to the event.

- *Play a short video or audio segment.* People respond well to visual messages. To do this well, however, remember that this will cut into your speaking time. The last thing you should do is play three minutes of

How would you toast the bride and groom?
© Shanta Giddens/Shutterstock.com

video for a six-minute speech. Your message content is the important thing, not your introductory audio or video. Thus, for a six- or seven-minute speech, the use of a video segment should be fifteen to thirty seconds, tops. It is important to explain to the audience what they will be watching and what they should look for. Imagine for a moment that you are an audience member and the speaker begins his speech by walking over to the DVD player and playing a clip from *The Terminator*. You have no idea why you are watching the film but you sit back and enjoy the action. After the clip, the speaker says, "I am here to talk to you today about violence in the media." In this example, the speaker failed to set up the visual so that it motivated the audience to listen. The speaker should have begun by stating, "I am going to show you a clip from the film *The Terminator*. Count how many violent acts you see." You would know why you were watching the clip and would engage in the set task. After playing the clip, the speaker follows up by stating, "There were a total of fifteen violent acts performed in fifteen seconds. Watching such violence desensitizes us to real life violence in our communities." By explaining the clip and linking it to the speech, the speaker has created a compelling attention getter.

Whatever attention-getting technique you choose to use, your attention getter should establish interest, should be relevant to the message, and should prepare the audience for the thesis statement about to come.

Revealing the Topic

After capturing your audience's attention, you want to clarify for your audience exactly what you will talk about. This is achieved by providing a clear and simple **thesis statement** (or topic sentence, or central idea), which announces in one sentence what your speech is about. It's not the same as your specific purpose statement, but it certainly echoes that focus. If your specific purpose was "to create awareness in my audience about the services provided by the American Red Cross in our community," then your thesis statement could be: "A simple rule of thumb is that you should be able to say it in one breath, and it answers this question: 'If I were to ask to give one focused sentence that introduces the subject of my speech, what would that be?'" Few things frustrate listeners more than sitting through a speech attempting to figure out what you are talking about.

Moving the Audience to Listening

Consider how your information could possibly impact the listeners. Could it save them money or time? Do they lack of information or perspective? Why not give your listeners a reason to listen? By listening to your speech, they could be improving their understanding for another course or important life issue. Your audience analysis will help to reveal what reasons might motivate your particular audience to listen. You know about how and why we fail at listening, and you have some strategies for helping your audience to overcome those barriers. Keep all those elements at the center of your message preparation.

To be audience-centered means to find a way to add value to your audience's lives through your speech. It means giving your audience more for their money. It means connecting your speech topic with the needs of the listener. Remember Maslow's hierarchy of needs that you read about in Chapter 12? There is the basis of your reflection: What needs can I connect to early on in my speech? The audience should not have to work to see the link between their needs and the topic you have chosen. The link should be obvious in the introduction. This is analogous to sales training. Salespeople are taught to answer for customers the question, "What's in it for me?" (W.I.F.M.). In other words, the audience is silently wondering, "Why should I buy your product?" If the salesperson tells us what we gain from the purchase, then she motivates us to listen further to her sales pitch. You can create this reason to listen by showing the audience that what they're about to hear impacts them directly. You don't have to spend a great deal of time on this idea, but you do have to give the audience direction on why the topic is worth listening to. This could be something as simple as a statement saying, "You might not own this, but you probably know someone who does," or, "You might not think that what happens here is part of your life, but your tax dollars are going to support this effort." Part of creating a compelling introduction is telling the audience what they have to gain by listening. When you do that, you show them that you've thought about their perspective, and you have their best interest at heart.

Establishing Credibility in the Introduction

You've already read about the concept of ethos or credibility. You know that it's the audience's perception of you, seen through the lenses of character, intelligence, goodwill, and charisma. By helping the audience consider why they should listen, you have established a sense of goodwill. Another way to increase people's motivation to listen to your message is by offering a statement of your expertise. People are certainly interested in what Steve Jobs or Bill Gates has to say about technology, but why should they believe you? By offering a bit of information about how you are knowledgeable on the subject you have chosen, you boost your credibility, increasing the chance that your audience will listen to your ideas. Your competence might be built on personal experience and firsthand knowledge, or it might come from classes, reading, or even the experiences that others have shared with you.

For example, if you have trained show dogs as a hobby for ten years, tell your audience about your experience in a speech about caring for pets. If your have recently learned about the risks related to nano-technology through a chemistry class, share that in a speech about nano-technology. If you have volunteered during an emergency or given blood at a Red Cross center, then tell your audience your experience as you discuss American Red Cross services. A credibility statement in the introduction may be as simple as telling the audience about the amount of research done to prepare the speech: "Over the past couple of months, I have read numerous articles, books, and interviews about the Red Cross's history and services." When you help your audience to perceive you as believable, you are also giving them the opportunity to identify with you. If they think that they're like you and the topic is important to you, then by extension, it's also important to them.

Previewing the Body through an Initial Summary

The **initial summary** or **speech preview** forecasts what main points are about to come in the body. You want to let the audience know what the main points include so that they have a perspective on what to focus on. You're telling the audience what you're about to tell them, providing an initial listening guideline. But an initial summary can do more than that. Not only does it preview what's to come, but it can serve as a reminder to you, too. By telling your listeners that you plan to cover the ingredients, process, and cautions of making mortar, you review for yourself one last time where you're about to go. In a similar fashion, that initial summary serves as a bridge to the first main point in the body; it signals that the main content (body) of the speech is about to come. The initial summary is typically presented at the end of your introduction and should flow naturally from your thesis statement. In the speech about the American Red Cross, it might sound something like this: "Today I will explain three major services offered by the Red Cross in our community: disaster relief, health services, and military support services." This preview should be short, specific, and easy to understand. Avoid the temptation to state your preview as a question; an initial summary should state clearly what the speech will cover and the order in which it will be covered.

The tone and direction of your message are established when you create an effective introduction. This is done by gaining attention, revealing the topic, suggesting a reason to listen, establishing credibility, and previewing the body through an initial summary.

HOW DO I CONCLUDE THE SPEECH?

If you did a good job in the introduction, you set the stage for your audience to listen. The end of the speech should wrap up your ideas through a final summary and create closure for you and the audience. Have you ever read a book or gone to a movie that left you unsatisfied at the end? Do you recall one of those times when you weren't sure that it was over? This **final summary** helps the audience recall the main points, improving overall recollection and comprehension. You could signal the coming end with a simple review of your main points. In the Red Cross example, it might appear like this: "You've learned today about the services provided by our American Red Cross, which include disaster relief, health and safety, and military family services." An effective **conclusion** gives the audience one last time to hear your main points. By this time, you've now repeated your main points three times: first in the initial summary, then in the body, and now in the final summary. The final objective of the conclusion is to *close the speech* as powerfully as you began. Two important pitfalls to avoid: Don't assume that you'll "know" how to end the speech when you're done (the "lightning will strike me" approach) and make sure that it's really the end. One mistake speakers make is that they assume some inspirational ending will come to them as they're speaking. It doesn't happen. You need to know what your final statements will be, and you need to practice them so you wrap up with direct eye contact and strong delivery. Equally irresponsible is saying, "In conclusion," and then not concluding. We've all suffered through speakers who use that signal one or more times but then continue to drone on.

So how do you create closure? How do you end a speech? In the introduction, you try to capture the listeners' attention with a *hook*. Any of those techniques could be employed again in the conclusion. If you began by hooking the audience with a story, your closing might offer the moral of the story. If you started with thought-provoking questions, you might wish to return to those questions and offer answers, or you might ask the audience to reflect again on their answers. You could use the conclusion for a final appeal or challenge to the audience, telling them what response you expect from them. The key is to create a sense of closure in the same way that a well-written novel or movie leaves the audience feeling complete or satisfied.

HOW DO I USE CONNECTIVES TO BRIDGE MAIN IDEAS?

Now you have explored the most obvious structural aspects of sequence: creating an introduction, body, and conclusion. There is one more sequencing strategy to consider as you craft your speech: How do you connect those three structural elements into a seamless yet dynamic message? Unlike an interpersonal dialogue, where you can jump from topic to topic and still share meaning, in a speech you have to link the main ideas through connectives.

Connectives create the dynamic flow of a speech and help listeners to remember and to recognize where they have been and what to expect next in a speech. They are a subtle aspect of speechmaking that can turn a good speech into a great speech. The most common kinds of connectives are transitions, signposts, internal previews, and internal summaries.

Transitions consist of phrases or key words that we use to link ideas; they're typically used to bridge "big" ideas in a speech, such as a link between introduction and body, between main points, or between body and conclusion. A transition usually signals that one idea is done and the speech is moving to something new. Examples of transitions are phrases such as, "As I move to the next point . . ." or, "The final idea I want to make is . . ." Even "in summary" is a transition.

Signposts alert the audience to something important about to come; think of them as pointing a spotlight on an idea. "What you should remember is . . ." and, "The only thing that you should know is . . ." are signposts. So are numbers ("*the first cause* of obesity is . . ." They warn the audience of the importance of the next remarks.

Previews do just that: They give the audience a prompt or advanced warning that movement is about to occur, but they do it in a bit more detail than signposts or transitions. They can serve the same function as your initial summary did in the introduction, except on a much smaller scale. An example would be, "In order to understand the problems of the dangers of parasailing, we need to know first about equipment and then about the process."

Finally, an **internal summary** reviews what has just happened; it is the opposite of your internal preview. It reminds the audience of what they just heard in a preceding point, and it allows the audience to understand how new information connects to previous information. By saying, "Now that I've covered the equipment used in parasailing . . ." you have reminded the audience what they should have heard.

These connectives are very subtle, and what's important is the movement that they'll supply to your message. They're the last part of sequencing that should be considered as you work on your speech. When you use connectives well, you can bridge gaps between and among ideas, adding to the unity of your message.

The decision strategy of sequencing allows you to arrange your ideas and evidence for the audience so that they have a better chance of grasping and sharing your meaning. How you structure ideas should be based on the needs of the situation and audience. The most basic step in developing sequencing is to think of the three basic elements of organization: introduction, body, and conclusion. Each of these elements has specific functions, but each allows you to use your own creativity in adapting your structure to your audience and purpose. You strategically choose among organizational patterns so you can achieve your intended result. Then you add in your supporting materials to flesh out those ideas. Connectives are considered last, because they function to join ideas; they tie the main points into one cohesive whole.

ENDNOTES

1. For some examples of how the communication field has studied the credibility concept, consider the following recent articles: David K. Berlo, James B. Lemert, and Robert J. Mertz, "Dimensions for Evaluating the Acceptability of Message Sources," *Public Opinion Quarterly* 33 (1969): 563–576. Also Lanette Pogue and Kimo Ahyun, "The Effect of Teacher Nonverbal Immediacy and Credibility on Student Motivation and Affective Learning," *Communication Education* 55 (3) (July 2006): 331–344; "Can Corporate Blogs Ever Really Be Credible?" *Business Communicator* 7 (2) (June 2006): 1–2; Spiro Kiousis and Daniela V. Dimitrova, "Differential Impact of Web Site Content: Exploring the Influence of Source (Public Relations versus News), Modality, and Participation on College Students' Perceptions," *Public Relations Review* 32 (2) (June 2006): 177–179 and J. Glascock and T. Ruggiero, "The Relationship of Ethnicity and Sex to Professor Credibility at a Culturally Diverse University," *Communication Education* 55 (2) (April 2006): 197–207.

2. Richard C. Jebb, (trans.). *The Rhetoric of Aristotle* (Cambridge: University Press, 1909): 69.

3. Max Weber defined charisma as a certain quality of an individual personality, by virtue of which s/he is set apart from ordinary people and treated as endowed with supernatural, superhuman, or at least specifically exceptional powers or qualities. These are such as are not accessible to the ordinary person, but are regarded as of divine origin or as exemplary, and on the basis of them the individual concerned is treated as a leader. "Max Weber," http://business.nmsu.edu/~dboje/teaching/503/weber_links.html (accessed Feb. 21, 2006). For some examples of communication research on the concept, see, for example, William L. Gardner, "Perceptions of Leader Charisma, Effectiveness, and Integrity," *Management Communication Quarterly*, 16 (4) (May 2003): 502; Mark Anderson, "Pancho Villa and the Marlboro Man: American-Style Charisma in the Marketplace of Ideas," *Media History* 7 (2) (Dec. 2001): 171–181.

4. For examples of different polls, see the Gallup organization at http://www.gallup.com/or the *Entertainment Weekly* polls at http://www.ew.com/ew/critmass/index.html. Also, two articles speak to media and charisma: T. Sheafer, "Charismatic Skill and Media Legitimacy: An Actor-Centered Approach to Understanding the Political Communication Competition," *Communication Research*, 28 (6) (Dec. 2001): 711; and B. Briller, "Heroes and Other Villains: Politics, TV and Charisma," *Television Quarterly* 30 (2) (Fall 1999): 31.

5. Peggy Anderson, (ed.) *Dwight D. Eisenhower, Great Quotes from Great Leaders*, (Lombard: Great Quotations, 1989).

6. "Importance of Eye Contact," http://www.synchronicsgroup.com/tips/eye_contact.html, The Synchronics Group San Francisco, CA (accessed Sept. 11, 2007). Copyright © 2007. Reprinted with permission.

7. Humane Society of the United States, "HSUS Pet Overpopulation Estimates," http://www.hsus.org/pets/issues_affecting_our_pets/pet_overpopulation_and_ownership_statistics/hsus_pet_overpopulation_estimates.html (accessed July 16, 2007).

8. Max Weber, *Max Weber: The Theory of Social and Economic Organization*, translated by A. M. Henderson and Talcott Parsons (New York: The Free Press, 1947). For examples of research on charisma, see R. J. House, and B. Shamir, "Toward the Integration of Transformational, Charismatic, and Visionary Theories," in M. Chemers and R. Ayman (eds.), *Leadership Theory and Research: Perspectives and Directions* (New York: Academic Press, 1993): 81–107 and J. M. Howell, "Two Faces of Charisma: Socialized and Personalized Leadership in Organizations," in J. A. Conger and R. N. Kanungo (eds.), *Charismatic Leadership: The Elusive Factor in Organizational Effectiveness* (San Francisco: Jossey-Bass, 1988), 213–236.

9. K. J. Klein and R. J. House, "On Fire: Charismatic Leadership and Levels of Analysis," *Leadership Quarterly* 6 (2) (1995): 183–198. Also Jane A. Halpert, "The Dimensionality of Charisma," *Journal of Business and Psychology*, 4, no. 4 (June 1990): 399–410 and Jeffrey D. Kudisch, Mark L. Poteet, Gregory H. Dobbins, Michael C. Rush and Joyce E. A. Russell, "Expert Power, Referent Power, and Charisma: Toward the Resolution of a Theoretical Debate," *Journal of Business and Psychology* 10 (2) (1995): 177–195.

10. Kenneth Burke, *A Rhetoric of Motives* (Berkeley: University of California Press, 1950), 3–46.

11. See a video example of the creation of an infomercial by NBC's *Dateline* at http://www.msnbc.msn.com/id/14856571/"From the inside out" John Larson (Sept. 15, 2006). For a simple history of Infomercials, see http://www.answers.com/topic/infomercial?cat=biz-fin.

12. MarthaStewart.com, http://www.marthastewart.com/ (accessed Sept. 14, 2007).

13. Donald Trump, "Martha Stewart, the Domestic Diva is Back." http://www.time.com/time/subscriber/2005/time100/builders/100stewart.html (accessed Sept. 14, 2007).

14. James C. McCroskey, *An Introduction to Rhetorical Communication*, 7th ed. (Boston: Allyn and Bacon, 1997), 91–101.

15. Alan Finder, "For Some, Online Persona Undermines a Résumé" (June 11, 2006), http://www.nytimes.com/2006/06/11/us/11recruit.html (accessed Sept. 13, 2007).

16. Warren Buffet quotation, http://thinkexist.com/quotation/it_takes-years_to_build_a_reputation_and_five/151205.html (accessed Sept. 13, 2007).

17. "Fan Frenzy over Harry Potter Book 7: Harry Potter and the Deathly Hallows—MuggleNet.com Book Tour," (May 17, 2007), http://www.randomsandiego.com/blog/2007/05/17/mugglenetcom-book-tour-fan-frenzy-over-harry-potter-book-7-harry-potter-and-the-deathly-hallows/ (accessed Sept. 11, 2007).

18. Michiko Kakutani, "An Epic Showdown as Harry Potter Is Initiated into Adulthood," http://www.nytimes.com/2007/07/19/books/19potter.html (accessed July 19, 2007).

19. Marty Dodge Book Review, "Harry Potter and the Deathly Hallows by J. K. Rowling," http://blogcritics.org/archives/2007/07/21/154457.php (accessed July 21, 2007).

20. http://www.ratemyprofessors.com/index.jsp

21. Maio, G. R., & Olson, J. M. (1998). Values as truisms: Evidence and implications. *Journal of Personality and Social Psychology*, 74, 294–311.

22. Maslow, A. H. (1970). *Motivation and personality* (2nd ed.). New York: Harper and Row.

23. Fukuyama, F. (1992). *The end of history and the last man*. New York: Avon.

24. Koltko-Rivera, M. E. (2006). Rediscovering the later version of Maslow's hierarchy of needs: Selftranscendence and opportunities for theory, research, and unification. *Review of General Psychology*, 10, 302–317.

25. Maslow, A. H. (1966). Comments on Dr. Frankl's paper. *Journal of Humanistic Psychology*, 6:107–112.

26. Csikszentmihalyi, M. (1997). *Finding flow: The psychology of engagement with everyday life*. New York: Basic Books.

27. Maslow, A. H. (1968). *Toward a psychology of being* (2nd ed.). New York: Van Nostrand Reinhold.

28. Kidder, R. M. (2005). *Moral courage*. New York: William Morrow.

29. Schwartz, S. H. (1992). Universals in the content and structure of values: Theory and empirical tests in 20 countries. In M. Zanna (Ed.), *Advances in experimental social psychology* (Vol. 25; pp. 1–65). New York: Academic Press.

30. Schwartz, S. H., & Bilsky, W. (1990). Toward a theory of the universal content and structure of values: Extensions and cross-cultural replications. *Journal of Personality and Social Psychology*, 58:878–891.

31. Feather, N. T., Volkmer, R. E., & McKee, I. R. (1992). A comparative study of the value priorities of Australians, Australian Baha'is, and expatriate Iranian Baha'is. *Journal of Cross-Cultural Psychology*, 23, 95–106.

32. Wheeler, E. *Tested public speaking*, 2nd ed. (New York: Prentice Hall, 1949), p. 35.

33. "Shocking Statistics: Beauty of a Woman," http://www.colorado.edu/studentgroups/wellness/NewSite/BdyImgShockingStats.html (accessed November 23, 2007).

34. "U.S. tourists kill mugger, Costa Rica says," *Los Angeles Times* (February 23, 2007), A10.

10

SPEECH PRESENTATION

COMMUNICATE CONFIDENTLY*

So far, we have probed within ourselves and moved outward toward exploring our connections to cultures. We noted the benefits of overcoming our anxieties and fears about interacting with other cultures. We now move to another type of interaction that may remain intimidating: public speaking. This section helps you develop confidence when you encounter other people as your audience.

If you fear public speaking, you are not alone. The Roman lawyer Cicero, one of the ancient world's greatest speakers, confessed that "the better the orator, the more profoundly is he frightened of the difficulty of speaking . . ." (1942, I.xxxvi.120). What made Cicero a great orator was that he treated fear as a call to act by preparing thoroughly for every presentation. Roughly 85 percent of Americans harbor anxiety about public speaking.[26] Problems arise only when fear overtakes reality. A 2001 national Gallup poll reported that 40 percent of Americans fear speaking in front of an audience—outranked only by snakes, feared by 51 percent of respondents.[27] We could add to the list a related fear that probably was pounded into our minds from early childhood: fear of strangers.

Comedian Jerry Seinfeld has joked that people fear giving the eulogy at a funeral more than being in the casket. Clearly, no one really would rather die than give a speech. In addition, meeting someone you don't know can actually be a positive experience. Communication anxiety is caused by a *false* perception of how awful the experience might be. This irrational perception causes damage when we don't replace it with more accurate ones. Medical studies have found that, *if unchecked,* fear of public speaking can induce symptoms of cardiac arrest.[28] In some medical studies,[29] researchers who wanted to simulate the symptoms of a heart attack simply placed subjects in situations where they faced the task of delivering a public speech!

Before you flee this course in terror, reconsider the last few sentences. Stage fright debilitates speakers *if* they continue unrealistic perceptions and *if* they don't control their reactions. We can't eliminate all fears associated with oral communication, but we can gain control over our perceptions and behaviors. A key to successful communication is controlling our anxieties instead of letting our anxieties control us. You can choose whether to dread communication or treat it as a productive opportunity to share ideas. Communication itself is as irksome or as inviting as you decide to make it. Overcoming fear requires breaking out of destructive feelings of helplessness, realizing that you can control your level of fear and how you react to public presentation situations.[30]

Communication apprehension (often abbreviated as CA) describes the feeling of anxiety about oral communication with others—and this dread applies to real or imagined situations.[31,32] The degree of apprehension varies depending on the type of communication: groups, pairs, and speeches.[33] The most documented—and most severe—area of communication apprehension is fear of public speaking, more commonly known as **stage fright**. Communication apprehension is nothing to be ashamed of. Everyone feels it to some degree and a change in circumstances can inflate or shrink anxiety levels. Speakers at all skill levels can experience CA.[29] In fact, some research reports that college honors students experience more stage fright than non-honors students.[34] So don't think "I'm dumb" if you dread public speaking.

The anxiety surrounding public speaking may take two forms. **Trait anxiety** is a general fear across different situations, while **state anxiety** is associated with particular settings, speech conditions, or times.[35,36] If you experience trait anxiety, you probably will find techniques that help you approach communication more calmly and positively prove most helpful. If you undergo state anxiety, then methods that give you greater confidence and control regarding your communication environment can empower you as a speaker.

You probably wonder, "Exactly what should I *do* to become a more confident communicator?" Not every technique for reducing communication apprehension works equally well for everyone. Try each of the following techniques to determine which of them work best for you. Regardless of how accomplished you consider yourself as a communicator, greater confidence will improve your effectiveness. The less nervous a speaker seems, the more competent and believable the audience will believe the person to be.[37,38]

Harnessing Nervousness

So, do we want to eliminate all feelings of nervousness about presentations? Absolutely not. Just ask any peak performer, such as an accomplished athlete, actor, or musician. Before a major performance, these performers want—indeed, crave—the adrenaline rush of anticipating doing what they have prepared to do. Feeling zero apprehension and no emotion results in lackluster performance: a sluggish game, a flat character, a song without soul. Not all nervousness is bad. Successful speakers still get nervous; they simply channel it productively.

Nervousness can be debilitating if you treat it as negative anxiety. Witnessing our own symptoms of nervousness can actually create more anxiety.[39] This is why it is important to understand how the body reacts to anxiety and why these reactions are so normal.

The symptoms that unskilled speakers dread—increased body temperature, more rapid heart rate, shallower breathing, etc.—merely signify arousal. When we were younger, we actually sought this sensation, eager to ride a new roller coaster, hoping to drive a car for the first time, or anticipating a first date. This arousal stimulates confident speakers to devote more energy to their presentation because they feel the energy surge as the presentation approaches.[40] The symptoms are negative only if we permit them to be.

To convert nervousness to positive energy, consider how you can channel your fear and convert it to more animated delivery. Deliberately plan some movement during your presentation so you can use some of that excess energy. Allow your arms and hands to gesture a bit. It's much tougher to have shaky hands and trembling legs if those body parts are in motion. Keep the movement within reason—just a few steps can dissipate energy and enliven a presentation. Some speakers also find that using a visual aid helps focus energy toward something other than their own nervousness. A visual aid in any form (poster, flip chart, PowerPoint, etc.) can reduce the feeling that you have to face the audience alone, since you have additional materials to clarify your points. If you do plan to add some sort of visual aid, read ahead in Chapter 8 for advice on choosing, constructing, and using your presentation materials. Remember that a visual aid adds a new dimension to any presentation, so make sure to include your aid (even before it is complete) in your practice sessions.

Immersion

Over time, the more you are exposed to what causes fear, the less fear you will feel. This process is called **habituation**. The more time you spend facing situations such as public speaking that cause fear, the calmer you become.[41] Gradually, you get more accustomed to making presentations—fear of the mysterious unknown dissolves into a comfortable routine.

Habituating yourself to communication requires seeking out opportunities to communicate. The technique of embracing what causes fear by doing it is called **immersion**. Volunteer for opportunities to speak throughout your campus or community. Presentations delivered to friendly audiences such as your favorite club or your religious congregation let you hone your skill without risking rejection. Take advantage of small ways to develop oral communication skills. Ask questions in your classes to help reduce shyness in conversations. Make at least one positive verbal contribution during each meeting you attend at work or in an organization. Try teaching key concepts to classmates who need help; you'll get practice explaining ideas while making new friends. Join groups such as choirs or competitive speech teams that reward participants for public performances. Volunteer for positions that emphasize oral communication, such as recruitment chair for a club or interviewing people for articles in a newsletter. Toastmasters International, with more than four million members throughout the world, is an organization devoted to public speaking. People join (or create) Toastmasters chapters in their community to encourage and gain experience in oral communication.

Just as you gain fluency in a language by reading and speaking it often, you feel more comfortable with making presentations if you keep doing them. Avoidance only magnifies fears. If you had a bad experience as a speaker, making more presentations increases the opportunities to have better experiences. You can't become a better speaker if you avoid speaking.

Not ready to give a full-fledged presentation yet? Specific techniques can get you to that point. The most effective method to develop confidence is through anxiety reduction techniques such as cognitive restructuring, systematic desensitization, and the other methods discussed in this chapter.[42] But you must actually *do* the techniques in addition to reading about them.

Cognitive Restructuring

To become more effective communicators, we need to identify negative influences that feed our fears.[43] Negativity can have devastating effects for speakers. Imagine telling yourself constantly: "I'm an incompetent speaker. I look like an idiot when making a presentation. I'll forget everything. Everyone will laugh at me." Self-fulfilling prophecy reminds us that these negative thoughts actually can create poor performance, regardless of your skill as a speaker. **Cognitive restructuring** transforms negative self-talk into positive self-talk. The technique replaces threatening thoughts about communication with more positive perceptions. Although your original self-talk was discouraging, your restructured self-talk helps you refocus on how you will cope with speaking.[44] Cognitive restructuring works best when your positive statements are specific, focusing on positive things you are can do (e.g., "I have note cards to eliminate the chance of forgetting content") or perceive (e.g., "The audience is watching me because they are interested") instead of vague reassurances (e.g., I'm a good public speaker). Your restructured statements should be realistic actions or thoughts that you can enact.[45]

To use cognitive restructuring properly, you should:

1. List specific negative thoughts associated with the communication event. Yes, actually write them. Writing your negative and positive thoughts by hand gives you a greater sense of ownership: These are your thoughts in your handwriting.
2. Now, evaluate each negative statement. Consider why the statement is irrational, unrealistic, or downright silly. You can work with friends or classmates to discover why the negative expectations are unfounded. List the objections to the negative thoughts.
3. Next, change each negative thought to a more positive version. These positive alternatives should be optimistic but realistic. For instance, if you say, "I will deliver a perfect speech," you are setting unrealistic expectations and inviting disappointment. Avoid negative or limiting statements.

<u>**Poor examples:**</u>
- I'm not a terrible speaker.
- I don't speak as quietly as some people say I do.

<u>**Better examples:**</u>
- I know my material because I practiced at least twice a day.
- My voice resonates to show pride in my work.

4. Keep the list of positive thoughts where you can see them and repeat them often (several times per day). You might keep your affirmations in your notebook or daily planner, post them on your refrigerator door, tape them to your mirror, use one or more as screen savers on your computer, text them to yourself, or write them on post-it notes so you can have them handy wherever you go. Don't just read them—say them aloud. Literally talk yourself into believing them. These affirmations, if repeated often and taken seriously, can reprogram you to expect success in speech-related tasks.

Figure 10.1 shows a sample cognitive restructuring worksheet prepared according to these guidelines. Remember: The restructured versions must be plausible, not simply wishes. For example, don't reassure yourself that you are well prepared if you slapped together your presentation the night before it was due.

Systematic Desensitization

Fear of public communication enacts a vicious cycle: We falsely reassure ourselves that we are safe by avoiding what causes the fear. Avoidance is exactly what makes stage fright and related maladies worse. By avoiding public speaking (or other forms of presentations), we think that we escape discomfort. True—for now. The longer we avoid public presentations, the more difficult they will become. We must confront our fears to conquer them.[43]

Fortunately, **systematic desensitization** can effectively reduce communication apprehension,[46] especially among people with high trait anxiety.[35] Systematic desensitization allows confrontation of a fearful condition in small steps. The method relies on an **incremental approach** with each stage of practice getting slightly closer to simulating the actual presentation conditions. Gradually, you approach whatever is causing the fear, exposing yourself more and more closely to the problem. This gradual approach lets you become used to a reduced version of whatever is causing the fear before bringing you closer

FIGURE 10.1 Sample cognitive restructuring worksheet.

Sample Negative Perception	Evaluation of Negative Perception	Positive Restructuring
My interview will be a complete fiasco.	1. Even the worst interview has some positive aspects. 2. Why? My most recent interview went well. 3. I'm not helpless—I can control how I prepare.	1. I have prepared well and will be confident in this interview. 2. My interview will contain strengths and some areas.
I hate it when everybody stares at me.	1. What do I expect my audience to do—shut their eyes? 2. What's to hate? I appreciate it when my friends look at me when I'm talking to them. 3. There's no reason to suspect the audience is staring because they want to ridicule me.	1. It's good to be the center of attention for a change. 2. My audience cares enough about my ideas to make direct eye contact.

to it. Figure 10.2 shows some possible stages of systematic desensitization to cope with the most common fear among Americans: fear of snakes.[27]

Here is how the method would work for public speaking. The number of stages will vary depending on how gradually you approach the actual presentation. Generally, the more anxiety you feel, the more steps you will need to reach your goal. Before entering each stage, relax your mind and body as much as possible. The following technique is a popular relaxation method that works on each area of your body from the feet up. You might find other relaxation methods (such as the technique described below for visualization) more helpful, but this procedure is a typical approach for systematic desensitization.

Rest comfortably in a seated or reclining position. Inhale and exhale deeply and slowly several times. Now totally relax your feet and toes, taking as long as necessary to let them feel almost weightless. When your feet feel absolutely relaxed, let the wave of relaxation pass gradually up to your calves. Let your calf muscles lose tension and feel light. Continue this relaxation method; release all muscular tightness for each area of your body, all the way up to your face. Remember to relax your jaw, eyes, and fingers. Feel your entire body rest and recover. When you have maintained this refreshed, calm (but not sleepy—this is relaxation for reassurance, not unconsciousness) feeling for a few minutes, you are ready to enter a stage of systematic desensitization. If at any time your fear resurfaces and produces uncomfortable anxiety during systematic desensitization, return to your relaxation mode until the anxiety becomes manageable. Then try the systematic desensitization stage again.

Figure 10.3 illustrates what the successive stages of systematic desensitization might be for a speaker. The number and content of stages vary, but some basic principles still hold: (1) You progress to the next stage only when you

FIGURE 10.2 Sample systematic desensitization stages for coping with fear of snakes.

Stage 1: View black-and-white sketches of snakes	**Least Level of Initial Anxiety**
Stage 2: View color drawings of snakes	
Stage 3: View black-and-white photos of snakes	
Stage 4: View color photos of snakes	
Stage 5: View short videos of snakes	
Stage 6: View longer videos of snakes with sound	
Stage 7: View live snakes at a zoo through a glass barrier	
Stage 8: View live snakes without a barrier	
Stage 9: Touch a live snake	**Greatest Level of Initial Anxiety**

The final stage does not seek extreme measures, such as having a pet snake or becoming a snake handler. The goal is to control reactions to the source of fear (snakes) so that extreme negative reactions no longer control you.

FIGURE 10.3 Sample stages of systematic desensitization for a speech.

Stage 1: Rehearse 30 seconds of speech alone (or to a household pet) while wearing pajamas lounging on the sofa at home	**Least Level of Initial Anxiety**
Stage 2: Rehearse 30 seconds of speech while wearing very casual clothes, seated at home in front of best friend	
Stage 3: Rehearse 1 minute of speech to 2-3 close friends while standing at home	
Stage 4: Rehearse 2 minutes of speech to 5-8 acquaintances while standing in your regular classroom	
Stage 5: Rehearse 3 minutes of speech to 10-12 acquaintances while standing in your regular classroom; solicit feedback from audience	
Stage 6: Rehearse entire 5-minute speech to 12-15 acquaintances while standing in your regular classroom, wearing clothes you will wear for the formal speech; solicit feedback from audience	
Stage 7: Deliver entire speech to 25 classmates and your instructor in classroom for a grade	**Greatest Level of Initial Anxiety**

feel comfortable with the current stage. If you feel serious anxiety, do your relaxation. If the anxiety persists after several attempts, go back to the preceding stage to regain your comfort level. (2) Move to more challenging stages systematically. Advancing through some stages might be rapid while other stages progress slowly. If you leapfrog stages—perhaps skipping from stage 2 to stage 6—your confidence will plummet and your rate of progress will slow. (3) The exact content of the steps may differ. Severe anxiety might enable you to begin simply by vocalizing sounds, even if they are not complete words. Maintain the incremental method: *gradually* and *systematically* approach a "real" presentation. For example, you might only want to add a few audience members at a time and then move toward making the setting more formal.

In Figure 10.3, the final condition for conquering anxiety was realistic. We did not seek the eloquence of Martin Luther King, Jr. Set achievable but ambitious goals that you can count as success. Systematic desensitization has brought many people's phobias to a more manageable level, but the method can take a lot of time depending on your anxiety level.

Visualization

Visualization invokes specific, positive images of successful performance so you program yourself to succeed. Relaxation with self-directed positive imagery allows you to be in control of that imagining and use it to your advantage rather than falling into disabling negative imagery. There are many forms of guided relaxation. Figure 10.4 describes one of the simplest methods.

Slow, rhythmic breathing should help you concentrate as you relax.[48] One requirement is that you actually did write/plan your presentation, you practiced it, and you practiced the relaxation and imagery several times before the actual event. There is no magic in this exercise, but it is very successful if combined with preparation and practice. The benefits of visualization extend to public speaking, interpersonal communication, and interviewing. Visualizing effective performance has proven consistently to reduce feelings of anxiety and increase the comfort level of speakers.[49] Not only can visualization reduce communication apprehension, but when done properly and consistently, it actually improves your performance.[50,51]

The more vividly you can imagine and describe your positive performance, the more effective your visualization will be.[52] Visualization should extend beyond visual images to involve multiple senses. Legendary bodybuilder Lee Haney, eight-time Mr. Olympia, used this technique: "Visualization is many times more effective if you strive to move beyond the imagined visual image and use your other four senses—touch, hearing, smell, and taste".[53(p375)] Images

FIGURE 10.4 Steps of relaxation with positive imagery.

1. Sit comfortably and close your eyes. Try not to cross your limbs—the pressure of limb on limb can become a distraction and cause tension.
2. Take several (at least three) very slow, deep breaths, with the inhale and exhale each lasting several seconds.
   a. After the first deep breath, begin to name the inhale something positive: "confidence," "calmness," "energy," "focus"—whatever positive trait that will be helpful to you in the situation.
   b. Name the exhale something you want to get rid of: "negative," "anxiety," "fatigue," "distraction,"—whatever you want to expel.
   c. Begin to imagine your breathing as a cleansing and reorienting process—taking in what is helpful, clearing away what is not.
   d. Continue breathing but allow it to slow down to a regular, gentle rhythm. This slow, regular pattern of breathing encourages relaxation—no whooshing sounds of forcing air into and out of your lungs.[47]
3. Once you begin to feel that you are relaxed and taking in what is good for you in the situation, you can begin to do more focused imagery in regard to giving a presentation in front of other people. Here is where it would be most helpful to have planned your personal imagery of a successful speech. What would you look and sound like if you were calm and confident, even having fun, talking there in front of an audience? What would you do that was "fun" and could keep you from being embarrassed if you happened to drop your speech or trip walking onto the stage? See yourself as in control, even if there is a mishap. We can't prevent accidents or mistakes, but we can control how we deal with them. It would be good to talk with a classmate or friend about your success image so you really have it set, then you can go through the image while in the relaxed state.
4. Also, while doing the relaxation and imagery, come up with a signal phrase (e.g., "I have practiced, I know my material, I can be calm") that you can use as a signal for your doing the speech in the positive way you've imagined.
5. Before actually giving the presentation, find a quiet place (or even, if sitting in class, create a small space in your mind by closing your eyes and breathing) where you can do your deep breathing, cleansing and taking in what you need, and imagining yourself successfully speaking.

experienced through multiple senses become more realistic, so your goal seems more achievable.

Having models of effective speaking can improve your visualization. Try observing some speakers you admire and substitute an image of yourself as the performer.[51] Your library and your instructor can recommend videos and audios of well-known speakers. Observing and learning from excellent student speeches tends to improve performance.[54] That's why you should pay close attention to the best speakers in your class. What techniques from their presentations might prove helpful to you? Take some notes on what these outstanding speakers did that impressed you. Try using a few of those techniques as you practice your next presentation.

Tech Talk

To find models of great speeches, you don't need to wait for recommendations from others. Try searching the Internet for audio and video presentations of speakers you admire. One excellent, frequently updated resource is American Rhetoric (http://www.americanrhetoric.com), where you'll find thousands of text, audio, and video versions of speeches.

Control Your Presentation Conditions

One excellent way to become a more confident communicator is to shape your communication environment instead of letting it affect you negatively. If you make a thorough, honest inventory of the concrete conditions that might damage your presentation, you should find that many of them can be prevented or improved. Work with your classmates and instructor to identify potential trouble spots in each of the following areas:

- Physical presentation environment.
- Nature of the audience and assignment.
- Your own physical, mental, and emotional condition.

FIGURE 10.5 Coping with conditions that produce anxiety.

Conditions That Produce Anxiety	Sample Coping Mechanisms to Reduce Anxiety
Large audiences	1. Gradually increase the number of listeners in your practice sessions until the audience size approaches the one you will address. 2. Practice in the room where you will give your speech.
The speech will be graded	Prior to your practice sessions, give listeners a copy of the evaluation form. Have your listeners use the form in your rehearsals.
The speech will be presented in front of "strangers"	1. Get a bit of brief information about your listeners through a survey or an informant. 2. Through informal conversations, get enough information about specific listeners that allows you to feel they aren't strangers (e.g., you find people who share your major, are from your hometown, etc.).
Criticism may be taken personally	1. Remember that only speeches are graded—speakers are not. 2. Ask your critics: "What would you suggest be changed in the speech?"
Uneasiness of direct eye contact with audience	1. Make some direct eye contact with each listener. 2. Keep direct eye contact with each person for only a few seconds (to avoid staring). 3. Experiment with movement to vary angles of vision (e.g., moving through the audience or changing where you stand).

One way to deal with potential hindrances is to incorporate ways of dealing with them in your practice sessions. For example, if you worry about feeling uncomfortable in dress clothing, try practicing your presentation while wearing your presentation outfit. Figure 10.5 illustrates several obstacles students actually have identified in this course. Each factor accompanies ways that students have found to deal with the matter effectively.

WHAT METHOD OF DELIVERY IS MOST APPROPRIATE?

You have four different choices to make for your overall delivery plan: all involve a decision about the extent to which the written word will play in your speech.

Scripted

Some speakers like to deliver prepared remarks from a manuscript. This is especially true when exact language is crucial, such as in diplomacy issues or for a commencement address before a large audience. It is common for heads of state to speak from a manuscript in order to ensure accuracy in their messages. In these cases, word-for-word delivery is essential. Time limits may also play a role in the use of a manuscript; a candidate who purchases a one-minute spot needs to nail down that time. However, most of us do not find ourselves in these unique situations.

Using a manuscript might seem like an easy way to present your speech, but it can also have drawbacks. Crafting a manuscript takes an inordinate amount of time; you find yourself concentrating on word choice and sentence development in a way that you wouldn't do in other forms of delivery. Written and spoken language are essentially different; the way you write in long sentences with complex structures doesn't work well in the spoken form, where brief phrases and even incomplete sentences are more natural. Speaking from a script limits the speaker to only those comments prepared in advance. You don't have the chance to stray from the prepared remarks, and if an audience member seems confused, you can't elaborate. It is common for new speakers to make the mistake of just reading from a manuscript, leading to a drop in eye contact and vocal variety. If you do look up from the manuscript, it's easy to lose your place. A manuscript requires you to make the words "come alive" through vibrant vocal delivery, and that requires skill. It's very easy to find yourself reading *at* the audience through a manuscript, rather than talking *with* them.

What should you expect if you feel a scripted speech is appropriate for your occasion? Be sure to practice out loud so that you don't falter over words. Pacing must be timed perfectly; you don't want to pause in the wrong place, and you don't want to rush through the speech. Consider vocal tone: how can you emphasize words so that they sound conversational rather than scripted? Create a manuscript that is easy to read in larger print so that you can still develop and maintain eye contact; you want to be able to move off the script to look at the audience, even though you are tied to the words. Roger Ailes, a political media consultant, suggests that if a manuscript is called for, you should type your words in short, easy-to-scan phrases on the top two thirds of the notes so you don't have to look too far down.[1] A manuscript doesn't have to mean boring the audience with a monotonous tone, lack of eye contact, and stilted pacing; it does mean, though, that you'll have to work hard to overcome those pitfalls.

Memorized

At some point, we have all probably been expected to memorize a speech or poem. Perhaps it was the preamble to the Constitution or the Declaration of Independence; maybe it was a poem or a prayer. You may have wondered why you needed this skill; after all, there is little call for long, memorized, complex speeches, and the effort you put into memorizing was painful. It's safe to say that while you might admire someone who can spout off long speeches from memory, it's probably not something you'd want to do yourself. However, the ability to memorize short passages still has its place in presentations. Memorization is a useful strategy to use for short speeches such as toasts, introductory remarks, or award acceptances. Even small portions of a speech where specific wording or language is important can utilize memorization. You just need to practice over and over, making sure to work on vocal variety as you do the words from rote memory.

The negatives of a memorized speech are apparent. First, in order to memorize, you must create a full manuscript document. That means that the pitfalls of a scripted speech play a role here. Second, memorizing anything takes time and practice, more than you probably need to spend on a presentation. More obvious, though, as a danger of memorization is that the stress of a speaking situation can lead to memory lapses and occasionally even a complete loss of what was memorized. If you forget where you were, it's nearly impossible to pick up smoothly. Not only will you panic, but the audience will likely become very uncomfortable. All-in-all, memorizing an entire presentation is more trouble than help.

Impromptu

What would you do if a television reporter cornered you to get a response about an incident that just happened, an issue that's in the public eye, or a comment about the weather? If you're able to give a competent immediate response, you could be on the evening news! Even if that scenario doesn't hold much appeal, your ability to think and speak on your feet is essential in life. Meetings, interviews, unexpected reports, instructing or supervising others, and participating in general conversation all require the ability to organize thoughts quickly and delivery them effectively.

Speaking **impromptu** means talking about a topic with little or no preparation. Mark Twain said, "It usually takes me more than three weeks to prepare a good impromptu speech,"[2] and he was probably correct. Most of the time when we speak "off the cuff" or say a "few words," we do so in situations where we've given thought to the issue we're about to speak on. So, you might find yourself doing an impromptu speech at a community meeting when your opinion is sought, when your boss asks you to report on some incident, or when you're at a social function and a toast is called for.

A spur-of-the-moment or impromptu speech doesn't carry the same expectations of perfection as might a scripted or memorized speech. An audience usually is more forgiving in an impromptu speech because they understand you haven't had hours or days to prepare. However, that doesn't mean that you need to go into an impromptu situation stone cold. If you're in a meeting or listening to a presentation, take notes of the major points; this activity will likely cause you to consider your own opinion. If time allows you to do so, jot a few notes or outline of the points you want to make in case you're asked to respond.

Let's imagine that you've been asked for impromptu remarks of a minute or two. You need to be spontaneous and demonstrate your quick wit. What quick strategies can you call on?

If you do nothing else, make a note of how you want to open and conclude your remarks; remember, the first thing and the last thing the audience hears may be that which sticks with them. Make sure you understand what you've been asked to remark on, and make sure you answer it. Then structure the body of the message with two or four points, using some simple strategies:

- The **SPREE method** offers four points: State your Position, provide your Reason(s), Explain by experience or example, End with summary.
- The **PPF method** utilizes Past, Present, and Future as the main points. You can say something like this: We used to do this . . . but now we find ourselves doing this . . . and in the future we'll need to do this . . .
- The **apples/oranges method** begins by acknowledging that "there are two sides to this argument . . ." and then state the positions: One position says this, the other says that. End by giving your position on the issue.
- The **simple 6 method** uses the common questions of who, what, when, why, where, and how as the main points. Don't try for all of them, but use them to structure ideas and to jog your memory.

When delivering an impromptu speech, there are a few pitfalls to avoid. Don't apologize for a lack of preparation. If it's truly an impromptu occasion, give the best effort you can on short notice. When you offer an excuse, you damage your credibility. Focus your delivery on strong eye contact and vocal variety; you can't do much more. Don't ramble; stick to those main points, give some support, and make it short and sweet. You don't want to be accused of talking without saying anything.

To really speak effectively, you'd like to be able to prepare in advance. Even if you don't have that opportunity, you can still provide your audience with a clearly organized, brief message that makes a point. After all, you do impromptus all the time—you have ample chances to experiment with developing an effective strategy for their presentation.

Extemporaneous

You might hear people confuse impromptu and extemporaneous methods; often, people think they're one and the same. However, an **extemporaneous (or extemp) speech** is one that is carefully planned and practiced, that works from an outline or series of notes yet leaves room for message adjustment, and that maintains a conversational style.

The key to extemp is that outline of ideas. From it, you can adapt the words to the audience as they listen. The advantages of an extemp speech arise from the best of the other three methods. You can write out key ideas, as in a scripted speech. You can commit some lines (key data, phrases, quotations) to memory so word choice is exact. You can remain spontaneous and adapt to the audience and the occasion as you speak, just like in an impromptu. In addition, the extemp speech encourages you to use a conversational style, one that sounds spontaneous even though it's been well thought out and practiced.

How do you prepare an extemporaneous speech? Create an outline of main ideas and say it out loud. As you do, consider the amount and kind of supporting points you're developing, along with the purpose and time of your speech. Then think, am I saying too much or too little? Do my ideas coherently flow? Do I know the supports well enough to be able to present them in an interesting yet clear fashion? How are my introduction and conclusion? Next, revise that outline into a speaking outline, keeping the amount of written material minimal. Practice the speech all the way through, using only the outline. You may forget a few supports the first couple of times, but that's OK—keep going! Your goal is to keep yourself focused on the ideas of the speech, not the perfection of the words or the delivery. If you plan to use presentational aids, bring them into practice. After several run-throughs, you'll find that you are able to get through the ideas and their supports pretty well by thinking, not by checking your notes, and then it's time to work on delivery. Watch for eye contact by recruiting an audience of family or friends, or even watch yourself in a mirror. Record the speech if possible; listening to yourself (or watching on video) can point out distracting mannerisms. The key is that you must practice more than once; a single practice is a recipe for catastrophe. By giving yourself time to think the speech through, you'll find your confidence growing.

A combination of styles may work best to present your message.
© ORKO/Shutterstock.com

Although each of these speaking styles is described separately, in reality, a combination of styles might be used in any given public speech or other communication situation such as an interview or meeting. You might consider memorizing a portion of the opening so that you can engage your audience without notes or other distractions. This lets you make strong eye contact with audience members and truly hook them into the speech. The body of a speech might involve the use of brief notes in an extemporaneous style. A question and answer session after a presentation resembles impromptu speaking, requiring a person to respond "in the moment." In meetings, you're called upon to offer your opinion on a plan: that's the place for an impromptu. Interviews are extemporaneous in the sense that you can plan and rehearse answers to questions, but you don't exactly know the directions those questions will take.

Remember: No one is born a great speaker. Effective public speaking takes practice, regular practice. The great thing about presenting a message is that, like riding a bike, when you can do it well, you can always do it well if you follow the same pattern of preparation, practice, and presentation.

WHAT STRATEGIES MAKE UP EFFECTIVE DELIVERY?

Do you want a surefire way to bore your audience to tears? To ensure audience members lose interest and drift away, stand in one place, never look up from your notes, use gestures minimally, and speak rapidly in a low-pitched, monotonous voice. Assuming that boring people isn't your goal, if you want to help the audience attend to, hear, and understand your message, you need to consider how to incorporate nonverbal delivery strategies.

Effective nonverbal delivery is critical in the success of any communication effort. This is true for any communication situation, whether it's interpersonal or small group, public or mediated. Effective delivery is a combination of verbal and nonverbal tactics, so factors such as eye contact, posture, vocal quality, and facial expression will play a major role in the audience's ability to listen and to follow your ideas. Even the presentational aids that supplement your words and nonverbal presence are aspects of effective delivery. Earlier in this chapter, you were told that a conversational style of delivery is the most desired, but you're probably thinking about more specifics, such as, "What do I do if I can't breathe?" or "What happens if my hands are shaking?" or "Is it OK to move around a little?" In order to impact the audience in a positive way and to answer those questions, let's consider some of the elements of effective vocal and physical delivery.

HOW DO I SPEAK TO CREATE UNDERSTANDING?

Have you ever met someone in person that you've spoken to on the phone many times? Was the image that you initially had skewed from his actual looks? Did you think he was older or younger than in reality? Was he taller or shorter? Did he dress as you thought he did? Were you shocked to learn that he was a she? Based on vocal cues, we do predict people's age, occupation, status, ethnicity, appearance, and a host of other things. Effective vocal delivery involves volume, rate, pitch, pauses, and the trio of articulation, pronunciation, and dialects, each of which can play a very important part in creating images and impressions. It's important that you present your ideas by using vocal delivery that enhances understanding and interest.

Volume

How can you use the volume of your voice for effect in your speech?
© 2008, JupiterImages.

Volume means projecting your voice loudly enough so that it can be clearly heard by those in your audience. Just how loudly you must speak depends on the room size, the audience size, and the amount and type of background noise. It's likely that your voice sounds louder to you than to your audience, but by watching your audience and adjusting to their feedback (leaning forward, looking puzzled, wincing), you can adjust the volume of your voice so that everyone in the audience can hear. If you have a soft voice, you don't want to cause your audience to strain to listen. They might decide it's not worth their effort. A quiet voice might require the use of electronic amplification, but realize that if you use a microphone awkwardly, the audience could interpret this as ineptness on your part. Your volume can also be manipulated for effect. Sometimes raising or lowering the volume can communicate importance or draw in the audience and emphasize a point. The key is to be aware of your volume and to adapt it according to your audience and setting.

Rate

Rate is the speed at which you speak. The normal rate of adult speech has been estimated to be between 120 and 150 words per minute. What matters is not how many words a speaker can get out, but how many (well-chosen) words are understood by the listener. People talk so fast because others around them do this, because they think erroneously that others will not take the time to listen to them, and because they do not realize the listeners are struggling. Speaking quickly doesn't mean you're unintelligible, however, and you can consider how using rate as a delivery strategy can enhance understanding.

Changing the speed of delivery to coordinate with different elements of your speech is one way to maintain audience interest. Varying your rate can improve the audience's ability to attend to your speech. You might start with a fast-paced, attention-getting story and then slow down as you reveal the topic and preview your main points. However, a study in 2000 found that speaking too quickly causes the audience to perceive you as tentative about your control of the situation.[3] A monotone rate, one that does *not* change, will lead your audience members to lose interest and make it more difficult for them to listen and learn from your message.

Pitch

Singing involves the alteration of the voice to produce the melody. That modulation of your voice is something you can also employ in effective delivery through awareness of pitch.

Pitch is your voice's intonation; how high or low in range your voice sounds to another. Your typical pitch is the range that you use when you're conversing normally, and in natural conversation, vocal pitch rises and falls and often helps listeners to understand a message. Your pitch may give others a perception of your mood and can show your enthusiasm for the topic or audience. Normally, women's voices are pitched higher than men's because women's vocal cords are shorter. However, individuals of each sex may display wide variations due to difference in physical structure. But keep in mind that no matter what nature supplies you for pitch, you still can manipulate it for strong effect.

In some cultures, inflection plays a major role in changing the meaning of words. Many of the languages of Southeast Asia and Africa are tone languages, meaning that they use pitch to signal a difference in meaning between words. In some of these languages, word meanings or grammar elements like tense depend on pitch level. Words can take on totally different meanings depending on their tones. In Mandarin Chinese, for example, the word *ma* means "mother" when spoken in the first tone, "hemp" when spoken in the second tone, "horse" in the third and a reproach in the fourth.[4]

Typically, our pitch in the United States goes higher when we ask a question and drops when we make a declaration of fact. Try the following activity. Say the following sentences, adding emphasis by raising your pitch on the italicized word each time.

This is a great class.

This *is* a great class.

This is a *great* class.

Now try it with a question mark at the end:

This is a great *class?*

Notice how the meaning shifts, depending on the emphasis of the words.

You can use this stress or inflection when you want to highlight a point, but don't overdo it. You might want to record a conversation with friends or family members and listen to changes in pitch to see what meanings you're suggesting. However, while it can assist you by underlining enthusiasm or importance, pitch change isn't a strategy you want to overdo.

Pauses

Pauses add emphasis and impact to your speech by stopping your message briefly. Where and how you pause in your speech can have a dramatic effect on meaning. Pauses can be used to stress a point, to gain attention, to create a transitional effect, and to allow you time to think and catch up. They often are necessary for your listener just to think about what you've just said. Read the following line: "Woman without her man is nothing." Now think about possible ways to interpret those words. Through strategic pausing, the message meaning could be very different. Read it two more times, pausing at the commas:

> Woman without her man, is nothing.

> Woman, without her, man is nothing.

How you decide to deliver that line, including pauses, is critical to the message you communicate. Listeners do not "see" the commas in your speech; they must "hear" them through your strategic use of pauses in delivery

Vocalized pauses such as "um," "like," "you know," "stuff like that," or "Uhhhhh" detract from your speech. These involuntary fillers or bridge sounds are understandable in their way, because they are unintentionally included by speakers in order to maintain control. You are uncomfortable with silence, so you fill it up with sounds. These do not function in the same way that intentional pauses do. In fact, they detract from meaning, rather than enhancing it. To avoid vocalized pauses, try this easy test: Call yourself and leave at least a one-minute message about an upcoming assignment. Then listen to your voice mail and count the number of vocalized paused in your message. Give it a try. How many vocal pauses do you count? How do they impact your message? Are you surprised by the frequency of your vocalized pauses? The bottom line is, most of us find vocalized pauses to be annoying; you can eliminate them by paying attention.

Articulation, Pronunciation, and Dialects

Articulation is the physical production of a sound clearly and distinctly. **Pronunciation** is saying a word in an accepted standard of correctness and sound. While the two are interdependent, they are not the same. You can articulate a word clearly but still mispronounce it; for instance, if you say the "s" in the word *Illinois*, you're articulating the sounds but pronouncing it wrong! An example of misarticulation comes from Ohio, where students sometimes say *fur* when they mean "for" and *doin'* instead of "doing." Because some words sound similar, they require the speaker's careful articulation to avoid audience confusion. Consider, for example, the difference between *persecution* and *prosecution*, or the difference between *asking* someone and *axing* someone. It's not uncommon to mispronounce words, because you may not know how to say it correctly. Alphadictionary.com offers a list of the 100 most mispronounced words in English, which includes *athlete* (some people say "ath-a-lete"), *card shark* (the correct words are "card sharp"), *escape* ("excape"), and *herb* (" 'erb").[5]

Articulation and pronunciation are further confounded by **dialects,** which are regional or ethnic speech patterns that have variations in grammar, accent, or even vocabulary. The United States has four major regional dialects: eastern, New England, southern, and general American. There are also many ethnic dialects, including African-American English, Hispanic English, Cajun English, and Haitian English.[6] Your dialect has been shaped by your background, and it has meaning for those who share it. However, if you're speaking to an audience who doesn't share your dialect, you would want to avoid regionalisms that point out your differences. We're all familiar with those: Do you drink pop or soda? What goes on ice cream: jimmies or sprinkles? When grocery shopping, do you use a buggy or a cart? When washing your car, do you attach your outside hose to the spigot or the faucet? What you should keep in mind is that a distracting dialect may cause listeners to make negative judgments about your personality or competence.[7] This can be an important consideration if you're a nonnative English speaker, because your dialect, along with articulation and pronunciation, may be an additional barrier.

Take a Closer Look

What strategies can you use to impact dialect, articulation, and pronunciation?

- Watch your audience's expressions to see if they seem to understand or if they look confused.
- Define your terms.
- Make sure you pronounce names or technical terms correctly.
- Slow down so you can articulate more clearly.
- Avoid regional words that may not mean the same thing elsewhere, or use both terms (yours and the local one) to show that they're synonyms.

All of these can aid you in avoiding confusing your audience with the way you say ideas!

Your vocal delivery is unique; no one sounds exactly like you (which is why the FBI uses voiceprints in its investigative work). You have the ability to impact the audience by strategically using aspects of vocal delivery that you can control.

HOW DOES MY PHYSICAL DELIVERY AFFECT UNDERSTANDING?

In Chapter 4 you learned about nonverbal communication, the messages you deliver with appearance, movement, posture, eye contact, facial expression, and use of space and objects. Your nonverbal messages can assist audience members in interpreting the verbal message, or they can distract from that understanding. You know the phrase, "Actions speak louder than words." When you consider physical delivery, keep that in mind: An audience expects that good communicators will present their ideas clearly and in an interesting fashion. Your delivery can create (or destroy) emotional connections with your audience. If your nonverbal delivery contradicts what you're saying, the audience will more likely believe the nonverbal rather than the verbal. Think about shaking your head no side-to-side while saying in a flat voice, "I really had a good time tonight." What message will really be believed—the words or the nonverbal one?

How you present yourself nonverbally is vital to your success as speakers. Effective physical delivery allows a speaker to develop immediacy with an audience and involves eye contact, facial expression, gestures, movement, and attire.

Your delivery can create emotional connections with your audience.
© 2008, JupiterImages.

Eye Contact

Eye contact is the direct visual contact made with another person. Ralph Waldo Emerson said, "One of the most wonderful things in nature is a glance of the eye; it transcends speech; it is the bodily symbol of identity."[8] The significance of eye contact tells us about meaning in various cultures. Some cultures feel that strong eye contact demonstrates interest and respect in the other person. Conversely, other cultures hold that (especially when you are young) you should not look at others in the eye when speaking, or you'll show disrespect. Some Latin American and Asian cultures show respect by avoiding the glance of authority figures. In the United States, we value meeting another's eyes, because it is seen as demonstrating honesty. People in Brazil engage in intensive eye contact; here, we'd consider it staring.[9]

But since you're in an American classroom, let's consider why eye contact is seen in the United States as important for at least two reasons.[10] First, it creates a strong connection between listener and speaker. Audience members who feel more connected likely will listen more closely. Second, the speaker is able to gather feedback from audience members if eye contact is frequent and effective. Generally speaking, the longer the eye contact between two people, the greater the intimacy is developed.[11]

What strategies can you employ to meet your audience's gaze comfortably? Try looking briefly from one person to the next (you can even think about a "pattern" of gaze, from one corner to another, one row to an adjacent one). This scanning can let you acknowledge individuals without ignoring others. If you are sitting around a table, make sure you share eye contact with everyone in the group. Look for friendly people; conversely, if you're in the audience, smile at the speaker, for encouraging that person can create a pleasant interaction. If you see audience members looking at you with interest, leaning forward and seeming eager for more, you can assume that you are connecting with your audience. If, on the other hand, you see people nodding off or staring at your overhead with confused expressions, these are good indications that a problem should be corrected. By watching the feedback offered by your audience through eye contact, you can make corrections and improve your speech in the moment. Consider the type and amount of notes you use. Generally, the guideline would be to speak from an outline or a key word page, but if you feel you must use more, then make sure your notes are clear, large, and numbered in case you drop them. Effective eye contact tells the audience that you have confidence in yourself and care about their ability to understand your message.

Facial Expression

Another way that you can display concern for the audience and passion for the subject is through your face. Research tells us that your face plays an essential role in expressing your thoughts, emotions, and attitudes.[12] Through your face, you have the initial opportunity to set the speech tone, even before you open your mouth. Think about it: when you don't like some kind of food, you probably make a face. That expression tells others how you feel about that morsel! The movements of your eyes, eyebrows, mouth, and facial muscles can build a connection with your audience.

Just like eye contact, your culture may dictate the kind and amount of **facial expression** you will display. For example, Koreans, Japanese, and Chinese do not usually show outward emotion through their faces, and in fact, may have learned to mask their emotions. Some Native American groups use far less facial animation than do other North Americans. Research also suggests that men and women use different facial displays.[13] In other cultures, people expect great animation when they speak, and they expect others to be similarly expressive. As a speaker, you need to be alert to the cultural norms of your audience.

Unfortunately, under the pressure of delivering a group presentation, many people solidify their expression into a grim, stone face, grimacing instead of smiling. Try to soften your face right from the start: when you greet the audience, smile! This is how you'd start a conversation with another, because you'd want to begin by establishing a warm, positive relationship. The same intent probably holds true for a speech. A relaxed smile to start your speech will help create a connection with the audience, perhaps even develop a closeness with them. You probably won't want to smile throughout the entire presentation, because your face should mirror your message. While figuring out how to "hold your face" isn't the most important delivery strategy you can employ, you need to make sure that your facial expressions are consistent with your words. Try taping yourself

Speakers must be alert to the cultural norms of the audience.
© 2008, JupiterImages.

to discover your expressions just to make sure they're not contradicting your words.

Gestures

Gestures include movement of your head, arms, and hands that you use to emphasize, to reinforce, or to illustrate ideas. You probably don't even notice your gestures when you're in a relaxed conversation, but when you are giving a speech or presenting an important message in a group, you may become very self-conscious. Not everyone is naturally expressive with their gestures; they may not use their hands, cock their head to the side, or even shrug their shoulders to express some feeling. Some speakers try to get rid of their hands by putting them in pockets; others fidget or play with things.[14] As with other delivery techniques, cultural influences impact gestures. For example, Arab and Italian cultures expect a great deal of animation; German and Japanese expect a reserved style.[15] You can see this in how we greet others: Do we shake hands? Do we bow? Do we place our hands crossed on our chest?

Gestures can be used to reinforce your message, such as holding up fingers to reinforce the spoken words *first, second,* and *third*. Gestures can also be used to add emphasis to words; pounding one's fist on the podium demonstrates conviction or emotion.

If you're not sure what to do with your hands, then think about where you will place them during the speech: Are you going to be playing with notes? Giving a podium a death grip? Playing with keys in your pocket? When you stand, do you naturally do it with your arms crossed in front of you? What message does that send? Honestly, gestures will probably take on the form of your normal conversational style, and it really doesn't matter so much if you use many gestures or not. What does matter is *how* you use those gestures. They should support your message, not detract from it.

Movement

Movement involves the positioning of your entire body as you speak. By moving closer to the audience, a speaker removes the physical and psychological barriers that distance him or her from the audience. What does a podium, lectern, or table do to that space? Does it impact the trust that the audience might be feeling? The more willing you are to move toward the audience, the more attentive the audience becomes and the more similarity they feel with you.

You have probably experienced this with a professor who greets you as you enter, calls students by name, makes frequent eye contact with students, and moves among them throughout the class session. Contrast this to the classroom with a teacher who remains tied to notes behind the podium, paces nervously at the front of the room, and flashes up slide after slide with little or no attempt to the audience. Which would you prefer? What message are you taking from each of these instructors?

Posture also is an aspect of movement; slouching probably signals a lack of enthusiasm on your part. Sitting down while giving a formal presentation probably doesn't work, either, because it's too informal; this is unlike giving a short impromptu to a small group seated around a table, where standing would seem presumptuous. Purposeful movement not only creates a connection, but it can signal changes in the speech. You can change position or location by moving a step or two; that not only shows confidence, but it demonstrates that something "new" has happened in your message.

Consider how you will approach and leave the front of the audience; how will you establish yourself, how will you end? By approaching in a confident fashion, your audience will perceive you as someone to listen to. If you start "packing up" and shuffling notes before your message is finished, your message may be lost and your credibility damaged. Developing speakers should "fake it until they make it," meaning that even if you do not feel confident, you should try to appear confident. By standing tall, looking at your audience, and moving with purpose, you are able to convey a sense of confidence that positively impacts how your audience views.

Distracting movement is aimless. If you move around the room constantly, you may be creating a burden on your audience: they have to follow you and try to maintain eye contact. You'll likely end up with people tuning out; no one enjoys watching someone else pace. Shifting back and forth on your feet suggests nervousness. If you move so that you're blocking the screen you're using, or if you find yourself placing your back to the audience so you can look at something behind you, you're signaling a disinterest in the audience. How can you perceive their feedback, how can they hear you, and what happens to your eye contact?

How can you develop purposeful movement? Again, taping yourself doing a speech is a good way to see how others perceive you. But you can also watch others (professors, peers, public figures) to see how they move; these models might provide you some positive ideas on what to do, as well as pointing out negatives to avoid.

Attire

Your personal appearance makes that first impression. An unkempt, untidy speaker suggests that the message that is about to come will also be lacking in polish or disorderly. If you fiddle with your hair or glasses, wear a hat that shades your eyes, play with jewelry, or wear something distracting (clothes, hair, makeup), your audience will be sidetracked by that rather than being focused on the message. Students often ask if they have to get dressed up when they give their speech. The answer is, of course, that it depends on what impression you wish to make on your audience. Think about what nonverbal messages your attire or appearance makes as you speak. Does your appearance reinforce or contradict your message? If you're trying to enhance your credibility on a topic, is it appropriate to wear something that indicates your identification with that issue (uniform, school tie, name badge, etc.) Typically in most situations, you'd dress a bit more formally than your audience, but you should be comfortable in what you wear. Your appearance should help you to feel confident, and it should boost your credibility with the audience.

Vocal and physical delivery surrounds your message; they help the audience to form initial impressions about the kind of person you are. The way you sound and the way you look can suggest confidence and concern or incompetence and unreliability. Your speech's impact is strongly impacted by how you deliver it. Having something important to say should take precedence, but saying it poorly will impact the audience's acceptance of your ideas. Good delivery presents your message in an interesting, clear way. One other group of strategies that can supplement your vocal and physical delivery involves the use of presentational aids. Let's examine how they can complement your message delivery.

HOW CAN PRESENTATIONAL AIDS AFFECT DELIVERY?

TV Guide selected NBC's Tim Russert's use of the dry erase whiteboard (November 7, 2000) on which Russert predicted "Florida, Florida, Florida" would be the pivotal state in the 2000 presidential election results, as number

68 of the "100 Most Memorable TV Moments" in history.[16] When Russert turned to a Tablet PC for election 2004, bloggers took note.[17] Why is the aid that the commentator used notable? Because Russert's use of presentational media demonstrated the advantages of this supplemental delivery strategy.

Presentational aids are any items developed for reinforcing a message. These include objects, models, charts, drawings, graphs, videos, and photographs. The importance of visual representations is reflected in common sayings across many cultures. A Saudi Arabian proverb says, "Believe what you see and lay aside what you hear." The Chinese are familiar with, "I hear and I forget, I see and I remember." In Nigeria, they say, "Seeing is better than hearing." Traditional American sayings are, "Seeing is Believing" and, "A picture is worth a thousand words." So what exactly are the advantages of presentational aids?

Advantages to the Speaker and Audience

Presentational aids add a dimension to your delivery. First, they help us to communicate clearly. If you are discussing an object, you can show it or a representation. If you're citing statistical trends, you can picture them. If you're explaining a technique, you can demonstrate it. All of these examples show that you can make your information more vivid to the audience by adding a visual element to your message. Hands-on instruction, math manipulatives, graphing, and recording data make learning easier for the visual and tactile learners, according to education researchers.[18] You may have been the recipient of such instruction, because you learned math more easily when you could see the number in a different way. The audience can see a sequence of events or process, so an actual demonstration or a series of visuals will reinforce how those procedures work.

Second, presentational aids can create and maintain interest and attention. Think of the difference between a newspaper, a textbook, and a web page. Which one springs to mind as having the most visual appeal? Where words might lack interest, a well-placed presentational aid can grab the audience's attention.

Third, presentational aids can help your audience to remember. Research tells us that in addition to aiding your audience's understanding, a well designed aid will reinforce ideas. Researchers estimate that you remember 10 percent of what you read, 20 percent of what you hear, 30 percent of what you see, and 50 percent of what you hear and see simultaneously.[19] Your memory might also be engaged by your presentational aids as they remind you of important aspects of your message.

Fourth (but not the most important reason to use them), some speakers feel that by using a presentational aid, the audience will focus on it rather than on them. You have to recall that an aid is only a supplement to you and your message; it won't speak for you, but it can be there to complement your ideas and your delivery.

Bob enjoyed these benefits of presentational aids when he chose to give a speech to his college classmates on how to hit a baseball. He included a baseball bat that allowed him to effectively demonstrate how to grip the bat, to hold it back off the shoulder, and to swing it properly. The bat also was comforting to him, as hitting a baseball was something he knew well. Although he was not menacing with the bat, it did give him a feeling of being in control and in power. For him, the presentational aid choice helped him communicate his message and feel more confident doing it.

Types of Presentational Aids

You have a wealth of aids to choose from; that selection depends on your purpose, your ability to create the aid, the context you'll be speaking in, and your

---

A Closer Look

Review your presentational aids. Do they

❒ Help clarify understanding?
❒ Create interest?
❒ Enhance memory and retention?

ability to use the aid successfully. Let's put the types into three categories: three dimensional, two dimensional, and multimedia.

Three-dimensional Presentational Aid

Three-dimensional presentational aids include people and other animate creatures, objects, and models. Ask yourself from the very start if there is another way that you could illustrate your point rather than employing something living, simply because there are pitfalls to their use that could be avoided fairly easily. Using *actual animate creatures* (people, pets, etc.) can be tricky. However, if you wanted to show how to style hair, demonstrate how certain tae-kwon-do moves work, or illustrate dance steps, then having a real person there might be fruitful.

Simple thought can make this easier on you and your model: Don't ask for spur-of-the-moment volunteers, don't bring that person up until needed, and make sure the person understands that she is simply a presentational aid, not your partner in delivering the message.

Animals require even more planning: You can't control their behavior most of the time in front of an audience, and it's easy for that creature to become the center of attention, even when it's not playing a role in the message at that moment. In addition, many creatures are difficult to see from all audience vantage points. Out of respect for you and your audience, think long and hard about using an animal as a presentational aid. You might think that it would be unique or more realistic to show the creature, but what if you have audience members who have fears or allergies, or what if the pet gets stressed out by the experience? Stories of "bad animal speeches" are legend in speech classes: the student who brought a live piranha in a zip-lock bag, which started to leak as the fish tried to attack the speaker's hand through the bag; the "how to bury your pet" speech, where the person brought in an actual dead rabbit he killed that morning; the speech about fear of snakes, accompanied by a burlap bag with two rather large boas in it, which, when shown, promptly sent the front row diving from their seats. Generally, it's better to consider other ways to illustrate or demonstrate your points, rather than using animate creatures, simply because the negatives likely outweigh any advantage you would get from them.

Objects can be either the actual item or a representation of it. Objects create interest because they're something the audience can see, hear, touch, and maybe even taste. We can respond to the real thing when we see it, because that tangible presence brings the idea to reality. The example of the baseball bat earlier in this section shows the use of an object. There are simple keys to using objects: Make sure that it's large enough to be seen, but not so large that you can't manipulate it (move, carry, etc.). Showing how to do a card trick may not work if you're not using a regular deck of cards: How do you perform that task with a normal deck? Make sure that there is no danger involved in the object's use (the swinging of a baseball bat could have tragic consequences in a classroom!). Practice how you will use the object, and keep it out of sight when you're not using it so that it doesn't become a focal distraction.

Models are useful when you can't bring the actual thing in but you want to help the audience visualize the object in a three-dimensional way. You can't show how to cut a real person's hair (think about those shaking hands holding scissors in front of an audience), but you can do the process on a wig. You can't bring a helicopter to class to explain why it flies, but you can bring in a model. Again, the use of models is pretty simple: Make sure it's large enough to be seen and practice its use.

Two-dimensional Presentational Aids

Two-dimensional presentational aids make up the most commonly used category in speeches. These include images such as drawings, photographs, maps, graphs, charts, and overhead transparencies, to name a few. Because of an increased availability of electronic projection equipment in classrooms, conference rooms, and meeting places, images are nearly expected by contemporary audiences as the part of any presentation. Most of these can be developed through presentation software such as Power-Point, which will be discussed after a brief review of the types of two-dimensional images you can utilize.

Two important cautions should be considered from the start. You must keep in mind the relevance of the image to your message. This is true for all types of presentational aids, but because images are so readily available, many speakers tend to go overboard in their creation. Second, you must ensure that proper permissions have been sought if the images used are protected by copyright or a trademark. Just

because it's available on a Web site or in a book doesn't mean you can automatically use it for your own purposes. Nearly every article, picture, photo, and cartoon is protected by copyright. Educational use of an image might be allowed in a single use, small audience situation. Repeated use of an image, even for educational purposes, might be a copyright violation.[20]

Drawings are inexpensive, can be designed for your exact needs, and are easily constructed with presentation software, so you don't have to be a master artist to create them. Simple drawings with large, dark lines are more effective for audience presentations than are detailed images. *Photographs* provide greater reality than drawings, but small detail is likely to be difficult to see, even when projected. Enlarging photographs to poster size is possible but relatively expensive (remember, ask yourself how necessary the photo is to your audience's understanding your message). Additionally, you don't want your speech to become a travelogue of "and then there's this," so you need to keep photos to a minimum, and make their impact strong. *Maps* share the size issue with photos; the detail on them is often difficult to see from an audience perspective.[21] Ali gave a speech to familiarize his classmates with his home country of Algeria. He was aware that helping them to picture Algeria's world location would be an essential part of the message. Ali found an image of Algeria in the *World Fact Book*, a resource available through www.cia.gov, which he incorporated into a PowerPoint presentation. In his speech he described where Algeria is located on the African continent and how Algeria was nearly three and a half times larger than the state of Texas. Using the visual aid shown here, along with his comparison to Texas, he was able to make his audience quickly understand both the country's size and location.

Graphs are representations of statistical data; while many in your audience might not understand numbers, they can grasp their meaning when shown visually. Bar graphs, pie graphs, line graphs, and picture graphs are able to show trends and relationships. Because most computer software programs have the ability to translate data into graphs, this is an easy way to include data in your message. The use of graphs can make information visually clear, something spoken numbers might not do. However, remember that the graph does not speak for itself. You must explain in words what the audience should be seeing.

Charts, like graphs, summarize information. They are easy to use in different formats: Flipcharts (large pads of paper on an easel) and whiteboards are inexpensive and low tech. However, because you often have to be writing while talking, their appearance is often unprofessional (not straight, hard to read), and speakers are prone to misspellings. Can you really think, talk, and write simultaneously in front of others? Won't you lose eye contact when you turn to write? The best charts are simple; their words use parallel structure or balanced points; their letters are large and bold. Don't overuse color (many colors might make the audience feel like you're enthralled with that new box of crayons). The audience needs to see a simple, plain image. Because presentation software is readily available, it's better in most cases to create a chart before you speak. However, if you're in a situation where an ongoing discussion requires writing while the message is being given, consider having someone else do the scribing for you.

Overhead transparencies are the precursor to contemporary electronic projection, using a plastic sheet called a *transparency*. Special markers are required for their creation, or you can usually print on them from a copy machine or home printer. This type of aid is simple to create, doesn't require you to dim the lights, lets you continue to face the audience while the transparency is projected, and can be developed prior to the speech but still allow you to add detail while speaking.

There are universal rules for the creation and use of all two-dimensional presentational aids. You should always practice their use, especially if you're going to be writing on them as you speak. If possible, go to the place where you'll be presenting and make sure that you can put the image's projector and image within easy view of the entire audience. Keep your images simple; bullet points and words or phrases are more effective than long sentences and paragraphs that will cause the audience to want to read. Watch your font size; what looks big to you when you're creating on your kitchen table or laptop may be tiny when projected. A simple rule of thumb is to use 32–36 point type for titles, 24 point type for subtitles, and 18 point type for the rest of the text. You want to use a simple font rather than a fancy, decorative, or specialized font. For example:

Times New Roman 24 point looks like this.

Brush Script 24 point looks like this.

Kuenstler Script Medium 24 point looks like this.

Imagine seeing this projected; which would satisfy your need for clarity and ease of recognition? Last, don't show your presentational aid until it's necessary, and when it's not, cover it up or insert a blank image. Again, you want to control the audience's focus on the message, not the image.

Many of these two-dimensional aids can be developed through graphics presentational software. Such software offers you a means to present information clearly and with visual interest, and they don't require great amounts of time or expertise on your part. Software allow you to create a uniform and distinctive look; save work as you prepare it; establish progression and timing of ideas; and offer the audience a printout or electronic copy for later use. Presentation software such as Microsoft's PowerPoint, Apple's Keynote, Corel Presentation, Astound Presentation, and Lotus Freelance Graphics all allow their users to include two-dimensional images, words, sound, and animation in a presentation. Remember, though, that the software shouldn't dictate what you talk about; it's just a tool for supplementing delivery. Nor should you let special effects such as transitions, music, animation, and video clips attached to slides overwhelm the audience with needless images. PowerPoint is probably the most familiar presentational software and is the industry leader[22] so let's consider guidelines for its use.[23] Dr. Corey Hickerson developed a simple list of "how to's" that you can employ.[24]

One last caution about relying on any electronic creation: Equipment might not work the way you want. Have a backup plan, such as overhead transparencies or a handout ready, just in case. Remember, if something can go wrong, it likely will!

Multimedia Presentational Aids

Multimedia presentations involve the combination of sound and sight to create interest and excitement, along with information that is best presented in an audiovisual format. When played via CDs, DVDs, flashdrives, or laptops, audio and visual materials are easily combined into a professional-looking package. For example, if you are giving a speech about the music of the recording artist Prince, incorporating some sound clips might help your audience appreciate and understand the artist more fully. The danger of clips, music, and Web sites is that the audience may be conditioned to use these products in a passive fashion. If you're inserting multimedia in a speech, you want to get the audience to use these media in an active way, as a means to enhance clarity. The same cautions you've read for other presentation aids apply here. Make sure that what you're showing is really necessary; a movie clip might be interesting, but is it meant to be shown as a snippet for a supporting detail? A projected Web site might have too much detail on it to serve as a complement to your speech. CDs, DVDs, and flashdrives can give you a quick way to retrieve audio or visual information, but the temptation may be to put too much on them because of their storage capacity.

When using any multimedia source, make sure you introduce and explain it first, so the audience knows what to be looking or listening for. From a practical perspective, avoid playing an audio track while you are speaking. It might seem like a cool idea to play music as a background to your spoken message, but in the end, the audience will struggle to hear you because they can't listen to both the audio track and you at the same time.

If you don't know how to use the software, then multimedia will take a great deal of time to learn to use effectively. Make sure you're familiar with how to move forward in the presentation; how will you continue the information? Just like any technology, there's always the chance for breakdown or system incompatibility; have a backup plan in place. What will you do if everything falls apart? Remember, use multimedia presentation aids in a sparse fashion so you're not overwhelming the message. Many speeches have been dampened by unsuccessful attempts to use multimedia that did not work at all, did not include audio, or was not visible due to lighting limits or projection problems.

Using Presentational Aids Strategically

The three categories of presentational aids (three dimensional, two dimensional, and multimedia) offer you a range of ways to supplement your ideas. All cultures seem to recognize the value of visual expression accompanying verbal ideas, and they've become an anticipated part of business and academic life. But just because presentational aids are possible doesn't mean they have to be incorporated into a speech. Ask yourself if you learn better when you read something, when you see something, or when you do it? Different learning tasks require different techniques, don't they? The same holds true for presentational aids; some are more effective in representing specific ideas than are others. At the same time, there are many messages we present verbally that don't have "obvious" visuals, so we need to encourage the audience's understanding with additional presentational aids. The skillful use of any aid has become an expectation in our world, and you should consider their inclusion in your message preparation.

While each category has its own strategies and pitfalls, there are some general guidelines for you to consider to avoid the ineffective and enhance the effective.

Prepare in Advance

Prepare your presentational aids in advance, and practice with them in the same way. You need to have the resources and time necessary to create clear, memorable, and effective presentational aids. If you prepare in advance, you have a greater chance to make sure your information is accurate (no words are misspelled, ideas aren't missing or organized in a confusing fashion). You also need to be able to practice with them in "real time," as you would when giving the presentation to your audience. Practice helps you focus on the spoken message and augment it with your visual message, as opposed to the other way around. Second, practice is essential to successfully using aids when speaking. Taking time to practice with your presentational aids, whether they are three dimensional, two dimensional, or multimedia, will increase your confidence and readiness for the actual speaking situation.

Keep It Simple

Keep your presentational aids simple. Remember, it's the speech, not the dazzling graphics or multiple images, that matters. Too often speakers add transition features, animations, and sounds to a presentation that add little to their message effectiveness. In the same vein, avoid incorporating too many backgrounds or transition sequences just because they are trendy or exciting. You want attractive features that will ensure audience members will see your visual aid, but you want them to focus on your ideas, not the other way around.

The rule of thumb to employ is that you should include in your presentational aid only those things needed to make your point. Obey the 3 × 5 rule, which means that no more than three words and five lines or five words and three lines should be on any one slide or transparency. Essentially, this means you should not write out whole sentences or paragraphs for the audience to read. Instead, short phrases should be used to provide a visual reinforcement of the spoken message. Clutter is out; clarity is in. Intricate, detailed, and complicated ideas don't belong on a presentational aid; that's counter to the purpose.

You also need to consider color and font, as discussed earlier. Color can add energy and focus to a presentation, but it can also serve as a interruption to thought. Selecting foreground and background colors that are high in contrast will help text and images to be easy to see.[25] Television producers select cool background colors, such as blues and greens, because they create less strain on viewers' eyes. Similarly, careful attention to font selection can also impact clarity and visibility. Too much font variety can be distracting; you might use two (one for the title, the other for the rest), but in any case, you want to use a block-type font that is easier to read. The number and use of images is also important, as crowding a slide with pictures, especially animated ones, can quickly turn an effective presentation into a distracting one.

Make It Visible

Make sure your presentational aids can be seen. Your well-thought-out and well-designed presentational aid is worthless if the audience can't see it. That seems obvious, doesn't it? In most instances, modern corporate boardrooms and classrooms are designed to ensure audiences will be able to clearly see the visuals when projected. But not all speaking venues are designed for that purpose, so a little bit of planning can help. One strategy to use is the "floor" test. If using a nonprojected presentational aid (three-dimensional, some two-dimensional), create your visual aid and then place it on the floor in front of you. From a standing position you should be able to read the words and see all images in adequate detail. If you can, they probably will be appropriately visible when projected. If not, then corrections are necessary. Practice with the projected images, and make sure you're not standing in front of the screen. You don't want to be blinded by the light, and you don't want to cast a shadow.

Display It Selectively

Display the presentational aid only when it's complementing your verbal message. If a presentational aid is visible, it will be looked at by someone in the audience. That may mean that person isn't listening to you because she is admiring the artwork, wondering what you're going to be doing with it, or thinking that she could do something better. Cover three-dimensional objects or keep them out of sight. If using a flipchart, keep the blank page up until you need to point out the visual aspects. Slides can be blacked out, or you can insert a plain one into the presentation. You don't want to distract your audience by an unnecessary or ill-placed display.

The same goes for the use of sound. Avoid incorporating sound with your visual aids unless that feature improves understanding of your message. Sure, many presentational software programs can add neat sounds like cars screeching to a halt or the sound of a camera shutter clicking, but why would you do that? Before incorporating multimedia features into your presentation, ask yourself, "Will this feature help my audience understand my message?" and, "Can I use it without creating distraction?" If not, then don't incorporate the feature.

Control It

Control your presentational aids; do not be controlled by them. When using presentational aids, it is easy to be a slave to the tool. Instead of using the aid to help communicate an idea, the aid becomes the message. Audiences sometimes pay more attention to the background style or transitions used in presentational software slides than the intended messages. Sometimes speakers speed up their presentations to avoid allowing the screen saver to activate. A common mistake made with the best of intentions was made by a speaker who thought he would use the "timing" feature in PowerPoint. Unfortunately, his timing in the live presentation was different from his practiced timing (as it should be if a speaker is responding to the feedback of an audience). The result was

Three T Method

1. Touch (or point to) the focal point
2. Turn your face to the audience
3. begin Talking

a slide presentation that appeared possessed by a demon, bent on destroying his presentation.

This strategy is a reminder that you should talk to your audience, not to your aid. It's pretty easy to lose eye contact when utilizing an actual object or a projection, and your audience probably is looking at that aid, too. The message is the important item here, not the means by which it is being presented. A simple way to avoid this downside of using presentational aids is the **three T method.** First, Touch (or point to) the place you want the audience to focus their attention. Second, Turn your face to the audience. Third, begin Talking.

With thought, preparation, and effort, presentational aids will enhance your delivery in an added dimension. Although they're not always required, they provide an appeal to multiple senses. Presentational aids can increase message clarity, interest, and retention. They can enhance your credibility when used effectively. Conceived of poorly, designed inaccurately, or used ineffectively, they'll frustrate or bore your audience. You have a tightrope to walk here: you want to enjoy the advantages of successful presentational aids and avoid the consequences of poor design and use. You should always base your strategic choice on this basic question: Will the effective use of presentational aids enhance my speech purpose?

ENDNOTES

1. Roger Ailes and Jon Kraushar, *You Are the Message: Getting What You Want by Being Who You Are* (New York: Doubleday, 1995), p. 37.

2. *http://www.brainyquote.com/quotes/quotes/m/marktwain100433.html* (accessed August 27, 2007).

3. K. J. Tusing and J. P. Dillard, "The Sounds of Dominance: Vocal Precursors of Perceived Dominance during Interpersonal Influence," *Human Communication Research* 26 (2000), 148–171.

4. D. Deutsch, T. Henthorn, E. Marvin, H. Xu, "Perfect Pitch in Tone Language Speakers Carries over to Music," (Nov. 9, 2004), *http://www.aip.org/148th/deutsch.html* (accessed Sept. 1, 2007).

5. "The 100 Most Often Mispronounced Words in English," alphaDictionary.com, *http://www.alphadictionary.com/articles/mispronouced_words.html* (accessed Sept. 3, 2007).

6. For information on American dialects, see, for instance, the American Dialect Homepage, *http://www.evolpub.com/Americandialects/AmDialhome.html* (accessed Sept. 3, 2007), and "Varieties of English, Language Samples Project," *http://www.ic.arizona.edu/%7Elsp/index.html* (accessed Sept. 3, 2007).

7. Mary M. Gill, "Accents and Stereotypes: Their Effect on Perceptions of Teachers and Lecture Comprehension," *Journal of Applied Communication Research* 22 (1994), 348–361.

8. World of Quotes, Ralph Waldo Emerson, *http://www.worldofquotes.com/topic/Eye/1/index.html* (accessed Sept. 4, 2007).

9. See, for example, R. Axtell, *Dos and Taboos around the World*, 2nd ed. (New York: Wiley, 1990); and L. Samovar and R. Porter, *Communication between Cultures*, 4th ed. (Belmont, CA: Wadsworth, 2001).

10. Steven A. Beebe, "Eye Contact a Nonverbal Determinant of Speaker Credibility," *Speech Teacher* 23 (1) (Jan. 1974): 21.

11. For more information about the importance of eye contact, see, for instance, J. B. Bavelas, L. Coates, and T. Johnson, "Listener Responses as a Collaborative Process: The Role of Gaze," *Journal of Communication* (September 2002): 566–580.

12. Paul Ekman, Wallace V. Friesen, and S. Tomkins, "Facial Affect Scoring Technique: A First Validity Study," *Semiotica* 3 (1971).

13. L. Samovar, *Oral Communication: Speaking Across Cultures* (Los Angeles, CA: Roxbury, 2000), 102.

14. For more information about gestures, see, for instance, G. Beattie and H. Shovelton, "Mapping the Range of Information Contained in the Iconic Hand Gestures that Accompany Spontaneous Speech," *Journal of Language and Social Psychology* 18 (4) (1999): 438–462. Also J. Cassell, D. McNeill, and K.-E. McCullough, "Speech-Gesture Mismatches: Evidence for One Underlying Representation of Linguistic and Nonlinguistic Information," *Pragmatics & Cognition* 7 (1) (1999): 1–33; M. Gullberg and K. Holmquist, "Keeping an Eye on Gestures: Visual Perception of Gestures in Face-to-face Communication," *Pragmatics & Cognition* 7 (1) (1999): 35–63; A. Kendon, "Do Gestures Communicate?: A Review," *Research on Language and Social Interaction* 27 (3) (1994): 175–200; A. Melinger and W. J. M. Levelt, "Gesture and the Communicative Intention of the Speaker," *Gesture* 4 (2) (2004): 119–141; J. Streeck, "Gesture as Communication I: Its Coordination with Gaze and Speech," *Communication Monographs* 60 (4) (1993): 275–299 and J. Streeck, "Gesture as Communication II: The Audience as Co-author," *Research on Language and Social Interaction* 27 (3) (1994): 239–267.

15. Samovar, 103.

16. 68. Tim Russert Tallies the Vote (11/7/00) Decision 2000, "TV Guide and TV Land present the 100 Most memorable TV moments," *http://www.tvland.com/originals/100moments/page2.jhtml* (accessed Sept. 4, 2007).

17. "Election 2004 geekery: Tablet PCs are the new whiteboards" Peter Rojas, Engadget, *http://www.engadget.com/2004/11/02/election-2004-geekery-tablet-pcs-are-the-new-whiteboards/* (accessed Sept. 4, 2007).

18. Susan C. Jones, "Memory Aids for Reading and Math," Final Report U.S. Department of Education's Christa McAuliffe Fellowship (1991).

19. M. Patterson, D. Dansereau, and D. Newbern, "Effects of Communication Aids and Strategies on Cooperative Teaching," *Journal of Educational Psychology* 84 (1992): 453–61.

20. Indiana University's Copyright Management Center, *http://www.copyright.iupui.edu/fairuse.htm* has a good discussion of what constitutes fair use and the limits of using materials. (accessed Sept. 5, 2007).

21. Most libraries have online databases of maps, images, and other media. Check with your research librarian for assistance. See, for example, Images, maps, news sources, and other media, Virginia Tech University Libraries, http://www.lib.vt.edu/find/othermedia.html.

22. For an opposing view, see Professor Edward Tufte's, "PowerPoint is Evil," in *Wired* on line at *http://www.wired.com/wired/archive/11.09/ppt2.html*. There is ample information about the construction of PowerPoint slides. See, for example, N. Amare, "Technology for Technology's Sake: the Proliferation of PowerPoint," *Professional Communication Conference,* 2004. IPCC 2004. Proceedings. International Publication Date: 29 Sept.–Oct. 2004.

23. *http://office.microsoft.com/en-us/powerpoint/default.aspx* is the main Web site for PowerPoint, including tips and training points (accessed Sept. 5, 2007).

24. Corey A. Hickerson, Ph. D., Assistant Professor of Communication Studies: James Madison University.

25. For a discussion of the use of color, Microsoft PowerPoint has a brief discussion on choosing the right colors at http://office.microsoft.com/enus/powerpoint/HA010120721033.aspx.

26. Motley, M. T. (1988, January 22). Taking the terror out of talk. *Psychology Today,* 46–49.

27. Brewer, G. (2001, March 19). Snakes top list of Americans' fears. *Gallup News Service*. Retrieved April 9, 2010, from http://www.gallup.com/poll/1891/snakes-top-list-americans-fears.aspx

28. Wittstein, I. S., Thiemann, D. R., Lima, J., A., Baughman, K.L., Schulman, S. P., Gerstenblith, G., Wu, K. C., Rade, J. J., Bivalacqua, T. J., & Champion, H. C. (2005). Neurohumoral features of myocardial stunning due to sudden emotional stress. *New England Journal of Medicine*, 352, 539–548.

29. Harlan, R. (1993). *The confident speaker: How to master fear and persuade an audience*. Bradenton, FL: McGuinn and McGuire.

30. Esposito, J. E. (2000). *In the spotlight: Overcome your fear of public speaking and performing*. Southbury, CT: Strong Books.

31. McCroskey, J. C. (1972). The implementation of a large-scale program of systematic desensitization for communication apprehension. *Speech Teacher*, 21, 255–264.

32. McCroskey, J. C. (1977). Classroom consequences of communication apprehension. *Communication Education*, 26, 27–33. McCroskey, J. C. (1984). The communication apprehension perspective. In J. A. Daly & J. C. McCroskey (Eds.), *Avoiding communication* (pp. 13–38). Beverly Hills, CA: Sage.

34. Butler, J. Pryor, B., & Marti, S. (2004). Communication apprehension and honor students. *North American Journal of Psychology*, 6, 293–296.

35. Bodie, G. D. (2010). A racing heart, rattling knees, and ruminative thoughts: Defining, explaining, and treating public speaking anxiety. *Communication Education*, 59, 70–105.

36. Harris, K. B., Sawyer, C. R., & Behnke, R. R. (2006). Predicting speech state anxiety from trait anxiety, reactivity, and situational influences. *Communication Quarterly*, 54, 213–226.

37. McCroskey, J. C. (1976). The effects of communication apprehension on nonverbal behavior. *Communication Quarterly*, 24, 39–44.

38. McCroskey, J. C., & Richmond, V. P. (1976). The effects of communication apprehension on the perception of peers. *Western Journal of Speech Communication*, 40, 14–21.

39. Witt, P. L., & Behnke, R. R. (2006). Anticipatory speech anxiety as a function of public speaking assignment type. *Communication Education*, 55, 167–177.

40. Beatty, M. J. (1988). Situational and predispositional correlates of public speaking anxiety. *Communication Education*, 37, 28–39.

41. Freeman, T. Sawyer, C. R., & Behnke, R. R. (1997). Behavioral inhibition and the attribution of public speaking state anxiety. *Communication Education*, 46, 175–187.

42. Allen, M., Hunter, J. E., & Donohue, W. A. (1989). Metaanalysis of self-report data on the effectiveness of public speaking anxiety treatment techniques. *Communication Education*, 38, 54–76.

43. Ashley, J. (1996). *Overcoming stage fright in everyday life*. New York: Three Rivers Press.

44. Fremouw, W. J., & Scott, M. D. (1979). Cognitive restructuring: An alternative method for the treatment of communication apprehension. *Communication Education*, 28, 129–133.

45. Krayer, K. J., O'Hair, M. J., O'Hair, D., & Furio, B. J. (1984). Applications of cognitive restructuring in the treatment of communication apprehension: Perceptions of task and content coping statements. *Communication*, 13(1), 67–79.

46. McCroskey, J. C., Ralph, D. C., & Barrick, J. E. (1970). The effect of systematic desensitization on speech anxiety. *Speech Teacher*, 19, 32–36.

47. Hittleman, R. L. (1964). *Yoga for physical fitness*. New York: Paperback Library.

48. Wood, E. (1962). *Yoga*. Baltimore: Penguin.

49. Ayres, J. (2005). Performance visualization and behavioral disruption: A clarification. *Communication Reports*, 18, 55–63.

50. Ayres, J., & Ayres, T. A. (2003). Using images to enhance the impact of visualization. *Communication Reports*, 16, 47–56.

51. Ayres, J., & Hopf, T. (1992). Visualization: Reducing speech anxiety and enhancing performance. *Communication Reports*, 5, 1–10.

52. Ayres, J., Hopf, T., & Edwards, P. A. (1999). Vividness and control: Factors in the effectiveness of performance visualization? *Communication Education*, 48, 287–293.

53. Weider, J., & Reynolds, B. (1991). *Joe Weider's Mr. Olympia training encyclopedia*. Chicago: Contemporary Books.

54. Ayres, J., & Sonandre, D. M. A. (2003). Performance visualization: Does the nature of the speech model matter? *Communication Research Reports*, 20, 260–268.

Name _____   Lab Time & Date _____

Chapter 10
Self-Analysis

Students are asked to analyze their recorded presentations. This means watching the recording on Canvas. Then write down what you liked about your speech performance. **BE SPECIFIC!** Also write down some things you didn't like about your speech performance, then type what you specifically plan to do to overcome that particular behavior. This should be typed and stapled if more than one page.

INFORMATIVE SPEAKING

WHAT TYPES OF INFORMATIVE MESSAGES MIGHT I CONSIDER? WHAT STRATEGIES ARE IMPORTANT?

The Descriptive Speech

Think about how often in your day you are asked to describe something: whom do you admire, what your class was like, what you thought of a movie, why you like a certain kind of food, where your favorite vacation spot is, what your progress is on a project, why you use a term in a certain way, when you expect to complete a task. Your answer, whether brief or extended, represents a descriptive speech. A **descriptive speech** attempts to clarify information or to create understanding through vivid language. You want your audience to develop a meaningful image of an idea, term, situation, feeling, and so on, with the intent of having them "get your picture" by the end of the speech. As you are about to see, language strategies are particularly useful to consider when creating a descriptive speech.

Strategy 1: Sharing Definitions

A main language strategy used to create understanding is sharing definitions: concise, simple statements that explain what you mean by a word or expression. You might think that "everyone" knows what a term means, but that is often not the case. Think of simple common sayings, such as, "Close, but no cigar." Can you explain what it means? Do you know why that phrase came into being? Perhaps by explaining in the old days, cigars were given out as prizes at carnivals, you can help your audience better understand the phrase.

An example from a Texas speech class demonstrates the need for definition. A west Texas student delivered a speech about clearing the range for cattle. His northern-born-and-bred teacher had never experienced such activity, so she was very interested. However, confusion soon set in, as the student described the need to "pull mesquite." He described all sorts of suggestions, including herbicides, napalm, improving the soil (mesquite apparently prefers poor soil), and digging it up by the roots. Unfortunately for the student, the instructor thought he was talking about *mosquitoes* and spent the majority of the speech wondering in awe about the size of Texas bloodsuckers that needed such desperate means of control. The instructor didn't know what mesquite was, let alone how or where it grew. Had the student begun the speech by defining mesquite as "any of several usually spiny trees or shrubs that often forms

---

Take a Closer Look

Strategies for Descriptive Speech

Strategy 1: Sharing Definitions

Denotative definitions provide the dictionary definition of a word in terms if its class and distinguishing features.

Amplifying techniques expand on the denotative definition to provide greater meaning:

- Explication: Defining terms in the definition
- Comparison/contrast: Relating the word to another word
- Synonyms: Relating a term to another term with the same meaning
- Antonyms: Relating a term to another term with the opposite meaning
- Example: Giving a specific use of the term
- Enumeration: Listing members of the class that distinguishes the term
- Etymology: Explaining the origin of the word
- Negation: Describing what the word is not

Strategy 2: Using Investigative Questions

Leading question words guide speakers in describing a subject.

The key questions are *who, what when, where, why,* and *how.*

Strategy 3: Using Imagery

Imagery uses vivid language to appeal to the senses, making it easier for listeners to remember the topic.

- Visual imagery: Paints a mental picture
- Tactile imagery: Elicits thoughts about how something feels to the touch
- Auditory imagery: Suggests sounds
- Olfactory imagery: Suggests smells
- Gustatory imagery: Suggests taste
- Kinetic imagery: Elicits feelings of movement

---

dense thickets,"[1] much of the confusion could have been erased. It wasn't just a matter of *how* something was said, but *what* was meant by it that would have resulted in clarity of description.

Defining a concept doesn't have to take a great deal of time, and there are several definitional strategies you can use. The most common type of definition is the use of a **denotative definition** (also known as formal or dictionary definition), consisting of three parts:

1. *Term or item.* This is the word to be clarified.
2. *Class.* The general group to which a word belongs is its class.
3. *Differentia.* Distinguishing features, qualities, or characteristics make this term different from others in its class.

The more narrow you can get when developing the differentia, the less chance there is for audience confusion. Differentia usually combine **intension** (a list of attributes/characteristics that something must have to be properly labeled as this term) and **extension** (examples of actual instances of the term in use). So, for instance, scissors (term) are a cutting instrument (class) for paper or cloth consisting of two blades, each having a ring-shaped handle, that are so pivoted together that their sharp edges work one against the other (differentia).[2]

However, sometimes a denotative definition doesn't quite give the clarity that you seek. You can then use amplifying techniques that extend the definition. Each of these is a method of sharing connotative meaning, or the

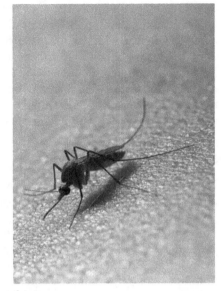

Mesquite and mosquito . . . two very different things.

© EuToch/Shutterstock.com   © Chia Yuen Che/Shutterstock.com

personal attributes you attach to the term. With **explication,** you simplify or further define other terms in the denotative definition. Let's say you have defined "apprehension" denotatively as "the faculty or act of apprehending, especially intuitive understanding; perception on a direct and immediate level."[3] You may need to follow up with a simple explanation of what words like *faculty* or *apprehending* mean in this context.

Another amplifying technique is **comparison/contrast;** you show how the term is similar or different to closely related terms the audience might know well. You demonstrate this every time you describe one of your classes by matching it up with another. **Synonyms** amplify your term by presenting another term having the same essential meaning, such as hurricane and tropical cyclone. **Antonyms** define your term by presenting another term having an opposite meaning: Freeze and boil are antonyms. You might choose to give an example, which is a specific instance of the word: A team mascot such as Brutus Buckeye helps to inspire fan spirit. **Enumeration** as an amplification technique lets you list all the members of the class to distinguish this one term (the grocery list approach). The word *style* can mean fashion, manner, behavior, typeface, sort, a slender tube, the slender part of a pistil, and so on. The **etymology** of a word explains the current meaning of the term based on the historical meaning or origin. Gravitas is from the Latin *gravitas,* "heaviness, seriousness," from *gravis,* "heavy, serious."

Hurricane or tropical cyclone?
Does it matter what you call it?
© Gregory Pelt/Shutterstock.com

Finally, the last amplification term is **negation,** which defines by saying what your term *is not;* you would use this when you want to stipulate new or specialized meaning that the audience is unfamiliar with. When rock hounds use the word *jargon,* they're not talking about slang. They're referring to a colorless (or pale yellow or smoky) variety of zircon.

No matter what techniques you use in defining your term, by clarifying your meaning and use of words, you'll show the audience concern for their understanding.

Strategy 2: Using Investigative Questions

A second strategy to consider when creating a descriptive message would be to answer the questions *who? what? when? where? why?* and *how?* All of these questions may not apply specifically to your message, but they can give you guides as to the depth of information that you might want to give. If you were asked to describe yourself, for instance, you could say *who* you model yourself after, *what* it was like to fail in a task and *how* you overcame that, *when* your least favorite time of life was, *where* you go when you need to escape, *why* you chose your major, and or *how* you view some current event. Each one of those prompts provides a different image to the audience, and each is more than they might learn by a simple demographic recital.

Strategy 3: Using Imagery

Finally, descriptive speeches call for vivid language. **Imagery** uses words and phrases that appeal to the senses (sight, touch, smell, hearing, and taste). By providing the audience visual, tactile, auditory, olfactory, gustatory, or kinetic experiences, you ask them to participate. The difficulty in speaking is that you don't want to become too literary. Remember, written words and spoken thoughts are different.[4] However, you can easily employ imagery in description. *Visual imagery* attempts to picture something; you can refer to color, size, or location. *Tactile* (touch) *imagery* elicits thoughts about texture, temperature, or feeling. *Auditory imagery* suggests sounds (pitch, volume, tone). *Olfactory imagery* reminds us of smells, where *gustatory* calls up tastes (sweet, sharp, bitter). *Kinetic imagery* evokes movement: speed, height, stillness, and so on. You don't have to get fancy with imagery, but a specific descriptive phrase such as, "You want the roux to be the texture and color of dark molasses with no black flecks," rather than saying, "Make the roux brown and thick," might make the difference between great crawfish étouffée and inedible smothered crawfish.

The more detailed the description of how the dish is made, the better chance you have of making it correctly.
© Tonic Valing/Shutterstock.com

Of course, organizing a descriptive speech is also important. You're trying to make something clearer or to enhance interest; how you structure those ideas is critical. Sometimes, the definition techniques that you've chosen will also dictate your structure; you move from formal, denotative meanings to informal, connotative ones. You move from simple example to extended illustration. You begin with the origin of a word or concept to its current meaning or status.

You'll probably find yourself using some of these descriptive language strategies as you develop more complex messages. The techniques used in a descriptive speech can be employed in other informative or persuasive speeches, because you may need to set up some common ground through definition or explanation before you can do anything more complex. However, if your primary goal is to develop a clearer image of an idea in the audience, then focus on the language strategies just described.

The Expository Speech

Another informative message often used in business and education is the expository, training, or *how-to* speech. An **expository message** focuses on teaching a person a process or skill or describing how some process occurs/happened. A person's first day on a new job often involves learning how to do aspects of the job in a particular way. Perhaps you've worked for a fast-food chain or retail store; it is likely that you've spent time watching training videos or working through online computer-based training activities that are in large part **how-to presentations.** The topics might include how to greet a customer, how to clean up a hazardous chemical spill, how to rotate stock on the grocery store shelf, or how to complete an employee performance evaluation.

Maybe you'd be interested in knowing how a package gets from source to destination, or how money gets circulated; you'll never actually do those tasks yourself, but knowing how the process works is of interest. Sometimes, you have to explain to someone how something happened. Imagine describing to your insurance agent just how your car got so damaged. All of these messages are expository.

Organizing an expository speech typically follows a chronological form. This simply means that when you explain how to do something or how something occurs, you follow time order. Think of it like making a cake or your favorite batch of cookies. You don't start by putting the ingredients in the oven. The order of priority follows a logical time sequence. First things go first and second things second, and so on. In a speech about cleaning up a hazardous spill, the first thing might be to alert others of the danger and to prepare for the clean-up by putting on the appropriate mask, eye protection, gloves, and coveralls. Without taking this first step, any subsequent step could be fatal and would certainly increase risk of personal injury.

If you're providing instructions about how to make some food item, you have to begin with a list of ingredients; there's nothing worse than starting to bake and finding out halfway through that some spice is needed that you don't have! Then you have to explain what and how to mix, how long to bake, how to plate and ice the cake, and so on.

When explaining how some process occurred (for instance, how Hurricane Katrina was born), you have to start with the place (a narrow area of tropical ocean), with a specific kind of temperature and wind, and so on. If you fall out of the chronological order, it is likely that your instructions will fail.

The other important strategy for expository speeches involves the use of language structural techniques such as mnemonic devices and transitions. They're about the most delicate language skill to develop for speaking, but they help to keep your audience focused and involved, and they move the instructions along. When done well, these can also assist the audience in retaining the instructions. Moreover, they may help to keep you on point, too!

A **mnemonic device** is a method you use for enhancing memory—both yours and the audience. The first language tactic, **alliteration,** involves the repetition of initial or matching sounds in neighboring words. You might be familiar with the tongue-twister "Peter Piper picked a peck of pickled peppers," but this isn't exactly the type of alliteration you might find useful. However, earlier in this chapter, you were exposed to the three Ps of an effective briefing: procedure, progress, and people. The repetitive *P* sound can create a memory peg for the audience. Other examples include the consonants in the four Cs of buying a diamond (cut, color, clarity, carat weight) or the four Ps of marketing (product, price, place, and promotion). Alliteration could be something as simple as "lefty loosie" to remember which way to turn a screwdriver.

You might remember to use the four Cs mnemonic devices when choosing a diamond.
© Stephen Lynch/Shutterstock.com

Another device is to use parallel structure. **Parallel structure** occurs when you use the same pattern of words to show that two or more ideas have the same level of importance, such as saying, "*Gather* ingredients, *mix* dry materials, *add* wet materials, *fold* into pan, *bake*, and *finish*." Each of these initial verbs help to move the ideas from step to step.

You might create an **acronym,** a word abbreviated in such a way that it creates a new word or phrase so that something (a concept or a process) is easy to remember. The "ABCs of CPR" describe the main points of rescue breathing: airway, breathing, circulation. If you were trying to remember the primary spectrum light, you'd probably recall ROY G. BIV: red, orange, yellow, green, blue, indigo and violet. FOIL is used in math to remember how to multiply two binomials; first, outside, inside, and last.

Acrostics create that memory by using the first letter of words to create a sentence. You learned the treble clef lines by "every good boy does fine (or *deserves fudge*)" and the mathematical order of operations by "Please Excuse My Dear Aunt Sally" (parenthesis, exponents, multiply, divide, add, subtract).

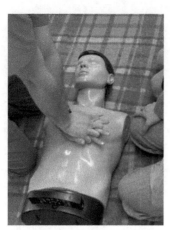

When you learn CPR, you use the ABCs.
© Prism_68/Shutterstock.com

As you're reading this, you're probably recalling such mnemonic devices from your past; when was the last time you dragged them up from your memory? That's the point: Once you give your audience a solid memory peg, they're more likely to remember the process you described.

Finally, don't forget **connective transitions**. They're the most subtle part of speaking, as they develop movement from point to point and create a seamless message. You've already learned about them in Chapter 13, so consider how you might employ transitions like "the next point is" or "in conlusion."

The expository message is one that you are exposed to daily: how to get someplace, how to do some task, how something happened. When you create one, remember the keys of chronological order and specific language use to create memory.

The Narrative Speech

Perhaps you've heard the story of how William S. Harley and Arthur Davidson started an American phenomenon in a 10 × 15-foot wooden shed back in 1903. These two men, later aided by brother Walter Davidson, created a product that continues to be sought over 100 years later.[5] Theirs is a story of personal sacrifice, determination, innovation, and imagination. The tale of the Harley-Davidson company is an American story, yet similar stories exist for many other companies and families throughout the world. These stories communicate powerful messages about sacrifice, misfortune, success, and family. Such stories are the personal narratives of our work, our lives, and our families.

A **narrative speech** tells a story that organizes our perceptions of the world, preserves our history, lets us experience other's lives or cultures without being there, entertains and engages us, promotes creativity, and connects each person involved in listening to the story. An effective speaker is one who can present a narrative that others can accept and that transcends differences in culture and experience. Before learning some strategies for developing narratives, you need to know what constitutes an effective one.

You've probably noticed that several of the chapters in this text begin with or include a story about someone's communication experience; our choice to do this reflects Walter Fisher's Narrative Paradigm, which says that humans are storytellers.[6] Fisher tells us, in essence, that we are more persuaded by a good story than by any other kind of communication. Robert Rowland echoed Fisher, reminding us that the idea that people are storytellers has been used in disciplines as diverse as history, anthropology, psychology, biology, and theology.[7] John Lucaites and Celeste Condit commented on "the growing belief that narrative represents a universal medium of human consciousness."[8] Fisher said that narratives are important because there are "ideas that cannot be verified or proved in any absolute way. Such ideas arise in metaphor, values, gestures, and so on."[9] According to Fisher, we experience the world as being filled with stories, and we have to choose from among them based on "good reasons." These "good reasons" are determined by biography, culture, and history.

Fisher defined *narrative* as a symbolic action: "words and/or deeds that have sequence and meaning for those who live, create, or interpret them."[10] If you agree with this definition, all communication is a narrative; it's a form of social influence. It isn't fiction or nonfiction; when you give an excuse to a parent or a partner for being late, when you read the headlines on the Web, when you watch a newscast, you're involved with narratives, all of which are shaping your reality. Narratives constitute our lives.

We make decisions about what narratives we'll accept and reject based on what makes sense to us, what Fisher calls *good reasons*. If you watch

Entertainment Tonight or *Access Hollywood*, you are presented with stories about celebrity behavior. Often, those narratives compete with stories in other tabloids or as told by the celebrity herself on a talk show. If you serve on a jury, you're presented totally opposite narratives of a crime: Who did what and why are not the same as seen through the eyes of the defense or prosecution. You have to decide which story to believe, and you do this by using an internal set of criteria called **narrative rationality**, our standard for judging which stories we should believe and which we should ignore. It is formed from two aspects, coherence and fidelity.

Coherence is the narrative's *internal* consistency: Does the story "hang together" by having all the points there, or are aspects left out or contradictory? You can see coherence by asking yourself about the flow (do the plot elements follow each other in a way you understand?), characters (are the people in the story believable?), and material (does this story seem to agree with other similar stories?). As an example, the film *Pulp Fiction* doesn't follow a traditional chronological flow, nor do all the characters interact. There are individual chapters involving some but not all; the timeline shifts. When a narrative skips around or characters seem to disappear and then suddenly reappear without explanation, you may judge its coherence as lacking.

Fidelity, the other aspect of narrative rationality, is the *external* standard for judging the truthfulness of a story. You probably got caught by your parents when you were younger, simply because some detail of the story you were giving as an explanation didn't ring true. Maybe they'd pursue the truthfulness by asking, "Now, if I called your friend's mom (or your teacher, or the storekeeper), would s/he say the same thing?" Fisher says that we judge fidelity by employing **good reasons**: a set of values that let us accept a story as true and worth acceptance. These good reasons include questions about facts (does anything seem to be omitted or distorted; does the narrative address significant or important issues of this case?) and values (are the values present appropriate? What would happen if I went along with those values? Are those values validated by my experience, and do they represent my ideals?).

Consider a couple of examples of narratives and Fisher's concepts, before you reflect on how narrative plays a role in your own communication behavior. The epic tales of Harry Potter, Luke Skywalker, and even Shrek the Ogre are all narratives that challenge our notions of coherence and fidelity. Do the events in the narratives seem to "ring true" to us? Are the characters believable? Do they stand for values to which we can relate? Do the stories seem to be congruent with our expectations based on other stories? Are there elements that have been left out, or that leave us wondering? Can you relate to elements in the narrative? In what way?

Do the stories that you read as a child still influence you today?
© digitalskillet/Shutterstock.com

Every night the evening news brings us narratives, some with greater depth of description, some with less: the stories of fires and floods, of heroism and despicable acts, of political issues and arguments. Legends, fables and folktales are at the heart of most cultures. From *Aesop's Fables* through the stories of the Han Chinese, Native American First People legend and Kumeyaay stories to Appalachian Jack tales and Russian folk tales,[11] we've all been told narratives that provide a glimpse into the past. These stories tell us about traditions and philosophies, crafts and foods, ways of living, and great battles and fearsome creatures.

Religious texts are filled with stories replete with values, heroes and villains, morals and ethical choices. You may view these stories in another way now than you did as a child, since your narrative rationality has become differently focused, but it's likely that these same narratives still play a role in your life. At the basis of Fisher's paradigm is the idea that we live in a world filled with stories, and as we choose among them, we experience life differently.

So what are the strategies for developing a narrative? They're pretty simple, and you've lived with them all of your life. You've developed your narrative rationality standards, and as you create your own narratives to share, keep those ideas of fidelity and coherence in mind.

Narratives provide listeners with a sense of action or drama by developing a plot, characters, dialogue, vivid descriptions, and narrative tension leading to resolution. When you develop a narrative, it must enhance the audience's experience, understanding, or appreciation of a person, event, or concept. Your story should connect to something within the audience's lives. The introduction must establish a context and pull the audience in from the start. You could set details or character descriptions, place the story in a larger context, or even tell the audience what the moral or outcome will be. As the narrative unfolds, remember chronological construction: Give description and don't ramble. The story must have coherence and fidelity, with characters, a plot, and values that make sense to listeners. The conclusion should leave a lasting impression with your audience. It should make the significance of the narrative clear to the audience.

Emotional sincerity and personal involvement are essential. A good story-teller employs vivid language choices and expressive delivery; both lend interest and animation. You've learned about techniques for language imagery earlier in this chapter, and Chapter 4 exposed you to effective delivery techniques.

Narratives often give detail to ideas that are shared from generation to generation. Stories develop characters and plots that help us make sense of sometimes difficult and unrelated ideas. They help to bridge difference in age, culture, gender and distance. Narratives stir emotions and generate interest in the minds and ears of listeners. We live in a world filled with narratives.

HOW IMPORTANT IS CREDIBILITY?

At the start of this chapter, you learned that informative messages instruct, clarify, and/or enlighten listeners. Through informative communication, your audience becomes more knowledgeable, gains new insight and new information, and understands complicated issues and feelings more fully. You can provide all the basic information to successfully create a well-developed informative message, but if you lack credibility, you will not be believed, nor will your information. Remember, credibility is developed through character, intelligence, goodwill, and charisma *as perceived by your audience.*

It is likely that you've had a teacher that you just didn't believe. Maybe that teacher contradicted something you learned before, didn't explain something clearly, used words you didn't understand, or told stories that were off topic. When informing, you are essentially acting in that teacher role, so you want to avoid those pitfalls. You can create a well-structured message and work on your language use, but are there other details you should consider?

Let's review some suggestions for you to try to enhance the audience's impression of your credibility and that of your message. Be prepared. Have a well-organized, well-supported message, and be flexible enough to alter it if needed. Be ready to answer questions competently. Use language that is adapted to the audience; you do not want to insult them by talking down, but if you have any doubts about their ability to comprehend your message, be sure to define, describe, and illustrate with examples. If you share group affiliation (because of your age, location, educational or work experiences, cultural background, or organizational membership), be sure to incorporate those affiliations into your message if appropriate by referring to them or using supporting materials that will reinforce them. Credibility is a changing factor, based on a number of perceptions. The only constant is that credibility exists within the mind of the audience, and your listeners or readers attribute character, intelligence, goodwill, and charisma based on their own unique perceptions.

Establish your qualifications to speak on this topic. Do you have experience? Is this your major? What you're trying to do here is show why we should listen to you in the first place. As you develop your ideas, be sure to share information accurately from credible sources. Credibility of sources can be established by reviewing the credentials of the information (or its source), including who said it, when they said it, and where it appears. This is as important in an educational setting as it is in any business environment. When you back yourself up with other credible sources, it enhances the audience's perceptions of whether or not to believe you; you're not the only one forwarding this idea. If you're defining something, you can easily cite the dictionary source that provided the original denotative meaning. If you're giving cautions in a process, there's probably a guidebook that you used at some point that reminded you of them. If you're explaining how an event got to the present point, why not provide testimony from those involved? If you fail to share accurate and credible information beyond yourself, you'll quickly be revealed for the shallowness of your contributions. Speakers who fail to acknowledge sources are charged with plagiarism, as you learned earlier in this text. Citing sources of evidence and using sources that the audience already accepts can add to your credibility.

You must also make sure that what you are saying is accurate when communicating an informative message, since such messages are often repeated. Misinforming a person either "accidentally" or intentionally has serious implications. If your audience is well informed and picks up on the misinformation, your credibility will be diminished, and your message will have lost its impact. On a more serious note, business people who knowingly share inaccurate information are quickly removed from positions of significance to ensure that they cannot harm the organization or its people. Alternatively, if the listener repeats the misinformation, more people are lead astray. If you forget to mention one step in a process, leave out one ingredient, or misspeak about a person involved in a narrative, you're deceiving the audience. Imagine the impact of one piece of misinformation shared in one speech to a group of twenty people who share that information with four other people, who share the information with two of their family members. In this scenario, 260 people are misled by one ill-informed or perhaps unethical speaker.

The creation of a credible persona is not easy. In fact, it carries some peril with it. When you open yourself up to others by sharing your ideas or values, you are taking a risk. What if others do not agree? What if they find your ideas to be ridiculous or wrong? When you attempt to establish yourself as someone to believe (in order to inform), others might think you lack expertise or are trying to come off as a know-it-all. Can you show that your point of view is believable, along with demonstrating that you should be perceived as a reliable authority? Because credibility is an essential factor in communication, it is worth the risk. There are some fairly simple, straightforward strategies that you can use to enhance your audience's perception of your credibility.

ENDNOTES

1. "Mesquite," *Dictionary.com*, http://dictionary.reference.com/browse/mesquite (accessed August 26, 2007).

2. "Scissors," Dictionary.com, http://dictionary.reference.com/browse/scissors (accessed August 26, 2007).

3. "Apprehension," Dictionary.com, http://dictionary.reference.com/browse/apprehension (accessed August 26, 2007).

4. There are all sorts of literary figures of speech you can see, such as metaphor, irony, hyperbole, and so on. However, these probably don't come quickly to mind while you're speaking. It's more likely that you'd find these useful when writing. Keep in mind that spoken language is simple rather than complex, concrete rather than abstract.

5. "History of Harley-Davidson," Harley-Davidson Company, http://www.harley-davidson.com/wcm/Content/Pages/H-D_History/history_1900s.jsp?loc=en_US (accessed August 26, 2007).

6. W. R. Fisher, *Human Communication as Narration: Toward a Philosophy of Reason, Value, and Action* (Columbia: University of South Carolina Press, 1985).

7. R. Rowland, "On Limiting the Narrative Paradigm: Three Case Studies." *Communication Monographs,* 56, (1989): 39–53.

8. J. L. Lucaites, and C. M. Condit, "Reconstructing Narrative Theory: A Functional Perspective." *Journal of Communication* 35, (1985): 90.

9. Fisher, 19.

10. Fisher, 58.

11. http://www.chinapage.com/story/story.html
http://www.firstpeople.us/FP-Html-Wisdom/sitemap.html
http://www.kumeyaay.com/
http://www.mwg.org/production/websites/jacktales/resources/appalachian_scholars.html
http://russian-crafts.com/tales.html

Chapter 11
Informative speech

Your Informative Speech will be the first speech you develop and give to your classmates. Here are the requirements for this speech:

- It must be between 5 and 8 minutes long. If you are still speaking at 12 minutes I'll stop you.
- For the topic you will choose three interpersonal communication principles – any idea in bold, any section label (for example haptics, biased language, connotation, assertiveness) – discussed in class earlier in the semester with one reflecting the experience you had working in your group for the group project. Tell your audience how these principles have affected your communication (hopefully for the better!) or changed the way you communicate, giving specific examples for each. Use concepts or principles from Chapters 1-7 in the text.
- On the day you speak hand in a final typed speech outline including transitional statements along with the Works Cited with at least 3 sources cited in MLA style. Staple the outline to the Works Cited. Indicate on the outline which informative organization pattern you used.
- Cite your sources within the speech.
- Wikipedia or Wikidictionary are not acceptable sources to use.
- You may use the lectern for this speech.
- Dress professionally.
- Deliver your speech in extemporaneous delivery style. You must use note cards.
- When your speech is ready review these requirements to make sure that you have everything ready when you speak:
  - ✓ Outline and Works Cited are stapled together!
  - ✓ You dressed professionally
  - ✓ You will cite your sources within the speech

When speaking what you say and how you say it are equally important in any oral presentation. Any speaking event is a performance and you want to make as positive an impression on your audience as possible. Your overall appearance and how you dress are a very important part of making an impression.

PERSUASIVE SPEAKING

ARE THERE DIFFERENCES BETWEEN INFORMATIVE AND PERSUASIVE GOALS?

As you have already learned earlier, communication serves many different purposes. When you construct a strategic message, it is important for you to consider what your goals are, and where you want to take the audience. Before we look at how you create strategic persuasion, it is important to consider how persuasive goals differ from informative goals, since these are the two kinds of messages you will give most often.

First, *informative communication clarifies, whereas persuasion urges choice.* Consider the role of an instructor. His mandate is to offer information so that the material becomes more comprehensible to the audience. Although you may already know something about the topic, the instructor's informative communication tries to help you understand it on a more complex level. Perhaps you will learn about the symptoms of depression in a psychology class. As opposed to the instructor, the persuader comes with the goal of choice: She wants you to take ideas and do something with them. That "doing" might be believing in a different way (changing your mind about people who suffer from depression), or it might be deepening your conviction (getting you to believe that you can make a change in your life to overcome depression).

A second distinction is related to the first: *where informative communication teaches, persuasion leads.* Consider this as a different role the source plays. If someone asks you for directions, you are expected to dispassionately offer

An instructor's role is to inform so students understand subjects on a more complex level.
© 2008, JupiterImages Corporation.

News journalists present the details of the day in an impartial manner.
© Florian ISPAS/Shutterstock.com

the turn-left-here details. A persuader is also an expert, but her job is to move the listener. If you were trying to persuade someone of the best route, you might say that there are three different ways to go: one offers greater scenic views, one passes shopping areas, and the third, your favorite, is the most time efficient.

Third, *where informative communication stresses understanding, persuasion does that and more: it adds the arousal of emotions.* As you will shortly learn, the impact of pathos, or emotional appeal, is a hallmark of persuasive strategy. The networks' evening news is supposed to be presented by impartial journalists who present the details of the day; Jon Stewart's *The Daily Show* may also cover those stories, but his ironic or sarcastic slant is designed to influence the way you perceive what happens in the world.

Finally, *informative communication calls for little audience commitment; persuasion requires it.* The audience for an informative speaker simply needs to receive the information; the source has no sense of whether the audience accepts it. As a persuader, you are consumed with a desire for commitment and approval. You want to see that your listener can use your message for future thought or upcoming action.

You might be thinking that there seems to be overlap on these two goals: Certain newsgathering organizations decide to cover a story in one way (or ignore it totally), while others provide a different slant. Is that informing or persuading? What if you provide a friend with statistics about the links between skin cancer and excess suntanning? Are you simply attempting to provide her with some enlightening data, or are you attempting to get her to stop using the tanning booths? What about the choices your instructor makes in thinking about course materials? When he tells a story to illustrate a point, does it come from his own value-laden experience, and might that be more influential, rather than being just a means of providing the wisdom of his discipline? In use, there is a fine line between informative and persuasive communication. The speaker's intent is the primary distinction here: What is the goal that the speaker has for the audience?

WHAT ARE THE TYPES OF PERSUASIVE CLAIMS?

Since this is a chapter primarily about persuasive public speaking, the focus will be on the speaker's task, but most of the fundamental aspects of public speaking can also be applied to other persuasive endeavors, such as interviewing for a job, pleading your case to another, creating an ad, selling a product or service, or designing a persuasive Web site. You already know that persuasion has an instrumental orientation. When you persuade, you do so with a strategic end result in mind. You can probably guess that persuasive speaking is a complex task, but it is a bit simpler when you think about it in terms of types of persuasive claims and their accompanying goals.

A **claim** serves the same purpose as a thesis statement in an informative speech: it represents the desired end result of the speech, the main idea that you want the audience to assume. Claims are also referred to as *conclusions* or *propositions*. Think of it this way: A conclusion is what you want the audience to reach by the end of your speech; a proposition is what you want them to accept. Just as there were different types of informative messages, the same is true in persuasion. There are three types of persuasive claims:

Persuasive skills come into play when you're trying to sell a product or service.
© Teze/Shutterstock.com

1. Claim of fact
2. Claim of value
3. Claim of policy

A **persuasive claim of fact** attempts to create a belief in an audience. Remember, a *belief* is your personal conception of reality—what you think "is." You might have beliefs about the existence of a supreme being, the existence of the Loch Ness Monster, or what the term *abortion* means. Those constitute your *facts* or *beliefs*. The goal of a claim of fact is to get your audience to think of something in a new way, or to get them to conceive of something they had never thought of before. You are attempting to create a shared reality. For example, a speaker might propose, "Nuclear power is an alternative form of energy to oil." The speaker is not just giving information about what constitutes nuclear power; he is trying to get you to see that it is an alternative to another form. A communication professor may find himself explaining the discipline as "not just an offshoot" of English, but rather as an ancient discipline with its own theories, strategies, and skills. A speaker wants you to make his reality into your reality when offering a persuasive claim of fact.

A **persuasive claim of value** goes beyond creation of reality. It attempts to get the audience to accept a judgment based on certain criteria. Using the nuclear power example, a speaker might say, "Nuclear power is the most efficient form of energy." If you are going to accept that claim, then you and he have to agree on what *most efficient* means. If you try to persuade another individual that Tom Hanks is the best actor of his generation, you are making a claim of value. How do you judge what a *best actor* is? Is it defined by the number of Oscars won, box office receipts, variety of roles, or number of films in a certain period? These become criteria by which "best actor" can be both understood and judged. When a friend asks you for an opinion about a class you took, you do not just repeat what was on the syllabus; you offer value judgments about the excellence of the professor, the importance of the book, the helpfulness of the assignments—or just the opposite. But when you make that claim that this is a "good" class, you are doing it on the basis of some value judgments on criteria that help to center you.

A **persuasive claim of policy** argues what should be done by the audience. Policy claims focus on the *oughts* or *shoulds* in our lives. You should not use tanning booths, you should have your pet spayed or neutered, you ought to dump your significant other, you ought to go see this movie starring Tom Hanks, you should vote for candidate X. Policy claims focus on future actions that the listener should consider; they are based on a foundation of shared beliefs and values. Once the speaker has gotten you to believe that nuclear power is an alternative to oil and that it is the most efficient form of energy, he can then attempt to persuade you that "the state should invest in nuclear power plants." This progression of claim of fact, to value, to policy illustrates another of the basic ideas about persuasion: it is rarely a one-shot opportunity. Persuasion takes time to develop; your persuasive goals may have to be incremental to get the desired end.

What kind of an argument might someone make if they are advocating nuclear power?
© Kristin Smith/Shutterstock.com

WHAT DO I NEED TO DEVELOP PERSUASIVE GOALS?

Let us look a bit deeper at these types of persuasive claims to examine their instrumental orientation. Consider a two-tiered approach to persuasive goals. The speaker has goals for the overall effect of the speech; the speaker also develops a specific goal for the audience. Every speech should have one level-one (or general) goal and one level-two (or specific) goal.

How does a coach heighten players' desire to win the game?
© Amy Meyers/Shutterstock.com

Level-one Goals

Level-one (general) goals might be considered the broad, overall goals of the speech. As the message creator, what is it that you hope to accomplish? Based on your audience analysis, what do you know about your audience that impacts the choices of rhetorical strategies you will use? It might be easy to think of level-one goals as being based on your perceptions of the audience at the start of your speech.

To Convince

If your goal is to **convince**, then you want to change the way your audience thinks or believes. You begin with the assumption that the audience disagrees with you, or perhaps they know nothing about your topic. For instance, what if you wanted to develop a speech that said, "Excessive suntanning is harmful." That is a claim of value, and you think that most people in your audience see nothing wrong with tanning booths or laying out in the sun. You want to influence them to change their minds.

To Stimulate

A goal to **stimulate** assumes that the audience already agrees with you, but you want to strengthen that conviction because it is built on a shaky foundation. "The Shroud of Turin is the burial cloth of Jesus" would be a claim of fact. The audience probably has heard of this Shroud, but perhaps they have not thought about why they believe or agree with you. You want to cement that agreement by heightening their belief. Speeches to stimulate are the ones coaches give before a game and at half-time; the team already wants to win, but the coach needs to stoke that fire.

To Actuate

Finally, the level-one goal to **actuate** means "to move to action." You are not satisfied with simply making the audience feel stronger in their belief; you want to get the audience up off their feet and doing something. "You should not purchase music with racist or sexist lyrics" is a policy speech where you assume the audience agrees with you but they are not doing anything about that agreement. By the end of your message, you want to push them to action.

Level-two Goals

Level-two (specific) goals mesh with level-one goals by providing a definitive, explicit goal for the audience. Think of these as specifying where you want the audience to be in mind or action at the end of the speech. What's the desired end result? You learned about three of these specific goals in Chapter 3 about critical thinking, but they are so essential to your creation of persuasion that a brief review and addition are important here.

To Adopt

To **adopt** means that you expect the audience to take on something new. A goal to adopt would assume that the audience does not know what you are talking about or isn't currently doing what you propose. The policy claim "Bravo

Company should be fined for dumping unused baby formula in third-world countries" is an example of the level-two goal to adopt. Your level-one goal would be to convince, because it's likely that the audience is ignorant about the issue. You want them to adopt a position that gets them to agree with your suggested policy.

To Discontinue

The goal to **discontinue** suggests the replacement of one idea or policy with another. Suppose you wanted the audience to agree to raise the drinking age to twenty-two. It's probably safer to assume that most people in your college-age audience will disagree. This would mean that your level-one goal is to convince. But what will you propose as an alternative? When you attempt to discontinue, you try to get the audience to abandon one way of thinking or behaving in favor of another.

To Continue

A goal to **continue** this speech is needed because you sense the audience's enthusiasm is flagging. It is usually paired with the level-one goal to stimulate. Now, you need to give them something specific to focus on to energize them again. Self-help groups use this message with frequency: You have not taken a drink (or a drug, or a hot fudge brownie sundae) for six months, so keep up the good work! You need to remind the audience why they started something in the first place, and you need to figure out a way to keep them on the right path.

To Deter

Finally, a level-two purpose to **deter** might be a bit unusual, for it means "to influence to stop something before you begin it." The anti-drug program D.A.R.E. has this purpose. Fifth graders probably do not know much about drugs and alcohol (to convince), and D.A.R.E.'s goal is to influence them through appeals to stop that behavior before the children reach middle school and are faced with decisions about alcohol or drugs.

When you consider your goals, you are not only thinking about your general purpose (level one) for speaking to this group, but also the end result (level two) you expect to reach with that audience. When you consider your goals, they should guide you in terms of the type of speech you need to give. More importantly, your goals will help you to strategize about what will form the content of your message. But before you can begin to strategize, you need to know as much as you can about your audience.

As explained in Chapter 12, part of the way you can work on your audience's perception and willingness to accept your claim is to have your own picture of them in order to target them most effectively. Because the individual members of your audience will possess her or his own blend of demographics and psychographics, it is probably impossible to really construct an accurate picture of the group. But the very nature of communication requires that you address people as though they are a known entity. Therefore, you need to be able to form some generalized beliefs about people and how they might react to your message and to you. A good message is audience-centered; your message needs to demonstrate in its content, organization, and language that you have placed the highest interest in the audience's needs and reactions.

Why is it important to know as much as you can about your audience?
© Igor Karon/Shutterstock.com

HOW DO THEORISTS DESCRIBE THE PERSUASIVE PROCESS?

Different theorists have discussed how persuasion actually works in influencing an audience, and you may have never thought about how influence has an effect on your daily life. Let's consider three theories that provide differing perspectives on the persuasive process. The **social judgment theory** suggests that attitude change is mediated by a judgment process, and it also supplies a way of thinking about how to persuade others.[1] In essence, people compare incoming persuasive messages to their present points of view. **Cognitive dissonance theory** says that dissonance resulting from inconsistent beliefs, attitudes, or behaviors is an uncomfortable feeling that motivates people to try to reduce it.[2] The **elaboration likelihood model** attempts to explain how people's attitudes are formed and influenced.

Social Judgment Theory

Your anchor positions will keep you centered, much like an anchor holds a boat in place.
© Kokhanchikov/Shutterstock.com

Social judgment theory says that people do not evaluate messages based on their merit alone; instead, their beliefs and attitudes are reference points for deciding whether to accept or to reject the persuasive message. Put simply, the success of persuasion is the end of a process when you compare your position to that of the persuasive message. This theory first suggests that we have core beliefs and values, called **anchor positions,** which serve to center our thoughts. Imagine being in a small boat out in the middle of a lake. Before fishing, you toss out the anchor that will keep you in the same stable area. Although your boat may move a bit, you will essentially stay put. That is what core anchors do. Second, according to this theory, we have **judgment categories** (latitudes or zones) that we use to evaluate incoming persuasive messages. Our opinions cannot be represented as points along a continuum, because we have degrees of tolerance around our positions. These latitudes include *the latitude of acceptance* (the range where incoming persuasion agrees with our core beliefs), the *latitude of rejection* (the zone where incoming messages deny something we believe or value); and *the latitude of noncommitment* (a neutral zone, where either we have no core anchors to judge the incoming message by, or we do not know enough to make that judgment).

As an example, let us say that you feel higher education is essential to a successful life. This anchor is made up of beliefs about what constitutes higher education (post-secondary), as well as some values about what makes up success. Your friend suggests that you take a special class that the community college is offering on emerging electronic technologies. Although you will not get academic credit for the class and it will cut into your limited free time, you put that message into the latitude of acceptance, because it agrees with your notion that higher education is valuable. But what if that friend comes to you and says that he thinks you should drop out of the classes you are taking this term, because they are a waste of time and you can make better money as a reality show cast member? That message will likely fall into your latitude of rejection; what your friend is telling you negates your beliefs in higher education and the definitions of success.

The next concept in the social judgment theory is about **ego-involvement;** it refers to the importance of an issue to you. You might be able to determine high ego-involvement by several characteristics:

- It includes membership in a group with a known stand (social conservatives, for example).
- Your latitude of noncommitment is nearly nonexistent (things are either accepted or rejected; there is no middle ground).
- You care deeply about the topic, and it's tied to your self-concept.

For example, for an adoptive parent, issues about adoption such as adoption law, adoption discrimination, and adoption costs are very important. The adoptive parent is ego-involved and may even have studied the topic more thoroughly than necessary for his own personal involvement. When that person hears stories about disrupted adoptions, adoption fraud, changing state adoption laws, or single-parent adoption, there is no middle ground for him. He knows where he stands, and why. In contrast, he may not be nearly as concerned with issues involving gun rights, legalizing marijuana, or forest clear-cutting. A person might be highly ego-involved with one issue but not involved in others. We are all susceptible to ego-involvement. Criticize a friend's parents or family, ridicule the way a girlfriend thinks, or make a disparaging comment about a new hairstyle, then wait for the ego-involvement to become apparent.

Social judgment theory suggests that persuasion works because we tend to make incoming information fit our judgment categories. These *distortions* of information are called assimilation and contrast effects.

An **assimilation effect** is said to occur when a person perceives the message to advocate a position closer to his or her own position than it actually does; the person minimizes the differences between the message's position and his position. For example, you might perceive the candidate from your political party as having the same attitudes as you do on issues of restarting the draft, school funding, and immigration reform, even though the person has made policy statements on those issues that don't really reflect what you think should be done. You minimize the distinctions between your position and your candidate's because you think that someone from your party must think like you, and you feel that policy statements are more political than personal on her part.

A **contrast effect** occurs when a person perceives the message as advocating a position further away from his position than it actually does; the person exaggerates the difference between the message's position and his own.[3] In the political example, this would be where you "push away" the ideas from a candidate from a different party, even though they're very similar to yours, because you can't believe that someone from that other party could think anything like you do.

Two important findings can be gathered from social judgment theory. First, if people judge a message as within their latitude of acceptance, they adjust their attitudes to accommodate it. This results in a positive persuasive effect. The most persuasive message is the one that is most discrepant from the receiver's position but still falls in his or her latitude of acceptance. Second, if a person judges a message to be within the latitude of rejection, she may adjust her attitude away from it.

This impact is complicated even more: For individuals with high ego-involvement, most messages that are aimed to persuade them that fall within their latitudes of rejection have the opposite effect, called the **boomerang effect.** By hearing something that is perceived as negating your position, you are made to feel even stronger about your position, rather than the desired persuasive effect of changing your mind.

How does the assimilation effect occur when you are comparing a politician's views to your own?

© 2008, JupiterImages Corporation.

Cognitive Dissonance Theory

Cognitive dissonance theory is based on the assumption that people need to see themselves as consistent in their thoughts and actions. When there is an inconsistency between cognitive elements (perceptions, beliefs, values, motives, and attitudes) and behavior, dissonance occurs. Think of dissonance as disharmony, stress, an uncomfortable feeling of being out of balance. We do not like living with inconsistencies in our lives; we prefer to be in balance. This theory suggests that competing cognitive elements will require something to change to eliminate the dissonance, and that is where persuasion comes in.

Say, for instance, that you have a project due at work on Monday, but you are invited to go skiing over the weekend. You feel dissonance because completing the project is important to your career, but skiing is really tempting fun. You must decide to do one or the other, but you consider the two sides. On one hand, completing the project will be tiring; you will be locked in your office all weekend; you are not sure if you have all the data you need; you do not want to disappoint your boss. On the other hand, you do not want to miss out on a ski weekend. Skiing is great exercise, which you really need; you desperately need a break; maybe you will meet someone new on the slopes. How do you deal with the dissonance created by this stressful dilemma?

According to dissonance theory, you have several choices.

- You could change your beliefs or attitudes about one of the choices (skiing becomes a dangerous physical activity rather than great exercise).
- You could add additional beliefs to one side of the equation (skiing is really expensive).
- You could make one of the choices seem to be less important than you originally did (your job will not be lost if the project is a day late).
- You might distort or misinterpret the information involved (you could claim that you did not know the project was due *this* Monday).

Cognitive dissonance is a fact of daily living. Let us look at another example. You are asked for your position on changing the immigration laws. On one hand, you acknowledge the mostly positive impact that immigrants have had on our nation. Your own grandparents were immigrants to the nation. You realize the economic influence they have. You work alongside people who have immigrated. On the other hand, you think that people who have come to the United States illegally should be deported; they have broken the law. You resent the fact that some immigrants resist learning English. You feel that your tax dollars are being used to support people who do not pay taxes.

To relieve this dissonance, you could reject the belief that tax dollars are being misused; you could remind yourself that your friend's adopted children were immigrants, and it took them three years to get here, but it was done legally, adding new beliefs to the mix; you could distort your beliefs about how many illegal immigrants there really are; you could seek out more information that supports one side or the other. In any case, the theory suggests that you will have to come down on one side or the other. Dissonance may be eliminated by reducing the importance of the conflicting beliefs, acquiring new beliefs that change the balance, or removing the conflicting attitude or behavior. In sum, dissonance occurs when you must choose between attitudes and behaviors that are contradictory.

As a communicator, you can employ dissonance theory to influence your audience. You might be able to create that dissonance and then help the audience to "solve" it by giving them ideas that support your position. This is the basis of most ads. You are told that a large number of people die needlessly because they are thrown from their cars for lack of a seatbelt, but this car has automatic seatbelts that stop that. You are reminded how little kids use too much toilet paper, resulting in stopped-up toilets and waste; however, buying this special toilet paper with marks on it will teach children how much to use. You are alarmed by statistics on the growing number of melanoma deaths, but your concerns are allayed by using this sun block lotion with SPF 50. Your audience will change by reorganizing their beliefs, attitudes, values, or actions because they cannot live with the imbalance they are feeling. You will have successfully persuaded!

Elaboration Likelihood Model

The elaboration likelihood model (ELM) attempts to explain how attitudes are formed and changed and how a person is influenced or persuaded.[4] This provides you with a third way to understand how theorists view persuasion. According to this theory, an individual's motivation toward change is developed through thought traveling through one of two routes. The **central route** suggests that people think actively about the message, evaluating information and weighing it against what they already know. To process a message centrally, the audience has to be motivated to respond and to think critically. **Elaboration** involves cognitive processes such as evaluation and recall. We use the central route to scrutinize ideas, determine their worth, and contemplate possible consequences. When people are motivated and able to think about the content of the message, elaboration is high. Your unique cognitive responses to the message determine the persuasive outcome (i.e., the direction and amount of your attitude change). If you're faced with a decision on buying a high-end product such as a car or a house, it's likely that you'll take time to list pros and cons, check out others' opinions, and take your time before you spend your money.

How much time would you take to decide to buy a big-ticket item such as a house?
© 2008, JupiterImages Corporation.

The **peripheral route** is used when we do not think about the message very much and are influenced more by the nonargumentative aspects of the message; this is low elaboration. It offers a way to accept or reject a message without any active thinking; you make quick decisions by relying on a variety of cues such as surface message features (the way a person looks, the number of supports given rather than their quality) or judgment heuristics (rules that guide thought, such as, "Professors know what they are talking about, so I should believe her").

This is typical of advertisements using celebrity endorsers; the hope is that you'll buy the product because someone you admire is using it. You don't think about the cost, your need, or any other important consideration. You want to be like that person, and by using that product, you will be one step closer. Persuasion can also occur with low elaboration. The receiver is not guided by a critical evaluation of the message, as happens in the central route; instead, the receiver decides to employ a decision rule that makes thinking simple.

As a speaker, you must determine whether the receivers are motivated to listen to the message and how much elaboration is likely to occur. Motivational factors could include the personal relevance of the message topic (ego-involvement), a person's need for information to think about and ability to examine that information, and factors such as the presence or absence of time pressures or distractions. One of the ways to motivate your listeners to take the central route is to make the message personally relevant to them. Fear can work in making them pay attention, but only you keep it moderate and give them a solution. Consider those ads that suggest you need a certain kind of energy drink, where someone just like you is pictured dragging through the day starting at about 2:00 P.M., just when you're supposed to be getting a project finished or meeting with an important client for a crucial presentation. Then the friendly announcer suggests that you could avoid that horrible scenario if you drank "High Energy Revitalizer," which costs under $2.00 per drink and is available in drink machines or your local convenience store. The end of the ad shows that person downing a delicious can of the drink, and minutes later she's no longer tired, the project gets completed, and the client loves the presentation! The ad moves you from fear to solution to visualizing success, all in thirty seconds.

Elaboration Likelihood Model

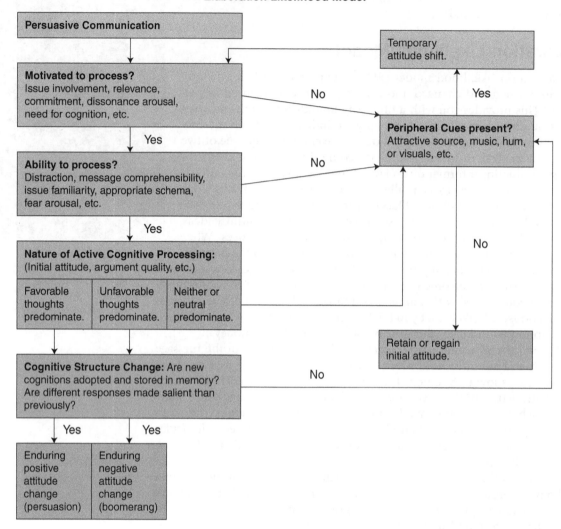

ELM explains the differences in persuasive impact produced by messages that have a large amount of information and compelling reasons, as compared to messages that rely on simplistic reaction to some issue, situation, or thing. The key variable in this process is involvement: how willing and able to elaborate the audience member is. Is he willing to put in the effort required to critically consider the issue being advocated and its supporting materials? When elaboration is high, the central persuasive route is likely to occur. Conversely, the peripheral route is the likely result of low elaboration.

ELM helps us to understand why and when messages and self-motivated efforts are more or less likely to lead to influence. Keep it in mind when you are puzzled by your audience's reaction to your well-thought-out ideas. Maybe they are just using the peripheral route to thinking they have developed: They're saying to themselves, "If a college student is saying that, it can't possibly be true."

There are many communication theories that explore how persuasion occurs. Social judgment, cognitive dissonance, and elaboration likelihood are three that show you the importance of influencing the audience by the information you develop in your message. Persuasion is not linear; you do not really change someone else. Instead, you give that person reasons to change himself in the direction you desire. Let us consider some persuasive strategies that you might employ.

WHAT PERSUASIVE STRATEGIES SHOULD I USE?

On January 23, 2006, President Bush told an audience at Kansas State University that the congressional resolution passed in the wake of the September 11 attacks that authorized the invasion of Afghanistan and other counterterrorism measures gave him the legal authority to initiate a domestic surveillance program. Bush reportedly authorized the National Security Agency to intercept communications between people (including American citizens) within the United States and terrorist suspects overseas without obtaining a court warrant. Critics such as the American Civil Liberties Union call the program illegal, saying that it threatens civil liberties and privacy rights.[5] Now, imagine yourself taking the position of one of the sides of this question. Is the policy necessary for the safety of the country? Does eavesdropping violate your right to privacy? How would you go about establishing your persuasive speech supporting your position?

Effective persuasion is accomplished through the creation and use of several different strategies. Based on your audience, your goals, and the speech purpose, you will establish common ground through credibility; you will appeal to the audience's beliefs, attitudes, and values; and you will create reasoned arguments that allow the audience to think clearly.

Enhancing My Credibility

One of the strategies that you are already familiar with is the concept of *credibility*, the sense that the audience believes in you as a persuasive advocate. At various points in this text, we've referred to the sender's credibility. Your listeners assess your character, intelligence, goodwill, and charisma while you present your message. Their belief in you may come from your looks, your status, your role, your degree, your expertise, your trustworthiness, or any mixture of all of these. That doesn't mean that you should leave such perceptions up to chance. You have the opportunity to use what you know about the perceptional processes of selection, organization, and interpretation to influence the audience to see you as worthy and deserving of attention. Some recommendations include the following.

Demonstrate Personal Involvement in the Subject

You know the role of ego-involvement, according to social judgment theory. Even though your firsthand experience doesn't make you an expert, it can show that you have a stake in it. A speech about problems of people rebuilding houses in hurricane-prone lowlands could be made more personal if you showed before-and-after pictures of your family's vacation home.

Cite Research

If you can use sources that are respected by your audience, not only will you show that you are well read, but also those sources will add objectivity to what you are saying. Make sure you cite those sources accurately, and don't falsify information. Someone who uses elaboration (as described in the elaboration likelihood model) will demand to have evidence so that they can think through the ideas you're presenting. They'll not be satisfied by simple personal involvement, as someone who uses the peripheral route might be.

Create Identification with the Audience

We usually trust speakers who seem to share many similar attitudes and beliefs with us. Show that your background is similar; share beliefs, attitudes, and values. Use *we* language to show that common ground. If your audience sees similarity with you, your ideas may more likely fall into their latitude of acceptance, simply because they feel they share anchor positions with you.

Deliver your Message Confidently and Forcefully

You've already read about delivery techniques. As a reminder, consider some of the findings from a study of nonverbal behaviors, credibility, and persuasion by communication researchers Judee K. Burgoon, Thomas Birk, and Michael Pfau, who wanted to create a more complete and accurate representation of the persuasive impact of nonverbal behaviors.[6] Among their findings:

- Greater vocal pleasantness, kinesic/proxemic immediacy, kinesic dominance, and kinesic relaxation were associated with greater persuasiveness.
- Vocal cues (specifically, fluency and pitch variety) played a larger role in competence and composure judgments than did kinesic/proxemic cues, while the reverse was true for sociability and character judgments (with immediacy most strongly implicated).
- Vocal, kinesic, and proxemic cues that connote pleasantness and immediacy foster favorable credibility judgments on all but the dynamism dimension.[7]
- Greater vocal pleasantness, kinesic/proxemic immediacy, kinesic dominance, and kinesic relaxation were associated with greater persuasiveness.

Credibility is but one of the strategic dimensions of persuasion that you can employ. Although you would like to have your audience perceive you in a positive light, a failure to use reason can cause persuasive breakdown.

Creating Reasoned Argument

As you attempt to persuade someone to accept your ideas, you are trying to influence the way that person thinks. Most of us feel that what we know is superior to what someone else thinks. As you try to get your audience to shift in their beliefs, values, attitudes, or actions, you must lead them through a series of reasons. In ancient terms, this aspect of message creation was called *logos*. With persuasion, you present a claim or position that is supported by reasons for its acceptance; this is known as **argument. Reasoning** is a systematic mental process of moving from one idea to another in order to reach a new conclusion.

Types of Reasoning

Two basic types of reasoning might be considered for persuasion. **Inductive reasoning** occurs as we mentally progress from a single impression or example to form a general conclusion. You see someone wearing a certain kind of clothing, and you assume something about that person's values. You see Johnny Depp in a pirate movie and assume that he must be a weird character in real life because of how he looks and acts on screen. You read a story about the famine in a third-world country, and you reason that all people who have emigrated from that country have left there to escape famine. Specific-example-to-general-conclusion reasoning is needed because we can only assimilate so much information. We create categories for generalizations, but sometimes

Based on appearance, what do you assume about her values?
© Ronald Sumners/Shutterstock .com

those generalized conclusions are based on limited or incorrect information. **Deductive reasoning,** by contrast, moves your thoughts from a generalized belief to a new specific instance. For example, if you believe that a certain type of ethnic food is too spicy, when offered a sample from that ethnic food group, you might pass it up without tasting it, reasoning that it will be too spicy, too. Television producers may believe that their target audience prefers reality programming; as a result, the newest offering is another reality show. Deduction allows you to take an audience from where they are to where you would like them to be by reasoning from general to specific. Your persuasive speech is a series of reasons, both inductive and deductive, created by the organization and manipulation of your supporting materials into logical structures. As you recall from Chapter 3, you can make use of five essential types of supporting materials, or kinds of evidence, but now you have to think about their successful application.

Let's briefly review three organizing strategies that are effective for persuasive messages and see how they display reasoning.

Cause-effect order is used to show a relationship between a source and its outcomes. You could also reverse the order and show how some effects can be traced back to their origins. Cause-effect order allows you to develop a reasoning chain that uses induction as it demonstrates that a certain end state (effect) is the result of specific causes. If you were giving a persuasive speech of fact that asserts, "Campus parking does not meet the needs of the campus community," you might develop your ideas by describing the locations of the lots, the conditions of the lots, and the number of permits given. By combining these three specific points, you can reason toward the proposition that parking does not meet the needs of the community. If you can get the audience to believe your three specific causes (locations, conditions, and permits), then you can lead them to effect (inadequate parking situation).

Problem-solution order structures ideas by pointing out a dilemma and offering (or supporting) its potential remedies. If you use this structure, you must first demonstrate that a dilemma exists, that it's serious, and that it impacts your audience. Then you are able to move into the potential solutions, perhaps even focusing on one resolution. Problem-solution order may be a more familiar persuasive pattern, and it often mixes inductive and deductive reasoning. It works especially well when you want to create dissonance and then resolve it.[8] Many advertisements begin by envisioning a problem such as "your house smells like a cat." They then suggest that their product will eliminate the problem: New "Cat No Smell" removes all tell-tale signs of Kitty. By getting you to consider that this problem may be occurring in your life, even though you were unaware of it, advertisers can successfully create dissonance and the desire to remove it. When a solution is made available immediately, you are more primed to consider it.

Can an advertisement make you think your house smells like the cat?
© 2008, JupiterImages Corporation.

Finally, there's Monroe's **motivated sequence,** that evolution of the problem-solution format that encourages your audience to take a specific action. As the name implies, the motivated sequence employs psychological principles, especially that of balance, as it moves the audience through five interrelated steps: attention, need, satisfaction, visualization, and action. In the *attention step,* you want to cause the listeners to focus tightly on you and your ideas. This step comes in the introduction of the speech. A speech arguing for the creation of Saturday morning classes could say, "Our college should institute Saturday morning classes." The next three steps constitute the body. *Need* demonstrates to the audience that a serious problem exists that demands change. Remember, in the need step of the body, you try to create in your audience an uncomfortable state of dissonance which they will want to alter. That's the essence of cognitive dissonance theory, which you learned about earlier. When people are made to feel dissonance, they want to resolve it. It is in the need step that you can join evidence with emotion.

The second part of the body, *satisfaction*, proposes a plan of action that will solve the need. It's here that you will describe your solution to the problems you just defined. There should be one overall solution to the entire need, not an individual solution to each problem you described. Here's a continuance of the example:

1. Repeat proposition statement: Our college should institute Saturday morning classes.
2. Describe major aspects of the plan: Supports here could be costs, time factors, and people involved.
3. If plan is used elsewhere, tell us about its success.

The third part of the body (or fourth step of the motivated sequence) is *visualization*, where you picture for the audience what the world will be like if your plan is adopted. This step projects the audience into the future to intensify their desire for change. It's important to remember that the conditions you picture must seem probable. The visualization step should be a logical counterpart to all of the ideas brought up in the need step. You may choose the positive, negative, or combination method.

The last step is *action*, where you urge the audience to do a specific, explicit act. You want to give them detailed information on how to accomplish this action, so that they will know how to commit themselves. One caution: Asking your audience to "think about this" isn't an action! What behavior do you want them to do? An example for this speech would urge the audience to attend the SGA meeting to be held on Tuesday in Squires at 7 P.M. to voice your support for this controversial change. This is an example of a "passive change" speech, since the audience can't actually make the plan occur.

Motivated Sequence Step	Topic: Proper Speech Organization (Informative)	Topic: Donate to Your University's Annual Fund (Persuasive)
1. Attention	Imagine getting lost on a deserted road in the middle of nowhere with no map and no contact with anyone. That's what it feels like not to have a clear organizational pattern.	Suppose you had to sit on the bare dirt in a classroom that was a cardboard box.
2. Need	As you advance in your career, people will look to you for direction and instructions. You will orient new employees and explain policies.	It takes money to hire the best faculty and maintain facilities, money that doesn't just appear from nowhere.
3. Satisfaction	Clear instructions require a plan. Chronological patterns detail the steps required to accomplish a task. Problem-solution design empowers you to troubleshoot difficulties on the job.	You could feel the pride of giving the next generation the education they deserve.
4. Visualization	(positive) Others will see you as a competent professional, always ready with a clear plan. (negative) Return to that lonely road without a map. Confusion turns to panic, as you wander aimlessly from point to point when addressing your co-workers. You hear whispers: "Clueless."	(positive) Imagine your name on a classroom or on the entire building. (negative) Think about trying to learn in rooms that are freezing in winter, broiling in spring.
5. Action	Learn and use the basic organizational patterns discussed in this chapter.	Donate to your university's annual fund. Make the future one that you shaped.

STRATEGIC FACTORS OF REASONING

Beyond order and reasoning come some other strategic considerations for persuasion. Remember, there are many variables that can impact your persuasive situation, so these ideas are simply pieces of experience for you to think about. It's impossible to establish the "perfect" template for any communication event.

Letting the audience know what is about to come, **forewarning**, might work well in informative speaking, but research suggests that for persuaders, the message is more effective when forewarning is minimized. There are some exceptions, however. If your receivers initially agree with you and you are seeking only small changes, it is okay to let them know what is coming. Reconsider that latitude of acceptance: Forewarning stimulates your audience to start thinking about things you want them to think about.

Message sidedness refers to the concept that there are two sides to every issue.[9] A *one-sided message* presents only one perspective; a *two-sided message* presents both sides. However, both types still advocate only one position. Where a one-sided message defends a position and avoids bringing up competing views, a two-sided message also defends a position and attacks the opposite. If a two-sided message simply mentions competing perspectives and there is no attack on the competition, it does no more than a one-sided message. The question is, which approach is better? One-sided messages are more effective when these factors are true:

- Your audience is friendly towards you.
- The audience already favors and/or agrees with your message.
- Listeners do not know much or anything about your topic.
- Counterarguments from the opposition will not be presented.
- You want immediate (not sustained) change, like buying an impulse purchase or signing a petition.

Two-sided messages are more effective when these factors apply:

- The audience is critical, skeptical or unfriendly.
- The audience is well-educated and expects to hear both sides.
- Opposing arguments from your competition are likely to be presented.
- You desire sustained change (you do not want them to agree or do only for the moment; you want them to continue this change).

Two-sided messages appear to be more fair and balanced. For an audience that is not thinking very carefully, two-sided messages make the persuader seem more credible. In addition, for the audience who is thinking carefully, the combination of defense and attack makes them think even more systematically about the issue and may start them questioning the validity of the "other" side. However, by pointing out something about the opposition, you run the risk of having the audience agree with that other side (remember the boomerang effect).

The variables of *primacy* and *recency* refer to a person's tendency to remember what he or she hears at the beginning or at the end of a message. This strategic consideration involves when you should present your *best evidence*. A *primacy effect* means that arguments presented first are more persuasive than later ones. Primacy is especially effective when you need to focus the audience's attention quickly or provide them structure and direction, along with comprehension. This means that primacy works when a topic is controversial or interesting, or when you have an issue that is highly familiar to your audience. The goal is to get to the major point quickly so as to focus them. *Recency,*

When you use an emotional appeal, you are evoking an emotional response from others.
© Nicholas Sutcliffe/Shutterstock
.com

presenting the most important arguments last for the greatest impact, works under conditions where the subject is uninteresting or the issues are relatively unfamiliar. You can work your way up to the important point you want the audience to act on.

HOW CAN I APPEAL TO THE AUDIENCE'S EMOTIONS?

Consider how often you encounter persuasion based on arousal of feelings of pride or love, sentiment or nostalgia, or those that manipulate our guilt, fear, and shame in an attempt to influence. **Pathos,** or *emotional appeal*, tries to captivate an audience's needs, values, motives, and attitudes. This emotional aspect of persuasion creates immediacy and power, often compelling us to act. When using an emotional appeal, you are trying to evoke a response from the audience based on an emotional response. It is important to remember that emotional appeals should only be used to support your position from its reasoned standpoint, not to distract, mislead, or misrepresent.

Emotion is a state of arousal affected by cognition (beliefs, awareness) and context (it is influenced by external cues). You respond to emotions as a reaction to ward off pain and to seek pleasure. Although emotional appeals do not last long, you may find that this aspect of persuasion has a compelling force, reinforcing the cognitive elements.

So-called *positive* emotional appeals result in warmth. Feelings like love, pride, affection, and comfort, often touched off by some form of association, result in positive attitudes toward issues. Put yourself in the place of a child being promised a McDonald's Happy Meal. The meal itself is "happy"—not only do you get food, but you get a toy. Another example of positive emotional appeal would be Pillsbury telling us that "nothin' says lovin' like somethin' from the oven."

On the opposite end of the spectrum is the most widely studied of all emotional appeals: reflective fear.[10] These are not simple stimulus-response reactions, such as the feelings you might have for a spider; you see it and are scared. In reflective fear, you actually have some cognitive processing behind the fear. You have probably heard the phrase, "Experience is the best teacher." It may be that you never feared living through a natural disaster until you experienced one. Now when a tornado warning comes on or a hurricane nears your coast, you feel fear set in. Maybe when you were younger you never thought that you could get an STD. However, as you learned about statistics for sexually active people and their chances of getting an STD, you began to fear that outcome.

Reflective fear also has varying intensity in an audience; the closer the threat is, the more the fear increases. You are probably not too worried about your final speech for this course today, but the night before it is due, you will feel that concern. Also, the perceived probability of the fear event occurring gets combined with the anticipated magnitude of damage that might happen. If you think something bad will happen *and* you think that is really bad, then more reflective fear will be felt. As a speaker, you may want to create reflective fear, but only if you are able to ease that fear as you influence. Think back to your earliest dentist visits. The hygienist attempted to get you to brush better; she showed you pictures of cavities forming on teeth and talked about how painful it can be to get rid of "Mr. Cavity." She gave you one of those red pills to chew that show where you miss brushing and where decay could set in. She showed you how to brush and floss; she gave you a free toothbrush and floss packet. In doing this, she was able to create fear by showing you that a real threat exists to you, and then she solved that problem.

After experiencing a natural disaster firsthand, you may feel fear at the thought of facing a similar situation.

© 2008, JupiterImages Corporation.

So how can a communicator use pathos, or emotional appeals? Remember, their effect is short-lived and they fade over time, so you need to repeat them through rich, vivid examples and meaningful statistics. There are five general findings to consider about your ability to use emotional appeals:

1. Emotional appeals should not be used in lieu of logical persuasion.
2. Higher credible sources are more able to use emotional appeals, because they are already believed. If you do not have much credibility, then emotional appeals might be seen by the audience as a distraction by an unbelievable source.
3. The more important the topic is to the audience, the less effective reflective fear appeals are. People who already believe do not need to be frightened or threatened.
4. The greater reflective fear you can create, the greater the persuasive effect is, up to a point. If you create too great an emotion, that high anxiety might create gridlock, wherein the person simply tunes out.
5. Emotional appeals may be called for and may succeed in specific situations, such as the following:
   - When you want to create interest, such as garnering attention to something the audience knows nothing about
   - When you need to create a difference between generic ideas or products
   - When you want to suggest superiority in a subjective area, like when you attempt to show that your school is the "best" in its student services offerings
   - When it is important to provide continuity across a series of messages in a campaign, such as when an advertiser uses the same slogan for many ads.

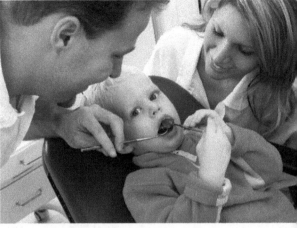

Remember how the dentist taught you how to brush and floss so you wouldn't get cavities?
© Répási Lajos Attila/Shutterstock.com

WHY DOES PERSUASION FAIL?

There are many ways in which persuasive efforts can fail. You have probably gathered that attempts to influence others can be a combination of credibility, emotion, and reason. It is important to remember that the audience is judging the mix; it is their perceptions that are important. Sometimes people do not listen well or critically. Sometimes they simply accept what they are being given. But more often, your audience will weigh what they are hearing, and so it is important to consider some of the ways that your persuasive choices may be in error. As an ethical communicator, it is your job to present the most well-crafted message possible; being human, you make mistakes. Let us see what some of those possible persuasion flaws are.

Defective Evidence

The first wrong choices you can make are with your supporting materials. The use of **defective evidence**, supports that do not create the belief you are seeking because something is wrong with that data, are pretty typical. The use of *defective data*, supporting materials that are false, is a relatively easy one to correct. For example, the U.S. Census Bureau reported in 2004 in its American Community Survey incorrect data for mean and median earnings for full-time, year-round workers sixteen years and older.[11] You can check your sources, review your statistics, and review your examples.

Hasty generalizations occur when you draw a conclusion from too little data; you supply one example and expect the audience to draw your conclusion from that. For instance, giving an example of one type of computer and then saying that all computers made by this company are the same would be a hasty generalization.

Authority appeals use unidentified or unqualified sources to support an idea. It is easy to identify a source; consider it *verbal footnoting* when you say, "As Barbara Walters said on *The View* on Monday . . ." and your audience will be in a position to judge the veracity of the source. The qualifications of your sources are equally important. Although Coach Krzyzewski of Duke is a wonderful basketball mentor, he should not be considered an expert on global warming. Misuse of statistics occurs when you use incomparable bases of comparisons. For example, if you say that Zander grew one inch last year and Russ grew two, arguing that Russ is catching up, those growth spurts are not necessarily indicative of a catching up. Sometimes, statistical misuse comes from the myth of the mean, the creation of averages where none really exists. Have you ever seen an "average American family," which, according to the Census Bureau, consists of 3.14 people?[12]

Defective Arguments

When you present **defective arguments** or use poor reasoning, your attempts to influence will also be weakened.

False analogies compare two things that are not really comparable. It is an easy step-off of logic to say, "Sue is an outstanding lacrosse player; she'll make a fine coach." Or "Romania, under the dictator Ceausescu, was a model for democratic voting; they held elections just like we do, and they had 100 percent voter turnout." In reality, the elections were staged and citizens voted because if they did not, they would be put in jail. What about a claim from a manufacturer such as, "You eat fruit for breakfast; why not try fruit-flavored gelatin?"

False cause reasoning supplies a linkage between a source and an effect that does not exist. The conclusion does not result from the reasons given, or the claim is unsupported by evidence. Examples would be statements such as, "If this marriage amendment does not pass, American family life is doomed," or "Candidate X did not serve in the military; he could not possibly function as commander-in-chief."

Slippery slopes occur when you mistakenly use the domino effect as your evidence. You supply one piece of evidence and suggest that it will result in a long chain of events, usually leading to doom. McDonald's once ran a television ad that wondered, "What if there was only one McDonald's in the world?" It showed all sorts of people from previous ads entering the sole fast-food restaurant, resulting in tipping the Earth off its axis, ricocheting around the rest of the solar system, and flying off into space. Or consider the argument that if the government restricts the private ownership of guns any more, the next step will be confiscation, and the next will be a total ban on all weapons, and when "they" come to get us, we will have no way to protect our family.

Ad hominem is an irrelevant attack on a source. Let us say, for example, that your opponent on an issue proposes a military draft for all eighteen-year-old males, not just for national defense but for a sense of discipline and responsibility. If you were to come back with the statement, "My opponent only wants this because she is female and forty," that would be an irrelevant attack. You are not arguing that the conclusion is a bad one; you are arguing falsely that the person who made it is not in a position to do so.

You have probably been caught up in *ad populum* errors. They are commonly known as the *bandwagon* approach: Someone argues that a conclusion is true because "most people" believe it. Examples would be, "You should vote for this project because it is going to win anyhow," or "Most people polled believe that fluoride in water may lead to cancer. Fluoride should be banned because of its consequences."

Finally, an *appeal to ignorance* suggests that because something has not been shown to be false or wrong, it must be right. When your friend asserts, "Of course life exists on other planets. No one has shown that it does not," he is using an appeal to ignorance.

Misused Language

The last group of persuasive errors involves **misused language.** *Equivocation* occurs when you use a term that could have multiple meanings, and you fail to clarify which one you mean. Say you are presenting an argument for the legalization of marijuana, and you state that the Bible says that God created the grass and said, "This is good." If you argue that, therefore, marijuana should be legalized because God liked grass, you are exhibiting equivocation.

Amphiboly means that your argument depends on the ambiguity of grammar. When you fail to clearly state something grammatically, it can be taken in multiple ways. One newspaper headline announced, "School needs to be aired." Does that mean that the place smells and needs some freshening, or is it that the school is lacking in something, and that an explanation is going to be talked about or broadcast? It may sound like clever word play to say, "Teacher strikes idle children," but what is it you really mean?

Emotive language appears to be simple description, but in fact it reveals more about values or attitudes. Let us say that you do not spend money frivolously. Are you best described as thrifty, cheap, or a miser? What about that relative of yours who is losing hair? Is he Mr. Clean, a cue-ball head, or just thinning on top?

Errors of evidence, reasoning, and language are very easy to make. We cannot always be correct when we speak, even though we've been schooled in it and usually try to sound appropriate. Most of the time, errors are unintentional and are easily corrected. But there are times when unethical communicators use such errors, or fallacies, in order to confuse or mislead. That is why it is important to be able to spot them and to understand why something is not right.

FINAL WORD ABOUT ETHICAL PERSUASION

Persuasion involves a complex mix of elements: speaker goals, audience demographics and psychographics, and strategies to implement. Although you are exposed to persuasive attempts every day, it may be overwhelming to consider how you can actually engage in successful persuasion, let alone be a competent consumer of persuasive messages. Finally, consider the responsibilities you have when you are a persuasive communicator. You are attempting to influence others—you want them to believe or to act in ways that can benefit or harm society. In 1972, the National Communication Association (then the Speech Communication Association), adopted the Credo for Free and Responsible Communication in a Democratic Society. This credo affirms basic principles essential to living in a free marketplace of ideas. Two paragraphs in particular resound with the concepts of responsibility, especially for the persuasive advocate who has the intent and power to influence others.

> WE ACCEPT the responsibility of cultivating by precepts and example, in our classrooms and in our communities, enlightened uses of communication; of developing in our students a respect for precision and accuracy in communication, and for reasoning based upon evidence and a judicious discrimination among values.

WE ENCOURAGE our students to accept the role of well-informed and articulate citizens, to defend the communication rights of those with whom they may disagree, and to expose abuses of the communication process.

(From "Credo for Free and Responsible Communication in a Democratic Society" by National Communication Association. Copyright © 1972 by National Communication Association. Reprinted by permission.)

This means that we believe that you are accountable for the ideas that you present. You know that you must have sound evidence that serves as the foundation for your message. You cannot exaggerate, stir up emotions in a way that is dangerous, or lie. You must present your position in a way that the audience can interpret and decide for themselves whether to accept it. Essentially, your responsibility is to show respect for the audience. The phrase "a judicious discrimination among values" reminds us that while you might firmly believe your position, the audience has the right to freedom of choice based on their values, which may conflict with yours. This is echoed in the second paragraph, which says that you must defend the rights of others with whom you may disagree. Your listener can disagree with you without penalty. In addition, by being a well-informed and articulate citizen, you have the following responsibility to yourself: You have to know what you are saying, to believe in it, and to present it in a compelling, ethical fashion. Communication professor Richard Johannesen reflected on these responsibilities, noting "To achieve these goals, we must understand their complexity and recognize the difficulty of achieving them."[13]

ENDNOTES

1. Carolyn W. Sherif, Muzafer Sherif, and Roger E. Nebergall, *Attitude and Attitude Change: The Social Judgment-involvement Approach* (Philadelphia: Saunders, 1965).

2. Leon Festinger. *A Theory of Cognitive Dissonance* (Stanford, CA: Stanford University Press, 1957).

3. A recent study of these effects was conducted by Zakary L. Tormala and Joshua J. Clarkson "Assimilation and Contrast in Persuasion," Personality and Social Psychology Bulletin 33 (4) (2007): 559–571, available at http://psp.sagepub.com/cgi/content/abstract/33/4/559.

4. See, for example, Richard E. Petty and John T. Cacioppo, *Attitudes and Persuasion: Classic and Contemporary Approaches* (Dubuque, IA: Wm. C. Brown, 1981). Also Richard E. Petty and John T. Cacioppo, *Communication and Persuasion: Central and Peripheral Routes to Attitude Change* (New York: Springer-Verlag, 1986).

5. Cnn.com, "White House steps up defense of domestic eavesdropping," Cable News Network, *http://www.cnn.com/2006/POLITICS/01/23/nsa.strategy/* (accessed February 24, 2006).

6. Research on delivery and its impact on credibility is vast. For example, Judee K. Burgoon, Thomas Birk, and Michael Pfau, "Nonverbal Behaviors, Persuasion, and Credibility," *Human Communication Research* 17 (Fall 1990): 140–169. Also Sheila Brownlow, "Seeing Is Believing: Facial Appearance, Credibility, and Attitude Change," *Journal of Nonverbal Behavior* 16 (2) (1992): 101–115; Joyce Newman, "Speaker Training: Twenty-Five Experts on Substance and Style," *Public Relations Quarterly* 33 (2) (1988): 15–21; Martha Davis, Keith A. Markus, Stan B. Walters, "Judging the Credibility of Criminal Suspect Statements: Does Mode of Presentation Matter?" *Journal of Nonverbal Behavior* 30 (4) (2006): 181–198; Lanette Pogue, Kimo Ahyun, "The Effect of Teacher Nonverbal Immediacy and Credibility on Student Motivation and Affective Learning," *Communication Education* 55 (3) (2006): 331–344; Katherine G. Hendrix, "Student Perceptions of Verbal and Nonverbal Cues Leading to Images of Black and White Professor Credibility," *Howard Journal of Communications* 8 (3) (1997): 251–273.

7. Burgoon, et al 162.

8. Just like Professor Harold Hill in *The Music Man,* you begin by picturing for your audience the extent of the horrible situation: a pool table will cause young boys to avoid chores, use bad language, stop listening to parents, and wallow in bad morals. (Yes, this is in essence a cause-effect order). Next, you say, "But wait! I have a solution that will resolve this issue! Your town needs a boys' band!" You describe the band's elements: uniforms, musical instruments, determined practice. And then to sell the point, you describe how that band will remove the temptations of avoiding chores, bad language, and so on. What Professor Harold Hill showed was that with a problem-solution order, you can create a need in the audience, and then resolve that need.

9. Mike Allen, "Meta-Analysis Comparing the Persuasiveness of One-Sided and Two-Sided Messages," *Western Journal of Speech Communication* 55 (4) (1991): 390–404.

10. Julia Wood. "A Preliminary Study of Cognitive Impairment as a Function of Reflective Fear-Arousal in Persuasion." http://eric.ed.gov/ERICWebPortal/Home .portal?_nfpb=true&_pageLabel=RecordDetails&ERICExtSearch_SearchValue_ 0=ED096706&ERICExtSearch_SearchType_0=eric_accno&objectId= 0900000b800e6b9e

11. This information was later corrected on the Census Bureau Web site: U.S. Census Bureau, "American Community Survey," United States Census Bureau, *http://www .census.gov/acs/www/UseData/Errata.htm* (accessed July 17, 2007).

12. U.S. Census Bureau, "Average Family Size 2000," United States Census Bureau *http://factfinder.census.gov/servlet/ThematicMapFramesetServlet?_bm=y&-geo_ id=01000US&-tm_name=DEC_2000_SF1_U_M00166&-ds_name=DEC_ 2000_SF1_U&-_MapEvent=displayBy&-_dBy=040,* (accessed July 17, 2007).

13. Richard L. Johannesen, "Perspectives on Ethics in Persuasion," in *Persuasion: Reception and Responsibility,* 7th ed. Charles U. Larson, (Belmont, CA: Wadsworth, 1995), 28.

Chapter 12
Persuasive speech

Your Persuasive Speech will be the second speech you develop and give to your classmates. Here are the requirements for this speech.

- It must be between 5 and 8 minutes long. If you are still speaking at 10 minutes I'll stop you.
- You will hand in a rough draft of your speech outline.
- On the day you speak, you will hand the instructor a final speech outline including transitional statements along with your typed Works Cited with at least 3 sources cited in MLA style. Indicate on the outline which *persuasive* organization pattern you used.
- Wikipedia or Wikidictionary are not acceptable sources to use.
- You may not use the lectern for this speech nor stand behind the desk
- You must have a presentation aid of some kind for this speech.
- Dress professionally.
- Deliver your speech in extemporaneous delivery style. You must use note cards.
- When your speech is ready review these requirements to make sure that you have everything ready when you speak:
  - ✓ Outline and Works Cited are stapled together!
  - ✓ You dressed professionally
  - ✓ You will cite your sources within the speech
  - ✓ You have a presentation aid

BRAINSTORMING TECHNIQUE

by Don Yoder, University of Dayton

Prescriptive approaches to group decision making assume that groups can make the best possible decision only if they have critically analyzed the problem, considered a variety of information relevant to the problem, and have a choice among a large variety of options. Notice that in the standard agenda model groups must thoroughly analyze a problem *before* they generate ideas about solutions. They also need to generate lots of alternatives, and they need to think about all the positive and negative consequences of each solution before they can choose the specific course of action they want to implement.

A common method groups use to help them accomplish the goal of thoroughly discussing a problem is *brainstorming*. Brainstorming is a group process designed for the simple purpose of generating ideas. To be successful, brainstorming relies on the *synergy* that comes from group interaction and the mutual stimulation of ideas. The interaction allows immediate "stimulus-response" reactions to generate ideas from each other's comments. One person's ideas can spark an idea in other group members that they may have never thought of without the stimulation. Brainstorming groups can generate more and different ideas than a single member working alone because the group members stimulate ideas through their interaction.

Group brainstorming is thus different than merely thinking out loud. Several barriers inhibit the free generation of lots of ideas, however, and groups must use procedures that minimize these barriers.

PROCEDURES FOR EFFECTIVE BRAINSTORMING

Brainstorming requires all members to state any and all ideas that come to mind. The following procedures help to ensure that group members have the time and motivation to generate as many ideas as they can:

1. *Define the problem before beginning the brainstorming session.* Group members should know specifically what they are to brainstorm about. It may be to generate ideas about the problems they are to solve. It may be that they are trying to generate ideas for a solution. Perhaps they are trying to anticipate all the possible consequences of a proposed course of action. Having a clear focus for the brainstorming session helps the members generate pertinent ideas.

2. *All members must participate.* Brainstorming is based on the premise that "many heads are better than one" and that group members stimulate each other to generate ideas they could not think of themselves. Thus, if an individual group member doesn't participate, not only are those ideas lost, but the stimulation those ideas may have for other group members is also lost.

A strong leader suppresses his or her own ideas. If there is a strong leader in the group, the leader should suppress his or her own ideas so as not to inhibit or unduly influence the other group members. In a work group, the supervisor or manager may have fate control over the other members. Group members may be reluctant to state ideas that are contrary to those of the leader, or they may wish to curry favor with the boss by simply echoing the boss's ideas. In this case, the leader should refrain from contributing ideas so that the members will have free rein to say whatever they think.

3. *No criticism of the ideas is allowed.* This is usually the most difficult criterion for group members to meet. It is natural to react to others' ideas and to make comments or criticisms. If an idea is criticized or laughed at, group members will be unwilling to make any further contributions or will refrain from making suggestions that are similar to the one criticized. Consequently, criticism can undermine the ability of group members to stimulate each others' ideas.

Even positive reactions can influence the group to generate only similar suggestions that will get a comparable positive response. Reactions can be verbal or nonverbal. Laughing, frowning, shaking the head, nodding the head, grimaces, and looks of shock can be as evaluative and detrimental to the brainstorming process as overt statements. Groups must remember that the goal of brainstorming is to *simply generate ideas.* Evaluation of the ideas will come later, after the brainstorming session is over.

Self-censorship also occurs in groups and inhibits the brainstorming process. Even if other group members make no overt criticisms of others' ideas, an individual group member could self-censor an idea. The person may decide that the idea is ridiculous, or that it won't work, or that it is trivial, or it will sound stupid and decide not to share it with the group. Remember that brainstorming relies on stimulating ideas in others. Any idea (even ones that initially sound stupid or wrong) may stimulate a great idea in someone else, something they may not have thought of if the member had let self-censorship overrule a contribution. In brainstorming, all ideas are equally valuable and must be expressed.

A good way to remember that all ideas are necessary and valuable is to adopt the adage of "the wilder, the better." Sometimes the most outrageous idea can be the one that stimulates the best solution. If the group adopts the approach that they should be generating "wild" ideas, the urge to criticize their own or others' ideas will diminish.

A story of corporate brainstorming that illustrates this principle takes place in an assembly plant. The workers in the packaging department were supposed to wrap porcelain figurines in paper and place them in cartons for shipping. To save money, the company used old newspapers, which they could get for free. However, the workers would sometimes stop and read the newspaper for a few seconds if a cartoon or headline caught their eye. It wasn't blatant or purposefully disruptive, but it happened frequently enough that there was always a holdup in the production line. The supervisors tried to solve the problem through traditional incentive plans, changing to non-English newspapers, and a variety of changes, but nothing worked. During a brainstorming session, one exasperated executive blurted out, "Maybe we should just turn off the lights and let them work in the dark—they couldn't read the newspaper then!" Obviously, this was a wild idea that could never be implemented. But it stimulated another executive to think of the actual solution. The company hired visually impaired workers for the packaging department! They were not distracted by the newspapers; they were very good workers, and the company received accolades for their diversity hiring. Whether this is a true story or an urban legend, it illustrates the process where the "wild" idea, stated without fear of criticism, stimulated the idea that was actually implemented.

4. *Members must stimulate each other's ideas.* The interaction necessary for effective brainstorming requires that group members carefully listen to each other. If members' ideas are going to stimulate ideas in each other, then people must listen closely to what other people are saying. There is a temptation to become absorbed in your own thinking process as you try to come up with additional ideas. You forget to listen to others and build from their ideas.

   To facilitate the interaction and mutual stimulation, group members should keep ideas brief. There is no need for elaborate explanation or justifications of an idea. Since group members are not evaluating ideas during the brainstorming session, it is not necessary to defend the idea or to explain it in any depth. The goal is to generate as many ideas as you can. Quantity of ideas is more important in brainstorming than quality of ideas. The longer a person takes to state, explain, and justify an idea, the less time available for others to contribute their ideas.

   It is often helpful to post ideas where everyone can see them. You can use a variety of media for posting ideas. You can write them on a posterboard, a flipchart, or blackboard, on PowerPoint, or even on a Web site designed for group work. It is important that the ideas are readily available so that they can continue to stimulate new ideas among the group members.

5. *Brainstorming takes time.* The effectiveness of brainstorming requires that groups interact for more than a couple of minutes. In the first few minutes of brainstorming, groups seldom generate more or different ideas than a single person could do alone. It takes time for the obvious ideas to be stated and for the mutual stimulation to take effect to bring out the creative ideas. As a rule of thumb, you should brainstorm for about five minutes per group member. (A four-person group would brainstorm for a minimum of 20 minutes.) Of course, the complexity of the problem being examined may require more or less time. If you are trying to think of a name for a product, you may need less time than if you are trying to solve a complex operational restructuring problem.

SUMMARY

Brainstorming is an effective method for generating ideas that can be used in any stage of the standard agenda model (or other models) of group decision making. The interaction among group members stimulates creativity and produces ideas that a single person cannot generate alone. When done in a climate of openness with no evaluation of ideas, group members can feel free to say whatever comes to mind. When the group members concentrate on the quantity of ideas rather than quality, and when they are willing to risk offering wild ideas to stimulate each others' thinking, brainstorming can help improve the quality of group decisions.

Index